L'ANNUAIRE DU MONDE DES AFFAIRES ANGLOPHONES A PARIS

Editor
David Applefield

Assistant Editor
Tanya Leslie

Production/Design
Cory McCloud

Assistants
Heidi Behrendt
Julia Alvarez-Grosser
Russell Roman

Paris-Anglophone, under license from The Apple Field Company, is published by Association Frank *(Loi de 1901)* with the participation of France-Telecom. Distributed in France by Editions Parigramme (Livredis) and in North America by Inland Book Company.

 Paris-Anglophone may be consulted electronically on the World Wide Web at **http://www.paris-anglo.com**.

Although every effort has been made to assure the accuracy of this volume, the Editors, Publisher, and its vendors cannot be held responsible in the case of error or change of directory contents.

We openly invite readers to send suggestions, corrections, questions, and comments as well as individual and trade orders, special and premium-sale orders, inquiries concerning print and electronic sponsoring, advertising, Web Page development, and our Customized Commercial & Cultural Consulting service (CC&CC) to:

Association Frank
32, rue Edouard Vaillant
93100 MONTREUIL / France
Tel: (33) (1) 48 59 66 58
Fax: (33) (1) 48 59 66 68
Email: 100265.1435@compuserve.com

 Dépôt légal juin 1995.
Printed in France by BCI, St Amand-Montrond, *n° d'impression : 1/1533.*
Cover stamp : Engraving by Pierre Gandon © SPADEM, 1995.
ISBN 2-84096-046-X

TABLE OF CONTENTS — TABLE DES MATIÈRES

Bienvenue à la 4e édition de **Paris-Anglophone !**

SACHEZ que cet annuaire de Paris s'adresse tout autant à vous qu'à un public anglophone. La nouvelle et quatrième édition de *Paris-Anglophone* compte aujourd'hui plus de 4200 adresses, dont 2000 nouveautés — un choix qui traduit l'importance économique de la communauté commerciale et culturelle anglo-américaine à Paris, et le rôle grandissant qu'elle a assumé au cours des dernières années. Si vous-même, votre société ou votre association êtes en relation avec le monde des affaires anglophones, ou si vous désirez multiplier les contacts que vous entretenez avec des firmes, des sociétés de services ou des particuliers américains, anglais, irlandais, canadiens et australiens, *Paris-Anglophone* deviendra vite un outil de travail indispensable.

Dans cette nouvelle édition, nous avons procédé à un reclassement des différentes activités afin de faciliter la tâche au lecteur. Nous avons également introduit de nouvelles rubriques . Multimédia, En Réseau, un chapitre entier consacré aux enfants, etc. La rubrique Shopping/Boutiques a été entièrement repensée: vous y trouverez tout, du tailleur Chanel au bouquet de roses, en passant par le whisky irlandais ! Le même souci de précision nous a amené à compléter et remanier la section Cafés/Restaurants: il vous est désormais possible de choisir entre un grand restaurant, un pub irlandais ou la cuisine végétarienne. Grâce à toutes ces améliorations, *Paris-Anglophone* est plus pratique, plus facile à consulter et surtout plus complet. Aucun autre annuaire anglophone de Paris ne présente un aussi large éventail d'activités, regroupées de manière simple et claire.

En dernier lieu, nous sommes fiers de pouvoir vous présenter l'édition Internet de *Paris-Anglophone*, hébergée sur notre propre *Site Web* — **http//www.paris-anglo.com** — un service qui permet aux utilisateurs de *Paris-Anglophone* de consulter notre annuaire sur le Réseau. Par ailleurs, nous avons établi des liens directs avec les "home pages" de nos sponsors/annonceurs. Ces derniers nous communiquent à la fois des images et des informations qui facilitent la vie à Paris. Ces innovations s'accompagnent de nouveaux services et de nouvelles rubriques — Galeries d'Art à Paris, Calendrier Culturel, Actualités Politiques, etc. — destinés à créer un environnement professionnel actif, propice aux échanges culturels et commerciaux entre les communautés anglophone et francophone.

Bienvenue au monde de *Paris-Anglophone* ! Si, d'une manière ou d'une autre, nous pouvons vous aider à renforcer vos relations avec les milieux d'affaires anglophones à Paris ou ailleurs, n'hésitez pas à nous contacter— par lettre, fax ou courrier electronique. **DA**

Welcome to the 4th Edition of **Paris-Anglophone!**

FOR over five years we have been building, updating, and publishing a list of professional, commercial and cultural activities in Paris that comprise the Anglo-American community. To that we have added other professional contacts and services essential for English-speaking residents and visitors of Paris.

The directory in its present 4th edition consists of over 4200 entries – more than 2000 new listings – a fact that reflects the rapid growth of Paris' Anglo-American commercial and cultural community.

In this new Edition, we have restructured the activities and created new categories of listings, such as Multimedia Paris and On-line Services. We have added greater specificity to our Shopping/ Boutique section and diversified the Wining & Dining category. On the whole, ***Paris-Anglophone*** is now increasingly user-friendly, practical, and above all, comprehensive. In fact, there is no other professional directory of English Paris as complete and broad-based as ***Paris-Anglophone***.

Lastly, we are pleased to introduce the Internet On-Line edition of ***Paris-Anglophone*** situated on our own Web Site – **http//www.paris-anglo.com**. Not only can ***Paris-Anglophone*** users consult the directory on-line, we have created direct links to the home pages of participating sponsors who are providing highly useful information and images for working and living in Paris – to which we are regularly adding new services and features such as our Paris Art Gallery, Cultural Calendar, and Political Update, all designed to create a dynamic professional environment for commercial and cultural exchange between the Francophone and Anglophone worlds.

If you work in or with France, aspire to increase your physical or virtual presence in France, or are seeking professional and cultural contacts, ***Paris-Anglophone*** is an essential tool. If you live in or around Paris or are planning a visit to the French capital, you will find ***Paris-Anglophone*** to be a great asset and friend.

In the spirit of wanting to continue to serve our readers in the most effective way possible, we invite you to send in your comments, corrections, and suggested additions. If you have a company or service in France and would like to be listed in ***Paris-Anglophone*** or to receive more information on sponsorship/ advertising possibilities in the book and Web Site editions, please send in the form located at the back.

We wish you continued success in all your endeavors in France. If we can be of assistance just phone, fax, or E-mail us and we'll try to help. **DA**

Accountemps
17, rue Jean Mermoz
75008 PARIS
Tel: 45 63 08 01
Fax: 45 63 08 45
Consultant: Delphine SALA

Anderson Consulting S.A. et Cie
Tour Gan
Cedex 13
92082 PARIS LA DEFENSE 2
Tel: 42 91 07 00
Fax: 42 91 08 00

Arthur D. Little France
15, rue Galvani
75017 PARIS
Tel: 40 55 29 00
Fax: 40 55 08 80
Managing Director: M. Jean-Luc FALLOU

Coopers & Lybrand
32, rue Guersant
75017 PARIS
Tel: 45 72 80 00
Fax: 45 72 22 19
President: M. P.B. ANGLADE
Accountants, tax consultants, lawyers

Deloitte Touche Tohmatsu
185, avenue Charles de Gaulle
92200 NEUILLY-SUR-SEINE
Tel: 40 88 28 00
Fax: 40 88 28 28
Telex: BDA 620 883F
Contact: M. Hervé BARDON
Audit, finance, management, productivity

Ernst & Young
Tour Manhattan
6, Place de l'Iris
92095 PARIS LA DEFENSE 2 Cedex 21
Tel: 46 93 60 00
Fax: 47 76 20 33
Director: M. Roy D. MITCHELL
Accounting, management, tax advice

Ex Com
48, Bd. des Batignolles
75017 PARIS
Tel: 44 90 84 00
Fax: 44 70 96 10

Factofrance Heller
Tour Facto
18, rue Hoche
36, avenue du Maine
92988 PARIS LA DEFENSE Cedex 88
Tel: 46 35 70 00
Fax: 46 35 69 10
Director: M. Michel AUSSAVY
Billing service

Fidulor
6, avenue du Prof. André Lemière
75980 PARIS Cedex 20
Tel: 43 63 72 73
Fax: 43 63 02 55
Director: M. Hervé GOHIN

Horwath France
12, rue de Madrid
75008 PARIS
Tel: 43 87 11 40
Fax: 45 22 78 87
Director: M. René AMIRKHANIAN

Inter Audit S.A.
21bis, rue Lord Byron
75008 PARIS
Tel: 43 59 58 73
Fax: 42 89 14 02
Director: M. R.J. TWIST
Bilingual accounting and auditing

KPMG Audit
47, rue de Villiers
92200 NEUILLY-SUR-SEINE
Tel: 46 39 44 44
Fax: 47 58 71 38
Partner: M. James WILD

KPMG Peat Marwick
53, avenue Montaigne
75008 PARIS
Tel: 45 63 15 40
Fax: 45 61 09 25
Senior Partner: M. Curtis BEHRENT

Lavigne Cogéval et Associés
88, avenue Niel
75017 PARIS
Tel: 42 27 24 10
Fax: 42 27 80 15

Marie-Line Fleuridas
2bis, rue Raymond Losserand
75014 PARIS
Tel: 43 20 09 94
Accounting, financial advice to foreign companies

Michèle Julien
59, rue Monge
75005 PARIS
Tel: 43 31 22 70
Fax: 45 35 63 14

Price Waterhouse
Tour AIG
34, Place des Corolles
Cedex 105
92908 PARIS LA DEFENSE
Tel: 41 26 16 00
Fax: 41 26 16 16
Senior Partner: M. Joël GARLOT
Management consultants, legal and fiscal

Raymond Chabot International
Tour Fiat
La Défense 6
92084 PARIS LA DEFENSE Cedex 16
Tel: 47 96 63 90
Fax: 47 96 63 96
Director: M. Yves LABAT

Richard A. Van Ham
74, avenue Marceau
75008 PARIS
Tel: 47 23 89 12
Fax: 47 20 15 07
USA tax accounting service

Sam Okoshken
51, avenue Montaigne
75008 PARIS
Tel: 44 13 69 50
Fax: 45 63 24 96
Income tax, property, setting up a business

Sefico
65, avenue Kléber
75116 PARIS
Tel: 47 27 65 98
Fax: 47 04 97 84
Contact: M. Jacques WENIG
Auditors, accounting and consulting services

Smith Barney
7, Place Vendôme
75001 PARIS
Tel: 42 96 10 66
Fax: 42 96 22 81
Manager: M. Christian PINCHART-DENY

Sogecc
12, rue Yves Toudic
75010 PARIS
Tel: 42 00 70 50
Fax: 42 39 13 43
President: M. Jean-Claude HAGEGE

Tucker Anthony Inc.
5bis, rue du Louvre
75001 PARIS
Tel: 42 61 57 68
Fax: 40 20 96 88
Manager: M. Hilary Gordon EDWARDS

Advertising Balloon Montgolfière
8, Villa Hallé
75014 PARIS
Tel: 40 47 61 04

Agence Annie Schneider
21, rue du Cirque
75008 PARIS
Tel: 42 66 10 34
Fax: 47 42 93 31
Press and public relations

AJIF S.A.R.L.
44, rue de Laborde
75008 PARIS
Tel: 43 87 19 41
Fax: 43 87 19 41
Director: M. Adrian FURTADO
Production of customised marketing publications, marketing events and electronic databases for Internet use

Bates France
11, rue Galvani
75017 PARIS
Tel: 44 09 59 59
Fax: 45 74 08 06

Bell Treasure Halas (B.T.H.)
14, Bd. Sébastopol
75004 PARIS
Tel: 42 71 40 90
Fax: 42 71 10 12

Data Reseach Publications
6, rue Mignard
75116 PARIS
Tel: 45 03 02 72
Fax: 45 03 02 96
Manager M. Pascal DUMAS
Market research (perfume, cosmetics)

Euro RSCG Worldwide
84, rue de Villiers
92683 LEVALLOIS-PERRET Cedex
Tel: 41 34 34 34
Fax: 41 34 45 67
President: M. Alain DE POUZILHAC

J. Stobbs Marketbase
107, avenue La Bourdonnais
75007 PARIS
Tel: 45 51 36 03
Fax: 47 53 72 85
Director: Mrs Johanna STOBBS
International marketing and communications

LLI Promotion
11bis, rue Baliat
92400 COURBEVOIE
Tel: 47 68 50 54
Fax: 43 34 18 24
Prints your advertising message on clothing

MBA Marketing and Business Analysis
114, avenue Félix Faure
75014 PARIS
Tel: 40 60 14 14
Fax: 45 39 17 31

MS Conseil
3, rue Achille Martinet
75018 PARIS
Tel: 42 23 64 52
Fax: 42 23 16 30
Consultant: Monique SALVAYRE
Market research

Paul Krob Media Representation
20, allée Darius Milhaud
75019 PARIS
Tel: 42 41 22 64
Fax: 42 41 75 71
Director: M. Paul KROB
Media representative and advertising advisor

Payrat & Associés
9, rue Denis Poisson
75017 PARIS
Tel: 40 68 12 12
Fax: 40 68 12 58

Promosalons
45, avenue George V
75008 PARIS
Tel: 47 20 93 79
Fax: 40 70 11 31
Contact: M. Pierre BONNAVE

Romance Alan
97, rue Vieille du Temple
75003 PARIS
Tel: 42 71 71 32
Fax: 42 71 12 86
Director: Mrs Alan ROMANCE

The Media Partnership France
149, quai Stalingrad
92130 ISSY-LES-MOULINEAUX
Tel: 40 93 08 09
Fax: 44 47 01 22

World Gold Council
1, avenue Bertie Albrecht
75008 PARIS
Tel: 49 53 04 61
Fax: 49 53 04 67
Manager: M. François DE LASSUS

Young & Rubicam France
23, allée Maillasson
B.P. 73
92105 BOULOGNE Cedex
Tel: 46 84 33 33
Fax: 46 84 32 72
Fax: 46 84 32 70
Director: M. Jean-Pierre VILLARET

15-34
58, avenue d'Iéna
75116 PARIS
Tel: 47 20 96 61

Agence Transatlantique
170, rue du Fbg. St. Antoine
75012 PARIS
Tel: 40 09 89 62
Specializes in the English-speaking world

Alabama
11, rue Moreau Vauthier
92100 BOULOGNE-BILLANCOURT
Tel: 46 99 15 30
Fax: 46 04 28 18

Alice
6, rue Escudier
92100 BOULOGNE-BILLANCOURT
Tel: 41 10 56 00
Fax: 41 10 57 48

American Banners Publicité
6, avenue de Boissy
94380 BONNEUIL-SUR-MARNE
Tel: 43 99 00 62
Fax: 43 39 05 87
Manager: M. Jacques CHETRIT

Austin Knight
129, rue de Turenne
75003 PARIS
Tel: 48 04 78 78

BCP France
8, rue de la Ferme
92100 BOULOGNE-BILLANCOURT
Tel: 46 21 77 33
Fax: 46 21 78 00
Managing Director: M. Jean LANGEVIN

BDDP
162, rue de Billancourt
92100 BOULOGNE-BILLANCOURT
Tel: 49 09 70 10
Fax: 48 25 04 19
President: M. Jean-Michel CARLO

Beaumont Bennett
63bis, rue de Sèvres
92100 BOULOGNE-BILLANCOURT
Tel: 46 84 85 00
Fax: 46 84 00 18

Bordelais Lemeunier Leo Burnett (B.L.L.B.)
122, rue Edouard Vaillant
92300 LEVALLOIS-PERRET
Tel: 41 49 73 00
Fax: 41 05 09 99
President: M. Jacques BORDELAIS

Brad Gorman
10, rue Michel Chasles
75012 PARIS
Tel: 40 19 94 94

Broad Romero International
236, Bd. St. Germain
75007 PARIS
Tel: 45 49 14 84
Fax: 45 49 09 12
Managing Director: M. Philippe BROAD
International public relations and marketing

Bureau International de Relations Publiques (B.I.R.P.)
17, avenue Ledru Rollin
75012 PARIS
Tel: 53 17 11 40
Fax: 53 17 11 45
Director: M. Jean-Pascal JEGU
Organizes exhibitions, congresses, seminars

Burke Marketing Research
78-80, avenue Général de Gaulle
Tour Galliéni 1
93174 BAGNOLET Cedex
Tel: 49 72 51 00
Fax: 49 72 51 06
Director: M. Gilles HUSTAIX

CLM-BBDO
2, allée Moulineaux
92130 ISSY-LES-MOULINEAUX
Tel: 41 23 41 23
Fax: 41 23 43 70
President: M. Alain POIREE

Colorado
71, rue Chardon Lagache
75016 PARIS
Tel: 45 27 80 00

Communication Business
137, rue du Fbg. St. Denis
75010 PARIS
Tel: 40 34 90 00
Fax: 40 34 10 19

Copywrite S.A.R.L.
1, passage Brady
75010 PARIS
Tel: 42 08 48 53
Fax: 42 38 14 08
Director: M. John FARR
Marketing and advertising

DDB Needham Worldwide
12, rue Médéric
75017 PARIS
Tel: 40 53 60 00
Fax: 47 66 80 66
Director: M. Hervé BROSSARD

Dun & Bradstreet International
Immeuble Défense Bergères
345, avenue Georges Clémenceau
92882 NANTERRE Cedex 9
Tel: 41 35 17 00
Fax: 41 35 17 77
Director: M. Bruno LEPROU
DE LA RIVIERE

Elektra Communications International
58, rue de Romainville
93260 LES LILAS
Tel: 43 60 01 43
Fax: 43 60 01 76
Minitel: 3615 NETWORK
Directors: M. Nick HARPER
& M. Hugh BARNARD
Design and construction of interactive and multimedia systems, including 3615 NETWORK and 3668 AngloPhone (see advertisement)

Euro Media
50, rue de Paradis
75010 PARIS
Tel: 42 46 61 15

Frost & Sullivan
8, rue de l'Arcade
75008 PARIS
Tel: 47 42 91 27
Fax: 47 42 91 29
Manager: M. Ian RUTHERFORD
Industrial market research

Fun Book France
85, rue de Maubeuge
75010 PARIS
Tel: 42 81 40 19

Grey Communication
63bis, rue de Sèvres
92514 BOULOGNE-BILLANCOURT
Cedex
Tel: 46 84 85 00
Fax: 46 84 00 18
President: M. Jan VAN AAL
Full range of media services

GT Partenaires
2bis, rue Descombes
75017 PARIS
Tel: 42 12 81 81
Fax: 42 12 01 85

Harper-Sklower
94, rue St. Honoré
75001 PARIS
Tel: 40 26 01 73
Fax: 40 26 03 22
Contact: M. Nick HARPER
Founded by two international agency directors to provide clients and agencies with an established business development resource

Havas Media International
78, avenue Raymond Poincaré
75016 PARIS
Tel: 45 01 54 55
Fax: 45 01 64 02

J. Walter Thompson
35, rue Baudin
92593 LEVALLOIS-PERRET
Tel: 41 05 80 00
Fax: 41 05 80 01
Director: M. Daniel COLE

Lintas
22, quai de la Mégisserie
75001 PARIS
Tel: 40 41 54 00
Fax: 42 33 43 56
President: M. Vincent NEGRE

Louis Harris France
5, Bd. Poissonnière
75002 PARIS
Tel: 44 82 25 25
Fax: 42 33 26 35
US polling institute

Lowe Quadrillage & Associés
96, avenue du Général Leclerc
92100 BOULOGNE-BILLANCOURT
Tel: 46 04 72 72
Fax: 46 04 72 73

Madison
3, rue Troyon
75017 PARIS
Tel: 47 64 04 45
Fax: 47 66 43 69

McCann-Erikson
48, rue de Villiers
92309 LEVALLOIS-PERRET Cedex
Tel: 47 59 34 56
Fax: 47 59 34 72
President: M. Claude DOUCE

Morales, Johancik & Associés
5, rue de Charonne
75011 PARIS
Tel: 43 14 81 40
Fax: 43 14 81 44
Advertising creation

Nielsen
9, avenue des Trois Fontaines
95007 CERGY-PONTOISE Cedex
Tel: 34 41 44 44
Fax: 30 38 60 77
President: M. Jean-Jacques MEYER

ODA - Régie Publicitaire des Annuaires France-Télécom
7, avenue de la Cristallerie
92317 SEVRES Cedex
Tel: 46 23 30 00
Fax: 46 23 32 86
Free call: 05 38 84 71

Ogilvy & Mather
36, rue Brunel
75017 PARIS
Tel: 40 68 60 00
Fax: 45 74 89 02
Chairman: M. Daniel SICOURI

Peaux Rouges
17, rue Hermel
75018 PARIS
Tel: 42 59 19 00
Fax: 42 59 18 48

Phil et Jeff
79bis, rue Lepic
75018 PARIS
Tel: 42 58 62 05

Publicis
133, avenue des Champs-Elysées
75008 PARIS
Tel: 44 43 70 00
Fax: 44 43 75 25
Communications Director:
Mme Laurence REY

Ray Lampard International Media
6, rue Bertin-Poirée
75001 PARIS
Tel: 40 28 01 19
Tel: 42 21 13 31
Fax: 40 26 34 33
Director: M. Ray LAMPARD
Media consultant and publications advertising representation

Revolver
8, Bd. de la Madeleine
75009 PARIS
Tel: 47 42 09 40
Fax: 47 42 09 44

Saatchi & Saatchi Business Communications Group
3, Bd. Georges Seurat
92523 NEUILLY-SUR-SEINE Cedex
Tel: 40 88 80 00
Fax: 46 40 19 41
Director: M. Christian LARGER

Saatchi & Saatchi Healthcom
30, Bd. Vital-Bouhot
92523 NEUILLY-SUR-SEINE Cedex
Tel: 40 88 40 00
Fax: 47 22 11 54
Health communications

Smartech Company
54, rue Moxouris
78150 LE CHESNAY
Tel: 39 63 30 60
Fax: 39 55 10 02
Director: Mme Martine MANDAR
Designs and makes all types of products

Taylor Nelson Vepro
14, rue de Silly
92100 BOULOGNE-BILLANCOURT
Tel: 48 25 66 44
Fax: 48 25 04 72

TBWA
25, rue du Pont-Neuf
75001 PARIS
Tel: 40 41 58 59
Fax: 40 26 62 50
Chairman: M. Jacques LEVY

Teatime Communications
43bis, rue d'Hautpoul
75019 PARIS
Tel: 42 40 14 00
Fax: 42 40 77 67
Director: M. Daniel BISSON
Public relations, marketing, design

Text Appeal International
113, rue des Pyrénées
75020 PARIS
Tel: 43 56 74 75
Fax: 43 56 80 84
President: M. Elliot H. POLAK
Cross-cultural advertising

Wallace Salmon
4, rue de la Paix
75002 PARIS
Tel: 40 15 09 67

Willard Publicité
13, rue de Liège
75009 PARIS
Tel: 48 74 48 25

William Greenwood
53, rue Monceau
75008 PARIS
Tel: 45 61 03 22

Winning International
96, rue du Fbg. Poissonnière
75010 PARIS
Tel: 44 63 52 00
Fax: 44 23 04 20

Work in Progress
57, rue Labrouste
75015 PARIS
Tel: 48 28 44 44

Your's And Go
2, rue Orteaux
75020 PARIS
Tel: 43 70 23 27
Fax: 43 70 49 22
Market surveys

Aer Lingus
47, avenue de l'Opéra
75002 PARIS
Admin: 42 66 93 61
Res: 47 42 12 50
Fax: : 42 66 36 62
Marketing Director: Mme Monika CASALI

Air Canada
10, rue de la Paix
75002 PARIS
Admin: 44 50 20 11
Res: 44 50 20 20
Fax: 42 60 99 99

Air France
1, Square Max Hymans
75015 PARIS
Admin: 43 23 81 81
Info: 44 08 24 24
Headquarters

Air France
2, rue Robert Esnault Pelterie
75007 PARIS
Tel: 44 08 24 24
Arrivals: 43 20 12 55
Departures: 43 20 13 55
Minitel: 3615 AF
Ticket Office

Air Inter
Aérogare des Invalides
75007 PARIS
Tel: 45 55 07 72
Fax: 45 51 01 78
Ticket Office

Air Inter
1, avenue Maréchal Devaux
91550 PARAY VIEILLE POSTE
Tel: 46 75 12 12
Fax: 46 75 12 22
Commercial Director:
M. Jean-Pierre BOURGNEUF
Headquarters

Air New Zealand
66, avenue des Champs-Elysées
75008 PARIS
Tel: 53 77 13 30

Air UK
3, rue de Choiseul
75002 PARIS
Admin: 49 27 98 01
Res: 44 56 18 08
Fax: 42 60 52 47
Sales Manager: Martine NERAUD

America West Airlines
66, avenue des Champs-Elysées
75008 PARIS
Tel: 53 77 13 20
Fax: 53 77 13 65

American Airlines
109, rue du Fbg. St. Honoré
75373 PARIS Cedex 08
Res: 42 89 05 22
Fax: 42 99 99 95
Director: M. Jacques ALONSO

British Airways
Tour Winterthur
Cedex 18
92085 PARIS LA DEFENSE
Tel: 49 03 93 00
Fax: 49 03 93 90
Contact: Mme Isabelle KOCH

British Midland Airways
4, Place de Londres
Continental Square
Roissypole
95700 ROISSY CDG
Tel: 48 62 55 52
Res: 48 62 55 65
Fax: 48 62 55 97
Sales Manager: M. Michel TURINI

Canadian Airlines International
109, rue du Fbg. St. Honoré
75373 PARIS Cedex 08
Res. 49 53 07 07
Fax: 42 99 99 33
Commercial Director:
Mme KIRCHER

Continental Airlines
92, avenue des Champs-Elysées
75008 PARIS
Admin: 42 99 09 48
Res: 42 99 09 09
Fax: 42 25 31 89
Director: Mme Annette BRAUNER
Continental One Pass
Tel: 42 99 09 10
Marketing: 42 99 09 45

Delta Air Lines
Immeuble Lavoisier
4, Place des Vosges
Cedex 64
92052 PARIS LA DEFENSE Cedex
Admin: 49 04 72 00
Res: 47 68 92 92
Fax: 47 68 52 82
Director France: Mme Reine CAVEY

Eurobelgian Airlines
20, rue de la Fédération
75015 PARIS
Tel: 45 75 75 00
Fax: 45 77 58 14

Jersey European Airways
2, rue Duphot
75001 PARIS
Tel: 42 96 02 44
Fax: 40 15 91 23
Manager: M. Rene GALLOW
Representative for Heli-USA

Northwest Airlines Inc.
16, rue Chauveau Lagarde
75008 PARIS
Tel: 42 66 90 00
Fax: 42 66 94 66

Qantas Airways
13, Bd. de la Madeleine
75001 PARIS
Admin: 44 55 52 05
Res: 44 55 52 00
Fax: 42 97 51 34

T.A.T.
17, rue de la Paix
75002 PARIS
Tel: 42 61 82 10
Fax: 49 27 06 65

Trans World Airlines (TWA)
6, rue Christophe Colomb
75008 PARIS
Admin: 40 69 70 00
Res: 49 19 20 00
Fax: 40 69 70 99

U.S. Air
23bis, rue Danjou
92100 BOULOGNE-BILLANCOURT
Res: 49 10 29 00
Fax: 49 10 00 07
Commercial Director: Anne-Marie PECHEUR

United Airlines
Les Mercuriales
40, rue Jean Jaurès
93176 BAGNOLET
Tel: 48 97 82 82
Headquarters

United Airlines
34, avenue de l'Opéra
75002 PARIS
Res: 48 97 82 82
Commercial Director: Mme Jenny RUELLAND
Ticket office

UTA
12, rue Chaussée d'Antin
75009 PARIS
Tel: 48 24 74 74
Fax: 45 23 22 27

Vacances Air Transat
69, Bd. Richard Lenoir
75011 PARIS
Tel: 43 55 44 11
Fax: 43 55 41 59
Director: M. Jean-Marc BATTA

Other Airlines
Autres Compagnies

Aeroflot
33, avenue des Champs-Elysées
75008 PARIS
Admin: 42 25 31 92
Res: 42 25 43 81
Commercial Director: M. Raphael BALIEV

Aerolineas Argentinas
77, avenue des Champs-Elysées
75008 PARIS
Res: 53 77 15 10
Fax: 53 77 15 18
Public Relations: M. Carlos FEENEY

Air Afrique
29, rue du Colisée
75008 PARIS
Admin: 44 21 32 00
Res: 44 21 32 32
Fax: 45 61 49 59

Air Algérie
28, avenue de l'Opéra
75002 PARIS
Tel: 47 03 74 00
Fax: 42 60 43 60

Air China
10, Bd. Malesherbes
75008 PARIS
Tel: 42 66 16 58
Fax: 47 42 67 63
Commercial Director: M. Pierre VALLVE

Air Gabon
4, avenue Franklin Roosevelt
75008 PARIS
Tel: 43 59 20 63
Fax: 45 63 60 54
Commercial Director: M. Guy CHABERT

Air India
1, rue Auber
75009 PARIS
Admin: 42 68 40 00
Res: 42 68 40 10
Fax: 42 66 22 02
Commercial Director: M. E. MAJRI

Air Lanka
2, rue des Moulins
75001 PARIS
Tel: 42 97 43 44
Fax: 42 86 83 20

Air Madagascar
29, rue des Boulets
75011 PARIS
Tel: 43 79 74 74
Fax: 43 79 30 33

Air Malta
8, Bd. de la Madeleine
75001 PARIS
Tel: 44 86 08 40
Fax: 44 86 08 41

Air Mauritius
8, rue Halévy
75009 PARIS
Tel: 44 51 15 63
Fax: 47 42 04 38

Alitalia
69, Bd. Haussmann
75008 PARIS
Tel: 44 94 44 00
Fax: 44 94 44 80
P.R.: M. Jean-Pierre GAILLARD

All Nippon Airways (ANA)
91, avenue des Champs-Elysées
75008 PARIS
Admin: 44 31 44 11
Res: 44 31 44 31
Fax: 40 70 93 25

Austrian Airlines
9, Bd. Malesherbes
75008 PARIS
Admin: 42 66 35 43
Res: 42 66 34 66

Aéromexico
12, rue Auber
75009 PARIS
Tel: 47 42 40 50
Fax: 47 42 02 35

Cameroon Airlines
12, Bd. des Capucines
75009 PARIS
Admin: 43 12 30 20
Res: 43 12 30 10
Fax: 49 24 93 98

Cathay Pacific Airways
267, Bd. Pereire
75017 PARIS
Admin: 40 68 61 00
Res: 40 68 61 61
Fax: 40 68 92 10

China Airlines
10, Bd. Malesherbes
75008 PARIS
Tel: 42 66 16 58
Fax: 47 42 67 63

Csa-Ceskoslovenske Aerolinie
32, avenue de l'Opéra
75002 PARIS
Tel: 47 42 18 11
Fax: 47 42 32 22

Cubana de Aviación
33, avenue du Maine
75015 PARIS
Tel: 45 38 31 12

Cyprus Airways
37, rue Jean Giraudoux
75016 PARIS
Tel: 45 01 93 38
Fax: 45 01 24 20

Egyptair
1bis, rue Auber
75009 PARIS
Tel: 44 94 85 00

El Al
35, Bd. des Capucines
75002 PARIS
Admin: 44 55 00 00
Res: 40 20 90 90
Fax: 44 55 00 13

Emirates Airlines
38, avenue des Champs-Elysées
75008 PARIS
Res: 44 95 95 44
Admin: 44 95 95 48
Fax: 44 95 95 49

Finnair
11, rue Auber
75009 PARIS
Admin: 44 51 02 51
Res: 47 42 33 33
Fax: 44 51 02 50

Garuda Indonesia
75, avenue des Champs-Elysées
75008 PARIS
Admin: 44 95 15 55
Res: 44 95 15 50
Fax: 40 75 00 52

Gulf Air
36, rue du Chemin Vert
75011 PARIS
Tel: 49 23 27 00
Fax: 49 23 27 38

Ibéria
11, Pont des Cinq Martyrs
Lycée Buffon
75014 PARIS
Admin: 42 79 11 20
Res: 40 47 80 90
Fax: 42 79 11 02

Icelandair
9, Bd. des Capucines
75002 PARIS
Tel: 44 51 60 51
Fax: 42 65 17 52

Iran Air
63, avenue des Champs-Elysées
75008 PARIS
Tel: 43 59 01 20
Fax: 42 89 85 58

Island Helicopters New York
5bis, rue du Louvre
75001 PARIS
Tel: 44 77 87 95

Japan Airlines
1, Rond-Point des Champs-Elysées
75008 PARIS
Admin: 44 35 55 25
Res: 44 35 55 00
Fax: 44 35 55 99

Kenya Airways
38, avenue de l'Opéra
75002 PARIS
Tel: 47 42 33 11
Fax: 49 24 00 42

KLM Royal Dutch Airlines
36, avenue de l'Opéra
75002 PARIS
Admin: 44 56 19 00
Res: 44 56 18 18
Fax: 44 56 19 09

Korean Airlines
5, rue d'Amboise
75002 PARIS
Tel: 40 20 02 02

Kuwait Airways
93, avenue des Champs-Elysées
75008 PARIS
Admin: 47 20 52 44
Res: 47 20 75 15
Fax: 47 20 55 08

LOT Polish Airlines
18, rue Louis le Grand
75002 PARIS
Tel: 47 42 05 60

Lufthansa
21, rue Royale
75008 PARIS
Tel: 42 65 37 35
Admin: 40 17 12 30
Fax: 42 65 74 72

Olympic Airways
3, rue Auber
75009 PARIS
Admin: 47 42 87 99
Res: 42 65 92 42
Fax: 40 07 03 04

Pakistan International Airlines
90, avenue des Champs-Elysées
75008 PARIS
Tel: 45 62 92 41
Fax: 45 63 64 58

Royal Air Maroc
38, avenue de l'Opéra
75002 PARIS
Res: 44 94 13 10
Fax: 47 42 28 97

Royal Jordanian Airlines
12, rue de la Paix
75002 PARIS
Tel: 42 61 57 45
Fax: 42 60 48 19

Sabena - Belgian World Airlines
19, rue de la Paix
75002 PARIS
Admin: 44 94 19 00
Res: 44 94 19 19
Fax: 47 42 58 88

Scandinavian Airline System
30, Bd. des Capucines
75009 PARIS
Admin: 42 66 93 53
Res: 47 42 06 14
Fax: 42 66 17 01

Singapore Airlines
43, rue Boissière
75016 PARIS
Admin: 45 53 52 44
Res: 45 53 90 90
Fax: : 47 05 93 26

Société Kilian
21, avenue St. Fiacre
Z.A.C. du Bel Air
78100 ST-GERMAIN-EN-LAYE
Tel: 30 61 08 35
Fax: 30 61 57 80
Commercial Director: M. Edgardo DEMARIA
Paris representative for Mexicana Airlines, Lan Chile and Avensa

Swissair
4-14, rue Ferrus
75014 PARIS
Admin: 40 78 10 00
Res: 45 81 11 01
Fax: 45 65 00 48

TAP (Air Portugal)
11bis, Bd. Haussmann
75009 PARIS
Admin: 44 86 89 50
Res: 44 86 89 89
Fax: 44 83 60 68

Thai Airways
23, avenue des Champs-Elysées
75008 PARIS
Admin: 44 20 70 15
Res: 44 20 70 80
Fax: 45 63 75 69

Turkish Airlines
1, rue Scribe
75009 PARIS
Res: 42 66 47 40
Fax: 42 66 47 39

Varig
38, avenue des Champs-Elysées
75008 PARIS
Tel: 40 69 50 50
Fax: 42 89 22 40

Alain Neymarc Architecte
5, rue Scipion
75005 PARIS
Tel: 47 07 99 50
Fax: 43 37 01 59
Director: M. Alain NEYMARC
Licensed in France and the USA

Alternative Architecture Association
103, rue Raymond Losserand
75014 PARIS
Tel: 45 41 03 32
Fax: 40 44 94 87
Architect: M. Jean LABERTHONNIERE

Arc International
96, rue de Rivoli
75004 PARIS
Tel: 42 72 00 43
Fax: 48 04 87 20
Interior architecture

Architecture by American Concept
14bis, rue du Maréchel Foch
77780 BOURRON-MARLOTTE
Tel: 64 45 75 74
Fax: 64 45 75 12

Armeco International S.A.
8, rue Parmentier
92800 PUTEAUX
Tel: 46 97 04 88
Fax: 46 97 04 24
Director: M. Afchine MARKAZI

Bailey et Smith Architectes
14, rue Denis Poisson
75017 PARIS
Tel: 45 72 35 59
Fax: 45 72 12 01
Commercial Director: M. Francis LEVANT

Bouygues Immobilier
19, rue de Sèvres
92100 BOULOGNE
Tel: 41 10 04 04

Claude Chauchet
50bis, rue Madeleine Michelis
92200 NEUILLY-SUR-SEINE
Tel: 46 24 78 85
Fax: 40 54 74 10
Interior design

Cyril Sweet & Partners
22, avenue de Friedland
75008 PARIS
Tel: 42 56 00 38
Fax: 42 25 26 08
Director: M. Christian BOUCHEL
Construction cost consultants

Fromanger & Adam
30, rue Vieille du Temple
75004 PARIS
Tel: 42 78 79 41
Fax: 42 78 37 43
Director: Mme FROMANGER

Gleeds International
38, rue des Mathurins
75008 PARIS
Tel: 42 66 04 99
Fax: 42 66 29 02
Director: M. Jean-Pierre PAJON
Construction economists

Jean-Luc Grimaud
38, rue des Marais
92190 MEUDON VAL FLEURY
Tel: 45 07 97 87
Trompe-l'œil, interior decoration

Joséphine & Guy Duval
54, avenue de Saxe
75015 PARIS
Tel: 45 67 16 85
Fax: 47 83 65 99
Contact: Joséphine DUVAL
Architecture and interior decoration

Kaufman & Broad
44, rue Washington
75008 PARIS
Tel: 45 61 70 00
Fax: 53 75 30 10
Minitel: 3615 KAUFMAN ET BROAD
President: M. Guy NAFILYAN
Builder/Promoter

Lavalin International
23, rue Vernet
75008 PARIS
Tel: 47 20 83 88
Fax: 40 70 09 47
Vice-President: M. Jean-Pierre MOUREZ

Litwin S.A.
Tour Chantecoq
3-5, rue Chantecoq
92808 PUTEAUX Cedex
Tel: 41 02 52 52
Fax: 41 02 52 90
Director: M. André RHOE

Mellett Architects
6, rue du Roi Doré
75003 PARIS
Tel: 40 29 06 01
Fax: 40 29 06 02
Director: M. Patrick MELLETT

NFA S.A.R.L.
31, quai de l'Horloge
75001 PARIS
Tel: 44 07 05 75
Fax: 44 07 05 72
Contact: M. Joe SOBEY

Patrick Roth
6, allée Jean de la Bruyère
78000 VERSAILLES
Tel: 39 54 42 08
Interior design, rehabilitation

Robert Adams
16, rue Vézelay
75008 PARIS
Tel: 43 59 65 01
Fax: (16) 37 47 45 60
Architect

Smart Building Engineering
8bis, rue d'Annam
75020 PARIS
Tel: 43 58 09 87
Fax: 43 58 45 87

Bucknall Thorne Wheatley
11, rue La Boétie
75008 PARIS
Tel: 42 66 21 80
Fax: 47 42 21 78
Director: M. Tim BAILEY

Wimpey S.A.
72, Grande Rue
B.P. 67
92312 SEVRES Cedex
Tel: 41 14 77 00
Fax: 45 07 22 00

A l'Enseigne des Oudin
58, rue Quincampoix
75004 PARIS
Tel: 42 71 83 65
Man Ray, Lapicque, Fluxus, New Realists

AJIF Gallery
44, rue de Laborde
75008 PARIS
Tel: 43 87 19 41
Fax: 43 87 19 41
Director: M. Adrian FURTADO
Exhibitions of drawings, lithographs, paintings and publication of lithographs by contemporary figurative artists

Art Service International
30, rue du Château d'Eau
75010 PARIS
Tel: 42 39 14 00
Fax: 42 39 14 02
Director: Bénédicte PESLE

Art's Sagot International
123, rue de la Pompe
75016 PARIS
Tel: 47 55 03 50

Artcurial
9, avenue Matignon
75008 PARIS
Tel: 42 99 16 16
Fax: 43 59 29 81
Features 20th century masters, as well as a fine arts bookstore, decorative arts, jewelry

Baudoin Lebon
38, rue Ste-Croix-de-la-Bretonnerie
75004 PARIS
Tel: 42 72 09 10
Fax: 42 72 02 20
Contemporary art

Brachot-Amélio
4, rue Jacques Callot
75006 PARIS
Tel: 43 26 54 58
Fax: 46 34 03 98
Surrealist leaning with works by Magritte and Delvaux. Also represents contemporaries such as Roland Cat, Gina Pane and Broodthaers

Christie's
6, rue Paul Baudry
75008 PARIS
Tel: 42 56 17 66
Fax: 42 56 26 01
Art auction house since 1766

Darthea Speyer
6, rue Jacques Callot
75006 PARIS
Tel: 43 54 78 41
American gallery with a selection of high quality works in all media

Down-Town
33, rue de Seine
75006 PARIS
Tel: 46 33 82 41
Furniture dating from the 1950s

Drouot Richelieu
9, rue Drouot
75009 PARIS
Tel: 48 00 20 20
Public auction room

Durand-Dessert
28, rue de Lappe
75011 PARIS
Tel: 48 06 92 23
Conceptual art, Arte Povera

Espace Cannibal Pierce
7, rue Samson
B.P. 224
93200 ST-DENIS
Tel: 48 09 94 59
Directors: M. Ken SHEPHERD
& June SHENFIELD
Australian art gallery and bookstore

Espace d'Art Yvonamor Palix
13, rue Keller
75011 PARIS
Tel: 48 06 36 70
Fax: 47 00 01 21
Director: YVONAMOR PALIX
Conceptual art, video, photography

Etude Tajan
37, rue des Mathurins
75008 PARIS
Tel: 53 30 30 30
Fax: 53 30 30 31
Director: Maître Jacques TAJAN
Auction house

Farideh Cadot
77, rue des Archives
75003 PARIS
Tel: 42 78 08 36
Fax: 42 78 63 61

Fiesta Galerie
7, rue Quincampoix
75004 PARIS
Tel: 42 71 53 34
Fax: 42 71 53 34
Contact: Marie AFLACO
American antiques from the 1950-1960s, restaurant decors

Galerie 1900-2000
8, rue Bonaparte
75006 PARIS
Tel: 43 25 84 20
Fax: 46 34 74 52
Contact: Marcel FLEISS

Galerie Alain Gutharc
47, rue de Lappe
75011 PARIS
Tel: 47 00 32 10
Fax: 40 21 72 74
Director: M. Alain GUTHARC
Exhibits range from installations to photography used as documentation. Artists include Endo, Queniaux, Hepworth and Gallo

Galerie Albert Loeb
12, rue des Beaux-Arts
75006 PARIS
Tel: 43 26 45 62

Galerie Ariel
140, Bd. Haussmann
75008 PARIS
Tel: 45 62 13 09
Contemporary art works

Galerie Arlette Gimaray
12, rue Mazarine
75006 PARIS
Tel: 46 34 71 80
Fax: 46 33 06 22
Director: Arlette GIMARAY
Contemporary painting and sculpture

Galerie Beaubourg
23, rue du Renard
75004 PARIS
Tel: 42 71 20 50
Promotes contemporary French art

Galerie Benjamin Derry
26, rue des Jardins St. Paul
75004 PARIS
Tel: 42 77 15 75

Galerie Chantal Crousel
40, rue Quincampoix
75004 PARIS
Tel: 42 77 38 87

Galerie Claire Burrus
16, rue de Lappe
75011 PARIS
Tel: 43 55 36 90
Fax: 47 00 26 03
Contemporary art

Galerie Claude Bernard
5-7, rue des Beaux-Arts
75006 PARIS
Tel: 43 26 97 07
Fax: 46 33 04 25
Director: M. Claude BERNARD
Contemporary art with a preference for figurative paintings

Galerie d'Art Bernheim-Jeune
27, avenue Matignon
75008 PARIS
Tel: 42 66 65 03
Manager: M. DAUBERVILLE
Shows modern and contemporary art

Galerie d'Auteuil
58, rue d'Auteuil
75016 PARIS
Tel: 42 24 89 62

Galerie Daniel Templon
30, rue Beaubourg
75003 PARIS
Tel: 42 72 14 10
Fax: 42 77 45 36
Specializes in Minimal and Conceptual art (Judd, Flavin and Morris), as well as works by Alberola, Chia, Fetting, Rauchenberg and Salle

Galerie de France
52, rue de la Verrerie
75004 PARIS
Tel: 42 74 38 00
Fax: 42 74 34 67
Director: Mme C. THIEK
Showing works by artists like Rebecca Horn, Martial Raysse, Soulages, Domela, Matta, Degottex

Galerie Donya Quiguer
1, rue Ste-Croix-de-la-Bretonnerie
75004 PARIS
Tel: 48 04 72 55
Contemporary artwork and glass creations

Galerie Fabre
6, rue Pont de Lodi
75006 PARIS
Tel: 43 25 42 63

Galerie Fanny Guillon-Laffaille
4, avenue de Messine
75008 PARIS
Tel: 45 63 52 00
Fax: 45 61 92 91
Director: Fanny GUILLON-LAFFAILLE
Work by the Ecole de Paris *artists along with contemporary creations*

Galerie Franck & Hervé Bordas
2, rue de la Roquette
75011 PARIS
Tel: 47 00 31 61
Emphasis on original lithographic prints

Galerie Hopkins-Thomas
2, rue de Miromesnil
75008 PARIS
Tel: 42 65 51 05
Modern and Impressionist painting

Galerie J.J. Donguy
57, rue de la Roquette
75011 PARIS
Tel: 47 00 10 94
Fluxus, new technologies, body art

Galerie Jacqueline Felman
8, rue Popincourt
75011 PARIS
Tel: 47 00 87 71
Promotes contemporary figurative work by younger artists (Michel Coquery, Buffoli, Hours and Riccardo Licata)

Galerie Krief
50, rue Mazarine
75006 PARIS
Tel: 43 29 32 37
Fax: 43 26 99 81
Director: Mme Elizabeth KRIEF

Galerie Maeght
12, rue St. Merri
75004 PARIS
Tel: 42 78 43 44
Director: M. Adrien MAEGHT
20th century masters such as Braque, Giacometti, Kandinsky and Matisse

Galerie Martin-Caille Matignon
75, rue du Fbg. St. Honoré
75008 PARIS
Tel: 42 66 60 71
Fax: 47 42 55 48
Painting gallery

Galerie MC
46, rue de Seine
75006 PARIS
Tel: 43 25 34 70

Galerie Patrice Trigano
4bis, rue des Beaux- Arts
75006 PARIS
Tel: 46 34 15 01

Galerie Pierre Boogaerts
44, rue Vieille du Temple
75004 PARIS
Tel: 42 74 44 68
Director: M. Pierre BOOGAERTS
Specialized in original art by American illustrators

Galerie Samia Saouma
16, rue des Coutures St. Gervais
75003 PARIS
Tel: 42 78 40 44
Fax: 42 78 64 00
Director: Samia SAOUMA
Sales of contemporary photography, paintings and drawings

Galerie Stadler
51, rue de Seine
75006 PARIS
Tel: 43 26 91 10
Fax: 46 34 73 97
Works by Rainer, Saura, Shirage, Thupinier

Galerie Yvon Lambert
108, rue Vieille du Temple
75003 PARIS
Tel: 42 71 09 33
Fax: 42 71 87 47

Gallery A.B.
63, passage Jouffroy
75009 PARIS
Tel: 42 47 05 17

Gilbert Brownstone et Cie
26, rue St. Gilles
75003 PARIS
Tel: 42 78 43 21
Fax: 42 74 04 00
Director: M. Gilbert BROWNSTONE
An American gallery, active in the field of Conceptual art. Promotes the work of Albers, Fontana, Gottfried Honnegar, Jesus-Raphael Soto and Raynaud

Jean Fournier
44, rue Quincampoix
75004 PARIS
Tel: 42 77 32 31
Fax: 48 87 34 65
Shows abstract work by an international group of artists such as Sam Francis, Claude Viallat, Joan Mitchell, Shirley Jaffé, Pierre Buraglio, Bernard Piffaretti

Lavignes-Bastille
27, rue de Charonne
75011 PARIS
Tel: 47 00 88 18
Fax: 43 55 91 32
Director: M. Jean-Pierre LAVIGNES
From neo-Expressionism to abstract art

Lelong
13, rue de Téhéran
75008 PARIS
Tel: 45 63 13 19
Fax: 42 89 34 33

Louis Carré
10, avenue de Messine
75008 PARIS
Tel: 45 62 57 07
Works by 20th century artists

Marcel Bernheim
18, avenue Matignon
75008 PARIS
Tel: 42 65 22 23
Fax: 42 65 27 16

Mathias Fels
138, Bd Haussmann
75008 PARIS
Tel: 45 62 21 34
New Realists, New Figurative movement

Paris American Art
4, rue Bonaparte
75006 PARIS
Tel: 43 26 79 85

Sagot Le Garrec
10, rue de Buci
75006 PARIS
Tel: 43 26 43 38

Sotheby's
3, rue Miromesmil
75008 PARIS
Tel: 42 66 40 60
Fax: 47 42 22 32
Prestigious auction house for works of art

Wally Findlay Galleries
2, avenue Matignon
75008 PARIS
Tel: 42 25 70 74
Fax: 42 56 40 45
President: M. Simone KAROFF

Zabriskie
37, rue Quincampoix
75004 PARIS
Tel: 42 72 35 47
Fax: 40 27 99 66
Director: Andréa HOLZHERR
Branch of the New York gallery

Manufacturers
Constructeurs

British Motors
58, rue de La Fontaine
75016 PARIS
Tel: 42 88 05 34
Fax: 45 27 23 83
Director: M. Edgar BENSOUSAN

Citroën
125, Bd. Jean Jaurès
92110 CLICHY
Tel: 42 70 17 17
Fax: 47 37 26 01

Delphi France
56-68, avenue Louis Roche
92231 GENNEVILLIERS Cedex
Tel: 40 80 70 00
Fax: 40 80 72 24
Director: M. Jean CAZADE
Division of General Motors

Ford France
344, avenue Napoléon Bonaparte
B.P. 307
92506 RUEIL-MALMAISON
Tel: 47 32 60 00
Fax: 47 32 60 16
Financial Director: M. Rainer PIRKL

Peugeot Automobiles
75, avenue de la Grande Armée
75116 PARIS
Tel: 40 66 55 11
Fax: 40 66 54 14

Renault S.A.
34, quai du Point du Jour
92109 BOULOGNE-BILLANCOURT
Cedex
Tel: 41 04 50 50
President: M. Louis SCHWEITZER

Rolls-Royce International Ltd
122, avenue Charles de Gaulle
92522 NEUILLY-SUR-SEINE Cedex
Tel: 47 22 14 40
Fax: 47 45 77 38
Regional Executive:
M. CHARLTON

Rover France S.A.
B.P. 32
95102 ARGENTEUIL Cedex
Tel: 39 98 40 40
Fax: 39 82 45 38
Managing Director:
M. Christopher T. FRANKLIN
Automobile importer

Dealers/Accessories
Concessionnaires/Accessoires

American Car Club de France
15, Fontaine du Perlan
78920 ECQUEVILLY
Tel: 34 75 57 79
Contact: M. Jean-Claude PETITPRE

Cadillac Jean Charles
50, avenue de New York
75116 PARIS
Tel: 47 20 00 40
Fax: 47 20 59 42

Chrysler
44, rue de la Convention
75015 PARIS
Tel: 45 79 30 30

Dixie Driver's Association
5, rue Drouhin
93150 BLANC-MESNIL
Tel: 48 67 33 24
Fax: 48 67 46 57
President: M. Michel
LAMOURANNE
Club of American cars

Franco Britannic Automobiles
21, avenue Kléber
75116 PARIS
Tel: 45 00 85 19
Fax: 47 58 79 57
Exclusive agent for Rolls-Royce, Bentley, Jaguar and Daimler

Harley-Davidson
48, rue de la Chapelle
75018 PARIS
Tel: 46 07 83 21
Fax: 42 05 96 49

Jaguar Wilson
116, rue du Président Wilson
92300 LEVALLOIS-PERRET
Tel: 47 39 92 50

Fax: 47 39 50 31

Mercedes-Benz
118, avenue des Champs-Elysées
75008 PARIS
Tel: 45 62 24 04
Fax: 42 25 64 83

Mustang Club de France
36, rue Roger Jourdain
92500 RUEIL-MALMAISON
Tel: 47 51 39 43
Fax: 47 29 07 27

Opel/GM/Oldsmobile René Petit
81, rue de Meaux
75019 PARIS
Tel: 44 52 40 00
Fax: 44 52 40 40
Dealership for General Motors, Buick, Pontiac, Cadillac and Chevrolet

SAAB
60, Bd. de Reuilly
75012 PARIS
Tel: 40 02 02 77
Fax: 40 02 08 62
Public Relations: Diane DORPHIN

Volvo Actena Mirabeau
56, avenue de Versailles
75016 PARIS
Tel: 44 30 82 30
Fax: 40 50 67 85
Contact: Mme LEMAIRE
Full range of Volvo vehicles and services (see advertisement)

Abbey National Bank
163, Bd. Haussmann
75008 PARIS
Tel: 44 95 00 95
Fax: 44 95 00 99
Free call: 05 10 10 11

ABN Amro Bank
3, avenue Hoche
75008 PARIS
Tel: 42 67 50 50

American Express Bank
11, rue Scribe
75009 PARIS
Tel: 47 14 50 00
Fax: 42 68 17 17
President: M. Pierrot GRANDI
Foreign currency and traveler's checks

American Express France
4, rue Louis Blériot
92561 RUEIL-MALMAISON
Tel: 47 77 77 07
Fax: 47 77 74 65
President: M. Charles PETRUCCELLI
Headquarters

Australia & New Zealand Banking Group Limited
6, rue de Berri
75008 PARIS
Tel: 40 75 05 37
Fax: 40 75 05 46
General Manager: M. Maurice LEMOINE
Specialized in export financing

Bank of America
43-47, avenue de la Grande Armée
75782 PARIS Cedex 16
Tel: 45 02 68 00
Fax: 45 01 77 89
Senior Vice-President:
M. Christian BARTHOLIN
Wholesale banking

Bank of Boston
104, avenue des Champs-Elysées
75008 PARIS
Tel: 40 76 75 00
Fax: 40 76 75 95
Director: M. Peter JETON

Bank of Credit and Commerce International
125, avenue des Champs-Elysées
75008 PARIS
Tel: 44 43 90 00
Fax: 47 20 56 43

Bank of India
3, rue Scribe
75009 PARIS
Tel: 42 66 50 04
Fax: 42 66 50 06

Bank of Korea
30, avenue George V
75008 PARIS
Tel: 47 20 74 58
Fax: 47 20 61 99

Bank of New York
36, Bd. Haussmann
75009 PARIS
Tel: 42 46 26 25
Fax: 42 47 02 36

Bank of Tokyo
4, rue Ste Anne
75001 PARIS
Tel: 42 61 58 33

Bankers Trust Company
12-14, Rond-Point des Champs-Elysées
B.P. 649-08
75367 PARIS Cedex 08
Tel: 42 99 30 00
Fax: 42 89 02 92
President: M. Philippe SOUVIRON

Banque Audi France
73, avenue des Champs-Elysées
75008 PARIS
Tel: 42 25 75 00
Fax: 42 56 09 74

Banque de France
39, rue Croix-des-Petits-Champs
75001 PARIS
Tel: 42 92 42 92
Fax: 42 96 04 23
Governor: M. Jean-Claude TRICHET

France Telecom

ce!

When we talk service, we're also talking about price/quality ratio.

And when you use France Telecom for your international calls:

- You get access to a global telephone network with 'round the clock supervision
- You're free to phone without a membership contract or other restrictions
- You get direct-dial access to parties in foreign countries
- The numbers you call remain confidential
- Rates stay constant despite currency exchange fluctuations
- You can take advantage of low rates by phoning or faxing during off-peak hours
- You have a highly competent, reliable team of people at your service whenever - and wherever - you need to phone.

Berlin
3.08 FF (excl. tax) per minute

Rabat
5.84 FF (excl. tax) per minute

Moscow
5.43 FF (excl. tax) per minute

Los Angeles
4.92 FF (excl. tax) per minute

France Telecom, the world's fourth largest carrier, means international calling with confidence.

For more information or for an English speaking representative contact the International Business Center :

N° Vert 05 05 05 75 APPEL GRATUIT or (33-1) 44 76 27 28.

And the world is closer.

Banque Française du Commerce Extérieur
21, Bd. Haussmann
75009 PARIS
Tel: 48 00 48 00
Fax: 48 00 41 51
International Director:
M. Erik LESCAR

Banque Indosuez
96, Bd. Haussmann
75008 PARIS
Tel: 44 20 20 20
Fax: 44 20 29 56
Vice-President: M. Jean-François LEPETIT

Banque Nationale de Paris (BNP)
16, Bd. des Italiens
75009 PARIS
Tel: 40 14 45 46
Fax: 40 14 23 81
Minitel: 3614 BNP

Banque Paribas
3, rue d'Antin
75002 PARIS
Tel: 42 98 12 34
Fax: 42 98 11 42
Communications Director:
Mme Véronique GUILLOT-PELPEL
Contact: M. Jean ROUGNON

Banque Sanpaolo
52, avenue Hoche
75382 PARIS Cedex 08
Tel: 47 54 40 40
Fax: 47 54 46 57

Banque Transatlantique
17, Bd. Haussmann
75009 PARIS
Tel: 40 22 80 00
Fax: 48 24 01 75
Manager: M. Anthony STONE
Deputy Director Banking:
M. Patrick J. DANO

Banque Wormser Frères
11bis, Bd. Haussmann
75009 PARIS
Tel: 47 70 90 80
Fax: 47 70 37 79

Barclays Bank
21, rue Laffitte
75009 PARIS
Tel: 44 79 79 79
Fax: 44 79 72 52
Intl Deputy Director: M. Arnaud DE MASCAREL
Headquarters - 38 branches around Paris

Baring Brothers
49, avenue d'Iéna
75116 PARIS
Tel: 53 67 11 11
Fax: 40 70 00 51

Brown Harriman Corporation
12-14, Rond-Point des Champs-Elysées
75008 PARIS
Tel: 43 59 89 04
Fax: 45 63 66 63
Partner: M. William MOORE

Chase Manhattan Bank
42, rue Washington
75008 PARIS
Tel: 53 77 10 00
Fax: 53 77 10 50

Citibank N.A.
Citicenter
19, Le Parvis
Cedex 36
92073 PARIS LA DEFENSE
Tel: 49 06 10 10
Fax: 47 67 07 04
Citiphone 24h/24h: 49 05 49 05
Minitel: 3615 CITIBANK
Expatriate Marketing Manager:
Mme Judith DAVIS
(see advertisement)

Commerzbank
3, Place de l'Opéra
75002 PARIS
Tel: 44 94 17 00

Corestates Bank
231, rue St. Honoré
75001 PARIS
Tel: 42 60 21 87
Fax: 49 27 95 02
Vice-President: M. John KNUTSON

Cortal
131, avenue Charles de Gaulle
92571 NEUILLY-SUR-SEINE Cedex
Free call: 05 10 15 20
All transactions by telephone

Deutsche Bank
3, avenue de Friedland
75008 PARIS
Tel: 44 95 64 00

Discount Bank
16, avenue Kléber
75016 PARIS
Tel: 45 01 23 00
Fax: 45 01 58 10

International Bankers
18, Bd. Malesherbes
75008 PARIS
Tel: 44 94 88 44

J.P. Morgan
14, Place Vendôme
75001 PARIS
Tel: 40 15 45 00
Fax: 40 15 44 77
President: M. Didier CHERPITEL

Kiosque American Express
19, avenue George V
75008 PARIS
Tel: 53 67 03 15
American Express cash dispenser

Kleinwort Benson France
11, avenue Myron T. Herrick
75008 PARIS
Tel: 44 95 05 05
Fax: 42 89 87 36

Lazard Frères et Cie
121, Bd. Haussmann
75008 PARIS
Tel: 44 13 01 11
Fax: 42 25 73 99

Legal and General Bank
58, rue de la Victoire
75009 PARIS
Tel: 48 74 35 72

Lehman Brothers Bank
56, rue du Fbg. St. Honoré
75008 PARIS
Tel: 44 56 41 00
Fax: 44 56 42 37
President: M. Simon NORA

Lloyds Bank
15, avenue d'Iéna
75016 PARIS
Tel: 44 43 42 41
Fax: 44 43 42 05
Director: M. Claude DEMARIA

Louis Dreyfus France
87, avenue de la Grande Armée
75016 PARIS
Tel: 40 66 11 11
Fax: 40 67 14 19

Midland S.A.
20bis, avenue Rapp
75332 PARIS Cedex 07
Tel: 44 42 70 00
Fax: 44 42 77 77
Director: M. Bernard POUY

Mitsubishi Bank Ltd
112, avenue Kléber
75016 PARIS
Tel: 44 34 00 99

Morgan Grenfell
39, rue Washington
75008 PARIS
Tel: 44 95 09 00
Fax: 53 75 05 90

Morgan Stanley
25, rue Balzac
75008 PARIS
Tel: 53 77 70 00
Managing Director: M. Patrick DE ST-AIGNAN

National Bank of Canada
123, avenue des Champs-Elysées
75008 PARIS
Tel: 47 20 37 52
Fax: 47 23 31 04
Director: M. Jean-Luc ALIMONDO

National Westminster Bank
18, Place Vendôme
75001 PARIS
Tel: 44 58 53 00
Fax: 40 15 07 37

Philadelphia National Bank
231, rue St. Honoré
75001 PARIS
Tel: 42 60 21 87

Republic National Bank of New York
20, Place Vendôme
75001 PARIS
Tel: 44 86 18 61
Fax: 42 60 05 62
President: M. Elo ROZENCWAJG

Riggs National Bank (Europe)
U.S. Embassy Office
2, avenue Gabriel
75382 PARIS Cedex 08
Tel: 47 42 37 22
Fax: 47 42 38 10
President: M. Robert WOODBRIDGE

Rothschild et Cie
17, avenue Matignon
75008 PARIS
Tel: 40 74 40 74
Fax: 45 61 48 52

Royal Bank of Canada Europe Ltd
29, rue de la Bienfaisance
75008 PARIS
Tel: 40 08 42 00
Fax: 42 93 32 11
Director: M. Hugues
DE GUITAUT

Royal Saint Georges
3, rue Scribe
75009 PARIS
Tel: 41 34 26 00
Fax: 41 34 25 46

S.G. Warburg Securities Sas
65, rue de Courcelles
75008 PARIS
Tel: 48 88 33 44

Saudi American Bank
51, avenue Hoche
75008 PARIS
Tel: 43 8000 80

Schroders Partenaires
41, avenue George V
75008 PARIS
Tel: 40 73 85 00
Fax: 40 70 11 08

Société Générale
29, Bd. Haussmann
75009 PARIS
Tel: 40 98 20 00
Fax: 40 98 27 01

State Street Banque
21-25, rue Balzac
75008 PARIS
Tel: 53 75 80 80
Fax: 53 75 80 09
Director: Monique BOURVEN
Contact: M. Alain CONTINI

Thomas Cook Bankers France
8, rue Bellini
75016 PARIS
Tel: 47 55 52 25
Fax: 47 27 37 22
Public Relations Director:
M. SOISSON

Woolwich Bank
87, avenue François Arago
B.P. 801
92000 NANTERRE
Tel: 40 97 40 00
Fax: 40 97 40 05
Headquarters

Woolwich Bank
120, avenue du Général Leclerc
75014 PARIS
Tel: 45 45 63 83
Fax: 45 45 63 11

World Bank
64, avenue d'Iéna
75116 PARIS
Tel: 40 69 30 00
Fax: 47 23 74 36

Exchange Bureaux
Bureaux de Change

Banque Régionale d'Escompte
66, avenue des Champs-Elysées
75008 PARIS
Tel: 42 89 10 99
Automatic teller for converting 10 and 20 US bills into francs

Change du Rond-Point
Galerie Elysées Rond-Point
47, avenue Franklin Roosevelt
75008 PARIS
Tel: 42 25 91 36
Tel: 42 25 91 37
No commission charge

Change St. Michel
5, quai St. Michel
75005 PARIS
Tel: 43 54 40 10

Chequepoint
150, avenue des Champs-Elysées
75008 PARIS
Tel: 49 53 02 51
Director: M. John GIANNI

Crédit Commercial de France
115, avenue des Champs-Elysées
75008 PARIS
Tel: 40 70 70 40

European Exchange Office
6, rue Yvonne Le Tac
75018 PARIS
Tel: 42 52 67 19
Fax: 42 52 58 20

Thomas Cook
8, rue Bellini
75016 PARIS
Tel: 47 55 52 25
Fax: 47 27 37 22
Public Relations Director:
M. Jacques SOISSON

Tradex Change
74, rue Rambuteau
75001 PARIS
Tel: 42 36 92 01
Contact: M. Edward STEWART

Beauty Salons
Instituts de Beauté

Astrid Beauté
228, rue du Fbg. St. Denis
75010 PARIS
Tel: 46 07 20 57

Clarins
4, rue Berteaux Dumas
92200 NEUILLY
Tel: 46 24 o1 81
Director: M. Christian
COURTIN-CLARINS
Beauty parlor

Guinot
4, rue de la Paix
75002 PARIS
Tel: 42 86 08 30

Institut Jeanne Piaubert
27, rue Jean Goujon
75008 PARIS
Tel: 53 77 55 31

Institut Maria Galland
7, avenue Marceau
75016 PARIS
Tel: 47 20 14 77

Institut Martin's Nails
35, rue Léon Frot
75011 PARIS
Tel: 43 48 68 38
Manicure, American nails

L'Onglerie
178, rue St. Martin
75003 PARIS
Tel: 42 77 20 60
Professional nail care

Look Lemon
10, rue Richepanse
75008 PARIS
Tel: 42 60 77 29
Beauty salon

Orlane
163, avenue Victor Hugo
75116 PARIS
Tel: 47 04 65 00
Beauty salon

Sothys
128, rue du Fbg. St. Honoré
75008 PARIS
Tel: 45 63 98 18
Beauty salon

Tyala Carita
39, rue du Cherche Midi
75006 PARIS
Tel: 45 49 13 57
Beauty institute

USA Health and Beauty
4, passage Prado
75010 PARIS
Tel: 48 01 08 71
Institute and home visits

Hairdressers
Salons de Coiffure

Christophe Milson
9, rue des Archives
75004 PARIS
Tel: 42 72 12 81
English-speaking coiffeur

Dean Coiffure Studio
Tel: 42 80 29 09
Have your hair cut and styled at home!

Françoise Raoult
8, rue St. Paul
75004 PARIS
Tel: 42 77 45 97
Hair salon in a quaint, old-fashioned setting

Institut Capillaire Elida
114, avenue des Champs-Elysées
75008 PARIS
Tel: 44 13 65 60

Institut René Furterer
15, Place de la Madeleine
75008 PARIS
Tel: 42 65 30 60
Fax: 42 65 00 14
Hair care institute

James Coiffure
51, rue Jouffroy
75017 PARIS
Tel: 42 27 13 84
Salon for men and women

Jean Claude Gallon
3, rue Paul Louis Courrier
75007 PARIS
Tel: 42 22 04 36
Hairdresser's salon for men and women

Marc Alengrin
29, avenue Duquesne
75007 PARIS
Tel: 47 05 17 63
Hairdresser

Michèle & Heinz Coiffeurs
4, rue de la Trémoille
75008 PARIS
Tel: 47 23 75 55
Contact: Susan TOURSEL
English-speaking coiffeur for men and women

S'Trim
130, avenue de Suffren
75015 PARIS
Tel: 47 83 24 74
English-speaking hairdresser's salon

Tiffy's Hair Design
21, rue Neuve St. Pierre
75004 PARIS
Tel: 42 77 61 04

English-Language Bookstores
Librairies de Langue Anglaise

Abbey Bookshop
29, rue de la Parcheminerie
75005 PARIS
Tel: 46 33 16 24
Fax: 46 33 03 33
President: M. Brian SPENCE
Literary and general stock, new and used. Will supply any book from the USA, UK and Canada and ship anywhere

Albion
13, rue Charles V
75004 PARIS
Tel: 42 72 50 71
Fax: 42 72 85 27
Anglo-American literature, history, science

American University of Paris Bookstore
American Church
65, quai d'Orsay
75007 PARIS
Tel: 40 62 05 92
Fax: 45 56 06 00
Manager: Julia FITZGERALD
University books, new and used, gifts

Attica Bookshop
64, rue de la Folie Méricourt
75011 PARIS
Tel: 48 06 17 00
Fax: 48 06 47 85
English section: 48 06 49 80
Over 300 languages, including of course American and English

Bookmaster
7, rue Bequet
92500 RUEIL-MALMAISON
Tel: 47 14 04 24
Fax: 47 32 09 67
Director: M. David HASTINGS
British/US books by mail order

Brentano's
37, avenue de l'Opéra
75002 PARIS
Tel: 42 61 52 50
Fax: 42 61 07 61
Director: M. Maurice DARBELLAY
Anglo-American literature, art books, magazines and newspapers. Book signings and events

Espace Cannibal Pierce
7, rue Samson
B.P. 224
93200 ST-DENIS
Tel: 48 09 94 59
Directors: M. Ken SHEPHERD & June SHENFIELD
Paris' only Australian bookshop and art gallery

Foot-Note
Bd. de Constance
77305 FONTAINEBEAU Cedex
Tel: 60 72 42 61
Fax: 60 72 43 42
E-mail: footnote@insead.fr
Director: Mme Chana WEINSTEIN
English business and management books, retail and mail order

Galignani
224, rue de Rivoli
75001 PARIS
Tel: 42 60 76 07
Fax: 42 86 09 31
Director: Marie PACCARD
Fine arts, Anglo-American literature, guidebooks, newspapers and magazines-the oldest English bookstore on the continent

Michael Neal
6, rue des Bas Jardins Feugères
91650 ST-YON
Tel: 64 58 40 64
Collector of everything by and about Edouard Roditi

Nouveau Quartier Latin
78, Bd. St. Michel
75006 PARIS
Tel: 43 26 42 70
Fax: 40 51 74 09
General Manager: Mme Anne WARTER
International bookshop

Shakespeare & Company
37, rue de la Bûcherie
75005 PARIS
No Telephone
Owner: M. George WHITMAN
The Rag & Bone Shop of the Heart. Open daily from noon until midnight

Tea and Tattered Pages
24, rue Mayet
75006 PARIS
Tel: 40 65 94 35
Fax: 39 50 33 76
Owner: Kristi CHAVANE
Manager: Karen PIGNATARO
Secondhand books, small tea room at the back. Open every day 11h00-19h00

The Book Cellar
23, rue Jean de Beauvais
75005 PARIS
Tel: 46 34 62 03

Tridias Bookshop
19, Place du Marché
78110 LE VESINET
Tel: 39 76 11 13
Fax: 39 76 60 70
Director: M. JUDD
British books, toys, gifts

Village Voice Bookshop
6, rue Princesse
75006 PARIS
Tel: 46 33 36 47
Fax: 46 33 27 48
Minitel: 3615 VILLAGE VOICE
Director: Mme Odile HELLIER
High-quality literary bookstore and reading series. Vast collection in modern and contemporary fiction, poetry and translations as well as works in the social and political sciences, philosophy, literary criticism, etc.
(see advertisement)

W.H. Smith
248, rue de Rivoli
75001 PARIS
Tel: 44 77 88 99
Fax: 42 96 83 71
Manager: M. Stuart WALKER
Marketing Manager: Dorothée BEN TAHAR
The only British-owned bookstore in Paris. Literature, guides, magazines and a good teaching resources section upstairs
(see advertisement)

Other Bookstores
Autres Librairies

Album
6, rue Dante
75005 PARIS
Tel: 43 54 67 09
Fax: 43 25 82 70
Contact: M. Philippe TOUBOUL
Comics, strip cartoons, US imports

Artcurial
9, avenue Matignon
75009 PARIS
Tel: 42 99 16 19

Aux Films du Temps
8, rue St. Martin
75004 PARIS
Tel: 42 71 97 25
Books and magazines about films

Chantelivre
13, rue de Sèvres
75006 PARIS
Tel: 45 48 87 90
Fax: 45 48 97 69
An excellent address for children's books and games

Elliot Klein S.A.R.L.
47, rue Saint-André-des-Arts
75006 PARIS
Tel: 43 29 62 68 (call for appt.)
Fax: 43 26 52 36
Rare & OP books on ethnology, etc.

Flammarion 4
La Maison Rustique
26, rue Jacob
75006 PARIS
Tel: 43 25 67 00
Fax: 40 51 05 95
Books on gardens and plants

Flammarion 4
107, rue de Rivoli
75001 PARIS
Tel: 42 96 21 31
Fax: 40 05 07 10
Fashion, decorative arts

FNAC Etoile
26-30, avenue des Ternes
75017 PARIS
Tel: 44 09 18 00
Books, records, photography

FNAC Forum
1, rue Pierre Lescot
Porte Lescot, Niveau -3
75001 PARIS
Tel: 40 41 40 00
Fax: 40 41 40 86
Books, records, photography

FNAC Montparnasse
136, rue de Rennes
75006 PARIS
Tel: 49 54 30 00
Fax: 49 54 30 03
Books, records, photography

Gibert Jeune
5, Place St. Michel
75005 PARIS
Tel: 43 25 70 07
Fax: 43 26 25 34
Travel, fiction, sciences, stationery

Gibert Jeune
27, quai St. Michel
75005 PARIS
Tel: 43 54 57 32
Fax: 40 46 97 02
New and used school books

Gibert Jeune
10, Place St. Michel
75005 PARIS
Tel: 43 25 91 19
Fax: 40 51 77 72
Foreign languages and literature

Gibert Joseph
26, 30, 32, Bd. St. Michel
75006 PARIS
Tel: 44 41 88 88
Fax: 40 46 83 62
French and foreign literature, travel guides, university texts

Golden Books
3, rue Larochelle
75014 PARIS
Tel: 43 22 38 56
Director: M. C. MANTEL
Books on New Age, psychology, natural health, astrology

Graphes
13, rue de Buci
75006 PARIS
Tel: 46 33 57 57
Director: M. Luc MONOD
Bookstore/Gallery (Avant-Garde, 20th-century illustrated books, photography)

L'Harmattan
16, rue des Ecoles
75005 PARIS
Tel: 43 26 04 52
Fax: 43 29 86 20
Director: M. PRYEN
Third World books and periodicals

L'Arbre à Lettres
2, rue Edouard Quenu
75005 PARIS
Tel: 43 31 74 08
Manager: Mme Martine DANTIN

La Chambre Claire
14, rue St. Sulpice
75006 PARIS
Tel: 46 34 04 31
Director: M. Fadi ZAHAR
Specialized in photography

La Documentation Française
29, quai Voltaire
75007 PARIS
Tel: 40 15 70 00 40 15 72 30
Non-fiction

La Hune
170, Bd. St. Germain
75006 PARIS
Tel: 45 48 35 85
Fax: 45 44 49 87
Manager: Mme Nicole RIEME
Fine arts, photo, dance, music, painting, literature

La Libre Errance
Librairie Luc Monod
5, rue de l'Echaudé
75005 PARIS
Tel: 46 33 19 84
Director: M. Luc MONOD
Early editions, 19th-century illustrated books (by appointment only)

Bookshop
WHSMITH
WHSMITH
WH SMITH

Les Archives de la Presse
51, rue des Archives
75003 PARIS
Tel: 42 72 63 93
Sells and buys back issues of all French newpapers and magazines going back to the turn of the century (Vogue, Le Petit Journal, Illustration, *etc.)*

Les Cahiers de Colette
12, rue Rambuteau
75003 PARIS
Tel: 42 72 95 06
Director: Colette KERBER
French fiction and biography, literary events

Les Femmes Savantes
73bis, avenue Niel
75017 PARIS
Tel: 47 63 05 82
Women's bookstore

Les Feux de la Rampe
2, rue de Luynes
75007 PARIS
Tel: 45 48 80 97
Devoted to the cinema

Librairie de l'UNESCO
7, Place de Fontenoy
75007 PARIS
Tel: 45 68 22 22
Newspapers and UNESCO publications

Librairie de la Communication Tekhné
7, rue des Carmes
75005 PARIS
Tel: 43 54 70 84
Media, technology, business

Librairie de la Fontaine
13, rue Médicis
75006 PARIS
Tel: 43 26 76 28
Vast collection of books, cards and posters on the cinema

Librairie des Entreprises
53, rue des Entrepreneurs
75015 PARIS
Tel: 40 59 00 38
Fax: 40 59 02 25
Management, finance, company law, corporate issues

Librairie des Femmes
74, rue de Seine
75006 PARIS
Tel: 43 29 50 75
Women's literature and books about women

Librairie du Commerce International
10, avenue d'Iéna
75016 PARIS
Tel: 40 73 34 60
Fax: 40 73 38 98

Librairie du Globe
2, rue de Buci
75006 PARIS
Tel: 46 33 43 93
Fax: 43 25 50 55
Russian bookstore: novels, poems, travel guides, calendars, cards, teaching methods

Librairie Gaël
19, rue du Cardinal Lemoine
75005 PARIS
Tel: 46 34 60 82
Fax: 46 34 61 01

Librairie Gilda
36, rue des Bourdonnais
75001 PARIS
Tel: 42 33 60 00
Contact: Bud
Secondhand books and records

Librairie Gourmande
4, rue Dante
75005 PARIS
Tel: 43 54 37 27
Fax: 43 54 31 16
Specialized in food and wine

Librairie Hachette Evasion
77, Bd. St. Germain
75005 PARIS
Tel: 46 34 89 51
Fax: 46 34 65 45
Vast collection of guides

Librairie Touzot
38, rue St. Sulpice
75006 PARIS
Tel: 43 26 03 88
Fax: 46 34 77 11

Maison du Dictionnaire
98, Bd. Montparnasse
75014 PARIS
Tel: 43 22 12 93
Fax: 43 22 01 77
Dictionaries, lexicons and encyclopaedias in a wide range of languages

Mode Information
67, Bd. Sébastopol
75002 PARIS
Tel: 40 13 81 50
Fax: 45 08 94 24
Fashion, clothing, haute couture

Sélection du Reader's Digest
212, Bd. St. Germain
75007 PARIS
Tel: 45 48 04 26 (store)
Tel: 46 74 84 84 (info)

Tour de Babel
10, rue du Roi de Sicile
75004 PARIS
Tel: 42 77 32 40
Fax: 48 87 53 72
Italian bookstore (fiction, poetry, biography)

Virgin Mégastore
52-60, avenue des Champs-Elysées
75008 PARIS
Tel: 49 53 50 00
Fax: 49 53 50 40
Books, records, video, hi-fi

Avis Location de Voitures
5, rue Bixio
75007 PARIS
Tel: 45 50 32 31
Fax: 45 51 47 97
Res: 46 10 60 60

Avis Location de Voitures
Tour Franklin
Défense 8
92042 PARIS LA DEFENSE
Tél: 49 06 68 68
Fax: 47 78 98 98
Director: M. Christian DU TILLET
Headquarters

Budget Rent-a-Car
81, avenue Kléber
75016 PARIS
Tel: 47 55 61 00
Fax: 44 05 96 21

Budget Rent-a-Car France
5, rue du Pont des Halles
Zone Hotelière Delta
94656 RUNGIS Cedex
Tel: 45 12 39 47
Fax: 45 12 39 02
President: M. David ARBUTHNOT
Headquarters

Car Rental
60, Bd. Diderot
75012 PARIS
Tel: 44 68 89 89
Fax: 44 74 95 00
Minitel: 3615 CAR RENTAL
Discount car & truck rentals and leasing

Euro-Rent
42, avenue de Saxe
75007 PARIS
Tel: 44 38 55 50
Fax: 40 65 91 94
Minitel: 3615 EURORENT

Europcar Interrent
5, avenue d'Italie
75013 PARIS
Tel: 42 16 80 80
Fax: 45 86 71 97
Reservation and information

Executive Car-Carey Limousine
25 rue d'Astorg
75008 PARIS
Tel: 42 65 54 20
Fax: 42 65 25 93
President: M. REINE
Chauffeur-driven cars

Hertz France
B.P. 305
78054 ST-QUENTIN-EN-YVELINES Cedex
Tel: 30 45 65 65
Fax: 30 58 46 21
Headquarters

Hertz France
Res: 47 88 51 51
Minitel: 3514 HERTZ
Booking service

International Limousines
182, Bd. Péreire
75017 PARIS
Admin: 53 81 14 10
Res: 53 81 14 14

Le Voiturium
68, avenue de Versailles
75016 PARIS
Tel: 42 88 51 88
Fax: 45 25 47 17
Director: M. Didier HEIDET

London Cab in Paris
16, rue Chevreul
75011 PARIS
Tel: 43 70 18 18
Fax: 43 56 78 35
Director: Mme Elisabeth ROSUEL
London bus and coach tours of Paris

Prestige Limousines
165, rue de la Convention
75015 PARIS
Tel: 42 50 81 81
Fax: 42 50 87 29

Promenades de Style
52, rue du Fbg. Poissonnière
75010 PARIS
Tel: 47 70 08 28
Fax: 48 24 05 60
Anglophone Chauffeur: Edward
1964 Lincoln convertible - Tours and events

Franco-American Chambers of Commerce (F.A.C.C.) – *Chapters in the USA*

Atlanta
999 Peachtree Street, N.E.
Suite 2095
Atlanta, GA 30309
(404) 874-2602
(404) 875-9452
Executive Director: Leslie Perry Wingate

Chicago
55 East Monroe Street
Suite 3710
Chicago, IL 60603
(312) 263-7668
(312)263-7860
Executive Director: Patrice Cavallo

Dallas-Ft. Worth
4835 LBJ Freeway
Suite 640
Dallas, TX 75244
(214) 991-4888
(214) 991-4887
Executive Director: Erin Petit

Detroit
PO Box 43959
100 Renaissance Tower
Detroit, MI 48297
(313) 567-6012
(313) 567-0142

Houston
1776 St James Place
Suite 425
Houston, TX 77056
(713) 960-0575
(713) 960-0495
Executive Director: Kathleen Riffe

Louisiana
World Trade Center
Suite 2938
New Orleans, LA 70130
(504) 524-2042
(504) 522-4003
Executive Director: Lou Johnson

Miami
141 Sevilla Avenue
Coral Gables, FL 33134
(305) 444-1587

Minneapolis/St. Paul
Foshay Tower / Suite 904
Minneapolis, MN 35402
(612) 338-7750
(612) 334-2781
Executive Director: Christine Heinerscheid

New England
15 Court Square
Suite 320
Boston, MA 02108
(617) 523-4438
(617) 523-4461
Executive Director: Betsy O'Brien

New York
1350 Avenue of the Americas
6th Floor
New York, NY 10019
(212) 715-4444
(212) 765-4650
Executive Directors: Lenir Drake & Vicki Banner

Philadelphia
4000 Bell Atlantic Tower
1717 Arch Street
Philadelphia, PA 19103
(215) 994-5373
(215) 994-5366
Executive Director: Susan Silverstein

Pittsburgh
c/o Reed, Smith, Shaw & McClay
435 Sixth Avenue
Pittsburgh, PA 15219
(412) 288-4174
(412) 288-3063
Executive Director: Janet Stiehler

San Francisco
425 Bush Street
Suite 401
San Francisco, CA 94108
(415) 398-2449
(415) 398-8912
Executive Director: Jean Ward Jacote

Seattle
2102 Fourth Street
Suite 2330
Seattle, WA 98121
(206) 443-4703
Executive Director: Jack Cowan

Southern California
6380 Wilshire Boulevard
Suite 1608
Los Angeles, CA 90048
(213) 651-4741
(213) 651-2547
Executive Director: Barbara Hearn

Washington, D.C.
1730 Rhode Island Avenue, NW
Suite 711
Washington, D.C. 20036
(202) 775-0256
(202) 785-4604
Executive Director: Susan Shillinglaw

American Chamber of Commerce in France
21, avenue George V
75008 PARIS
Tel: 47 23 70 28
Fax: 47 20 18 60
Executive Director: W. Barrett DOWER

Austrade - Centre Australien du Commerce Extérieur
4, rue Jean Rey
75724 PARIS Cedex 15
Tel: 40 59 33 00
Fax: 40 59 33 22
Marketing, investment

Chambre de Commerce Franco-Indienne
4, avenue Daniel Lesueur
75007 PARIS
Tel: 43 06 88 97
Fax: 40 65 09 56
President: M. Francis DORE

Chambre de Commerce France-Canada
9-11, avenue Franklin Roosevelt
75008 PARIS
Tel: 43 59 32 38
Fax: 42 56 25 62

Chambre de Commerce Internationale
38, cours Albert Ier
75008 PARIS
Tel: 49 53 28 28
Fax: 49 53 28 59

Franco-American Chamber of Commerce
7, rue Jean Goujon
75008 PARIS
Tel: 43 59 63 35

Franco-British Chamber of Commerce
41, rue de Turenne
75003 PARIS
Tel: 44 59 25 20
Manager: Catherine YAOUAN
Helps bring together British and French firms

Franco-Irish Chamber of Commerce
33, rue Miromesnil
75008 PARIS
Tel: 47 42 36 28
Fax: 40 06 02 73
Secretary: Mrs Christine LISCOUET

Hong Kong Trade Development Council
18, rue d'Aguesseau
75008 PARIS
Tel: 47 42 41 50
Fax: 47 42 77 44

Japanese Chamber of Commerce
1, avenue de Friedland
75008 PARIS
Tel: 45 63 43 33
Fax: 45 61 08 62

Office du Commerce Irlandais en France
33, rue Miromesnil
75008 PARIS
Tel: 42 65 98 65
Fax: 47 42 84 76

Nannies/Babysitters
Nurses/Babysitters

Ababa
8, avenue du Maine
75015 PARIS
Tel: 45 49 46 46
Babysitters

ABC Puériculture
9, rue la Fontaine
75016 PARIS
Tel: 40 50 13 64
Babysitters

Alliance Française
101, Bd. Raspail
75006 PARIS
Tel: 45 44 38 28
English-speaking babysitters

Allô Maman Poule
4, rue Greffulhe
92300 LEVALLOIS
Tel: 47 48 01 01
Babysitting service

Alpha Baby
8, avenue Joffre
94160 ST MANDE
Tel: 43 65 58 58
Babysitters

Baby Sitting Service
18, rue Tronchet
75008 PARIS
Tel: 46 37 51 24
Fax: 42 66 52 45

Good Morning Europe
68, rue de Charenton
75012 PARIS
Tel: 44 87 01 22
Fax: 44 87 01 42
Live-in and live-out childcare positions

Home Service
2, rue Pierre Semard
75009 PARIS
Tel: 42 82 05 04
Babysitters

International Nannies
14, avenue de Villars
75007 PARIS
Tel: 47 05 41 33
Fax: 47 05 41 43
Nannies and mother's helps with serious references

Irish Nannies
16, rue de Schlumberger
92430 MARNE-LA-COQUETTE
Tel: 47 41 64 52
Fax: 47 41 26 52
Nannies and au pairs

Kid Services
159, rue de Rome
75017 PARIS
Tel: 47 66 00 52
Fax: 42 67 76 88
Director: Mme Anne MANSOURET
Babysitting, mother's helps, nanny searching

Nannies Incorporated
8, rue du Dobropol
75017 PARIS
Tel: 45 74 62 74
Carefully selected nannies, nurses and housekeepers

Nurse Au Pair Placement
Tel: 47 64 48 20
Fax: 47 64 48 20
Contact: Carolina GONÇALVES
Qualified and experienced au pairs, nannies and mother's helps in Europe and the USA

Soames International
B.P. 28
16, rue du Château
77302 FONTAINEBLEAU
Tel: 64 22 99 26
Fax: 64 22 03 08
Nannies, maternity nurses, au pairs

Childcare
Pédiatres

Dr André Nodot
30-32, rue de Fleurus
75006 PARIS
Tel: 45 48 19 29
Pediatrician

Dr Guy Viterbo
6, rue Champfleury
75007 PARIS
Tel: 47 34 68 09
Pediatrician for the American Hospital

Dr Joyce Ducellier
38, rue des Sablons
75116 PARIS
Tel: 44 05 01 50
Fax: 44 05 06 63
Pediatrician

Dr Pierre Bitoun
8, rue Jarente
75004 PARIS
Tel: 42 77 74 37
Pediatrician

Clothing
Habillement

Agnès B
2, rue du Jour
75001 PARIS
Tel: 40 39 96 88

Boutique Clayeux
80, avenue Victor Hugo
75016 PARIS
Tel: 47 55 15 24

Chattawak
125, rue St. Dominique
75007 PARIS
Tel: 45 55 76 85

Coup de Coeur
2, avenue des Ternes
75017 PARIS
Tel: 43 80 59 40

Du Pareil au Même
7, rue St. Placide
75006 PARIS
Tel: 40 49 00 33

Kenzo
3, Place des Victoires
75001 PARIS
Tel: 40 39 72 87

Natalys
92, avenue des Champs-Elysées
75008 PARIS
Tel: 43 59 17 65

Petit Bateau
81, rue de Sèvres
75006 PARIS
Tel: 45 49 48 38

Repetto
22, rue de la Paix
75002 PARIS
Tel: 44 71 83 00
Clothing for dance and gym enthusiasts

Tartine et Chocolat
105, rue du Fbg. St. Honoré
75008 PARIS
Tel: 45 62 44 04

Tony Boy
9, avenue Niel
75017 PARIS
Tel: 45 72 62 82

Miscellaneous
Divers

A la Poupée Merveilleuse
9, rue du Temple
75004 PARIS
Tel: 42 72 63 46
Fax: 44 59 85 87
Party novelties, masks, fancy dress, tricks, fireworks

Bebel le Magicien
Tel: 42 55 10 69
Magician for children's parties

C'est ma Chambre
45, rue des Archives
75003 PARIS
Tel: 48 87 26 67
Manager: Mme DESORMEAUX
Charming bedroom furniture and accessories for children

Chantelivre
13, rue de Sèvres
75006 PARIS
Tel: 45 48 87 90
Fax: 45 48 97 69
An excellent address for children's books and games

Children's Academy on Tour
66, avenue des
Champs-Elysées, no. 74
75008 PARIS
Tel: 44 95 14 31
Contact: Sabrina SCOTT
A children's organization for cultural awareness

Children's Parties
108, rue Lourmel
75015 PARIS
Tel: 40 60 03 60
Contact: Christine SERIE
Magicians, puppets and games for birthday parties, Halloween, Christmas...

Cité des Sciences et de l'Industrie
Parc de la Villette
30, avenue Corentin Cariou
75019 PARIS
Tel: 40 05 70 00
Minitel: 3615 VILLETTE
The world of Science and Technology presented in an original manner with many interactive video games

Disneyland Paris
B.P. 100
77777 MARNE-LA-VALLEE
Admin: 64 74 40 00
Res: 64 74 60 65
Info: 60 30 60 30
Minitel: 3615 EURO DISNEY
Director: M. Philippe BOURGUIGNON
Disney theme park 32 km. east of Paris

English Juniors' Club
16, rue de la Liberté
75019 PARIS
Tel: 42 03 66 87
Contact: Monique IFERGAN
English courses for children aged 3 to 12

Eurobaby
Tel: 47 48 11 84
Contact: Kathy
Short and long term rental of baby equipment: cots, car seats, push chairs, etc.

Hoppmann
10, rue Carnot
93100 MONTREUIL
Tel: 48 59 80 06
Fax: 48 59 80 00
Shows for kids (mime, clown, following)

La Pelucherie
84, avenue des Champs-Elysées
75008 PARIS
Tel: 43 59 49 05
Fax: 42 89 25 18
Plush toys for children

Le Paris des Tout Petits
Editions d'Annabelle
8, rue d'Anjou
75008 PARIS
Tel: 47 42 01 61
Fax: 47 42 42 14
Director: Mme ROLLAND
A children's guide to Paris in French

Little Dragons
2, rue Jacquemont
75017 PARIS
Tel: 42 28 56 17
Fax: 47 00 53 39
Kindergarten

Musée en Herbe
Jardin d'Acclimatation
Bois de Boulogne
Tel: 40 67 97 66
Children's museum

Stepping Stones
1, Route du Grand Pont
78110 LE VESINET
Tel: 30 53 14 73
Director: Mme S. TAYLOR
Activities for anglophone children 3-5 years old

Steve & Suzy
38bis, rue Lamarck
75018 PARIS
Tel: 42 62 71 14
Contact: M. Steven MURRAY
Entertainment for children's parties: games, prizes, music, clowns, magic, tricks

The Disney Store
44, avenue des Champs-Elysées
75008 PARIS
Tel: 45 61 45 25

Toys-R-Us
Centre Commercial "Les Quatre Temps"
92092 PARIS LA DEFENSE
Tel: 47 76 29 78
Admin: 60 76 83 00
Toy store

Anacomp
B.P. 60023
95970 ROISSY CDG Cedex
Tel: 49 38 49 49
Fax: 48 63 22 58
Director: M. RONEZ

AT&T France
Tour Horizon
52, quai de Dion-Bouton
92806 PUTEAUX Cedex
Tel: 47 67 47 67
Fax: 47 67 47 71
Free call: 05 48 51 11 (customer service for AT&T calling card)
Director General:
M. Stéphane GANTZER
Marketing Director:
Mme Sandra LUCIDI-AZERA
Marketing Assistant:
Catherine DEL GUERCIO
(see advertisement)

AXS Telecom
19, rue Auguste Chabrières
75015 PARIS
Tel: 45 57 54 40
Fax: 45 57 54 45
Discount call-back service

Bouygues Télécom
88, Bd. Villette
75019 PARIS
Tel: 44 84 69 00
Fax: 42 38 32 42

British Telecom France
Immeuble Jean Monnet
Cedex 56
92061 PARIS LA DEFENSE
Tel: 46 67 25 00
Fax: 47 68 95 76
Marketing Manager: M. Richard VIEL

Cable & Wireless France
Les Collines de l'Arche
Bâtiment Madeleine
92057 PARIS LA DEFENSE
Tel: 46 92 91 00
Fax: 49 01 01 09
Director: M. Robert TREHIN

Canal France International
59, Bd. Exelmans
75016 PARIS
Tel: 40 71 11 71
Fax: 40 71 11 72
Satellite TV network

Charlocom
39, rue du Dr Blanche
75016 PARIS
Tel: 47 61 69 70
Fax: 46 21 05 95
Contact: M. ROYER
Portable, cordless and fixed telephones

CNIT - Centre des Nouvelles Technologies et Industries
4, Place de la Défense
92053 PARIS LA DEFENSE
Tel: 46 92 12 12
Fax: 46 92 24 49

Desef S.A.R.L.
7, rue du Maine
75014 PARIS
Tel: 44 10 89 44
Fax: 44 10 89 22
Contact: M. François FRANÇAIS
International discount telephone service

Dynatech Communications France
Bâtiment GAIA
9, Parc Ariane
78284 GUYANCOURT Cedex
Tel: 30 48 83 00
Fax: 30 48 83 10
Manager: M. Christopher JACKSON
Constructor and distributor of telecommunication equipments

Elektra Communications International
58, rue de Romainville
93260 LES LILAS
Tel: 43 60 01 43
Fax: 43 60 01 76
Minitel: 3615 NETWORK
Directors: M. Nick HARPER
& M. Hugh BARNARD
Design and construction of interactive and multimedia systems, including 3615 NETWORK and 3668 AngloPhone
(see advertisement)

France-Télécom/ Direction des Réseaux et Services Internationaux
37-39, avenue Ledru Rollin
75012 PARIS
Tel: 43 42 68 55
Fax: 43 42 81 50
Communications & Marketing Director: Mme Constance CAPDENAT
Public Relations Director: Mme Sylvaine ROUSSEAU
Marketing & Development: Mme Sylvie JACQUEMIN
Worldwide networks and services (see advertisements)

Gandalf France
16, Burospace
Route de Gisy
91572 BIEVRES
Tel: 69 33 18 55
Fax: 60 19 38 60
General Director: M. Michel CARDIET
Telecommunications

Hughes Network Systems
2, rue de la Renaissance
92184 ANTONY Cedex
Tel: 40 96 10 10
Fax: 40 96 05 11
Manager: J. MARCHALOT
Telecommunications

Hutchison Telecom
131, avenue Charles de Gaulle
92200 NEUILLY-SUR-SEINE
Tel: 46 41 91 00
Fax: 46 41 91 53
Contact: Laetitia GEORGES

Intercarte International
24, rue Feydeau
75002 PARIS
Tel: 40 26 31 96
Fax: 40 26 03 62
Contact: M. ROYER

International Telecommunications
110, avenue Pierre Brossolette
92240 MALAKOFF
Tel: 46 56 78 78
Fax: 47 46 90 10
Director: M. Laurent SAVARY

Interworld
256, Bd. St. Germain
75007 PARIS
Tel: 45 49 93 88
Fax: 45 49 93 96
Contact: M. Bes DE BERC
Cheap telephone rates

Mailboxes Etc.
208, rue de la Convention
75015 PARIS
Tel: 44 19 60 20
Fax: 44 19 60 29

Matra Communication
Rue Jean-Pierre Timbaud
B.P. 26
78392 BOIS D'ARCY Cedex
Tel: 34 60 70 00
Fax: 34 60 74 16

MCI International (France)
125, avenue des Champs-Elysées
75008 PARIS
Tel: 47 20 50 80
Fax: 47 20 49 51
Director: M. Alexandre DEMIDOFF
International telecommunications services

Micro Tempus
16, avenue du Québec
LP 633
91965 LES ULIS Cedex
Tel: 69 28 83 00
Fax: 69 28 66 51
Director: M. André MARECHAL

Newbridge Networks S.A.
Les Collines de l'Arche
Opéra C
92057 PARIS LA DEFENSE
Tel: 46 93 06 00
Fax: 49 00 11 05
Director: M. Lionel HOVSEPIAN
Telecommunications

Nortel Matra Cellular
Rue Jean-Pierre Timbaud
B.P. 31
78392 BOIS D'ARCY Cedex
Tel: 34 60 82 17
Fax: 34 60 87 84
Telecommunications

Northern Telecom France
NT Meridian
Parc Léonard de Vinci
15, avenue Alexandre Bell
77607 BUSSY ST GEORGES Cedex
Tel: 64 76 76 76
Fax: 64 76 76 00

Octel Communications
21, Bd. de la Madeleine
75001 PARIS
Tel: 44 86 05 35
Fax: 42 60 53 43
Voice processing systems

Pitney Bowes France
Z.I. des Marais
1, avenue Louison Bobet
94124 FONTENAY SOUS BOIS Cedex
Tel: 45 14 67 00
Fax: 48 76 52 41
Vice-President: M. Cyril YOUSSOV

Rockwell Télécommunications
Tour Gan
18, Place de l'Iris
92082 PARIS LA DEFENSE 2
Cedex 13
Tel: 49 06 39 80
Fax: 49 06 39 90
Director: M. Olivier ROBERT

Scientific Atlanta S.A.
19, avenue de l'Ile St. Martin
92737 NANTERRE Cedex
Tel: 46 52 27 80
Fax: 46 52 27 81

Sprint International France
164bis, avenue Charles de Gaulle
92526 NEUILLY SUR SEINE
Tel: 46 43 34 00
Fax: 46 43 34 34
President: M. Paolo COLOMBI
Telecommunications networks and services

Telecash Distribution B.V.
145, rue Jean-Jacques Rousseau
92130 ISSY-LES-MOULINEAUX
Tel: 41 08 33 33
Fax: 41 08 33 30
Interactive cable TV networks

Telegroup France
B.P. 3
78910 ORGERUS
Tel: 30 21 78 49
Fax: 39 53 23 86
Sales Representative:
Judy BROWN
45% discount on European and Transatlantic calls

Telegroup France
8, rue Témara
B.P. 234
78104 ST GERMAIN EN LAYE
Tel: 30 87 99 00
Fax: 39 21 15 66
Contact: Mme SOSTRIN
Director: M. George APPLE

Telematics
13, avenue Morane Saulnier
Nungesser
78140 VELIZY
Tel: 34 63 04 80
Fax: 39 46 21 18
Director: M. Raphael BERDAH

Telextel
60bis, rue des Peupliers
92100 BOULOGNE
Tel: 46 21 17 00
Minitel: 3614 TEX

Transeurope Communications France
17, rue Ramponneau
75020 PARIS
Tel: 40 33 01 55
Fax: 40 33 04 11
Sales Director: M. David ATIA

Télétam
Tel: 46 44 40 00
Contact: M. Bruno LECLERC
Provides a strictly personal phone number to those without their own telephone, including a voice mailbox

Western Union International
4, rue Cloître-Notre-Dame
75004 PARIS
Tel: 43 54 46 12
Fax: 47 54 92 79
International telecommunications services

Addform
19, rue Roger Bacon
75017 PARIS
Tel: 45 72 25 34
Fax: 45 72 28 97
Commercial Director:
M. Jean-Claude BRUNEAU

Allied Telesyn International S.A.
3, avenue du Canada
91940 LES ULIS
Tel: 69 28 16 17
Fax: 69 28 37 49
President: M. Robin HAYS
Manufactures Ethernet network products

Amdahl France
1, Rond-Point Victor Hugo
92137 ISSY-LES-MOULINEAUX
Cedex
Tel: 47 65 78 00
Fax: 47 65 78 78
President: M. Yvon LE ROUX
Computers

American Power Conversion
4, rue Saint Claire de Ville
77185 LOGNES
Tel: 64 62 59 00
Fax: 60 17 80 29
President: M. Darrell LUCENTE
Equipment for protecting computerized networks

Ampex
2, rue Curnonsky
75017 PARIS
Tel: 41 27 92 30
Fax: 47 56 16 95
Manager: M. Alain DARRAS

Amstrad
28, rue de Châteaudun
75009 PARIS
Tel: 42 81 13 68

Apple Computer Europe Inc.
15, avenue Edouard Belin
92566 RUEIL-MALMAISON Cedex
Tel: 47 14 64 00
Fax: 47 14 12 26
Vice-President New Media:
M. Satjiv CHAHIL

Apple Computer France
12, avenue de l'Océanie
Z.A. de Courtaboeuf
91956 LES ULIS Cedex
Tel: 69 86 34 00
Fax: 69 28 74 32
Director: M. Frank LANNE

Apple France Systèmes
217, quai de Stalingrad
92134 ISSY-LES-MOULINEAUX
Tel: 45 29 90 90
Fax: 45 29 90 91

AST Computer
296, avenue Napoléon Bonaparte
92500 RUEIL-MALMAISON
Tel: 47 52 22 22
Fax: 47 49 48 48

AT&T Gis France
Tour Neptune
20, Place de Seine
92086 PARIS LA DEFENSE
Cedex 20
Tel: 49 03 29 00
Fax: 47 73 06 07
President: M. Christian LHUSSIER

AWS
7, rue Gay Lussac
75005 PARIS
Tel: 43 25 09 09
Fax: 43 29 68 78
Director: M. William SETRUCK
Apple dealership and self-service bureau

Bearware Engineering
25, Place Georges Pompidou
92300 LEVALLOIS-PERRET
Tel: 47 59 96 19
Fax: 47 48 09 64
E-mail: bearw@ibm.net
Director: M. TUOMINEN
Computer consultants

Bell & Howell France
32, rue Fernand Pelloutier
92110 CLICHY
Tel: 41 06 28 00
Fax: 47 37 01 04
Fax: 40 87 11 14
President: M. William VELTEN

BMC Software France
Immeuble Le Michelet
6, cours Michelet
92064 LA DEFENSE Cedex 52
Tel: 46 92 77 77
Fax: 47 74 74 44

Bull Europe
68, route de Versailles
78434 LOUVECIENNES Cedex
Tel: 39 66 60 60
Fax: 39 66 60 62

Bull S.A.
Tour Bull
Cedex 74
92039 PARIS LA DEFENSE
Tel: 46 96 90 90

Business Applications
9, rue du Mail
75008 PARIS
Tel: 42 96 15 62

Calcomp
Immeuble Le Clémenceau
205, avenue Georges Clémenceau
92024 NANTERRE Cedex
Tel: 47 29 55 00
Fax: 47 29 13 72
Marketing Manager:
M. Dominique COMTE
Graphic peripherals manufacturer

Cincom Systems France
208, rue Raymond Losserand
75014 PARIS
Tel: 40 44 38 00
Fax: 45 45 40 08
Contact: N. ZIDI

Comdisco France
93, Cour des Petites Ecuries
77185 LOGNES
Tel: 64 62 86 80
Fax: 64 80 70 11
Sale and rental of computer equipment

Compagnie Française Philips
2, rue Benoît Malcon
B.P. 313
92156 SURESNES Cedex
Tel: 47 28 10 00
Fax: 47 28 12 80
Minitel: 3615 PHILIPS

Compaq Computer Iris
49, rue de la Convention
75015 PARIS
Tel: 44 37 07 07

Computer Associates
14, avenue François Arago
92003 NANTERRE Cedex
Tel: 40 97 50 50
Fax: 40 97 51 51

Computer Products France
5 Route Nationale 10
78310 COIGNIERES
Tel: 30 66 37 62
Fax: 30 62 60 63
Commercial Director: M. Bernard JOUINEAU

Computer Technology
Immeuble Le Debussy 77
Boulevard de la République
92250 GARENNE-COLOMBES
Tel: 42 42 02 32
Fax: 47 82 55 65

Computer Vision
1bis, rue du Petit Clamart
B.P. 25
78141 VELIZY-VILLACOUBLAY Cedex
Tel: 40 83 60 00
Fax: 40 83 60 03
Director: M. François DULIEGE

Computer World Communications
2, Place des Vosges
92051 PARIS LA DEFENSE
Tel: 49 04 80 00
Fax: 49 04 80 80
Director: Mme Catherine DUMAZET
Computer consulting

Computerland
126, avenue du Général Leclerc
92100 BOULOGNE
Tel: 46 99 42 60
Fax: 48 25 82 31

Comshare
73, Bd Haussmann
75008 PARIS
Tel: 42 68 04 11
Fax: 42 68 04 10

Connect Data
112-114, avenue du Général Leclerc
78220 VIROFLAY
Tel: 30 24 26 27
Fax: 30 24 39 22
Director: M. Patrice RICCO

Continuum France
102, Ten. Boieldieu
92800 PUTEAUX
Tel: 47 17 47 47
Fax: 47 73 65 63

Crown Technologies
45-47, rue de Villeneuve
Silic 430
94583 RUNGIS Cedex
Fax: 45 60 44 66
Micro-computers and peripherals

CSPI-France
44bis, Bd. Félix Faure
92320 CHATILLON
Tel: 46 55 11 88
Fax: 41 17 03 38
Sales Manager: M. Michel PLANTIER
Sells array processors' VME boards

Data General France
4, avenue du Maréchal Juin
92366 MEUDON-LA-FORET Cedex
Tel: 40 94 60 00
Fax: 46 30 06 42

Data Recording Instrument
655, avenue Roland Garros
B.P. 68
78534 BUC
Tel: 30 97 40 00
Fax: 30 97 40 19
General Director: Mme Martine BRAGEOT

Datapoint International Headquarters
5-7, rue Montalivet
75008 PARIS
Tel: 40 07 37 37
Fax: 40 07 3738
Executive Assistant:
Mme Sylvia MULLEN

David Anteby
15, rue Georges Lafenestre
92340 BOURG LA REINE
Tel: 46 61 06 47
Computer applications for small businesses

Dell Computer France
Immeuble Plein Jour
12bis, rue Jean Jaurès
92800 PUTEAUX
Tel: 47 62 69 00
Micro-computer manufacturer

Digital Equipment France
2, rue Gaston Crémieux
91004 EVRY Cedex
Tel: 69 87 51 11
Fax: 69 87 54 44
Director: M. Jean-Paul NERRIERE

Digitco
29, Bd. Henri IV
75004 PARIS
Tel: 42 72 90 04
Fax: 42 72 58 63
Contact: Mme Soheila ANQUETIL
Apple dealership specializing in service to the anglophone community
(see advertisement)

EDS
Le Guillaumet
Cedex 70
92046 PARIS LA DEFENSE
Tel: 46 93 46 93
Fax: 46 93 41 00
Managing Director: M. Alain RICHARD

Emroll
9-11, rue Raymond Lefèvre
B.P. 11
93190 LIVRY-GARGAN
Tel: 43 83 56 21
Fax: 43 85 47 97
Director: M. Yann ZAMPILLI

Epson France
68bis, rue Marjolin
B.P. 320
92305 LEVALLOIS-PERRET Cedex
Tel: 40 87 37 37
Fax: 47 37 15 10
Director: M. Claude HOFFSTETTER

Eurelys
131bis, rue de Billancourt
92100 BOULOGNE-BILLANCOURT
Tel: 47 12 32 64
Fax: 47 12 06 26
Director: Sylviane DINEAUX

Eurequat Technologies
25, rue Michael Faraday
78180 MONTIGNY-LE-BRETONNEUX
Tel: 30 45 75 75
Fax: 34 60 57 94

FNAC Micro
71, Bd. St. Germain
75005 PARIS
Tel: 44 41 31 50
Fax: 44 41 31 79
Retail store for microcomputer software

GCC Technologies France
104, rue de Castagnary
75015 PARIS
Tel: 45 33 51 51
Fax: 45 33 33 51
Manager: M. Ernest Joseph YASSO

General Datacomm, International
Parc du Colombier
14, rue Jules Saulnier
93200 ST-DENIS
Tel: 48 13 34 70 42 43 0021
Vice-President: M. Peter HAUSER
Modems and other périphériques for computers

Harris Adacom
58, rue Roger Salengro
Les Dolomites
94126 FONTENAY-SOUS-BOIS Cedex
Tel: 49 74 25 25
Fax: 48 76 02 08
Director: M. Robert DEVOS
Computer services

Harris EDA
(Electronic Design Automation)
2, avenue de l'Europe
78941 VELIZY Cedex
Tel: 30 70 88 40
Fax: 34 65 95 31
Sales Representative: M. COX
Distribution of CAD software

Hewlett Packard France
Parc d'Activité du Bois Briard
2, avenue du Lac
91040 EVRY Cedex
Tel: 69 91 80 00
Fax: 69 91 84 32
President: M. Kléber BEAUVILLAIN

Honeywell
4, rue Ampère
78180 MONTIGNY-LE-BRETONNEUX
Tel: 30 58 80 00
Fax: 30 44 30 64

IBM Europe
Tour Pascal
92034 PARIS LA DEFENSE
Cedex 40
Tel: 47 67 60 00
Fax: 47 67 69 69

IBM France
224, Bd John Kennedy
91100 CORBEIL ESSONNES
Tel: 60 88 51 51

IBM France
Tour Descartes
2, avenue Gambetta
92066 PARIS LA DEFENSE
Cedex 50
Tel: 49 05 70 00
Fax: 49 05 99 70
Free call: 05 03 03 03
Minitel: 3615 IBM
President: M. Bernard DUFAU

ICL France
24, avenue de l'Europe
B.P. 70
78141 VELIZY Cedex
Tel: 34 65 80 70
Fax: 34 65 00 82
Director: M. Michel CLAY
Computer equipment manufacturing

IDEAssociates France
Métropole 19
134-140, rue d'Aubervilliers
75019 PARIS
Tel: 44 65 22 00
Fax: 40 35 46 88
President: M. Pierre VIOLO

IFA
10, rue Chevreuil
92150 SURESNES
Tel: 41 38 94 23
Fax: 41 38 27 79
Director: M. BOUHMENDIL
Distributor of video conference communications

Inforama S.A.
7, rue Pasquier
75008 PARIS
Tel: 47 42 14 40
Fax: 47 42 11 93
President: M. Robert GUILLAUMOT
International consultants for the computer industry

Information Service International
30, chemin de la Sandlach
B.P. 94
67502 HAGUENAU Cedex
Tel: (16) 88 05 16 00
Fax: (16) 88 05 16 79

Informix Software France
Les Collines de l'Arche
92057 PARIS LA DEFENSE Cedex
Tel: 46 96 36 36
Fax: 46 96 36 03
Vice-President Southern Europe:
M. Jean-Paul MINARRO

International Data Corporation
Immeuble Lafayette
2, Place des Vosges
92051 PARIS LA DEFENSE 5
Tel: 49 04 80 00
Fax: 49 04 80 80
Director: M. Gérard BIDAL

IP Systèmes
9, avenue du Canada
Parc Hightech
91966 LES ULIS Cedex
Tel: 69 28 68 50
Fax: 69 28 83 89

JD Edwards France
Immeuble Wilson
70, avenue du Président Wilson
92058 PARIS LA DEFENSE Cedex
Tel: 46 96 52 00
Fax: 46 96 52 52
Marketing Director: M. Alexandre WALKER

Laser Express Services
83, Bd. St. Michel
75005 PARIS
Tel: 46 33 27 98
Fax: 43 26 31 83
Computer services, scanning

Lotus Development
Boulevard des Chênes
Bâtiment Neptune 5
B.P. 219
78051 ST-QUENTIN-EN-YVELINES Cedex
Tel: 30 12 58 00
Fax: 30 12 58 99
Director: M. Didier ROCHEREAU

M.A.I. France
6-30, rue Roger Salengro
Péripole 177
94134 FONTENAY-SOUS-BOIS Cedex
Tel: 49 74 24 00
Fax: 48 73 57 08
Director: M. DUPONT
Computer maintenance

Macsimmum
18, rue de la Michodière
75002 PARIS
Tel: 42 66 40 78
Fax: 42 66 41 31
Director: M. Christian ALBERT
Apple distributor specializing in the graphic arts. Organizes special Internet training programs.

Memorex Télex
3, rue Maurice Ravel
B.P. 141
92300 LEVALLOIS-PERRET
Tel: 45 60 89 00
Fax: 42 70 53 83

Micromania
84, avenue des Champs-Elysées
75008 PARIS
Tel: 42 56 04 13
Fax: 53 75 01 37

Microsoft Europe
Tour Pacific
11, cours Valmy
92977 PARIS LA DEFENSE Cedex
Tel: 46 35 10 10
Fax: 46 35 10 30
President: M. Bernard VERGNES

Microsoft France
18, avenue du Québec
91957 LES ULIS Cedex
Tel: 69 86 46 46
Fax: 64 46 06 60
Technical support: 69 86 10 20

Microsoft France
18, avenue du Québec
Z.A. de Courtaboeuf 1
91957 LES ULIS Cedex
Tel: 69 86 46 46
Fax: 64 46 06 60
Director: M. Jean-Philippe COURTOIX

Microsoft Neurones
205, avenue Georges Clémenceau
92000 NANTERRE
Tel: 41 37 41 37

Modcomp France
Centre d'Affaires La Boursidière
Bâtiment Estérel
92357 LE PLESSIS ROBINSON Cedex
Tel: 45 37 70 91
Fax: 45 37 70 70
Commercial Director: M. Philippe GAUTIER

Nashuatec NRG France
70, avenue du Général de Gaulle
94022 CRETEIL Cedex
Tel: 48 98 20 00
Fax: 43 77 02 89
President: M. Gérard CARDO

Network Systems France
185, avenue Charles de Gaulle
92200 NEUILLY-SUR-SEINE
Tel: 46 43 70 00
Fax: 46 43 70 11
President: M. Philippe GALAIS

Novell Wordperfect
Tour Fiat
1, Place de la Coupole
Cedex 16
92084 PARIS LA DEFENSE
Tel: 47 96 60 00
Fax: 47 98 94 72
President: M. Jean-Loup DESAMAISON-COGNET

OCE France
32, avenue du Pavé Neuf
93160 NOISY LE GRAND
Tel: 45 92 50 00
Fax: 43 05 12 15

Oracle France
65, rue des Trois Fontanots
92732 NANTERRE
Tel: 47 62 20 20
Fax: 47 62 21 15
General Director: M. Michel ROCHER
Software publisher

Perot Systems
3, avenue du Centre
Les Quadrants
Guyancourt
78280 ST-QUENTIN-EN-YVELINES
Tel: 30 44 90 49
Fax: 30 44 92 00
Computer systems design

Pilot Software
101-109, rue Jean Jaurès
92300 LEVALLOIS-PERRET
Tel: 42 70 91 91
Fax: 42 70 95 00
President: M. Christophe DUMOULIN

Q.M.S. France
1bis, rue du Petit Clamart
78147 VELIZY Cedex
Tel: 41 07 93 93
Fax: 40 83 01 10
Laser Printers

Rank Xerox
7, rue Touzet Gaillard
93586 ST-OUEN Cedex
Tel: 49 48 47 46
The document company

Raymark France
51, rue du Président Wilson
92300 LEVALLOIS-PERRET
Tel: 41 06 66 36
Fax: 41 06 66 33
Manager: M. Olivier DESSART

SAS Institute
Domaine de Gregy
B.P. 5
77166 GREGY-SUR-YERRES
Tel: 60 62 11 11
Fax: 60 62 11 99
Director France: M. D. DELORGE

Scan Data
47, Grande Allée du
12 Février 1934
Noisiel B.P. 267
77442 MARNE-LA-VALLEE
Cedex 2
Tel: 64 62 51 40
Fax: 64 80 44 19
Managing Director: M. Jean-Gérard
GALVEZ
Computer sales and equipment

SCII International
32, Bd. Victor Hugo
92110 CLICHY
Tel: 47 56 94 94
Fax: 47 56 92 77
Human Resources Director:
Mme Marilyn TRIOU

SDRC
Immeuble Le Capitole
55, avenue des Champs Pierreux
92012 NANTERRE Cedex
Tel: 46 95 97 97
Fax: 46 95 97 98

SICOB
Comité des Expositions de Paris
55, quai Alphonse le Gallo
92107 BOULOGNE
Tel: 49 09 61 13
Fax: 49 09 60 03
Salon International d'Informatique

Siemens Nixdorf
14, avenue Béguines
95802 CERGY-ST-CHRISTOPHE
Tel: 34 20 34 20
Minitel: 3615 SIEMENS

Software Publishers
Association Europe
57, rue Pierre Charron
75008 PARIS
Tel: 45 63 02 02
Fax: 45 63 02 31
Managing Director: M. Gérard
GABELLA

Speedware France S.A.
92, avenue des Champs-Elysées
75008 PARIS
Tel: 40 74 01 10
Fax: 45 62 85 16
President: M. Guy EICHELBRENNER

Sterling Software
Immeuble Wilson
Cedex 59
92058 PARIS LA DEFENSE
Tel: 47 67 40 40
Fax: 47 67 40 41

Storage Technology France
3, avenue du 8 Mai 1945
78280 GUYANCOURT
Tel: 30 12 35 53
Fax: 30 12 35 00

Storagetek
Quartier des Chênes
3, avenue du 8 Mai 1945
78284 GUYANCOURT Cedex
Tel: 30 12 35 53
Fax: 30 12 35 00
President: M. Claude FER

Sun Microsystems France
13, avenue Morane Saulnier
78140 VELIZY-VILLACOUBLAY
Tel: 30 67 50 00
Fax: 30 67 53 00
President: M. Alain PECHON

Synercom S.A.
11, rue Tronchet
75008 PARIS
Tel: 47 42 07 00
Fax: 47 42 05 07
President: M. Martin TUNSTALL

Syntel Informatique
12ter, rue Jonquoy
75014 PARIS
Tel: 40 52 07 17
Fax: 45 41 57 13
Computer technology

Tandem Computers
1, avenue de la Cristallerie
92316 SEVRES Cedex
Tel: 41 14 64 00
Fax: 41 14 64 50
E-mail: hervieux_pascale@tandem.com
Marketing Assistant:
Mme Pascale HERVIEUX
Computer manufacturer

Terminal Image
54, rue David d'Angers
75019 PARIS
Tel: 42 49 21 06
Fax: 42 02 40 65
Director: M. Eric SALES
3-D computer graphics and animation technology

Texas Instruments France
8, avenue Morane Saulnier
B.P. 67
78141 VELIZY
Tel: 30 70 10 01

Texas Instruments France
821, avenue Jack Kilby
B.P. 5
06271 VILLENEUVE-LOUBET Cedex
Tel: (16) 93 22 20 01
Fax: (16) 93 20 30 11
Chairman: M. Christian TORDO

Thomas & Betts
29, rue de Monthléry
Silic 120
94513 RUNGIS Cedex
Tel: 41 80 16 00
Fax: 46 87 42 87
Director: M. Georges GOLDBERG
Manufacturing and sales of electronic components

Tracor France
1, allée de la Chartreuse
CE 1447
91020 EVRY Cedex
Tel: 60 91 42 49
Fax: 60 91 42 48
Manager: M. Yves DALLE
Computer peripherals

Unisys France
2, Bd. de l'Oise
La Palette Orange
95015 CERGY-PONTOISE Cedex
Tel: 30 73 37 37
Fax: 30 38 40 25
Minitel: 3614 UNISYS
President: M. Jacques BOUIN
Computer manufacturer

Vox Technology
37, rue du Château
92500 RUEIL-MALMAISON
Tel: 47 14 13 41
Fax: 47 14 19 08
Director Europe: M. Maxime GOUSSE

Wang France
Bâtiment B3
10, Place de la Coupole
94227 CHARENTON-LE-PONT Cedex
Tel: 46 76 61 00
Fax: 46 76 61 61
Director: Jimmy ANIDJAR

Wyse Technologies
Z.A. de Courtaboeuf
21, avenue du Québec
91951 LES ULIS Cedex
Tel: 69 82 91 00
Fax: 69 82 92 43

Ziff Davis France
14, Place Marie-Jeanne Bassot
92300 LEVALLOIS-PERRET
Tel: 46 39 55 00
Fax: 46 39 02 06
Contact: M. Pascal RIVIERE
Newsletters, computing publisher

Arapaho
30, avenue d'Italie
75013 PARIS
Tel: 53 79 00 11
Fax: 45 83 43 10
President: M. Philippe MAHER
Rental of concert halls, production management

Casino de Paris
16, rue de Clichy
75009 PARIS
Tel: 49 95 99 99
Fax: 42 85 10 99

Cité de la Musique
211, avenue Jean Jaurès
75019 PARIS
Tel: 44 84 44 84

Eglise Saint-Eustache
75001 PARIS
Tel: 42 36 31 05
Venue for classical concerts

L'Elysée Montmartre
72, Bd. Rochechouart
75018 PARIS
Tel: 44 92 45 49

L'Olympia
28, Bd. des Capucines
75009 PARIS
Res: 47 42 25 49

La Cigale
120, Bd. Rochechouart
75018 PARIS
Tel: 49 25 81 75
Fax: 42 23 67 04
Director: Corinne MIMRAM
Fashion shows, seminars, banquets, cocktails, private parties

La Villette
La Grande Halle
211, avenue Jean Jaurès
75019 PARIS
Info: 40 03 75 03
Admin: 40 03 75 00
Venue for "Halle that Jazz" Festival

Le Bataclan
50, Bd. Voltaire
75011 PARIS
Tel: 48 06 21 11

Maison de la Radio
116, avenue Président Kennedy
75016 PARIS
Tel: 42 30 15 16

Musée National du Moyen Age
Thermes de Cluny
6, Place Paul Painlevé
75005 PARIS
Tel: 43 25 62 00
Communications Director:
M. Michel MAUNIER
Medieval art collections, music and poetry, performances

Orchestre des Concerts Lamoureux
Salle Pleyel
252, rue du Fbg. St. Honoré
75008 PARIS
Tel: 45 63 44 34
Fax: 45 62 05 41
Administrator: Annie FOULTIER
Symphony concerts

Palais des Congrès
2, Place Porte Maillot
75017 PARIS
Tel: 40 68 22 22

Palais des Sports
1, Place Porte de Versailles
75015 PARIS
Tel: 48 28 40 48

Palais Omnisports de Paris Bercy
8, Bd. de Bercy
75012 PARIS
Admin: 40 02 60 60
Res: 44 68 44 68
Minitel: 3615 BERCY

Sainte Chapelle
4, Bd. du Palais
75001 PARIS
Tel: 43 54 30 09
Venue for classical and baroque music

Salle Gaveau
45, rue La Boétie
75008 PARIS
Tel: 45 62 69 71
Res: 49 53 05 07

Théâtre Dunois
108, rue Chevaleret
75013 PARIS
Tel: 45 84 72 00

Zénith
211, avenue Jean Jaurès
75019 PARIS
Tel: 42 08 60 00

Opera Houses
Opéras

Opéra Comique
5, rue Favart
75002 PARIS
Tel: 42 96 12 20
Fax: 42 86 85 78

Opéra de Paris-Bastille
120, rue de Lyon
75012 PARIS
Info: 43 43 96 96
Res: 44 73 13 00

Opéra de Paris-Garnier
8, rue Scribe
75009 PARIS
Info: 40 17 35 35
Res: 47 42 53 71
Prestigious opera house.
Ceiling decorated by Chagall

A.T. Kearney
48, rue Jacques Dulud
92200 NEUILLY-SUR-SEINE
Tel: 46 41 93 93
Fax: 47 45 36 21
President: M. Jacques TASSEL

Allan, Chanut, Perron
7, rue Royale
75008 PARIS
Tel: 47 42 51 31
Fax: 42 65 19 91
Partner: M. Peter ALLAN

Allen et Associés
11, rue La Boétie
75008 PARIS
Tel: 42 65 88 57
Fax: 42 65 02 80
Director: M. Ross ALLEN

American Banners
6, avenue de Boissy
94380 BONNEUIL-SUR-MARNE
Tel: 43 99 00 62
Fax: 43 39 05 87

Arrow Consultants
114bis, rue Michel Ange
75016 PARIS
Tel: 40 71 28 42
Fax: 40 71 28 19

Arthur Andersen et Associés
Tour Gan
Cedex 13
92082 PARIS LA DEFENSE 2
Tel: 42 91 06 06
Fax: 42 91 09 90
President: M. Gérard VAN KEMMEL

Arthur D. Little France
15, rue Galvani
75017 PARIS
Tel: 40 55 29 00
Fax: 40 55 08 80
Managing Director: M. Jean-Luc FALLOU

B.L.I.T.S.
41, rue Dauphine
75006 PARIS
Tel: 43 54 79 61
Business Language International Training Services

Bain & Co.
21, Bd. de la Madeleine
75001 PARIS
Tel: 44 55 75 75
Fax: 44 55 76 00
Director: M. Jean-Marie PEAN
Manager: M. Marc-André KAMEL

Barbara Romer
27, allée du Valois
60500 CHANTILLY
Tel: 44 57 30 48
Fax: 44 57 30 48
Personalized advice for business executives on how to improve their image

Bernard Krief Consultants
115, rue du Bac
75007 PARIS
Tel: 45 44 38 29
Fax: 42 22 91 36
Director: M. Bernard KRIEF

Berndtson Paul Ray
73, avenue des Champs-Elysées
75008 PARIS
Tel: 53 77 22 00
Fax: 53 77 22 09
Partner: M. Roger SOOLE

Bood & Partners
152, rue St. Honoré
75001 PARIS
Tel: 42 96 62 27
Fax: 42 86 92 14
Director: M. Maurice BOOD

Booz Allen & Hamilton, Inc.
112, avenue Kléber
75770 PARIS Cedex 16
Tel: 44 34 31 31
Fax: 44 34 30 00
Senior Vice-President:
M. Pierre RODOCANACHI
Top management consulting services

Bourse Européenne pour le Commerce et l'Industrie (BECI)
15-17, avenue de Ségur
75007 PARIS
Tel: 45 55 71 27
Fax: 45 51 27 48

Boyden Executive Search
1, Rond-Point des Champs-Elysées
75008 PARIS
Tel: 44 13 67 00
Fax: 44 13 67 13

Broadmark
20, avenue Kléber
75016 PARIS
Tel: 45 00 00 01
Fax: 45 00 82 82
Franco-American business consultancy

Brothers International Connections
11, rue Brochant
75017 PARIS
Tel: 42 28 05 71
Convention arrangements

Buck Consultants
7, rue La Fayette
75009 PARIS
Tel: 48 78 50 78
Fax: 40 23 95 46
Contact: M. Claude VALA
Compensation and benefits advice

Burson-Marsteller
11, rue Paul Baudry
75008 PARIS
Tel: 42 99 93 93
Fax: 40 74 07 14
Vice-President: Gail LAVIELLE

Business Group Consultants
60, avenue de New York
75016 PARIS
Tel: 45 24 50 09
Fax: 45 24 40 49

Business Perspectives
22, rue de Lubeck
75116 PARIS
Tel: 47 27 28 00
Fax: 47 27 22 80

Business Strategist
103, rue de la Pompe
75116 PARIS
Tel: 53 70 80 35

Cabinet Joublin McCann
62, avenue de Wagram
75017 PARIS
Tel: 47 63 09 25
Fax: 47 63 09 18
Contact: M. Patrick McCann
Bilingual recruitment consultants

Caldwell Consultants and Training
18, rue Rambuteau
75003 PARIS
Tel: 48 04 03 56
Fax: 42 72 88 09
Director: Mme Nancy CALDWELL
Consulting and training in negotiation, intercultural communication and creative problem solving

Camdi International Design
70, rue Mouffetard
75005 PARIS
Tel: 45 35 19 19
Fax: 45 35 93 00
Director: M. Yves MONPETIT

Capic
18, rue Volney
75002 PARIS
Tel: 42 61 03 27

Connell Speirs & Associates
54, rue Monceau
75008 PARIS
Tel: 42 89 13 23
Director: M. James SPEIRS

Coopers & Lybrand
32, rue Guersant
75017 PARIS
Tel: 45 72 80 00
Fax: 45 72 22 19
President: M. P.B. ANGLADE

Cottray Training and Development
11, Grande Rue
95470 FOSSES
Tel: 34 68 95 26
Fax: 34 72 55 25
Director: Gillian COTTRAY
Communication, teamwork, leadership

Cray Research France
18, rue Tilsitt
75017 PARIS
Tel: 44 09 14 00
Fax: 44 09 14 05
President: Mme Michèle NEYRET

Dames and Moore
2, rue Marly le Roi
78150 LE CHESNAY
Tel: 39 63 35 35
Fax: 39 55 35 71
Managing Director: M. René BONAZ
Consulting engineers in earth and environmental sciences

DBM France
17, 19, 21, rue du Fbg. St. Honoré
75008 PARIS
Tel: 44 51 52 80
Fax: 44 51 52 81
General Manager: M. Alain TOULOUSE

Deloitte Touche Tohmatsu
185, avenue Charles de Gaulle
92200 NEUILLY-SUR-SEINE
Tel: 40 88 28 00
Fax: 40 88 28 28
Telex: BDA 620 883F
Partner: M. Hervé BARDON

Destination Business
18, avenue des Champs-Elysées
75008 PARIS
Tel: 40 74 35 33

Dun & Bradstreet International
Immeuble Défense Bergères
345, avenue Georges Clémenceau
92882 NANTERRE Cedex 9
Tel: 41 35 17 00
Fax: 41 35 17 77
Director: M. Bruno LEPROU DE LA RIVIERE

Ecomail
54, rue Moxouris
78150 LE CHESNAY
Tel: 39 63 30 60
Fax: 39 55 10 02

Expatriate Management Consultants (EMC)
62, avenue Foch
92250 LA GARENNE-COLOMBES
Tel: 47 81 12 85
Fax: 42 42 39 63
Consultant: V. ALLEMANE
International Assignment Policy

Enomfra S.A.
6, 8, 10, avenue Eiffel
77220 GRETZ-ARMAINVILLIERS
Tel: 64 06 47 76
Fax: 64 06 47 59
General Manager: M. Jean VASEUX

Ernst & Young Conseil
Tour Manhattan
6, Place de l'Iris
Cedex 21
92095 PARIS LA DEFENSE 2
Tel: 46 93 60 00
Fax: 47 76 20 33
Advice about information technologies

Euromanagement Consultants
222, rue du Fbg. St. Honoré
75008 Paris
Tel: 49 53 01 96
Tel: 49 53 07 09
Fax: 40 75 00 42
Recruitement consultants

Essentiel Communication
6, rue de la Victoire
75009 PARIS
Tel: 49 95 96 96
Fax: 49 95 97 16
Director: M. Tony HARDINGHAM
Public Relations consultants

Euro-Marketing Associates
10, rue de la Paix
75002 PARIS
Tel: 42 61 56 08
Fax: 40 20 98 98
Managing Director: M. Bill DUNLAP
Development of European market for high-tech US companies

European Business Consultant
123, avenue de Versailles
75016 PARIS
Tel: 42 15 25 30

European Investment Managers
38, rue François Ier
75008 PARIS
Tel: 43 67 85 85
Fax: 53 67 85 86

European Leveraged Investment Group
59, avenue Marceau
75116 PARIS
Tel: 40 70 06 71
Fax: 40 70 04 61

European Safety Consultants
18, Bd. Malesherbes
75008 PARIS
Tel: 44 51 14 74
Fax: 44 51 14 77

Eurosearch Consultants
6, avenue de Messine
75008 PARIS
Tel: 45 61 96 03

Forgeot Weeks
128, rue Fbg. St. Honoré
75008 PARIS
Tel: 45 63 35 15
Director: M. Alain FORGEOT
Career consultants

Frank Facts
7, rue de Belfort
75011 PARIS
Tel: 43 79 99 37
Director: Mme Betty ABU GHEIDA
Information networking, intermediacy services

French Links
6, rue Deguerry
75011 PARIS
Tel: 43 14 91 59
Fax: 43 14 91 59
Director: Rachel KAPLAN
Franco-American public relations and cultural tourism company

Gary Cantor
6, rue Crétet
75009 PARIS
Tel: 48 78 08 47
Fax: 42 85 45 59
Bilingual financial consultant

Groupe Courtaud
26, rue de Berri
75008 PARIS
Tel: 45 62 20 00
Fax: 45 62 30 04
Career consultants

Hay Management Consulting Group
Tour Kupka B
92906 PARIS LA DEFENSE Cedex
Tel: 46 53 71 71
Fax: 46 53 71 50
Director: M. Laurent DUFFETEL

Heidrick and Struggles Intl.
112, avenue Kléber
75016 PARIS
Tel: 44 34 17 00
Fax: 44 34 17 17
Director: M. Gerard CLERY

Hill and Knowlton Actis
78, avenue Raymond Poincaré
75116 PARIS
Tel: 45 00 41 79
Fax: 45 00 14 98
Chairman: M. Alain DELESQUE

Horwath France
12, rue de Madrid
75008 PARIS
Tel: 43 87 11 40
Fax: 45 22 78 87
Director: M. René AMIRKHANIAN
Specialist consultancy for the hotel, catering, tourism and leisure industries

Hudson Research International
6, rue des Fonds Verts
75012 PARIS
Tel: 43 07 34 10
Fax: 43 07 34 10
Director: M. Duncan JAMES
Publications/Consulting

Inforama S.A.
7, rue Pasquier
75008 PARIS
Tel: 47 42 14 40
Fax: 47 42 11 93
President: M. Robert GUILLAUMOT
International consultants for advanced technology and the computer industry

Information et Entreprise
7, rue du Pasteur Wagner
75011 PARIS
Tel: 49 29 12 12
Fax: 48 06 55 65
Director: M. T. FOLLIN
Public relations consulting

Institut de Gestion Sociale
25, rue François Ier
75008 PARIS
Tel: 53 67 84 00
Fax: 40 70 10 74
Management, language and knowledge transfer

J. Stobbs Marketbase
107, avenue La Bourdonnais
75007 PARIS
Tel: 45 51 36 03
Fax: 47 53 72 85
Director: Mrs Johanna STOBBS
Marketing and communications

Jean-Pierre Frankenhuis
4, rue Jasmin
75016 PARIS
Tel: 45 25 97 64
Fax: 45 20 62 94

John Hardman Associates
B.P. 03
24210 AZERAT
Tel: (16) 53 05 28 74
Fax: (16) 53 05 28 73
Director: M. John HARDMAN
Focus on Franco-British and US marketing strategy

John Taylor
86, avenue Victor Hugo
75016 PARIS
Tel: 45 53 25 25
Fax: 47 55 63 97
Real estate consultants

Josiane Agard Développement
67, avenue Georges Mandel
75016 PARIS
Tel: 45 04 69 56
Fax: 45 04 68 57

Kepner Tregoe
91, rue du Fbg. St. Honoré
75008 PARIS
Tel: 05 90 87 03
Fax: 05 90 87 10
Manager: M. Mike FREEDMAN
Management and training consultants

Korn/Ferry Carré/ Orban International
166, rue du Fbg. St. Honoré
75008 PARIS
Tel: 45 61 66 60
Fax: 45 63 56 67
Managing Partner: M. Charles DE TOULOUSE-LAUTREC
Specialized in recruiting senior executive staff

KPMG Peat Marwick
53, avenue Montaigne
75008 PARIS
Tel: 45 63 15 40
Fax: 45 61 09 25
Senior Partner: M. Curtis BEHRENT

Leaders Trust International
32, avenue Kléber
75116 PARIS
Tel: 45 02 17 00
Fax: 45 00 56 07
Director: M. Gérard SAKAKINI
Management consultants

Leroy Consultants
32, rue d'Armaille
75017 PARIS
Tel: 40 68 38 38
Fax: 40 55 95 12

Louis Berger
71, rue Fondary
75015 PARIS
Tel: 45 78 39 39
Fax: 45 77 74 69
Manager: M. François FARHI

Margaret R. O'Shea
12, rue d'Enghien
75010 PARIS
Tel: 42 46 28 27
Fax: 42 46 43 47
Financial and cultural consultant

MBA Marketing & Business Analysis
114, avenue Félix Faure
75015 PARIS
Tel: 40 60 14 14

McKinsey & Company
29, rue de Bassano
75008 PARIS
Tel: 40 69 14 00
Fax: 47 20 44 85
Director: M. Peter KRALJIC

MG Services
3, rue de Verdun
78590 NOISY-LE-ROI
Tel: 34 62 05 49
Fax: 34 62 02 32
Director: M. Jean-Marc BLOT
Linguistic training, translating services

Moody's France S.A.
22, rue des Capucines
75002 PARIS
Tel: 53 30 10 20
Fax: 42 96 14 28
Director: M. Eric DE BODARD

Multi Services International
40, rue des Pâquerettes
94240 L'HAY-LES-ROSES
Tel: 46 86 26 58
Fax: 46 86 02 61
General Manager: M. Albert HAMMOND
Management services marketing

Nancy Willard-Magaud
4, allée de la Tuilerie
78430 LOUVECIENNES
Tel: 39 58 15 20
Fax: 39 58 11 08
College counseling

Nick Harper & Associates
5, rue des Saussaies
75008 PARIS
Tel: 42 66 42 41
Fax: 44 94 00 04
Contact: M. Nick HARPER
European creative and marketing resource specializing in start-ups and strategic planning for new products and services

PA Consulting Group
114, avenue Charles de Gaulle
92200 NEUILLY-SUR-SEINE
Tel: 40 88 79 79
Fax: 47 45 48 65

Pab Consultants
5, rue Vercingétorix
75014 PARIS
Tel: 43 35 57 20

Peat Marwick Consultants
Tour Fiat - Cedex 16
92084 PARIS LA DEFENSE
Tel: 47 96 20 00
Fax: 47 96 20 58
Dataid & Peat Marwick Systems: 47 96 21 21
Head hunters and consultants

Pellemon
27, rue Louis Vicat
75738 PARIS Cedex 15
Tel: 46 38 34 76
Fax: 46 38 34 82
Director: M. VALLANTIN-DULAC

Price Waterhouse
Tour AIG
34, Place des Corolles
Cedex 105
92908 PARIS LA DEFENSE
Tel: 41 26 10 00
Fax: 41 26 16 16

Proudfoot Crosby France S.A.
9, avenue Franklin Roosevelt
75008 PARIS
Tel: 42 56 46 59
Fax: 42 56 46 27
Management consultants

Raymond Chabot International
Tour Fiat
La Défense 6
Cedex 16
92084 PARIS LA DEFENSE
Tel: 47 96 63 90
Fax: 47 96 63 96
Director: M. Yves LABAT

Research & Business Partners Solutions
8, rue Halévy
75009 PARIS
Tel: 44 51 14 30
Fax: 44 51 14 31

Robins Communications
7, rue Campagne Première
75014 PARIS
Tel: 43 22 43 81
Fax: 43 21 84 89
Director: M. ROBINS
Business to business communications

Russell Reynolds Associates
7, Place Vendôme
75001 PARIS
Tel: 49 26 13 00
Fax: 42 60 03 85
Managing Director:
M. Stephen D. NEWTON

S3IC
29, rue d'Argenteuil
75001 PARIS
Tel: 40 15 09 02
Fax: 40 15 08 14
Consultant: M. Ronald MARKS
International "vecteurs". Specialists for Southern Africa

Sally Huet Travel Consultants
6D, avenue Francis Chaveton
92210 ST-CLOUD
Tel: 46 02 96 97
Fax: 47 71 85 20
Free holiday planning, worldwide travel

Shopping Plus
99-103, rue de Sèvres
75006 PARIS
Tel: 47 53 91 17
Fax: 44 18 93 68
Contact: Irene ADAMIAN
Shopping consultants

Shulman Associates
7, rue Leroux
75116 PARIS
Tel: 45 01 99 93
Fax: 45 00 83 47
Director: Valerie SHULMAN

SMC Internationale
6, rue des Frères Caudron
B.P. 98
78143 VELIZY Cedex
Tel: 39 46 42 05
Fax: 39 46 37 72
Chairman: M. Frank S. RATHGEBER

Spencer Stuart & Associates
39, avenue Franklin Roosevelt
75008 PARIS
Tel: 53 76 81 23
Fax: 53 76 81 00
President: M. Jean-Jacques PIC

Strategy Analysis International
2, avenue de Messine
75008 PARIS
Tel: 45 63 63 63
Fax: 45 61 11 93

T.P.F.C.
57, Bd. de Montmorency
75016 PARIS
Tel: 46 47 47 47
Fax: 46 47 58 65
Director: M. Philippe POINCLOUX

TASA International
6, avenue Marceau
75008 PARIS
Tel: 47 23 53 31
Fax: 47 20 59 19
Managing Director:
Mme Christiane CELLIER
Recruitment consulting

Tennessee Associates International
43, Bd. du Maréchal Joffre
92340 BOURG-LA-REINE
Tel: 46 11 86 15
Fax: 46 11 86 17

The Boston Consulting Group
4, rue d'Aguesseau
75008 PARIS
Tel: 40 17 10 10
Fax: 42 65 03 48
Vice-President: M. Gérard
DE LA FORTELLE

Tocqueville International
16, avenue de Friedland
75008 PARIS
Tel: 53 77 20 00
Financial consultants

Warren Thomas Busch
3, rue Darboy
75011 PARIS
Tel: 43 14 99 84
Representing Mondial International Financial Services

Wertheim & Cie
137, rue du Fbg. St. Honoré
75001 PARIS
Tel: 44 20 65 00
Fax: 44 20 65 01
President: M. Geoffrey
DE FARAMOND

William H. Wainwright Business and Financial Communication
9, rue de la Croix Blanche
78610 ST-LEGER-EN-YVELINES
Tel: 34 86 36 12
Managing Partner:
M. W.H. WAINWRIGHT
Communication, advertising

Workplace
17, rue Emile Dubois
75014 PARIS
Tel: 45 88 77 18
Fax: 45 65 23 43
Director: Brenda DEAN
Consulting and seminars on career management and job hunting

Write Angle
10, rue Chaudron
75010 PARIS
Tel: 40 35 96 69
Fax: 40 35 98 89
E-mail:
100042.2175@compuserve.com
Director: M. Henry BLOUNT
Business communications services

Alcoholics Anonymous
c/o American Church
65, quai d'Orsay
75007 PARIS
Tel: 46 34 59 65

American Aid Society
US Consulate
2, rue St. Florentin
75001 PARIS
Tel: 43 12 47 90
President: Mme Adèle ANIS
Helps US citizens who encounter problems in France

Brendan Flanagan
36, rue de Chabrol
75010 PARIS
Tel: 48 00 07 48
Fax: 48 00 96 11
Singles/Couples, NLP, Hypnotherapy

British Women's Association
7, avenue des Mésanges
77360 VAIRES-SUR-MARNE
Tel: 60 20 86 90
Contact: Valerie CHEMAMA

Cancer Support Group
4, avenue des Jonchères
78121 CRESPIERES
Tel: 30 54 94 66
Fax: 30 54 94 67
Contact: Elizabeth DE VULPILLIERES
Support for cancer patients and friends

F.A.C.T.S (Free AIDS Counseling Treatment and Support)
190, Bd. de Charonne
75020 PARIS
Tel: 44 93 16 32
Fax: 44 93 16 60
Coordinator: M. Chris WHITNEY
HIV services for anglophones

F.A.C.T.S. (AIDS Support Group)
American Church
65, quai d'Orsay
75007 PARIS
Tel: 45 50 26 49
Director: M. Irving LEVIN
Services for HIV, AIDS-related illnesses and families of people affected

Focus on the Family
St. Michael's Anglican Church
5, rue d'Aguesseau
75008 PARIS
Tel: 47 42 70 88
Fax: 47 42 70 11
Contact: Tessa CORBET
Bi-monthly meeting on Tuesday afternoon

Gay Counseling Center
Tel: 45 23 12 39
In French and English

Institut Relationnel et Loisirs
10, rue St. Anastase
75003 PARIS
Tel: 42 71 25 62

Inter Service Parents
5, impasse du Bon Secours
75011 PARIS
Tel: 44 93 44 93
Telephone counseling on childcare, education, law, schooling, leisure activities and family relationships

International Counseling Service
65, quai d'Orsay
75007 PARIS
Tel: 45 50 26 49
Individual, couple and family therapy, educational guidance

Jane Grey
47, Bd. Montparnasse
75006 PARIS
Tel: 42 22 33 35
Corporate and personal consultant and trainer in Applied Intuition

La Méthode Silva (Mind Control)
Cedex 16
27490 AUTHEUIL-AUTHOUILLET
Tel: 45 00 91 18
Tel: (16) 32 34 45 42
Fax: (16) 32 34 64 89
Director: M. Michael DODSON
Stress control, relaxation, personal and mental development

Message
10, rue du 10 Mai 1945
78290 CROISSY-SUR-SEINE
Tel: 34 80 05 88
Contact: Moira CLARK
Friendly support for mothers and pregnant women

Parenting Plus
Tel: 46 21 64 29
Contact: Mme Julie DAVIS
NLP, psychotherapy

Paris Therapy Center
27, rue Daubenton
75005 PARIS
Tel: 47 07 74 14
Director: M. GRILL, Ph.D.
Individual, couple and group therapy, sliding price scale

SOS Help! Crisis Line
B.P. 239-16
75765 PARIS Cedex 16
Tel: 47 23 80 80
Contact: Plum LE-TAN
A friendly listener daily 15h00-23h00

Sprint Parents' Action Network (SPAN)
30, avenue de l'Alliance
95600 EAUBONNE
Tel: 39 59 10 64
President: Rosemary LAUNAY
Support group for parents of children with special needs

The British Charitable Fund
12, rue Barbès
92300 LEVALLOIS-PERRET
Tel: 47 59 07 69
For British citizens in need or hardship

The Victoria Home
1, rue des Dardanelles
75017 PARIS
Tel: 30 53 21 33
Contact: Mme LONGLEY
Home for elderly British people

Voice Dialogue
66, rue Château des Rentiers
75013 PARIS
Tel: 45 85 03 38
Fax: 44 23 71 60
E-mail: diana-L1@verifone.com
Contact: Diana SMITH
Personal and professional development

Weight Watchers France
51, rue du Rocher
75008 PARIS
Tel: 45 22 78 76
Fax: 43 31 45 96
Minitel: 3615 WW

Air Express International
B.P. 10406
Zone Roissytech
1, rue du Pré
Bâtiment 3317
95707 ROISSY CDG
Tel: 49 19 68 68
Fax: 48 62 49 94
President: M. Marcel ETIEN

Airborne Express
9, Bd. Ney
75018 PARIS
Tel: 40 05 18 84

Burlington Air Express France
Aéroport Charles de Gaulle
B.P. 10287
95704 Roissy CDG Cedex
Tel: 48 64 63 63
Admin: 48 62 70 63
Sales Manager: M. Robert BELLIER

Chronopost
41, rue Camille Desmoulins
92442 ISSY-LES-MOULINEAUX Cedex
Tel: 46 48 10 00
Fax: 46 48 10 50
President: M. Frédéric TIBERGHIEN

DHL International
Z. I. Paris Nord II
241, rue de la Belle Etoile
95957 ROISSY CDG
Tel: 49 38 70 70
Fax: 49 38 72 97
Commercial Director:
M. Dominique LIETAR

Federal Express France
125, avenue Louis Roche
92230 GENNEVILLIERS
Tel: 05 33 33 55
Fax: 47 94 21 52
Director: Mme Marie-Pierre ROGERS

Jet Services Courier
Rue de la Belle Borne
B.P. 10136
95701 ROISSY CDG
Tel: 48 62 62 22
Fax: 48 62 62 46
Director: Gilles SOCOLOWSKI
Express transportation of documents and small parcels

May Courier International
13, rue Oberkampf
75011 PARIS
Tel: 43 38 77 00
Fax: 43 38 51 44

TNT-IPEC
83, rue Blaise Pascal
93600 AULNAY-SOUS-BOIS
Tel: 48 19 48 19
Fax: 48 19 49 19

United Parcel Service (UPS)
87, avenue de l'Aérodrome
B.P. 39
94310 ORLY VILLE
Tel: 49 79 30 00
Fax: 48 92 51 07
Commercial Director:
M. Warren WILTZ

American Express
11, rue Scribe
75009 PARIS
Tel: 47 77 77 07
Card services, traveler's checks, etc.

American Express France
4, rue Louis Blériot
92561 RUEIL-MALMAISON
Tel: 47 77 70 00
Fax: 47 77 74 40
Lost: 47 77 72 00
President: M. PETRUCCELLI
Headquarters

Diners Club de France
Tour Berkeley
19-29, rue du Capitaine Guynemer
92903 PARIS LA DEFENSE
Info: 47 62 75 00
Lost: 47 62 75 75
Tel: 40 90 00 00
Fax: 47 62 75 59
Minitel: 3615 DINERS CLUB
President: M. Alain PACAUD

Eurocard-Mastercard
16, rue Lecourbe
75015 PARIS
Tel: 45 67 53 53
Lost: 45 67 47 67
Intl: 43 23 25 96
Minitel: 3615 EM

Mastercard International Inc.
Tour Maine Montparnasse
33, avenue du Maine
75015 PARIS
Tel: 45 38 40 00

Visa-Carte Bleue
41, Bd. des Capucines
75002 PARIS
Admin: 40 15 00 74
Lost: 42 77 11 90
Minitel: 3615 CB VISA

Alliance Française
101, Bd. Raspail
75006 PARIS
Tel: 45 44 38 28
Fax: 45 44 25 95
Deputy Director: M. BAILLY

American Center
51, rue de Bercy
75592 PARIS Cedex 12
Tel: 44 73 77 77
Fax: 44 73 77 55
Contact: Nathalie AUBERGE
Exhibitions, conferences, films, stage performances

British Council
9-11, rue de Constantine
75007 PARIS
Tel: 49 55 73 00
Fax: 47 05 77 02
Public Relations: M. Duncan JACKMAN

Centre Culturel Canadien
5, rue de Constantine
75007 PARIS
Tel: 47 51 35 73
Fax: 47 05 43 55
Minitel: 3614 CANADA
Cultural Attaché: M. Emile MARTEL

Centre Culturel Indo-Français
12, rue Notre-Dame-de-Nazareth
75003 PARIS
Tel: 42 78 80 53

Centre Culturel Suédois
11, rue Payenne
75003 PARIS
Tel: 44 78 80 20
Fax: 44 78 80 27
Public Relations: Mme Birgitta EGESTROM-RABOT
Exhibitions, literary events, concerts, films, research center

Collège des Irlandais
5, rue des Irlandais
75005 PARIS
Tel: 45 35 59 79 (college)
Tel: 45 35 32 07 (cultural center)
Fax: 45 35 72 09
Administrator: Mme Roisin DOCKERY
Cultural and residential exchanges between Ireland and France

Délégation Générale du Québec
Cultural Service
66, rue Pergolèse
75116 PARIS
Tel: 40 67 85 70

Fondation C. Gulbenkian
51, avenue d'Iéna
75016 PARIS
Tel: 47 20 86 84
Fax: 40 70 98 79

Franco-Australian Cultural Association
11, avenue Maréchal de Lattre de Tassigny
92100 BOULOGNE
Tel: 46 03 01 92
Fax: 46 03 48 16
President: M. Jean-Paul DELAMOTTE

Goethe Institute
17, avenue d'Iéna
75016 PARIS
Tel: 44 43 92 30
Fax: 44 43 92 40
Director: Dr Klaus-Peter ROOS
German courses, lending library

Institut Culturel Italien
50, rue de Varenne
75007 PARIS
Tel: 44 39 49 39
Fax: 42 22 37 88
Director: M. Paolo FABBRI
Library, conferences, educational services

Institut Néerlandais
121, rue de Lille
75007 PARIS
Tel: 47 05 85 99
Fax: 45 56 00 77
Public Relations: Mme Elisabeth VAN BOETZELAER
Dutch cultural center: exhibitions, concerts, films, Dutch language courses, library

Korean Cultural Center
2, avenue d'Iéna
75016 PARIS
Tel: 47 20 83 86
Fax: 47 23 58 97

Bazar de l'Hôtel de Ville (BHV)
52, rue de Rivoli
75004 PARIS
Tel: 42 74 90 00
Fax: 42 74 96 79
President: M. Jean-Pierre BOULOT
Good Do-It-Yourself section in the basement

Galeries Lafayette
40, Bd. Haussmann
75009 PARIS
Tel: 42 82 34 56
Fax: 48 78 25 19
President: M. Georges MEYER

Galeries Lafayette
22, rue du Départ
75015 PARIS
Tel: 45 38 52 87
Fax: 43 22 09 44

La Samaritaine
19, rue de la Monnaie
75001 PARIS
Tel: 40 41 20 20
Fax: 40 41 28 28

Le Bon Marché Rive Gauche
5, rue de Babylone
75007 PARIS
Tel: 44 39 80 00
Fax: 44 39 80 50
Director: M. Philippe DE BEAUVOIR

Le Printemps
64, Bd. Haussmann
75009 PARIS
Tel: 42 82 50 00

Marks & Spencer
B.P. 252
75424 PARIS Cedex 09
Tel: 44 53 50 00
Fax: 40 16 13 73
President: M. J.M. GENIS
Headquarters

Marks & Spencer
88, rue de Rivoli
75004 PARIS
Tel: 44 61 08 00
Fax: 44 61 08 01

Marks & Spencer
37, Bd. Haussmann
75009 PARIS
Tel: 47 42 42 91
Fax: 42 66 59 92

Agnès B.
17, rue de Dieu
75010 PARIS
Tel: 40 03 45 00
Fax: 40 03 45 50
President: Agnès TROUBLE
Administrative offices

Burlington Worsteds International
383, rue de la Belle Etoile
95700 ROISSY-EN-FRANCE
Tel: 48 17 83 00
Fax: 48 17 83 17
Textile manufacturer

Cerruti 1881
3, Place de la Madeleine
75008 PARIS
Tel: 53 30 18 81

Chambre Syndicale de la Couture Parisienne
100, rue du Fbg. St. Honoré
75008 PARIS
Tel: 42 66 64 44
Fax: 42 66 94 63
Organization of Parisian fashion houses

Christian Lacroix
73, rue du Fbg. St. Honoré
75008 PARIS
Tel: 42 65 79 08

Céline
38, avenue Montaigne
75008 PARIS
Tel: 49 52 08 79

Emmanuel Ungaro
2, avenue Montaigne
75008 PARIS
Tel: 47 23 61 94

Emmanuele Khanh International
39, avenue Victor Hugo
75116 PARIS
Tel: 44 17 31 00
Fax: 45 00 20 71

Fashion Gradation International
10, rue des Jeûneurs
75002 PARIS
Tel: 45 08 17 16
Fax: 45 08 00 46
Patterns and sizes for clothing

Fashion Group of Paris
9, rue St. Florentin
75008 PARIS
Tel: 49 27 04 95

Fashion Institute of Technology
20, rue du Commandant Mouchotte
75014 PARIS
Tel: 43 35 10 12

Fra For
1, cours Jacquin
10000 TROYES
Tel: (16) 25 76 26 00
Fax: (16) 25 80 35 29
President: M. Robert SCHMID
Licensed Levi's manufacturer

Fruit of the Loom
167, rue Chevaleret
75013 PARIS
Tel: 44 06 83 83
Fax: 45 83 58 82
Contact: M. Alan WADE

Givenchy
3, avenue George V
75008 PARIS
Tel: 44 31 50 00
Fax: 47 20 44 96

Jean-Louis Scherrer
51, avenue Montaigne
75008 PARIS
Tel: 42 99 05 79

Kevin's Business
43, rue Popincourt
75011 PARIS
Tel: 48 07 26 63
Fax: 48 07 81 27
Women's clothing (wholesaler)

Lee Cooper France
Rue le Tintoret
80045 AMIENS Cedex
Tel: (16) 22 54 66 66
Fax: (16) 22 54 66 00

Levi Strauss Continental France
6, avenue du Pacifique
B.P. 115
91944 LES ULIS Cedex
Tel: 69 86 89 98
Fax: 64 46 54 78

Milliken Fabrics
37, rue Nouveau Monde
80240 ROISEL
Tel: (16) 22 86 61 15
Fax: (16) 22 86 59 09
Director: C.F. JEANES
Specialized in industrial knitwear

Playtex
6, rue de Penthièvre
75008 PARIS
Tel: 42 66 90 91
Fax: 42 66 66 91
President: M. Gaby FERTOUT
Makes, distributes and markets Playtex underwear

Prestige & Collections
6bis, rue des Graviers
92521 NEUILLY-SUR-SEINE Cedex
Tel: 46 40 58 14
Fax: 46 40 58 38
Marketing Director: M. Eric JOLY

Promostyl
31, rue de la Folie Méricourt
75011 PARIS
Tel: 49 23 76 00
Fax: 43 38 22 59
President: M. Sébastien DE DIESBACH
Leader in fashion design and trend forecasting. Author of the guide Cities of Fashion

Revlon
Charles of the Ritz
23, rue Boissière
75016 PARIS
Tel: 44 05 55 55
Director: M. LESIEUR

Sara Lee Personal Products
28, rue Jacques Ibert
92300 LEVALLOIS-PERRET
Tel: 46 39 38 38
Fax: 47 58 02 20
Distributor of hosiery (Dim), textiles and beauty products (Cacharel)

Sperry Top-Sider Europe
215, rue St. Honoré
75001 PARIS
Tel: 44 86 03 09
Fax: 44 86 03 00
General Manager:
M. Michel ROUEAU
Markets shoes. French subsidiary of the American firm Striderite Corporation S.A.

Spirit of Extasy
25, rue de Turbigo
75003 PARIS
Tel: 45 08 03 90
Fax: 42 36 33 63
Contact: Esther VOISIN
Unusual and exciting accessories for film and fashion

Warner's Aiglon
66, rue du Fbg. St. Honoré
75008 PARIS
Tel: 47 42 81 32
Fax: 42 66 14 15
Director France: M. François KLOTZ
Distributor of Warner lingerie in France

Yves Saint-Laurent
5, avenue Marceau
75016 PARIS
Tel: 47 23 72 71
Fax: 47 23 69 73

ACOFAB
Rue Bouvreuil
95612 CERGY-PONTOISE
Tel: 30 37 63 30
Fax: 30 37 46 36
Director: M. Gilbert LEPELTIER

ADT Sécurité Systèmes
10, rue Alphonse de Neuville
75017 PARIS
Tel: 47 66 04 19
Fax: 43 80 91 13
President: M. Paul PARMENTIER

Advanced Micro Devices S.A.
Z.I. Orlytech
5, allée du Commandant Mouchotte
91781 WISSOUS Cedex
Tel: 49 75 10 10
Fax: 49 75 10 13
Director: M. MERONE

Allen-Bradley Servovision S.A.
Energy Park
36, avenue de l'Europe
78140 VELIZY
Tel: 30 67 72 00
Fax: 34 65 32 33
Director: M. SALEUR
Industrial computerized automation

ALSIM Electronics
69, rue d'Aguesseau
92100 BOULOGNE-BILLANCOURT
Tel: 46 10 50 00
Fax: 43 75 85 70
Contact: M. Marc GRUNER

AMP de France
29, chaussée Jules César
B.P. 39
95301 PONTOISE
Tel: 34 20 88 21
Fax: 34 20 86 06
Director: M. Raymond WANDELL
Electronic connectors

Automatic Systems
57, rue Alphonse
B.P. 136
92223 BAGNEUX Cedex
Tel: 40 92 74 44
Fax: 40 92 74 43
Public Relations:
Mme N. LE CORRE

Augat S.A.
46, Place de la Seine
94513 RUNGIS
Tel: 46 75 99 00
Fax: 46 75 37 64
Director: M. Glyn DENNEHY
French subsidiary of the US-based firm Augat. Sells electronic components

Auxitrol
1, rue d'Anjou
B.P. 241
92603 ASNIERES
Tel: 47 90 62 81
Fax: 40 86 26 46
Director: M. Henri VERGES

Basler Electric International
P.A.E. "Les Pins"
67310 WASSELONNE
Tel: (16) 88 87 10 10
Fax: (16) 88 87 08 08
Director: M. Mark HENDEL

Belden Electronics
Tour Anjou
33, quai de Dion-Bouton
92814 PUTEAUX Cedex
Tel: 40 81 03 70
Fax: 40 81 02 22
Director: Jean-Jacques ERNOULT

BFI-IBEXSA Electronique
1, rue Lavoisier
91430 IGNY
Tel: 69 33 74 00
Fax: 69 33 74 99
Director: M. A. HUARD
Retailer

Bourns Ohmic
21-23, rue des Ardennes
75019 PARIS
Tel: 40 03 36 05
Fax: 40 03 36 14
President: M. Dietmar SCHAUER
Supplier of electronic components

Branson Ultrasons
Zone Industrielle
B.P. 247
74106 ANNEMASSE Cedex
Tel: (16) 50 43 96 50
Fax: (16) 50 37 67 10
President: M. Jost WERNER

Burr Brown International S.A.
18, avenue Dutartre
78152 LE CHESNAY Cedex
Tel: 39 54 35 58
Fax: 39 54 87 03
Director: M. VINCIGUERRA
Electronic components

Cherry S.A.R.L.
1, avenue des Violettes
Z.A. des Petits Carreaux
94384 BONNEUIL-SUR-MARNE
Tel: 43 77 29 51
Fax: 43 77 20 84
Manager: M. Claude MENANT
Distributor of electronic components

Crosfield Electronics
16, rue Georges Besse
92160 ANTONY Cedex
Tel: 46 74 20 00
Fax: 46 74 20 75
Sales of mainframe scanners

Curtis Instruments
98, Bd. Victor Hugo
92110 CLICHY
Tel: 47 31 61 10
Fax: 42 70 34 26
Director: M. Edward MARWELL

Datel
P.A. de Bois d'Arcy Nord
9, rue Michael Faraday
78180 MONTIGNY-LE-BRETONNEUX
Tel: 34 60 01 01
Fax: 30 58 21 30
Contact: M. Philippe KLEJTMAN

Eaton Controls
Avenue des Sorbiers
B.P. 5
74311 THYEZ CLUSES
Tel: (16) 50 89 37 00
Fax: (16) 50 96 08 80
Director: M. Didier DURANT

EG et G Instruments
1, rue du Gevaudan
Z.I. Petite Montagne Sud
CE 1734
91047 EVRY Cedex
Tel: 60 86 93 66
Fax: 60 86 18 37
Director: M. Louaye MOUDARRES

Emerson Europe S.A.
8, rue de l'Estérel
Silic 502
94623 RUNGIS Cedex
Tel: 46 87 51 52
Fax: 46 87 83 14
Commercial Director:
M. Christian PHILIPPE
Manufactures power supply systems

Erico
Rue Benoît Fourneyron
Z.I. Sud
B.P. 31
42161 ANDREZIEUX-BOUTHEON Cedex
Tel: (16) 77 36 56 56
Fax: (16) 77 36 59 98
Manager: J.C. FUCHS

EuroFax Muirhead
16, rue Médéric
75017 PARIS
Tel: 42 12 40 20
Fax: 42 67 68 66
Director: M. Renaud BAIN-THOUVEREZ

European Television Center
76, rue de Sèvres
75007 PARIS
Fax: 43 06 53 67
Television production

General Electric
Information Services
19, avenue Léon Gambetta
B.P. 338
92541 MONTROUGE Cedex
Tel: 46 73 16 00
Fax: 46 73 16 01
Director: M. Michel DANON

Genrad
6, rue Vincent Van Gogh
93364 NEUILLY-PLAISANCE
Tel: 49 44 22 00
Fax: 49 44 22 99
Director: M. Pierre GUILLEMAUD

IA Corporation
4, chemin de Malacher
ZIRST 4401
38944 MEYLAN Cedex
Tel: (16) 76 90 22 00
Fax: (16) 76 41 14 61
President: M. Charles MALKA

ILC DDC Electronique
10, rue Carle Hebert
92400 COURBEVOIE
Tel: 43 33 58 88
Fax: 43 34 97 62
Manager: M. Michel CAZOR

Ingram Micro
Carrefour de l'Europe
59810 LESQUIN
Tel: (16) 20 88 58 00
Fax: (16) 20 88 58 88
Director: M. Philippe JOSEPH

Intel Corporation
1, rue Edison
B.P. 303
78054 ST-QUENTIN-EN-YVELINES
Cedex
Tel: 30 57 70 00
Fax: 30 64 60 32
Director: M. Gilles GRANIER
Microcomputers

ITT Composants et Instruments
507, rue des Blains
92220 BAGNEUX
Tel: 46 65 50 90
Fax: 46 65 96 96
President: M. Jacques PASCAL

ITT Semi Conductors France
157, rue des Blains
92223 BAGNEUX
Tel: 45 47 81 81
Fax: 45 47 83 92
Selling of semiconductors

JP2 S.A.
15, rue Le Corbusier
Z.A. Europarc
94035 CRETEIL Cedex
Tel: 43 99 47 32
Fax: 43 99 07 58
President: M. Jean-Paul
PARMENTIER
Retail trade of electronic equipment for cable television

K-Tron France
Z.I. de l'Abbaye, B.P. 60
38780 PONT EVEQUE
Tel: (16) 74 85 94 25
Fax: (16) 74 57 66 25
Manager: M. Michel JAMEY
The leader in machinery for electronic measuring and weighing

Keithley Instruments
3, allée des Garays
B.P. 60
91122 PALAISEAU Cedex
Tel: 60 11 51 55
Fax: 60 11 77 26
Manager: M. Hermann HAMM

Kenwood France
13, Bd. Ney
75018 PARIS
Tel: 44 72 16 16
Director: M. KITAHARA
Auto radio imports

KLA Instruments France
25, rue Michael Faraday
78180 MONTIGNY-LE-
BRETONNEUX
Tel: 30 45 30 03
Fax: 30 45 26 69

Lambda Electronique
Route de Grivery
Gometz le Chatel
B.P. 77
91943 LES ULIS Cedex
Tel: 60 12 14 87
Fax: 60 12 27 94
Director: M. LEGRAND
Distributor of electronic materials

Litton Precision
Products International
58, rue Pottier
B.P. 75
78151 LE CHESNAY Cedex
Tel: 39 55 21 04
Fax: 39 55 50 68
Commercial Director:
M. Jean-Claude SIBI
Importer of electronic components

Morton International
2, rue Ampère
Zone Industrielle, B.P. 36
91430 IGNY
Tel: 69 41 03 45
Fax: 69 41 86 25
Director: J. WOUTERS

Motorola Semi Conducteurs
Avenue Général Eisenhower
Le Mirail
B.P. 1029
31023 TOULOUSE Cedex
Tel: (16) 61 19 90 00
Fax: (16) 61 40 44 99
Director: M. Robert ASCHIERI

Narda France
67, avenue Jean Jaurès
91122 PALAISEAU
Tel: 69 20 40 10
Fax: 69 20 36 04
President: M. Bernard LEIBOWITZ
Imports electronic components

National Instruments France
CA Paris Nord
B.P. 217
93153 LE BLANC MESNIL
Tel: 48 14 24 24
Fax: 48 14 24 14
E-mail: info@natinst.com
Contact: M. Louis-Paul DOCO
Measuring equipment and software

National Semi-Conductor France
Bâtiment ZETA
Z.A. de Courtaboeuf
3, avenue du Canada
91966 LES ULIS Cedex 16
Tel: 69 18 37 00
Fax: 69 18 37 69
President: M. Hans ROHRER

Newport Electronique
9, rue Denis Papin
78190 TRAPPES
Tel: 30 62 14 00
Fax: 30 69 91 20
Manager: M. René GERVAIS

Proner
38-40, allée du Closeau
Z.I. des Richardets
93161 NOISY-LE-GRAND
Tel: 45 92 79 00
Fax: 43 03 42 18
President: M. BLANCHER
Electric and electronic conductors

Quorum International
62, avenue de Wagram
75017 PARIS
Tel: 47 63 09 21
Fax: 47 63 09 18
Contact: M. Patrick McCann
Electronic security products

Raychem
2, Bd. du Moulin-à-Vent
B.P. 8300
95802 CERGY-PONTOISE Cedex
Tel: 34 20 21 22
Fax: 34 24 03 12
Director: M. Alain TEITELBAUM
Electronic components

Siliconix-Temic
3, avenue du Centre
B.P. 309
78054 ST-QUENTIN-EN-YVELINES
Tel: 30 60 70 48
Fax: 30 60 70 02
Director: M. GRU
Marketing of electronic components

Solectron France
Chemin Départemental 109
B.P. 6 Canejan
33611 CESTAS Cedex
Tel: (16) 56 75 75 75
Fax: (16) 56 89 81 36
President: M. Charles DICKINSON

Sprague France
8, avenue du Danemark
37100 TOURS
Tel: (16) 47 51 42 71
Fax: (16) 47 51 53 70
President: M. Gérard SERER

Tektronix
Z.A.C. de Courtaboeuf
6, rue de la Terre de Feu
91941 LES ULIS Cedex
Tel: 69 86 81 81
Fax: 69 07 09 37
Director: M. Patrick GENINA

Telectronics
118, rue de Tocqueville
75017 PARIS
Tel: 46 22 77 04
Fax: 47 66 47 96
Director: M. BRUNIER

Teradyne
Z.A.C. Kléber
Bâtiment F
165, Bd. de Valmy
B.P. 54
92706 COLOMBES Cedex
Tel: 46 13 15 00
Fax: 46 13 15 01
Marketing Manager: Mme Régine CHRETIEN

Thomas & Betts
55-57, Place de la Seine
Silic 120
94513 RUNGIS Cedex
Tel: 46 87 23 85
Fax: 46 87 42 87
Director: M. George GOLDBERG
Study, sale & marketing of electronic components

Ultimate
30, avenue de l'Europe
78140 VELIZY-VILLACOUBLAY
Tel: 30 67 21 00
Fax: 30 70 68 69
Manager: M. Alexandre PHOCAS

Universal Instruments
86, avenue Louis Roche
92230 GENNEVILLIERS
Tel: 47 92 12 22
Fax: 47 92 35 20
Manager: M. Maxime SAUGE
Sells equipment designed for the electronics industry

Veeder Root
8, Place de la Loire
Silic 422
94583 RUNGIS Cedex
Tel: 46 87 09 81
Fax: 46 86 80 04
Manager: M. Jean WILTZ
Electronic meters, counters and gauges

Vishay Micromesures
98, Bd. Gabriel Péri
B.P. 51
92242 MALAKOFF Cedex
Tel: 46 55 98 00
Fax: 42 53 67 94
President: M. Jean-Luc LE GOER

Yes Alarms
125, avenue de Villiers
75017 PARIS
Tel: 42 27 30 20
Security systems

Australia
4, rue Jean Rey
75724 PARIS Cedex 15
Tel: 40 59 33 00
Visas: 40 59 33 06
Fax: 40 59 33 10
Minitel: 3614 AUSTRALIE

Canada
Consulate
30, Bd. de Strasbourg
31000 TOULOUSE
Tel: (16) 61 99 30 16

Canada
Consulate
77, rue Bonnel
69003 LYON
Tel: (16) 72 61 15 25

Canada
Consulate
35, avenue Montaigne
75008 PARIS
Tel: 44 43 29 00
Visas: 44 43 29 16
Fax: 44 43 29 99

Great Britain
Consulate
24, avenue Prado
13006 MARSEILLE
Tel: (16) 91 53 43 32
Fax: (16) 91 37 47 06

Great Britain
Consulate
353, Bd. du Président Wilson
33200 BORDEAUX
Tel: (16) 57 22 21 10
Fax: (16) 56 08 33 12

Great Britain
Consulate
11, square Dutilleul
59800 LILLE
Tel: (16) 20 57 87 90
Fax: (16) 20 54 88 16

Great Britain
Consulate
Victoria Center
20, Chemin Laporte
31300 TOULOUSE
Tel: (16) 61 15 02 02

Great Britain
Consulate
11, rue de Paradis
06000 NICE
Tel: (16) 93 82 32 04

Great Britain
Consulate
24, rue Childebert
69002 LYON
Tel: (16) 78 37 59 67

Great Britain
Embassy
35, rue du Fbg. St. Honoré
75008 PARIS
Tel: 42 66 91 42
Fax: 40 07 03 65
Fax: 42 66 95 90
Minitel: 3615 GBRETAGNE

Great Britain
Consulate
9, avenue Hoche
75008 PARIS
Tel: 42 66 38 10
Fax: 40 76 02 87

India
Consulate
20-22, rue Albéric Magnard
75116 PARIS
Tel: 40 50 71 71
Fax: 40 50 09 96

India
Embassy
15, rue Alfred Dehodencq
75016 PARIS
Tel: 40 50 70 70
Fax: 40 50 09 96

Ireland
Consulate
4, rue Desparmet
69008 LYON
Tel: (16) 78 76 44 85

Ireland
152, Bd. John Kennedy
06160 CAP D'ANTIBES
Tel: (16) 93 61 50 63

Ireland
4, rue Rude
75116 PARIS
Tel: 45 00 20 87
Fax: 45 00 84 17
Minitel: 3615 IRLANDE

Malta
92, avenue des Champs-Elysées
75008 PARIS
Tel: 45 62 53 01
Fax: 45 62 00 36

New Zealand
7ter, rue Léonard de Vinci
75116 PARIS
Tel: 45 00 24 11
Fax: 45 01 26 39

Singapore
22, avenue Victor Hugo
75016 PARIS
Tel: 45 00 11 83
Fax: 45 00 61 37
Economic Development Board

South Africa
59, quai d'Orsay
75007 PARIS
Tel: 45 55 92 37
Fax: 47 53 99 70

United States of America
Consulate
15, avenue d'Alsace
67000 STRASBOURG
Tel: (16) 88 35 31 04

United States of America
Consulate
2, rue St. Florentin
75001 PARIS
Tel: 42 96 14 88 (tape)
Tel: 42 61 80 75
Fax: 42 86 82 91

United States of America
Embassy
2, avenue Gabriel
75382 PARIS Cedex 08
Tel: 43 12 22 22
Fax: 42 66 97 83
Fax: 42 45 05 33

United States of America
Consulate
7, quai Général Sarrail
B.P. 2073
69226 LYON Cedex 2
Tel: (16) 78 24 68 49

United States of America
Consulate
12, Bd. Paul Peytral
13006 MARSEILLE
Tel: (16) 91 54 92 00

United States of America
Consulate
31, rue du Maréchal Joffre
06000 NICE
Tel: (16) 93 88 89 55
Tel: (Com (16) 93 82 30 98

United States of America
Consulate
22, cours du Maréchal Foch
33000 BORDEAUX
Tel: (16) 56 52 65 95

Other Embassies
Autres Ambassades

Austria
6, rue Fabert
75007 PARIS
Tel: 45 55 95 66
Fax: 47 20 25 80

Bahrain
3bis, Place des Etats-Unis
75016 PARIS
Tel: 47 23 48 68
Fax: 47 20 55 75

Belgium
9, rue de Tilsitt
75017 PARIS
Tel: 44 09 39 39
Fax: 47 54 07 64

Brazil
34, cours Albert Ier
75008 PARIS
Tel: 45 61 63 00
Fax: 43 59 82 80

Bulgaria
1, avenue Rapp
75007 PARIS
Tel: 45 51 18 68

Cyprus
23, rue de Galilée
75008 PARIS
Tel: 47 20 86 28
Fax: 40 70 14 68

Czech Republic
15, avenue Charles Floquet
75007 PARIS
Tel: 40 65 13 00

Denmark
77, avenue Marceau
75116 PARIS
Tel: 44 31 21 21
Fax: 44 31 21 88

Egypt
56, avenue d'Iéna
75016 PARIS
Tel: 53 67 88 30
Fax: 47 23 06 43

Federal Republic of Germany
Embassy
13-15, avenue Franklin Roosevelt
75008 PARIS
Tel: 42 99 78 00
Fax: 43 59 74 18

Federal Republic of Germany
Consulate
34, avenue d'Iéna
75016 PARIS
Tel: 42 99 78 00
Visas: 42 99 79 61
Fax: 47 20 01 60

Finland
Consular Section
18 bis, rue d'Anjou
75008 PARIS
Tel: 47 05 35 45
Fax: 45 55 51 57

Finland
Embassy
39, quai d'Orsay
75007 PARIS
Tel: 47 05 35 45
Fax: 45 55 51 57

Georgia
104, avenue Raymond Poincaré
75016 PARIS
Tel: 45 02 16 16
Fax: 45 02 16 01

Greece
17, rue Auguste Vacquerie
75116 PARIS
Tel: 47 23 72 28
Fax: 47 20 70 28

Hungary
5bis, avenue Foch
75016 PARIS
Tel: 45 00 41 59
Fax: 45 01 66 00

Iceland
8, avenue Kléber
75016 PARIS
Tel: 40 67 91 19
Fax: 40 67 99 96

Israel
3, rue Rabelais
75008 PARIS
Tel: 40 76 55 00
Fax: 40 76 55 55

Italy
51, rue de Varenne
75007 PARIS
Tel: 49 54 03 00
Fax: 45 49 35 81

Japan
7, avenue Hoche
75008 PARIS
Tel: 48 88 62 00
Fax: 44 09 20 77

Korea
125, rue de Grenelle
75007 PARIS
Tel: 47 53 01 01
Fax: 47 53 00 41

Lithuania
14, Bd. Montmartre
75009 PARIS
Tel: 48 01 00 33
Fax: 48 01 03 31

Luxembourg
33, avenue Rapp
75007 PARIS
Tel: 45 55 13 37
Fax: 45 51 72 29

Macedonia
21, rue Sébastien Mercier
75015 PARIS
Tel: 45 77 10 50
Fax: 45 77 14 84

Malaysia
32, rue Spontini
75116 PARIS
Tel: 45 53 11 85
Fax: 47 04 52 48

Mexico
9, rue de Longchamp
75016 PARIS
Tel: 45 53 76 43
Fax: 47 55 65 29

Morocco
5, rue Le Tasse
75016 PARIS
Tel: 45 20 69 35
Fax: 45 20 22 58

Norway
28, rue Bayard
75008 PARIS
Tel: 53 67 04 00
Fax: 53 67 04 40

Pakistan
18, rue Lord Byron
75008 PARIS
Tel: 45 62 23 32

Poland
1-5, rue de Talleyrand
75343 PARIS Cedex 07
Tel: 45 51 60 80
Fax: 45 55 72 02

Portugal
3, rue du Noisiel
75016 PARIS
Tel: 47 27 35 29
Fax: 47 55 00 40

Republic of China
11, avenue George V
75008 PARIS
Tel: 47 23 36 77
Fax: 47 20 24 22

Romania
5, rue de l'Exposition
75007 PARIS
Tel: 40 62 22 08
Fax: 45 56 97 47

Russia
40, Bd. Lannes
75016 PARIS
Tel: 45 04 05 05
Fax: 45 04 05 01

Slovenia
21, rue Bouquet de Longchamp
75116 PARIS
Tel: 47 55 65 90
Fax: 47 55 60 05

Spain
22, avenue Marceau
75008 PARIS
Tel: 44 43 18 00
Fax: 47 23 59 55

Sri Lanka
15, rue d'Astorg
75008 PARIS
Tel: 42 66 35 01
Fax: 40 07 00 11

Sweden
17, rue Barbet de Jouy
75007 PARIS
Tel: 44 18 88 00
Fax: 44 18 88 40

Switzerland
142, rue de Grenelle
75007 PARIS
Tel: 49 55 67 00
Fax: 45 51 34 77

The Netherlands
7-9, rue Eblé
75007 PARIS
Tel: 40 62 33 00
Fax: 40 56 01 32

Tunisia
25, rue Barbet de Jouy
75007 PARIS
Tel: 45 55 95 98
Fax: 45 56 02 64

Turkey
16, avenue Lamballe
75016 PARIS
Tel: 45 24 52 24
Fax: 45 20 41 91

Yugoslavia
54, rue de la Faisanderie
75016 PARIS
Tel: 40 72 24 24
Fax: 40 72 24 11

Zimbabwe
5, rue de Tilsitt
75008 PARIS
Tel: 47 63 48 31
Fax: 44 09 05 36

Antoinette Lefevre
3, rue de Duras
75008 PARIS
Tel: 42 66 26 26

Arrow Consultants
114bis, rue Michel Ange
75016 PARIS
Tel: 40 71 28 42
Fax: 40 71 28 19

Axel Assistance
5bis, rue Keppler
75116 PARIS
Tel: 47 23 67 20
Temporary and permanent employment agency

Berndtson Paul Ray
73, avenue des Champs-Elysées
75008 PARIS
Tel: 53 77 22 00
Fax: 53 77 22 09

BEPA
6, rue de Madrid
75008 PARIS
Tel: 43 87 48 13

Boyden Consulting
38, rue Vauthier
92100 BOULOGNE-BILLANCOURT
Tel: 46 99 18 18
Fax: 46 99 18 19
Managing Partner:
M. Eric C. MACKENTHUN
Executive search

Britt
23, Bd. des Capucines
75002 PARIS
Tel: 47 42 06 12
Fax: 47 42 18 66

Cabinet Joublin
62, avenue de Wagram
75017 PARIS
Tel: 47 63 09 25
Fax: 47 63 09 18

Coopers & Lybrand
32, rue Guersant
75017 PARIS
Tel: 45 72 80 00
Fax: 45 72 22 19
President: M. P.B. ANGLADE

Dernis Organisation
23, avenue de Wagram
75017 PARIS
Tel: 45 72 91 11
Fax: 45 72 91 12
Director: M. Jean-Philippe DERNIS
Office and secretarial service

Ecco
26, rue Gramont
75002 PARIS
Tel: 42 96 96 30
Contact: Mme HOMESCOUX
The specialist in temporary help

Egon Zehnder International
12, avenue George V
75008 PARIS
Tel: 47 23 51 06
Fax: 47 20 39 82

Euro-Pair Services
13, rue Vavin
75006 PARIS
Tel: 43 29 80 01
Fax: 43 29 80 37
Contact: Mme DAVAY
Au Pair Placement (USA, Europe)

Eurosearch Consultants
6, avenue de Messine
75008 PARIS
Tel: 45 61 96 03

Fischer
1, rue Léo Chavez
75020 PARIS
Tel: 40 30 02 27
Headhunters

Forgeot Weeks
128, rue du Fbg. St. Honoré
75008 PARIS
Tel: 45 63 35 15
Fax: 40 07 00 67
Director: M. Alain FORGEOT

GR Interim
12, rue de la Paix
75002 PARIS
Tel: 42 61 82 11
Fax: 47 03 40 49
Director: M. G.P. GROCHOWSKI
Delegating bilingual and trilingual office personnel

Heidrick and Struggles Intl
112, avenue Kléber
75116 PARIS
Tel: 44 34 17 00
Fax: 44 34 17 17
President: M. Gérard CLERY-MELIN

I.B.D. Algoe
28, avenue de Messine
75008 PARIS
Tel: 45 61 95 33
Fax: 40 74 02 02
Director: M. DESJEUX

John Stork International
10, rue des Saussaies
75008 PARIS
Tel: 42 65 26 13
Fax: 42 68 13 23
Director: M. F. GRANDCLAUDE
Executive search

Kelly Services
73, Bd. Haussmann
75008 PARIS
Tel: 44 94 64 64
Fax: 44 94 64 65
Director: M. TOMASINI
Administrative offices

Kelly Services
130 bis, avenue Charles de Gaulle
92521 NEUILLY-SUR-SEINE
Tel: 47 47 41 18
Director: Annie COUTANCEAU
Agency

Magnitude
90, avenue des Champs-Elysées
75008 PARIS
Tel: 53 76 11 76
Temporary employment agency

Manpower France
7-9, rue Jacques Bingen
B.P. 53
75825 PARIS Cedex 17
Tel: 44 15 40 40
Fax: 42 67 76 66
Director: M. Michael GRUNELIUS
Temporary help agency

Marie Gilmert Conseil
91, rue du Fbg. St. Honoré
75008 PARIS
Tel: 45 24 31 88
Fax: 42 66 15 60
Director: Marie GILMERT

Marketing Search
61, avenue Marceau
75116 PARIS
Tel: 40 70 10 70
Fax: 40 70 99 66
Director: Mme Camille VOLKER
Recruitment consulting

MCS International
2, passage St. Philippe du Roule
75008 PARIS
Tel: 42 89 27 85
Temporary trilingual staff agency

Metropolitan Models
7, Bd. des Capucines
75002 PARIS
Tel: 42 66 52 85
Fax: 42 66 49 72
Modeling agency

Minerve Intérim
422, rue St. Honoré
75008 PARIS
Tel: 42 61 76 76
Fax: 42 60 22 62
Temporary assignments for secretaries, receptionists, hostesses

Ordinter
16, rue Auber
75009 PARIS
Tel: 47 42 74 07
Fax: 47 42 83 73
Contact: M. Jean-Marc GUERIN

Pelissier Mennesson
82, avenue du Château
B.P. 7025
95050 CERGY-PONTOISE Cedex
Tel: 34 64 08 08
Fax: 34 64 31 22
Contact: M. Dominique GUYON

Personnel Research
27, rue des Mathurins
75008 PARIS
Tel: 49 24 95 11

Plus International
60, rue de l'Arcade
75008 PARIS
Tel: 40 08 40 30
Fax: 45 22 49 53
Contact: Mme CHAMBERS
Multilingual recruitment

Profile International
43, rue de Châteaudun
75009 PARIS
Tel: 44 53 49 12
Fax: 44 53 49 21
Consultant: Sally DAVIES
Executive personnel (catering, leisure industries)

Right Associates
Tour Winterthur - 14ème étage
Cedex 18
92085 PARIS LA DEFENSE 2
Tel: 46 96 65 65
Fax: 46 96 65 66
Director: M. John WOODGER

Selective Executive Assistants
91, rue du Fbg. St. Honoré
75008 PARIS
Tel: 44 71 35 16
Fax: 42 66 15 60
Director: Mme Sibyl VIDAL
Recruitment of bilingual executive secretaries

Selpro
43, rue Lafayette
75009 PARIS
Tel: 42 80 92 12
Fax: 42 80 90 99
Bilingual and trilingual secretarial personnel for short or long-term positions

Sheila Burgess
62, rue St. Lazare
75009 PARIS
Tel: 44 63 02 57
Fax: 44 63 02 59
Recruitment consultants

Spencer Stuart & Associates
39, avenue Franklin Roosevelt
75008 PARIS
Tel: 45 62 62 20
Fax: 42 25 61 28
Director: M. Jean-Jacques PIC

Synerval
11, rue Tronchet
75008 PARIS
Tel: 47 42 73 43
Fax: 47 42 05 07

T.M. International
18, rue Volney
75002 PARIS
Tel: 47 42 71 00
Fax: 47 42 18 87
Managing Director:
Mme Tanya IRELAND
Secretarial recruitment

University Services for Americans
5, rue Mizon
75015 PARIS
Tel: 43 35 23 26
Contact: M. Thomas MOODIE

AAA
71, rue du Fbg. St. Antoine
75011 PARIS
Tel: 44 75 70 70
Fax: 44 75 70 80

African American Films
26, rue de la Pépinière
75008 PARIS
Tel: 44 70 05 29
Fax: 44 70 04 75

Art Video Film
69, rue Dutot
75015 PARIS
Tel: 45 32 39 59
Fax: 45 32 50 75
Director: Mlle LENAEUR

Arts International Corporation
8bis, rue Campagne Première
75014 PARIS
Tel: 42 79 07 99
Fax: 42 79 83 39
Director: M. Milan WENDYGRAD
Script development and consultation for feature films

Atlantic Film
36, avenue Hoche
75008 PARIS
Tel: 45 63 32 60
Fax: 45 61 18 49
Director: M. Claude FUSEE
Production and distribution of films

Boréales
4, rue de Pontoise
75005 PARIS
Tel: 43 25 13 13
Fax: 43 25 17 87
Audiovisual production

Buena Vista Home Entertainment
10, rue Treilhard
75008 PARIS
Tel: 42 99 58 00
Fax: 42 99 58 58
Duplicate and distribute video tapes

Columbia Tristar Films France
131, avenue de Wagram
75017 PARIS
Tel: 44 40 63 00
Fax: 44 40 62 01
Director: M. Richard DASSONVILLE

Davis Film and Video Production
116bis, avenue des Champs-Elysées
75008 PARIS
Tel: 42 25 85 99

Film Media Consultant
76, rue Blanche
75009 PARIS
Tel: 48 78 36 06

Film Office
63, avenue des Champs-Elysées
75008 PARIS
Tel: 53 77 18 00
Fax: 42 56 03 75

France Animation
51, rue Gaston Lauriau
93100 MONTREUIL
Tel: 48 70 44 44
Fax: 48 58 36 62
Animation technology

Franklin Partner
41-43, avenue Marceau
92411 COURBEVOIE Cedex
Tel: 43 34 50 50
Fax: 43 33 64 73
Multi-media & visual communication

Gaumont
30, avenue Charles de Gaulle
92200 NEUILLY-SUR-SEINE
Tel: 46 43 24 14

GMCM Films
75, rue du Fbg. St. Honoré
75008 PARIS
Tel: 47 42 56 20
Fax: 47 42 55 48
Director: Mme Janet GREENBERG
Production of short films

Golden Film International
116, avenue des Champs-Elysées
75008 PARIS
Tel: 44 21 81 16

GPO
8, rue Michelet
93100 MONTREUIL
Tel: 48 58 07 90
Fax: 48 58 07 40
TV production & antenna installation

Les Films du Losange
22, avenue Pierre Ier de Serbie
75016 PARIS
Tel: 44 43 87 10
Tel: 44 43 87 15 (Distribution)

Les Films Singuliers
20, rue Michelet
93100 MONTREUIL
Tel: 42 87 02 02
Tel: 42 87 59 08
Fax: 42 87 01 89
Manager: M. Michel POIRIER

Locatel Rentals
86, Bd. St. Marcel
75013 PARIS
Tel: 47 07 77 99
Television and video rentals and sales

Media-Bis
B.P. 274
75625 PARIS Cedex 13
Tel: 45 83 61 38
Director: M. Kevin COLLETTE
Movies and television documentation

Metropolitan Films
1, rue Lord Byron
75008 PARIS
Tel: 45 61 11 67

MK2
55, rue Traversière
75012 PARIS
Tel: 43 07 92 74
Fax: 43 41 32 30
Major French film distributor

Motion Picture Export Association of America Inc.
26, rue de la Pépinière
75008 PARIS
Tel: 44 70 06 18

Office National du Film du Canada
5, rue de Constantine
75007 PARIS
Tel: 44 18 35 40
Fax: 47 05 75 89
Contact: Mme Germaine WONG
Canadian film representative group

Paramount Films
1, rue Meyerbeer
75009 PARIS
Tel: 47 42 56 31
Fax: 42 66 31 16

Parev Productions
135, rue du Mont Cenis
75018 PARIS
Tel: 42 64 10 18
Film and video production. Bilingual communication workshops using theater techniques

Paris-New York Productions
5, rue de Charonne
75011 PARIS
Tel: 48 06 29 43
Fax: 40 21 65 52
Director: M. Claude KUNETZ
Production of feature-length films, television series, publicity

Philips Videocommunications
4, rue du Port aux Vins
92156 SURESNES Cedex
Tel: 40 99 60 00
Fax: 40 99 64 31

PSC Video
8, rue Bellini
75016 PARIS
Tel: 47 27 00 73
Fax: 47 27 24 54

Reels on Wheels
35, rue de la Croix Nivert
75015 PARIS
Tel: 45 67 64 99
Fax: 45 67 69 51
Wide range of English-language films in V.O., delivered to your home

Remanence Production
42, rue Trousseau
75011 PARIS
Tel: 43 38 63 71
Fax: 43 38 63 89
Director: M. Bruno VENZAL
Corporate video, audiovisual production, clips

Reuilly Video
73, rue de Reuilly
75012 PARIS
Tel: 43 45 16 62
Movies rental in V.O, video conversion (NTSC, PAL, SECAM)

Rozon
6, rue Christophe Colomb
75008 PARIS
Tel: 53 67 88 88
Fax: 40 70 09 50
Managing Director:
M. Jean-Yves ROBIN
Production house (TV, festivals)

Sirius Films S.A.R.L.
93, rue de Maubeuge
75010 PARIS
Tel: 49 29 90 56
Fax: 49 29 94 77
Audiovisual production

Susan Friedman
9, rue Yvon-de-Villarceau
75116 PARIS
Tel: 45 00 79 63
"American in Paris" Film Co-Productions

Twentieth Century Fox
8, rue Bellini
75016 PARIS
Tel: 44 34 60 00
Fax: 47 27 24 54
Director: M. Gérard LEFEVRE

Téléfilm Canada
5, rue de Constantine
75007 PARIS
Tel: 44 18 35 30
Fax: 47 05 72 76

U.G.C.
78, avenue des Champs-Elysées
75008 PARIS
Tel: 45 74 95 40

United International Pictures
1, rue Meyerbeer
75009 PARIS
Tel: 40 07 38 38
Fax: 47 42 57 16
Director: M. Daniel GOLDMAN
Film distribution

V.O. Only
25, Bd. de la Somme
75017 PARIS
Tel: 42 67 76 17 (VHS)
Tel: 43 80 70 60
Fax: 42 27 04 90

Victoria Film Production
19, rue la Trémoille
75008 PARIS
Tel: 47 20 72 22
Fax: 47 20 90 32

Walt Disney Company (France)
44, avenue des Champs-Elysées
75008 PARIS
Tel: 44 20 55 00
Fax: 45 63 81 11
President: M. Pierre SISMANN

Warner Bros.
67, avenue de Wagram
75017 PARIS
Tel: 44 01 49 99
Cinema Director: M. Steven RUBIN

Warner Home Video
67, avenue de Wagram
75017 PARIS
Tel: 44 01 49 99

World Marketing Film
8, rue Lincoln
75008 PARIS
Tel: 42 25 84 20
Fax: 42 25 67 52

Zapp Video
39, rue des Peupliers
75013 PARIS
Tel: 45 80 59 70
Fax: 45 80 59 70
Director: M. Pierre-Yves MENKHOFF
Video report and conversion

Film Festivals
Festivals de Film

Cannes International Film Festival
99, Bd. Malesherbes
75008 PARIS
Tel: 42 66 92 20
Fax: 45 61 97 60
President: M. VIOT

Deauville Festival
36, rue Pierret
92000 NEUILLY-SUR-SEINE
Tel: 46 40 55 00
Fax: 47 38 10 10
President: M. CHOUCHAN
American films

Alpha Patrimoine
Investissement S.A.R.L.
36ter, rue de la Tour d'Auvergne
75009 Paris
Tel: 45 26 19 16
Fax: 48 78 02 11

American Tax Institute
4, rue Lamennais
75008 PARIS
Tel: 42 56 33 70
Fax: 42 56 00 45
Director: M. Bernard PFRUNDER

Bache France
6, rue Royale
75008 PARIS
Tel: 49 27 90 00
Fax: 40 15 98 94
Director: M. Gustavo DELLI PAOLI

Barney Inc.
7, Place Vendôme
75001 PARIS
Tel: 42 96 10 66
Fax: 42 96 22 81
Director: M. PINCHART-DENY

Bear Stearns
21-25, rue de Balzac
75008 PARIS
Tel: 42 99 60 60
Fax: 42 99 60 50

Bond & Stock Trader
164, rue du Fbg. St. Honoré
75008 PARIS
Tel: 44 13 62 80
Fax: 40 75 02 47
Contact: M. Yves PERBEN

Bunting Warburg
65, rue de Courcelles
75008 PARIS
Tel: 48 88 34 17
Fax: 48 88 32 54
Contact: M. Matthieu DEBOST

Datar
1, avenue Charles Floquet
75007 PARIS
Tel: 40 65 10 06
Fax: 40 65 12 40
Director: Mme Gabrielle GAUTHEY
Foreign investment advisor

Donaldson, Lufkin & Jenrette
6, rue Christophe Colomb
75008 PARIS
Tel: 49 52 69 00
Fax: 40 70 16 96
Director: M. GONNEAU

Dow Jones Telerate
128, rue du Fbg. St. Honoré
75008 PARIS
Tel: 42 89 05 09
Fax: 42 25 04 97
Sell real time financial data

Du Pasquier & Cie
31, avenue des Champs-Elysées
75008 PARIS
Tel: 40 76 03 03
Fax: 40 74 03 32
Manager: M. Philippe
DE MONTMARIN
American financing and investments

Dun & Bradstreet International
Immeuble Défense Bergères
345, avenue Georges Clémenceau
92882 NANTERRE Cedex 9
Tel: 41 35 17 00
Fax: 41 35 17 77
Chairman: M. Bruno LEPROU
DE LA RIVIERE

European American
Consulting Group
50, avenue de la Grande Armée
75017 PARIS
Tel: 40 55 02 14
Fax: 45 72 12 27
Merger and acquisition consulting, financial investments

European Credit Insurance
and Collection Agency
67, rue de l'Assomption
75016 PARIS
Tel: 45 25 03 97
Fax: 45 24 59 44

European Retail and Catering
Investments Company
137, Bd. Malesherbes
75017 PARIS
Tel: 47 66 97 97
Fax: 40 53 03 03

Eurostock
Rue des Frères Lumière
Z.I. des Chanoux
93330 NEUILLY-SUR-MARNE
Tel: 43 00 96 70
Fax: 43 00 50 44
Director: Mme DECHAMPS

Exco Paris
7, rue de Madrid
75008 PARIS
Tel: 44 70 30 00
Tax consultant

Expatriate Financial Services
11bis, rue de Prony
75017 PARIS
Tel: 46 22 53 39
Fax: 47 64 01 29
Director: M. Hendrick VRIESEN
Financial and educational consulting

First Marathon Securities
2, rue Chauveau Lagarde
75008 PARIS
Tel: 42 66 66 77
Fax: 42 66 96 78
Contact: M. Robert CHARBONNEAU

France Capital S.A.
4, rue St. Augustin
75002 PARIS
Tel: 45 00 42 53
Fax: 45 00 02 38
Contact: M. Roger CRUISE
Portfolio management for individuals

Frank De Saxce
103, avenue Emile Zola
75015 PARIS
Tel: 45 77 58 54
Tax consultant

Gordon Capital Corporation
10, rue de la Paix
75002 PARIS
Tel: 49 27 08 08
Fax: 42 60 59 36
Contact: M. Jean-Yves LE FLOCH

Hambros France S.A.
16, Place Vendôme
75001 PARIS
Tel: 42 60 57 17
Fax: 42 86 90 19
Director: M. DE NADAILLAC

J.C.B.-S.I.E.-F.B.C.
B.P. 102
75022 PARIS Cedex 01
Director: M. J. CHARLES
Recovery agents for the refund of previously paid UK income tax

Lewis Kirkpatrick
48, rue de Longchamp
75008 PARIS
Tel: 47 47 51 02
Tax consultant

Loewen, Ondaatje, McCutcheon et Company Ltd
16, avenue George V
75008 PARIS
Tel: 40 73 81 00
Fax: 47 20 27 26

Lyons Capital Inc.
18, avenue Victor Cresson
92130 ISSY-LES-MOULINEAUX
Tel: 46 42 51 20
Fax: 46 42 51 20
Business Development
Representative: Sharjeel MUFTI
Financing of businesses, mergers and acquisitions. Joint venture partnerships. Private placement of securities

Merrill Lynch, Pierce, Fenner & Smith
96, avenue d'Iéna
75116 PARIS
Tel: 40 69 10 00
Tel: 40 69 15 00
Fax: 40 69 11 90
Director: M. Jeronimo VILLALBA

Paine Webber International S.A.
56, rue du Fbg. St. Honoré
75008 PARIS
Tel: 44 71 13 00
Fax: 42 66 58 47
Director: M. Eric BERTIER
Brokerage and financial advisory

Porter & Dunham
5, rue Cambon
75001 PARIS
Tel: 42 61 55 77
Tax consultant

Price Waterhouse
Moisand et Associés
Tour AIG
34, Place des Corolles
Cedex 105
92908 PARIS LA DEFENSE
Tel: 41 26 40 00
Fax: 41 26 41 26

RBC Dominion Securities
29, rue de la Bienfaisance
75008 PARIS
Tel: 45 22 62 00
Fax: 43 87 57 90
Director: M. Paul NAGY

Robertson Taylor France
94, rue St. Lazare
75009 PARIS
Tel: 48 74 41 37
Fax: 48 74 41 27
Brokerage house

Russell Reynolds Associates
7, Place Vendôme
75001 PARIS
Tel: 49 26 13 00
Fax: 42 60 03 85
Managing Director:
M. Stephen D. NEWTON

Salomon Brothers
4, avenue Hoche
75008 PARIS
Tel: 47 63 79 07

Schneider S.A.
64-70, avenue Jean-
Baptiste Clément
92646 BOULOGNE
Tel: 46 99 70 00
Fax: 48 25 51 28
Director: M. Didier PINEAU-
VALENCIENNE
Holding company

Shearson Lehman Hutton
8, rue Bellini
75008 PARIS
Tel: 47 27 20 21
Fax: 47 27 04 71

Sullivan & Cromwell
8, Place Vendôme
75001 PARIS
Tel: 44 50 60 00
Fax: 44 50 60 60

Technology Investment Partners
196, avenue Victor Hugo
75116 PARIS
Tel: 45 03 04 14
Fax: 45 04 83 99

Tendler Beretz International
72, rue du Fbg. St. Honoré
75008 PARIS
Tel: 40 07 86 98
Fax: 40 07 80 46
Managing Director:
M. Anthony ACAMPORA

The Europe Company
26, rue de la Pépinière
75008 PARIS
Tel: 45 22 13 77
Fax: 45 22 13 70
Brokerage house

Tim Ellis
76940 N-D-DE-BLIQUETUIT
Tel: (16) 35 96 27 42
Private consultant for US income taxes

Warren Thomas Busch
3, rue Darboy
75011 PARIS
Tel: 43 14 99 84
Expatriate broker, tax-free investments.
Representing Mondial International
Financial Services

Wertheim & Cie
137, rue du Fbg. St. Honoré
75001 PARIS
Tel: 44 20 65 00
Fax: 44 20 65 01
President: M. Geoffrey
DE FARAMOND

Yorkton Securities
42, avenue de la Grande Armée
75017 PARIS
Tel: 40 68 96 08
Fax: 40 68 96 09
Director: M. Daniel P. BROOKS

Australian Import Center (A.I.C.)
2, rue Ernest Renan
75015 PARIS
Tel: 45 65 24 74
Fax: 45 80 57 70
Australian wines at the best prices

Allied Domecq Spirits and Wine
90, quai de Bercy
75610 PARIS Cedex 12
Tel: 44 74 57 00
Fax: 46 28 60 81

Baskin-Robbins
Bercy Expo
90, quai de Bercy
75610 PARIS Cedex 12
Tel: 44 74 58 74
Fax: 44 74 58 78
Director: M. Stéphane KLEIN
American ice cream manufacturer

Biscuiterie Nantaise
Avenue Lotz Cossé 5X
44040 NANTES Cedex 01
Tel: (16) 40 47 10 22
Fax: (16) 40 89 59 98
President: M. Guy SCHERRER
Only supplies restaurants

Biscuits Delacre
24, rue de Penthièvre
75008 PARIS
Tel: 45 95 05 50
Fax: 49 95 05 88

British Meat
114, rue La Boétie
75008 PARIS
Tel: 49 53 96 86

Burger King France
1, Place Victor Hugo
92400 COURBEVOIE
Tel: 46 91 95 95
Fax: 47 68 57 43
Administrative offices

Béto
6, rue Louis Saillant
Z.I. La Fosse à la Barbière
93601 AULNAY-SOUS-BOIS
Tel: 48 67 52 61
Fax: 48 67 52 75
Director: M. Alvaro LEMOS
Wholesale Mexican and American food products

Chamco Sea Food France
6, Place Louis XIII
94150 RUNGIS
Tel: 41 80 00 69
Fax: 46 87 04 45

Champagne Moët et Chandon
20, avenue de Champagne
51200 EPERNAY
Tel: (16) 26 54 71 11
Fax: (16) 26 54 84 23
President: M. LETZELTER
Supplies the public as well as the catering industry

Champagne Perrier-Jouet
24-28, avenue de Champagne
B.P. 31
51201 EPERNAY Cedex
Tel: (16) 26 55 20 53
Fax: (16) 26 54 54 55
Fax: (16) 26 54 27 29
President: M. Pierre ERNST

Champagne Taittinger
9, Place St. Nicaise
51100 REIMS
Tel: (16) 26 85 45 35
Fax: (16) 26 85 44 39
Export Director:
Mme SCHILLIGER

Coca-Cola France
11, rue Leblanc
75015 PARIS
Tel: 40 60 26 00
Fax: 40 60 29 39
Director: M. Michel I. D'ORNANO

Cointreau
152, avenue des Champs-Elysées
75008 PARIS
Tel: 44 13 44 13
Fax: 45 62 82 52
Chairman: M. Pierre COINTREAU
CEO: M. Emile ELOY
Spirits production

Colorado Cookie Company
4, rue Becquerel
E.A.E. de la Tuilerie
77645 CHELLES Cedex
Tel: 64 72 00 55
Fax: 64 72 10 30
Contact: Heather McEVOY

Contrex
18, rue de Courcelles
75008 PARIS
Tel: 40 75 38 00
Fax: 45 63 22 99
Mineral water

Cookie Connexion
160, avenue Ledru Rollin
75011 PARIS
Tel: 43 79 16 79
Fax: 43 56 11 33

Courvoisier
2, Place du Château
B.P. 59
16200 JARNAC
Tel: (16) 45 35 55 55
Fax: (16) 45 35 55 00
President: M. James D.N. FORD
Cognac and grape brandy manufacturer

CPC France
379, avenue du Général de Gaulle
92142 CLAMART
Tel: 40 94 52 52
Fax: 40 94 52 00
Director: M. Olivier DEFORGES

Daniel Chotard
18300 CREZANCY-
EN-SANCERRE
Tel: (16) 48 79 08 12
Fax: (16) 48 79 09 21
Producer of fine Sancerre wines

David's Western Cookies
253, avenue du Président Wilson
93214 LA-PLAINE-ST-DENIS
Tel: 48 20 30 00
Fax: 48 20 50 00
Contact: M. David FRIEDMAN
American bakery products for professionals

Dole Europe
16, avenue Kléber
75116 PARIS
Tel: 44 17 30 60
Fax: 44 17 30 70
Director: M. Freeney WILLIAMS

Epicerie Saint Georges
49, rue Burgaud Desmarets
17100 SAINTES
Tel: (16) 46 74 44 94
Fax: (16) 46 92 16 49
Managing Director:
M. Andrew BAKER
Importer of fine teas and delicacies from Britain

Fauchon
7, rue Vignon
75008 PARIS
Tel: 47 42 60 11
Fax: 47 42 83 75
Communications Director:
Mlle LE SOUDER
Administrative premises

Food From Britain
114, rue La Boétie
75008 PARIS
Tel: 42 25 01 86
Fax: 42 25 01 85

France Quick
40, rue Jean Jaurès
93170 BAGNOLET
Tel: 49 72 13 00
Fax: 43 63 59 13
Fast food chain

GH Mumm
Vinicole de Champagne
17-19, avenue Montaigne
75008 PARIS
Tel: 44 43 15 00
Fax: 44 43 15 01

Group Saman
36, 2ème avenue
13127 VITROLLES
Tel: (16) 42 15 15 15
Fax: (16) 42 79 28 46
Director: M. Christian SAMAN
Dried fruit import/export firm

Géant Vert
69-71, avenue Pierre Gresier
92100 BOULOGNE-BILLANCOURT
Cedex
Tel: 46 94 63 00
Fax: 46 94 62 03
General Manager: M. Yves LEPAGE
Premium quality vegetables

Häagen-Dazs
69-71, avenue Pierre Grenier
92100 BOULOGNE
Tel: 46 94 62 00
Fax: 46 94 62 08
Administrative offices

Kellogg's France
Tour Bureau de Rosny 2
93118 ROSNY-SOUS-BOIS Cedex
Tel: 49 35 21 21
Fax: 48 54 81 33

Kentucky Fried Chicken
31, Bd. Sébastopol
75001 PARIS
Tel: 40 26 61 14

Kraft General Foods France
B.P. 116
13, avenue Morane Saulnier
78148 VELIZY-VILLACOUBLAY
Cedex
Tel: 34 88 70 00
Fax: 34 88 70 08
Director: M. Luc VANDEVELDE

Lamy Lutti France
B.P. 100
Z.A.C. Ravenne-les-Francs
59587 BONDUES Cedex
Tel: (16) 20 11 31 00
Fax: (16) 20 11 31 30
Managing Director: M. Herman
HOEFNAGELS
Confectionery group

Mars Alimentaire
3, chemin de la Sandlach
B.P. 36
67501 HAGUENAU Cedex
Tel: (16) 88 05 10 01
Fax: (16) 88 05 10 02

McDonalds France
1, rue Gustave Eiffel
78045 GUYANCOURT Cedex
Tel: 30 48 60 00
Fax: 30 48 63 00
Headquarters

Moët-Hennessy
30, avenue Hoche
75008 PARIS
Tel: 44 13 22 22
Fax: 44 13 22 23
Cognac, Champagne

Nestlé France Noisiel
Boulevard Pierre Carle
77446 MARNE-LA-VALLEE Cedex
Tel: 60 05 91 20
Fax: 64 80 56 31

Pepsi-Cola France
Les Collines de l'Arche
Immeuble Madeleine
92057 PARIS LA DEFENSE
Cedex 24
Tel: 47 67 10 00
Fax: 47 67 10 10
Director: M. Thierry CASSEVILLE

Perrier
18, rue de Courcelles
75008 PARIS
Tel: 40 75 38 00
Fax: 45 63 22 99
Commercial Director:
M. GIRADOT

Pizza Hut
1bis, avenue de Paris
94300 VINCENNES
Tel: 43 74 14 14
Administrative offices

Premier Brands France
4, rue Bernard Palissy
B.P. 21
92802 PUTEAUX Cedex
Tel: 47 75 05 07
Fax: 47 75 36 28
Director: M. RICHENBACH
Supply biscuits to supermarkets

Quaker France
40, Bd. de Dunkerque
13002 MARSEILLE
Tel: (16) 91 91 91 48
Fax: (16) 91 91 20 12
Manager: M. Denis CANS
Pet food

Ralston Purina Europe Inc.
B.P. 301
78054 ST-QUENTIN-EN-YVELINES
Cedex
Tel: 30 12 59 00
Fax: 30 12 59 01
Director: M. Michel SZERADZKI
Pet food

Remy Martin & Cie
20, rue de la Société Vinicole
B.P. 37
16102 COGNAC Cedex
Tel: 45 35 16 16
Export Service: M. PELOUX
Cognacs

Roche Claire
190, rue Estienne d'Orves
92700 COLOMBES
Tel: 41 19 75 75
Fax: 47 82 31 61
High quality spring water

San Francisco Muffin Company
41, rue Linois
75015 PARIS
Tel: 45 79 09 09
Fax: 45 79 03 50
Director: Mme Lisa KOBLENTZ
American bakery - retail and wholesale
Boutique: 35, rue du Dragon, 75006, Paris

Schweppes France
12, rue Belgrand
92300 LEVALLOIS
Tel: 49 68 70 00
Fax: 49 68 00 04

Seagram France Distribution
Tour Gamma A
193-197, rue de Bercy
75582 PARIS Cedex 12
Tel: 40 04 46 00
Fax: 40 04 45 50
Distributor of fine wines, whiskeys and spirits: Four Roses, Absolut Vodka, Chivas Regal, Glen Grant, Crown Royal, Seagram's VO...

Seagram Global Brands Division
17-19, avenue Montaigne
75008 PARIS
Tel: 44 43 15 00
Fax: 44 43 15 01
President: M. Hubert MILLET
Wines and spirits

Société des Eaux Volvic
60, Bd. Maréchal Joffre
92340 BOURG-LA-REINE
Tel: 46 11 88 88
Fax: 46 11 88 89
Mineral water

Société Shaver
89330 ST LOUP D'ORDON
Tel: (16) 38 97 91 46
Fax: (16) 38 97 92 99
President: M. Yves GOETZ
Free-range poultry

Solgar France
79, rue Diderot
94300 VINCENNES
Tel: 48 08 15 50
Fax: 48 08 20 53
Vitamins, minerals, herbal remedies and many other Gold Label products

Unisabi
B.P. 7
45550 ST-DENIS-DE-L'HOTEL
Tel: (16) 38 59 61 61
Fax: (16) 38 59 61 72
President: Pierre LAUBIES
Pet food

Vignerons de France
39, rue Servan
75011 PARIS
Tel: 48 05 28 85
French wine-making cooperative

Vine Import
143, rue du Château
75014 PARIS
Tel: 42 79 98 46
Fax: 42 79 82 51
Director: M. SORBELLO
France's largest California wine importer/distributor, wholesale & retail

Weight Watchers Food
89, rue La Boétie
75008 PARIS
Tel: 53 77 17 17
Fax: 53 77 17 18

Wrigley
B.P. 29
68600 BIESHEIM
Tel: (16) 89 72 19 19
Fax: (16) 89 72 64 21
President: M. René CISERI

Culinary Schools/Caterers
Ecoles de Cuisine/Traiteurs

A la Carte
5, rue Paul Valéry
75116 PARIS
Tel: 44 05 02 02
Fax: 44 05 02 04
Manager: M. Stéphane DE MAINTENANT
Lunch/Dinner delivered to your home or office, business menus

C.I.D.D.
45, rue Liancourt
75014 PARIS
Tel: 43 27 67 21
Contact: Melba MAUVIEL
Wine-tasting courses in English

Chavy
90, avenue Charles de Gaulle
92200 NEUILLY-SUR-SEINE
Tel: 47 47 27 70
Catering services

Cross-Channel Catering Company
116, rue de Maubeuge
75010 PARIS
Tel: 44 53 75 55
Fax: 42 85 49 44

Dalloyau
Tel: 42 99 90 00
Takes care of formal receptions, cocktail parties

Découverte du Vin
45, rue Liancourt
75014 PARIS
Tel: 43 27 67 21
Fax: 43 20 84 00
Information center on wine. Oenology courses available in French, English and Japanese

Fauchon
7, rue Vignon
75008 PARIS
Tel: 47 42 60 11
Prestige events, weddings, banquets

In Your Home Catering
41, rue des Bartoux
92150 SURESNES
Tel: 46 97 07 87
Contact: Susan KUTNER
Handmade meals prepared to order

La Cuisine de Marie-Blanche
18, avenue La Motte-Picquet
75007 PARIS
Tel: 45 51 36 34
Fax: 45 51 90 19
Cookery classes, French etiquette, entertaining

La Toque d'Or
55, rue de Varenne
75007 PARIS
Tel: 45 44 86 51
Fax: 45 44 86 51
Director: Sue YOUNG
Cookery demonstrations and classes. Guided market and gourmand tours in Paris

La Varenne
Château du Fey
89300 VILLECIEN
Tel: (16) 86 63 18 34
Fax: (16) 86 63 01 33
Director: Marah STETS
French culinary school

Le Cordon Bleu
8, rue Léon Delhomme
75015 PARIS
Tel: 53 68 22 50
Fax: 48 56 03 96 (school)
Fax: 48 56 03 77 (store)
Director: Mme Lizabeth NICOL
Cooking and pastry classes

Maison de la Vigne et du Vin de France
21, rue François Ier
75008 PARIS
Tel: 47 20 20 76
Fax: 47 23 07 21
Contact: Sophie PERROMAT
Wine tasting, documentation, boutique

Muslin Tree Catering
Tel: 45 47 11 60
Contact: Ellen COHAN
Cocktails, receptions, bilingual bartenders, party set-up and clean-up

Oldies but Goodies
16, rue du Bourg Tibourg
75004 PARIS
Tel: 48 87 14 37
Caterers

Reels on Wheels
35, rue de la Croix Nivert
75015 PARIS
Tel: 45 67 64 99
Fax: 45 67 69 51
Tex-Mex and Indian food delivered to your home or office

Ritz-Escoffier Ecole de Gastronomie Française
38, rue Cambon
75001 PARIS
Tel: 43 16 30 50
Fax: 43 16 31 50
Assistant Manager:
Susan STURMAN
Cooking and pastry classes

Thanksgiving
20, rue St. Paul
75004 PARIS
Tel: 42 77 68 29
Director: Judith BLUYSEN
Catering services

Wine Business Club
16, rue St. Petersbourg
75008 PARIS
Tel: 42 93 10 43
Fax: 42 93 10 08
President: M. Alain MARTY
Oenology classes, wine-tasting

Centre de Renseignements des Douanes
23, rue de l'Université
75007 PARIS
Tel: 40 24 65 10
Customs Information Service

Centre Français du Commerce Extérieur
10, avenue d'Iéna
75783 PARIS Cedex 16
Tel: 40 73 30 00
Fax: 40 73 39 79
Euro Info: 40 73 34 67 (European trade regulations)
French Foreign Trade Board

Greffe et Registre du Commerce
1, quai de Corse
75004 PARIS
Tel: 43 29 06 75
Minitel: 3415 INFOGREFFE
Companies Registration Office

Hôtel Matignon
57, rue de Varenne
75007 PARIS
Tel: 42 75 80 00
Fax: 45 44 15 72
Prime Minister: M. Alain JUPPE
Secretary of State: M. François BAROIN

INPI
26bis, rue St. Petersbourg
75008 PARIS
Tel: 42 94 52 52
National Bureau of Patents & Trademarks

Mairie de Paris
4, Place de l'Hôtel de Ville
75196 PARIS R.P.
Tel: 42 76 40 40
Fax: 42 76 60 65
Mayor of Paris: M. Jean TIBERI
City of Paris Town Hall

Ministère de l'Economie et du Budget
139, rue de Bercy
75012 PARIS
Tel: 40 04 04 04
Fax: 43 44 51 88
Finance Minister:
M. Alain MADELIN

Ministère de l'Education Nationale
110, rue de Grenelle
75007 PARIS
Tel: 49 55 10 10
Minister of Education:
M. François BAYROU

Ministère de l'Industrie
20, avenue de Ségur
75007 PARIS
Tel: 43 19 36 36
Minister of Industry:
M. Yves GALLAND

Ministère de l'Intérieur
Place Beauvau
75008 PARIS
Tel: 40 07 60 60
Interior Minister:
M. Jean-Louis DEBRÉ
Minister in charge of Information Technologies and Communications:
M. François FILLON

Ministère de la Culture
3, rue de Valois
75001 PARIS
Tel: 40 15 80 00
Minister of Culture:
M. Philippe DOUSTE-BLAZY
Publishes Festivals et Expositions, *a comprehensive guide to cultural and artistic events throughout France (see advertisement)*

Ministère de la Défense
14, rue St. Dominique
75007 PARIS
Tel: 42 19 30 11
Tel: 42 19 30 12
Minister of Defense:
M. Charles MILLON

Ministère de la Jeunesse et des Sports
78, rue Olivier de Serres
75015 PARIS
Tel: 40 45 11 66
Fax: 45 32 32 16
Minister of Youth and Sport:
M. Guy DRUT

Ministère de la Justice
13, Place Vendôme
75001 PARIS
Tel: 44 77 60 60
Fax: 44 77 60 00
Minister of Justice:
M. Jacques TOUBON

Ministère des Affaires Etrangères
37, quai d'Orsay
75007 PARIS
Tel: 47 53 53 53
Fax: 47 53 47 53
Minister of Foreign Affairs:
M. Hervé DE CHARETTE
Minister in charge of Cooperation:
M. Jacques GODFRAIN
Minister in charge of European Affairs: M. Michel BARNIER
Minister in charge of Tourism:
Mme Françoise DE PANAFIEU

Ministère des Entreprises et du Développement Economique
101, rue de Grenelle
75007 PARIS
Tel: 43 19 24 24
Minister for Economic Expansion:
M. Jean ARTHUIS

Ministère des Transports
19, rue Franqueville
75116 PARIS
Tel: 45 24 97 10
Minister of Transport:
M. Bernard PONS

Ministère du Logement
1, Parvis de la Défense
92055 PARIS LA DEFENSE
Cedex 04
Tel: 40 81 21 22
Minister of Housing:
M. Pierre-André PERISSOL

Ministère du Travail, du Dialogue Social et de la Participation
127, rue de Grenelle
75007 PARIS
Tel: 40 56 60 00
Tel: 44 84 42 86
Minister of Employment:
M. Jacques BARROT

Préfecture de Police
7, Bd. du Palais
75004 PARIS
Tel: 53 71 53 71
Tel: 53 73 53 73
Admin: 53 71 31 11
Lost/Found: 45 31 14 80
Cartes Grises: 45 71 39 00 (car registry)
Central Police Authority

Employment

Organismes Professionnels

AGESSA
21bis, rue de Bruxelles
75009 PARIS
Tel: 48 78 25 00
Social Security Office for Authors

ANPE
123, rue Oberkampf
75011 PARIS
Tel: 49 23 33 00
National Employment Agency

ASSEDIC de Paris
4, rue Traversière
75012 PARIS
Tel: 40 19 25 00
Fax: 43 42 53 53
Employment Agency for Industry and Trade

Inter Europe Emploi - ANPE
69, rue Jean-Baptiste Pigalle
75009 PARIS
Tel: 48 78 37 82
Fax: 48 74 42 53
Helps French people find work in other European countries

La Maison des Artistes
11, rue Berryer
75008 PARIS
Tel: 45 63 32 82
Fax: 45 63 94 97
Social Security Office for Artists

URSSAF
3, rue Franklin
93518 MONTREUIL Cedex
Tel: 49 20 10 10
Fax: 48 51 75 75
Minitel: 3615 UR75
Social Security Office for Self-Employed Workers

Hospitals/Clinics
Hôpitaux/Cliniques

American Hospital of Paris
63, Bd. Victor Hugo
B.P. 109
92202 NEUILLY-SUR-SEINE Cedex
Tel: 46 41 25 41
Fax: 46 41 25 17
Director: Mme Joyce GRAY

Clinique Spontini
68bis, rue Spontini
75116 PARIS
Tel: 47 04 81 81
Fax: 47 04 86 61
Director: Dr FRIEDMAN
Surgical and obstetrical private hospital

Hertford British Hospital
3, rue Barbès
92300 LEVALLOIS-PERRET
Tel: 46 39 22 22
Fax: 46 39 22 26
General medicine, surgery

Hôpital des Quinze-Vingt
28, rue de Charenton
75012 PARIS
Tel: 40 02 15 20
Specialized in ophthalmology

Hôpital Hôtel Dieu
1, Place Parvis Notre Dame
75004 PARIS
Tel: 42 34 82 34

Hôpital la Pitié Salpétrière
47, Bd. de l'Hôpital
75013 PARIS
Tel: 42 16 00 00
Fax: 42 17 60 06

Hôpital Pasteur
209, rue de Vaugirard
75015 PARIS
Tel: 40 61 38 00

Hôpital Rothschild
33, Bd. Picpus
75012 PARIS
Tel: 40 19 30 00

Hôpital Saint-Louis
1, avenue Claude Vellefaux
75010 PARIS
Tel: 42 49 49 49

Institut National de la Santé et de la Recherche Médicale
149, rue de Sèvres
75015 PARIS
Tel: 45 67 08 11
Children's research hospital

Professionals
Médecins

Annie Motei
34, Bd. de l'Hôpital
75005 PARIS
Tel: 47 07 04 72
Massage therapist:Alexander Technique

Barbara Cox
115, rue du Théâtre
75015 PARIS
Tel: 45 75 74 61
Psychologist, Psychotherapist and Grief Counselor

Cabinet Chiropractique Précloux
43, rue de Richelieu
75001 PARIS
Tel: 42 60 42 36
Fax: 42 60 47 88
USA licensed Doctor of Chiropractic

Caroline Sauvan
92, rue St. Antoine
75004 Paris
Tel: 40 27 81 51
Allergist

Chiropractic "International Center"
119, rue de l'Université
75007 PARIS
Tel: 45 51 38 38
Contacts: Dr CHIAPPINELLI, Dr LAMBERT, Dr LEGAGNOUX
Back pain, arthritis, sciatica, wry neck? Team of highly-qualified chiropractors from the USA. Specialized in personal treatment. Contact our Paris office for information

Chiropractic Office Tourneur
44, rue Laborde
75008 PARIS
Tel: 43 87 81 62
Fax: 40 08 09 89
Director: Dr Marc TOURNEUR
USA licensed chiropractor

Claire Mathijsen
11, rue de Sèvres
75006 PARIS
Tel: 42 22 06 23
Psychotherapist

David Safier
36, avenue de Suffren
75015 PARIS
Tel: 40 65 96 10
Psychotherapist

Debra Berg
4, rue Ledru Rollin
92240 MALAKOFF
Tel: 46 55 96 96
Psychotherapist

Dr Alain Nys, M.D.
63, Bd. Victor Hugo
92202 NEUILLY-SUR-SEINE
Tel: 46 41 25 25
Fax: 46 41 29 96
Orthopedic medicine - Rehabilitation

Dr Alan D. Thal
52, Bd. de Vaugirard
75015 PARIS
Tel: 42 79 04 96
Fax: 42 79 80 61
Psychotherapist specialised in hypnosis and alternative medicine: US trained M.D. combines kinesiology, homeopathy and acupuncture in a unique way that can dramatically relieve chronic allergic states such as headaches, asthma, arthritis, colitis, herpes, stress, etc.

Dr Anne-Isabelle Richet
109, rue de l'Université
75007 PARIS
Tel: 45 51 82 32
English-speaking gynecologist

Dr Celine Bismuth
7, rue Bernard de Clairvaux
75003 PARIS
Tel: 48 87 61 61
Dentist

Dr Christian Ficat
63, Bd. Victor Hugo
92202 NEUILLY-SUR-SEINE
Tel: 46 41 25 25
Orthopedist

Dr Claude Guichard
37, rue du Départ
75014 PARIS
Tel: 43 22 22 96
Fax: 43 20 78 46
General practitioner

Dr Claude Huard
63, Bd. Victor Hugo
92202 NEUILLY-SUR-SEINE
Tel: 46 41 25 25
Orthopedics

Dr Claude Lemoine
16, avenue du Président Wilson
75016 PARIS
Tel: 47 23 06 63
Fax: 47 23 74 18
Dentist

Dr Dan Le Buisson
63, Bd. Victor Hugo
92202 NEUILLY-SUR-SEINE
Tel: 46 41 25 25
Fax: 40 99 98 49
Ophthalmologist: ocular surgery

Dr Daniel Rignault
63, Bd. Victor Hugo
92202 NEUILLY
Tel: 46 41 25 25
Tel: 43 50 14 13
Fax: 43 50 14 47
General and laparoscopic surgery

Dr Denis Adrai
69-71, avenue Raymond Poincaré
75116 PARIS
Tel: 47 04 39 09
Fax: 44 05 94 49
Dentist

Dr Diane Winaver
109, rue de l'Université
75007 PARIS
Tel: 45 51 82 32
English-speaking gynecologist

Dr Edouard Cohen
20, rue de la Paix
75002 PARIS
Tel: 42 61 65 64
Dentist

Dr Fitterer
9, avenue Bosquet
75007 PARIS
Tel: 47 05 52 43
Ophthalmologist

Dr Francis Manière
64, rue de Rennes
75006 PARIS
Tel: 45 44 03 21
Fax: 45 49 19 96
Sports medicine

Dr François Rolet
63, Bd. Victor Hugo
92202 NEUILLY-SUR-SEINE
Tel: 46 41 25 25
Gynecologist

Dr Gauthier
47, av Hoche
75008 PARIS
Tel: 47 66 33 25
Dentist (Master of Science)

Dr Gilbert Lancry
63, Bd. Victor Hugo
92202 NEUILLY-SUR-SEINE
Tel: 46 41 25 25
General Practitioner

Dr Guillaume Dufour
63, Bd. Victor Hugo
92202 NEUILLY-SUR-SEINE
Tel: 46 41 25 25
Orthopedist

Dr H.R.S. Nagpal
65, rue Pascal
75013 PARIS
Tel: 47 07 55 28
Fax: 43 37 11 47
Secretary: Ms. Constance SWEET
Psychoanalysis, psychiatry, group therapy with a special interest in problems of displacement, bilingualism and cultural difference

Dr Henri Frajder
35, Bd. Malesherbes
75008 PARIS
Tel: 42 66 25 44
Dentist

Dr Hubert Gamon
20, rue Cler
75007 PARIS
Tel: 45 55 79 91
General practitioner

Dr Hubert Godard
97, rue de Charenton
75012 PARIS
Tel: 43 47 45 53
Massage therapist: Rolfing

Dr Jean Rachinel
63, Bd. Victor Hugo
92202 NEUILLY-SUR-SEINE
Tel: 46 41 25 25
Ear, Nose, Throat

Dr Jean-François Tecucianu
174, rue de Courcelles
75017 PARIS
Tel: 46 22 40 82
Dental surgeon

Dr Jean-Jacques Aron
63, Bd. Victor Hugo
92202 NEUILLY-SUR-SEINE
Tel: 46 41 25 25
Opthalmologist

Dr Jean-Luc Pruvost
98, avenue Kléber
75016 PARIS
Tel: 45 53 84 84
Orthodontist

Dr Jean-Paul Clot
63, Bd. Victor Hugo
92202 NEUILLY-SUR-SEINE
Tel: 46 41 25 25
Surgeon

Dr Jean-Pierre Desgrez
63, Bd. Victor Hugo
92202 NEUILLY-SUR-SEINE
Tel: 46 41 25 25
Urologist

Dr Jeanette Mitchell Vigneron
58, rue du Cherche Midi
75006 PARIS
Tel: 45 44 19 27
American veterinarian

Dr John Relland, M.D., F.A.C.S.
American Hospital of Paris
63, Bd. Victor Hugo
92202 NEUILLY-SUR-SEINE
Tel: 46 41 27 07
Fax: 46 41 27 00
General and cardiovascular surgery

Dr Karl Naeher
12, allée des Orgues de Flandre
75019 PARIS
Tel: 40 34 36 35
Chiropractic and rolfing

Dr Linda Abitbol
41, avenue Bosquet
75007 PARIS
Tel: 45 55 65 45
Ophthalmologist

Dr Marchal
40, av Bosquet
75007 PARIS
Tel: 45 51 04 40
Dermatologist

Dr Metter
29, avenue Franklin Roosevelt
75008 PARIS
Tel: 43 59 88 17
Dermatologist, wrinkle treatment, laser

Dr Michael Specter
63, Bd. Victor Hugo
92202 NEUILLY-SUR-SEINE
Tel: 46 41 25 25
Cardiologist

Dr N.R. Gittins
47, rue St. Charles
75015 PARIS
Tel: 40 59 04 76
British veterinarian

Dr Olivier Burgun
20, rue du Renard
75004 PARIS
Tel: 48 04 94 81
Physiotherapist/Osteopath

Dr Philippe Vialatte
63, Bd. Victor Hugo
92202 NEUILLY-SUR-SEINE
Tel: 46 41 25 25
Urologist

Dr Pierre Raygot
32, Bd. Haussmann
75009 PARIS
Tel: 47 70 81 81
Fax: 47 70 39 39
Dentist - DDS from University of Southern California

Dr R. Derycke
66, avenue Victor Hugo
75016 PARIS
Tel: 45 01 88 02
Fax: 45 00 10 45
Dental surgeon

Dr Regis Lisfranc
63, Bd. Victor Hugo
92202 NEUILLY-SUR-SEINE
Tel: 46 41 25 25
Orthopedist

Dr Robert Natali
63, Bd. Victor Hugo
92202 NEUILLY-SUR-SEINE
Tel: 46 41 25 25
Ear, Nose, Throat

Dr Robert Steinmetzer, M.D., F.A.C.S.
American Hospital of Paris
63, Bd. Victor Hugo
B.P. 109
92202 NEUILLY-SUR-SEINE Cedex
Tel: 46 41 27 04
Fax: 46 41 27 00
Internal medicine

Dr Rosine Bretton
63, Bd. Victor Hugo
92202 NEUILLY-SUR-SEINE
Tel: 46 41 27 60
Fax: 46 41 27 00
Dermatologist and hair specialist

Dr Sarrot
6, avenue Sully-Prudhomme
75007 PARIS
Tel: 45 56 03 30
Gynecologist

Dr Stephen Wilson
44, avenue de Ségur
75015 PARIS
Tel: 45 67 26 53
General Practitioner

Dr Sylvie Homareau
American Hospital of Paris
63, Bd. Victor Hugo
92202 NEUILLY-SUR-SEINE
Tel: 46 41 27 24
Fax: 46 24 49 38
Dermatologist

Dr Tatiane Oppenheim
17, Bd. du Temple
75003 PARIS
Tel: 48 87 22 63
Gynecologist

Dr Thomas Hewes
63, Bd. Victor Hugo
92202 NEUILLY-SUR-SEINE
Tel: 46 41 25 25
Gastroenterology

Dr Yvan Abitbol
63, Bd. Victor Hugo
92202 NEUILLY-SUR-SEINE
Tel: 46 41 25 25
Ophthalmologist

Emmanuelle Ansart, M.D.
43, rue La Bruyère
75009 PARIS
Tel: 48 78 04 60
Psychiatrist

Dr. Georges Krygier
63, avenue Franklin Roosevelt
75008 PARIS
Tel: 43 59 47 67
Dental surgeon

Gilles Bourgoin et Philippe Mareuil
29, avenue Poincaré
75116 PARIS
Tel: 47 04 79 97
Orthodontists

Hugh Dobbs
2, allée des Rosiers
92230 GENNEVILLIERS
Tel: 47 90 33 40
Psychotherapist

Jill Bourdais
19, quai aux Fleurs
75004 PARIS
Tel: 43 54 79 25
Fax: 43 54 79 25
Psychotherapist, couple counselor

Joseph Shesko
4, rue Michel Chasles
75012 PARIS
Tel: 43 47 19 72
Fax: 43 47 19 72
Psychotherapist/Psychoanalyst

Marois Pierre
32, Bd. Haussmann
75009 PARIS
Tel: 47 70 81 81
Fax: 47 70 39 39
Dentist

Nancy Sadowsky
12, rue Marie Stuart
75002 PARIS
Tel: 42 33 10 07
Clinical psychologist, psychotherapist

Patricia Boulay
361, rue des Pyrénées
75020 PARIS
Tel: 47 97 59 93

Pedro de Alcantara
10, rue Hittorf
75010 PARIS
Tel: 42 02 00 17
Certified teacher of the F.M. Alexander technique

Radiology Center - Dr Philippe Lebar
199, rue de Grenelle
75007 PARIS
Tel: 45 55 08 09
Fax: 44 18 32 17
Owner/Radiologist:
M. Philippe LEBAR
X-rays, ultra sounds, dopplers, MRI, encephaloscan. Emergency appointments accepted, English spoken

Rebecca Sager
8, rue des Anglais
75005 PARIS
Tel: 43 25 95 21
Pre and post natal instruction

Reiki
62, rue Vasco de Gama
75015 PARIS
Tel: 48 28 38 02
Contact: Terence COLEMAN
Relief from stress, pain and illness. Reiki energy strengthens one's capacity to release underlying physical, mental and emotional causes

Reiki, Numerology
18, avenue Victor Cresson
92130 ISSY-LES-MOULINEAUX
Tel: 46 42 51 20
Fax: 46 42 51 20
Contact: Angelika ROMANET
Healing techniques based on philosophy, psychology and holistic sciences

Miscellaneous
Divers

Active Relaxation
71, rue du Cardinal Lemoine
75005 PARIS
Tel: 43 54 91 00
Fax: 43 54 98 39
Director: Sarah PETLIN
Program of exercise, visualization and relaxation techniques to relieve back pain and reduce stress

Alain Afflelou
5, rue des Mathurins
75009 PARIS
Tel: 42 66 33 73
Fax: 42 66 33 83
Chain of opticians

Alain Afflelou
47, rue de la Boucle
Nouveau Forum
75001 PARIS
Tel: 40 26 47 87
Fax: 40 26 46 73
Chain of opticians

Anglo-American Pharmacy
6, rue de Castiglione
75001 PARIS
Tel: 42 60 72 96
Contact: Mme ROCHER

British and American Pharmacy
1, rue Auber
75009 PARIS
Tel: 47 42 49 40
Fax: 42 65 29 42

Centre de Dépistage de SIDA
3-5, rue de Ridder
75014 PARIS
Tel: 45 43 83 78
Fax: 45 42 63 08
Director: M. André HOUETTE
Free AIDS testing

Centre de Vision
40, rue St. Honoré
75001 PARIS
Tel: 42 33 97 24
Optometrists and opticians

Centre Médico-Social
218, rue de Belleville
75020 PARIS
Tel: 47 97 40 49
Free AIDS testing. For other medical centers consult Minitel 3615 SIDA or call 05 36 66 36

Confort et Vision
95-97, rue de Passy
75016 PARIS
Tel: 42 24 66 80
English-speaking optical house, free tax for import

European Respiratory Society
60, rue de Vaugirard
75015 PARIS
Tel: 45 48 93 10
Fax: 45 44 34 11

Health Data Management Partners
34, Bd. Haussmann
75009 PARIS
Tel: 48 24 10 67

Health Network International
25, avenue Ferme des Hézards
78112 FOURQUEUX
Tel: 39 73 49 01
Contact: Charlotte COYNE
Network for health professionals

Laboratoires Alcon
4, rue Henri Ste Claire Deville
92563 RUEIL-MALMAISON Cedex
Tel: 47 10 47 10
Fax: 47 10 47 03
President: M. Thierry CLIDIERE
Ophthalmology

Laboratoires Allergan
1198, avenue du Dr Maurice Donat
B.P. 42
06251 MOUGINS
Tel: (16) 92 92 44 00
Fax: (16) 92 92 44 10
Vice-President: M. BOUCHARA
Clinical product testing in the healthcare industry

Laboratoires Roche Nicholas
33, rue de l'Industrie
74240 GAILLARD
Tel: (16) 50 87 70 70
Fax: (16) 50 87 70 77
President: M. Nils CLEMENCIN
Medicine

Laboratoires Sherwood Medical
Z.I. des Bordes
9-11, rue Henri Dunant
91070 BONDOUFLE
Tel: 69 36 17 00
Fax: 60 86 40 36
Manager: M. Jean-Pierre CHARON
Disposable medical appliances

Lissac
1, rue Auber
75009 PARIS
Tel: 47 42 57 80
Fax: 49 24 95 66
Optical house

Medtronic France
1, avenue Edouard Belin
92566 RUEIL-MALMAISON Cedex
Tel: 47 14 60 00
Fax: 47 08 49 80
President: M. Jean-Henri TANGUY
Pacemakers

Pharmacie "Les Champs"
84, avenue des Champs-Elysées
Galerie "Les Champs"
75008 PARIS
Tel: 45 62 02 41
Fax: 45 63 83 79
Director: Dr. Sylvia DERHY
Open 24h every day of the year

Pharmacie Lambart Laignier
149, Bd. St. Germain
75006 PARIS
Tel: 42 22 80 00
Open until 02h00 in the morning

Pharmacie Swann
6, rue de Castiglione
75001 PARIS
Tel: 42 60 72 96

RMO-Europe
Parc d'Innovation
Rue Geiler de Kayserberg
67400 ILLKIRCH
Tel: (16) 88 40 67 40
Fax: (16) 88 67 96 95
Sales Manager: Lyn E. TURNER
Dental equipment

Shiatsu
6, rue du Maréchal de
Lattre de Tassigny
94370 SUCY-EN-BRIE
Tel: 45 90 10 83
Shiatsu Practitioner: Carey DOWNER
Shiatsu treatment and classes

SMS France Snc
Bâtiment 7
1006, rue de la Croix Verte
Parc Euromédecine
34198 MONTPELLIER Cedex 5
Tel: (16) 67 04 11 43
Fax: (16) 67 04 11 45
Country Manager: M. LEPREVOST
Hospital information systems

Stryker France
B.P. 50040
95946 ROISSY CDG Cedex
Tel: 48 63 22 90
Fax: 48 63 21 75
Managing Director: M. Alain GUEZ
Medical equipment

Victoire sur le Tabac
16, rue du Colisée
75008 PARIS
Tel: 42 25 66 46
Fax: 43 59 53 03
Director: M. Patrice ELLEQUAIN
Health center to give up smoking. Personal growth seminar, rebirth and creative thought

Walter's Paris
107, rue St. Dominique
75007 PARIS
Tel: 45 51 70 08
Fax: 45 51 04 42
Optician - 25% discount on frames and contact lenses for AUP students

A l'Hôtel du Bois
11, rue du Dôme
75116 PARIS
Tel: 45 00 31 96
Fax: 45 00 90 05
Commercial Director:
M. Olivier TARRON
Hôtel de charme - British management

Best Western Hôtel
74, avenue du Docteur
Arnold Netter
75012 PARIS
Tel: 44 87 40 80

Château de Lesvault
58370 ONLAY
Tel: (16) 86 84 32 91
Fax: (16) 86 84 35 78
Director: Bibbi LEE

Château Golf des 7 Tours
Courcelles de Touraine
37330 CHATEAU-LA-VALLIERE
Tel: (16) 47 24 69 75
Fax: (16) 47 24 23 74
Hotel/Restaurant offering tourist and leisure activities

Claridge Belmann
37, rue François Ier
75008 PARIS
Tel: 47 23 54 42
Fax: 47 23 08 84
Director: M. PLOUSEAU

Flatotel Expo
52, rue Oradour sur Glane
75015 PARIS
Tel: 45 54 93 45
Fax: 45 54 93 07

Hilton International Paris
18, avenue de Suffren
75740 PARIS Cedex 15
Tel: 44 38 56 00
Fax: 44 38 56 10
Director: M. Oskar
VON KRETSCHMANN
Hotel/Restaurant

Holiday Inn Worldwide
45, rue Anatole France
92300 LEVALLOIS-PERRET
Tel: 47 57 35 00
Fax: 47 57 31 50

Hôtel Adagio
257-263, rue de Vaugirard
75015 PARIS
Tel: 40 45 10 00
Fax: 40 45 10 10
Contact: M. Pierre GUINARD
187 exclusive rooms and extensive conference and meeting facilities overlooking the Eiffel Tower

Hôtel Américain
72, rue Charlot
75003 PARIS
Tel: 48 87 58 92
Fax: 48 87 48 03

Hôtel Beaumarchais
3, rue Oberkampf
75011 PARIS
Tel: 43 38 16 16
Fax: 43 38 32 86
Quiet hotel in the Marais, reasonable prices

Hôtel Bedford
17, rue de l'Arcade
75008 PARIS
Tel: 42 66 22 32
Fax: 44 94 77 97
Director: M. LE ROLL

Hôtel Bouquet de Longchamp
6, rue Bouquet de Longchamp
75116 PARIS
Tel: 47 04 41 71
Fax: 47 27 29 09

Hôtel Concorde La Fayette
3, Place du Général Koenig
75017 PARIS
Tel: 40 68 50 68
Fax: 40 68 50 43
Sales & Marketing Director:
Mme Christine DESSEANT

Hôtel Concorde St. Lazare
108, rue St. Lazare
75008 PARIS
Tel: 40 08 44 44
Fax: 42 93 01 20
Director: M. Eric BRIAL
First-class traditional hotel

Hôtel de Castiglione
40, rue du Fbg. St. Honoré
75008 PARIS
Tel: 44 94 25 25
Fax: 42 65 12 27
Director: M. Eric MOUEZ
Hotel with restaurant

Hôtel de Crillon
10, Place de la Concorde
75008 PARIS
Tel: 44 71 15 00
Fax: 44 71 15 02

Hôtel de la Herse d'Or
20, rue St. Antoine
75004 PARIS
Tel: 48 87 84 09
Cheap prices

Hôtel de la Trémoille
14, rue de la Trémoille
75008 PARIS
Tel: 47 23 34 20
Fax: 40 70 01 08

Hôtel des Etats-Unis
16, rue d'Antin
75015 PARIS
Tel: 47 42 43 25
Fax: 47 42 82 83

Hôtel du Louvre
Place André Malraux
75001 PARIS
Tel: 44 58 38 38
Fax: 44 58 38 01
Directeur: M. Richard D'HARCOURT
Brasserie du Louvre, Bar Le Defender, Conference Center

Hôtel George V
31, avenue George V
75008 PARIS
Tel: 47 23 54 00
Fax: 47 20 40 00

Hôtel Ibis
122, rue La Fayette
75010 PARIS
Tel: 45 23 27 27
Fax: 42 46 73 79

Hôtel Intercontinental
3, rue de Castiglione
75001 PARIS
Tel: 44 77 11 11
Fax: 44 77 14 60
Public Relations: Mme Suzanne GRYNER

Hôtel La Lousiane
60, rue de Seine
75006 PARIS
Tel: 43 29 79 30
Fax: 46 34 23 87
Home to many American jazzmen in the past

Hôtel Les Jardins d'Eiffel
8, rue Amélie
75007 PARIS
Tel: 47 05 46 21
Fax: 45 55 28 08
Contact: M. RECH
80 rooms with a view of the Eiffel Tower - 32 garages

Hôtel Lutétia
45, Bd. Raspail
75006 PARIS
Tel: 49 54 46 46
Fax: 49 54 46 00
Director: M. DE MARJORIE

Hôtel Mercure Paris Vaugirard
69, Bd. Victor
75015 PARIS
Tel: 44 19 03 03
Fax: 44 19 03 02
Director: Anne-Marie THIAULT

Hôtel Mercure Royal Madeleine
29, rue de l'Arcade
75008 PARIS
Tel: 42 66 13 81
Fax: 42 66 02 27
Director: Mme JOBERT

Hôtel Meurice
228, rue de Rivoli
75001 PARIS
Tel: 44 58 10 10
Fax: 44 58 10 16
Director: M. ROCHE

Hôtel Plaza Athénée
25, avenue Montaigne
75008 PARIS
Tel: 47 23 78 33
Fax: 47 20 20 70

Hôtel Pullman Paris
20, avenue Charles de Gaulle
94656 RUNGIS Cedex
Tel: 46 87 36 36
Fax: 46 87 08 48

Hôtel Ritz
15, Place Vendôme
75041 PARIS Cedex 01
Tel: 43 16 30 30
Res: 43 16 36 69
Fax: 43 16 31 78
Commercial Director:
Mme HOLTMANN
Private "Ritz Club," Cooking School Ritz-Escoffier, Ritz Health Club, Restaurant L'Espadon

Hôtel Sheraton Prince de Galles
33, avenue George V
75008 PARIS
Tel: 47 23 55 11
Fax: 47 20 96 92

Hôtel Westminster
13, rue de la Paix
75002 PARIS
Tel: 42 61 57 46
Res: 42 61 39 64
Fax: 42 60 30 66
Contact: Mlle Isabelle LANGLOIS
Hotel/Restaurant with conference facilities

Le Bristol
112, rue du Fbg. St. Honoré
75008 PARIS
Tel: 42 66 91 45
Fax: 42 66 68 68
Commercial Director:
Mme HIRN
Restaurant

Le Fauconnier
11, rue Fauconnier
75004 PARIS
Tel: 42 74 23 45
A cross between a youth hostel and a proper hotel in the heart of Paris

Le Méridien Paris
81, Bd. Gouvion-St.-Cyr
75017 PARIS
Tel: 40 68 34 34
Fax: 40 68 31 31
Director: M. LECOULS

Le Warwick Champs-Elysées
5, rue de Berri
75008 PARIS
Tel: 45 63 14 11
Fax: 43 59 00 98
Sales Manager: Jennifer DEMNI
147 rooms and apartments, gourmet restaurant

Resinter Hotel Reservations
2, rue de la Mare Neuve
91021 EVRY Cedex
Tel: 60 77 27 27
Fax: 69 91 05 63
Director: M. MOUCHENE
All Sofitel, Pullman, Novotel, Mercure, Ibis and Arcade hotels

Saint James Paris
43, avenue Bugeaud
75116 PARIS
Tel: 44 05 81 81
Fax: 44 05 81 70
Director: M. Tim GODDARD
The only "Château-Hôtel" in Paris

Trusthouse Forte Hotels
23, Place Vendôme
75001 PARIS
Tel: 42 61 10 65
Fax: 42 86 05 40
Commercial Director:
Mme LAMBERT

3i Group
141, avenue Charles de Gaulle
92521 NEUILLY Cedex
Tel: 47 15 11 00
Fax: 47 45 31 24
Director: M. Frédéric DE BROGLIE
Corporate investments, acquisition of holdings

A. Schulman
10-12, rue Andras Beck
92366 MEUDON-LA-FORET Cedex
Tel: 41 07 75 00
Fax: 40 94 02 58
Director: M. Otto H. BRUDER
Plastics

A.M. International
60, rue Berthelot
92402 COURBEVOIE Cedex
Tel: 43 34 31 21
Fax: 43 34 96 80
President: M. Claude GUERARD

A.T. Cross France
11, rue Laugier
75847 PARIS Cedex 17
Tel: 42 67 15 37
Fax: 42 27 99 75
Director: M. Philippe MEURGER
Ballpoint manufacturer

A.V.X.
B.P. 213
91941 LES ULIS Cedex
Tel: 69 18 46 00
Fax: 69 28 73 87
Managing Director:
M. J.P. RONZEAU

Abbott France
12, rue de la Couture
Silic 233
94528 RUNGIS Cedex
Tel: 45 60 25 00
Fax: 45 60 04 98
Managing Director:
M. André GARCIA
Pharmaceutical laboratory

Ace/North Hills
Bâtiment Atria
Avenue Edouard Belin
92500 RUEIL-MALMAISON
Tel: 47 08 48 00
Fax: 47 08 47 32
President: M. Christian HONORE

ACG France
56-58, avenue Louis Roche
92231 GENNEVILLIERS Cedex
Tel: 40 80 70 00
Fax: 40 80 72 24
President: M. CAZADE
Automobile spare parts

Acheson France
Z.I. Ouest
Rue Georges Besse
B.P. 68
67152 ERSTEIN Cedex
Tel: (16) 88 59 01 23
Fax: (16) 88 59 01 00
President: G.N.B. LYNAM
Lubricants

Acu-Rite
2, avenue de la Cristallerie
92316 SEVRES Cedex
Tel: 46 26 15 85
Fax: 45 07 24 02
Manager M. Gilles BENARD
Clock-making industry

ADT Sécurité Systèmes
10, rue Alphonse de Neuville
75017 PARIS
Tel: 47 66 04 19
Fax: 43 80 91 13
Electronic surveillance, security

Agfa Gevaert
274, avenue Napoléon Bonaparte
B.P. 301
92506 RUEIL-MALMAISON Cedex
Tel: 47 32 71 11
Fax: 47 32 70 99
Director: M. MARAZZI
Photography, radiology and micrography

Air Products
Centre Paris Pleyel
93521 ST-DENIS Cedex 01
Tel: 48 09 75 00
Fax: 48 09 75 40
President: M. Bernard GUERINI
Manufactures and supplies industrial gas

Airbus Industrie
12bis, avenue Bosquet
75007 PARIS
Tel: 45 51 40 95
President: M. Jean PIERSON
Aircraft industry

Ajay Europe
Z.I. Grand Verger
53600 EVRON
Tel: (16) 43 01 35 35
Fax: (16) 43 01 76 18
Manager: M. Michel PICHON
Mineral salts

Alcoa France
113-121, avenue du
Président Wilson
93210 LA PLAINE ST DENIS
Tel: 49 17 87 00
Fax: 42 43 99 65
Director: M. Gérard PUPILE
Aluminium products

Allied Signal
126, rue de Stalingrad
93700 DRANCY
Tel: 43 11 50 00
Fax: 43 11 53 50
President: M. Jean-Claude
TRUPIANO
Automobile brakes

Allied Signal
4, avenue de la Baltique
Z.A. de Courtaboeuf
91946 LES ULIS Cedex
Tel: 69 07 00 89
Fax: 64 46 42 12
Basic components for printed circuits

Allied Signal Turbo
Route d'Oncourt Z.I.
B.P. 19
88150 THAON-LES-VOSGES
Tel: (16) 29 68 29 68
Fax: (16) 29 68 29 00
President: M. Philippe GALLIN
Turbo-compressors

Ameron France
9, avenue des Pommerots
78400 CHATOU
Tel: 30 71 50 50
Fax: 30 53 49 07
Industrial paint

Amica SA
5, rue Volta
B.P. 53
92800 PUTEAUX Cedex
Tel: 46 25 84 00
Fax: 46 25 83 83
Director: M. Alain CHOMONT
Electrical equipment

Ampco Metal France
20, rue Claude Bernard
B.P. 22
78311 MAUREPAS Cedex
Tel: 30 51 24 27
Fax: 30 62 63 96
General Director:
Mme Charles-Henri SOULARD
Trades in non-ferrous metals

Amphenol Socapex
5, rue du Président Kruger
B.P. 5
92403 COURBEVOIE
Tel: 49 05 39 22
Fax: 43 33 11 25
Director: M. Luc WALTER
Optical and electric connectors

Amway France
14, avenue François Sommer
B.P. 140
92185 ANTONY Cedex
Tel: 46 74 21 80
Fax: 46 74 21 81
Director: M. Nicolas LEFRANC
Distributor of Amway products

Anagram France
1, rue Etienne Dolet
93400 ST-OUEN
Tel: 49 45 00 09
Fax: 49 45 00 19
Director: M. BODEL
Markets mylar ballons

ANF Industrie
Place des Ateliers
B.P. 1
59154 CRESPIN
Tel: (16) 27 23 53 00
Fax: (16) 27 35 16 24

Applications Industrielles du Verre
Z.I. de l'Ecartelé
B.P. 444
35304 FOUGERES
Tel: (16) 99 94 50 50
Fax: (16) 99 94 57 19
President: M. Joel ROCHARD
Transformers for the glass-making industry

Applied Materials
Bâtiment E
Parc de la Julienne
91830 LE COUDRAY-MONTCEAUX
Tel: 69 90 61 00
Fax: 69 90 40 45
Manager: M. Pete RATH
Semi-conductors

Arco Chimie France
55-57, avenue Kléber
75016 PARIS
Tel: 44 34 67 39
Fax: 45 53 02 26
Commercial Director:
M. Pedro EMPIS

Armstrong World Industries
5, rue Louis Lejeune
92128 MONTROUGE Cedex
Tel: 47 46 73 00
Fax: 47 46 04 49
Director: M. Jean-Yves MARRON
Ceilings, floors, double glazing

Aro S.A.
1, avenue de Tours
72500 CHATEAU-DU-LOIR
Tel: (16) 43 44 74 00
President: M. Didier LOMBARD
Welding equipment

Associated Merchandising Corporation
17, rue St. Florentin
75008 PARIS
Tel: 42 60 34 03
Fax: 42 60 20 48
Director: Cheryl MOTTIN

AT&T Gis France
Tour Neptune
20, Place de Seine
92086 PARIS LA DEFENSE
Cedex 20
Tel: 49 03 29 00
Fax: 47 73 06 07
President: M. Christian LHUSSIER
Computer technology

Atal S.A.
7, rue Mariotte
75017 PARIS
Tel: 43 87 80 00
Fax: 43 87 01 38
Chairman: M. DOMINIONI
Office planning workspace

Aussedat Rey
1, rue du Petit Clamart
B.P. 5
78141 VELIZY-VILLACOUBLAY
Cedex
Tel: 40 83 44 12
Fax: 40 83 00 21
Director of Communications:
Marie-Christine MALINGRE
Paper manufacturer

Auto Suture Europe
Z.A. Clef de St. Pierre
78990 ELANCOURT
Tel: 30 79 82 00
Fax: 30 79 82 12
Surgical instruments

Autotrol
230, rue Robert Schman
Z.A. des Uselles
77350 LE MEE-SUR-SEINE
Tel: 64 10 20 00
Fax: 64 37 92 11
Director: M. SANDERSON
Water-processing equipment

Auxitrol
1, rue d'Anjou
B.P. 241
92604 ASNIERES-SUR-SEINE
Tel: 47 90 62 81
Fax: 47 86 26 46
Director: M. VERGES
Temperature, flow and level sensors

Babcock Entreprise
80, rue Emile Zola
93123 LA COURNEUVE
Tel: 49 37 31 31
Fax: 43 52 27 70
Director: M. ORPHELIN
Boilers

Badger S.F. Raytheon Engineers and Constructors
14, rue Gardines
78100 ST-GERMAIN-EN-LAYE
Tel: 34 51 60 75
Fax: 34 51 43 59

Baker Hughes Inteq
164-166, avenue Joseph Kessel
78960 VOISINS
Tel: 30 48 70 00
Fax: 30 48 70 01
Director: M. SCOTT
Drilling equipment

Baltek
61, rue de la Fontaine
75016 PARIS
Tel: 46 47 58 50
Fax: 46 47 66 58
Director: Mme Isabelle KOHN
Balsa wood traders

Barnier
9-11, rue Edouard Branly
B.P. 126
26001 VALENCE Cedex
Tel: (16) 75 44 80 00
Fax: (16) 75 81 24 47
Adhesive tape manufacturer

Bausch & Lomb France
Route de Levis St. Nom
B.P. 51
78320 LE-MESNIL-ST-DENIS
Tel: 30 69 65 00
Fax: 34 61 70 35
President: M. Guy MAYENOBE
Contact lense distributor

Baxter
Avenue Louis Pasteur
B.P. 56
78311 MAUREPAS Cedex
Tel: 34 61 50 50
Fax: 34 61 50 25
President: M. Michel GIBAULT
Pharmaceutical products

Bayer S.A.
49-51, quai de Dion-Bouton
92815 PUTEAUX Cedex
Tel: 49 06 50 00
Fax: 49 06 52 19

Bechtel France S.A.
38, rue Bassano
75008 PARIS
Tel: 47 20 53 04
Fax: 47 20 55 06
Director: M. CORI
Engineering research consultancy

Beckman Instruments France
92-94, Chemin des Bourdons
93220 GAGNY
Tel: 43 01 70 00
Fax: 43 81 16 80
Director: M. Alain GRANGER
Supply hospitals and laboratories with medical equipment

Becton Dickinson France
Rue Aristide Berges
B.P. 4
38800 LE PONT DE CLAIX
Tel: (16) 76 68 36 36
Fax: (16) 76 68 36 82
President: M. Werner DE BACKER
Surgical instruments

Benoist Girard & Cie
203, Bd. de la Grande Delle
B.P. 8
14201 HEROUVILLE-ST-CLAIRE Cedex
Tel: (16) 31 46 33 00
Fax: (16) 31 47 48 36
Manager: M. Lionel BARON
Manufactures orthopedic implants and artificial limbs

Best Power Technology
Z.I. Les Iles Cordées
38113 VEUREY VOROISE
Tel: (16) 76 53 86 19
Fax: (16) 76 53 86 26
Managing Director: M. Pierre-Henri CASTETS

Betz Industries
Allée 1 Mai
77183 CROISSY-BEAUBOURG
Tel: 60 37 59 60
Fax: 60 37 59 37

Big Drum France
1, rue Fondation Prud'Homme
88026 EPINAL Cedex
Tel: (16) 29 69 66 10
Fax: (16) 29 69 66 15
President: M. VECIANA
Ice cream packaging

Bijur Products Inc.
Z.I. de Courtaboeuf
5, avenue de l'Atlantique
B.P. 50
91942 LES ULIS Cedex
Tel: 69 29 85 85
Fax: 69 07 76 27
Commercial Director:
M. DELEEUW
Oil and grease lubrification

Bissell
Z.I. de Villemilan
27, avenue Ampère
91320 WISSOUS
Tel: 69 30 03 49
Fax: 69 30 69 62
President: M. John BISSELL
Automatic sweepers and household appliances

Black and Decker
Le Paisy
69570 DARDILLY
Tel: (16) 72 20 39 20
Fax: (16) 72 20 39 01
Director: M. Alain BRUNELLE
Sells Black & Decker products to retail outlets

Black Clawson Europe
30, avenue Pierre Curie
B.P. 90
33270 FLOIRAC
Tel: (16) 56 86 37 75
Fax: (16) 56 86 39 63
Director: M. Christian LASTERA
Paper machine manufacturer

Blackhawk
Centre Eurofret
Rue du Rheinfeld
B.P. 5
67026 STRASBOURG
Tel: (16) 88 65 76 30
Fax: (16) 88 65 76 31
President: M. Jean-Paul BARTHELME

Boeing International Corporation
2, avenue Montaigne
75008 PARIS
Tel: 47 23 55 49
Fax: 47 20 08 55
President: M. Andrew
Patrick FINNEGAN
Presents Boeing in Europe

Boet Système Actif
26, rue Paul Doumer
B.P. 704
59657 VILLENEUVE D'ASCQ
Tel: (16) 20 41 04 36
Fax: (16) 20 41 31 77
Director: M. Jean-Paul BOET
Industrial soundproofing

Borden France
3-5, rue Barbet
B.P. 102
76250 DEVILLE-LES-ROUEN
Tel: (16) 35 74 23 01
Fax: (16) 35 75 02 99
President: M. Gilles-Etienne
JACQUIN

Bose
6, rue St. Vincent
78100 ST-GERMAIN-EN-LAYE
Tel: 30 61 63 63
Fax: 30 61 41 05
Director: M. Andy SMAGA
Hi-fi and professional sound systems

Bostik
B.P. 46
77252 BRIE-COMTE-ROBERT Cedex
Tel: 64 42 12 12
Fax: 64 06 61 43
Chairman: M. LE HENAFF
Adhesives

Boston Scientific
4, avenue des Trois Peuples
78180 MONTIGNY-
LE-BRETONNEUX
Tel: 30 12 14 14
Fax: 30 57 44 97
President: M. Hans Peter
STROHBAND
Medical products

Bou-Matic Europe
2-4, rue de la Plaine
78860 ST-NOM-LA-BRETECHE
Tel: 30 80 43 43
Fax: 30 80 43 50
Director Europe: M. Dale GORDON
Manufactures and distributes equipment for the dairy industry

Bougie Champion
33, Place des Corolles
92400 COURBEVOIE
Tel: 46 93 03 00
Fax: 47 75 21 44
Spark plugs

BP France
8, rue des Gémeaux
95866 CERGY-PONTOISE Cedex
Tel: 34 22 40 00
Fax: 34 22 48 32
Contact: M. Philippe LAMBERT

Brady
B.P. 362
91959 LES ULIS Cedex
Tel: 69 31 19 20
Fax: 69 31 10 68
Commercial Director:
M. Randy OUDEMANS
Labels, label printers

Braillon Magnétique
P.A. de la Grande Ile
B.P. 6
73806 MONTMELIAN Cedex
Tel: (16) 79 84 21 45
Fax: (16) 79 84 14 49
Director: M. Jean-Michel GAMBUT
Magnetism

Brink's
49, rue de Réaumur
75003 PARIS
Tel: 42 71 27 70
Fax: 42 71 63 71
President: M. Paul LECOQ
Security firm specialized in the transportation of funds

British Steel
3, rue de l'Arrivée
75015 PARIS
Tel: 44 10 50 50

British Steel France
21, rue des Trois Fontanots
92024 NANTERRE Cedex
Tel: 46 14 03 00
Fax: 47 21 83 24
Contact: P. HAESMANS

BTR Valves S.A.
30, rue Jean Jaurès
B.P. 20
42240 UNIEUX
Tel: (16) 77 40 18 77
Fax: (16) 77 56 30 95
President: M. TALBOTT
Faucet trade (valves, couplings)

C.A.L. Pfizer
27, avenue Ste Lorette
B.P. 94
06333 GRASSE Cedex
Tel: (16) 93 36 08 69
Fax: (16) 93 36 81 73
Executive Assistant:
Mlle ANTONETTI
Essential oils and compositions for flavors and fragrances

C/S Steel
1, rue de la Cressonnière
27950 ST-MARCEL
Tel: (16) 32 64 84 00
Fax: (16) 32 64 84 12
Director: M. Philippe LUGUET
Wall covering, sunblinds, handrails

Cabot Europe Ltd
2, rue Marcel Monge
92158 SURESNES Cedex
Tel: 46 97 58 00
Fax: 47 72 66 47
General Manager:
M. Patrick EDEL
Chemical industry

Cadillac Plastic
8, rue Marc Sequin
77290 MITRY MORY
Tel: 64 67 44 24
Fax: 64 67 44 29
Director: M. SCHLOUPPE
Semifinished plastics trader

California Pellet Mill, Co.
34, avenue Albert Ier
B.P. 35
92502 RUEIL-MALMAISON Cedex
Tel: 47 49 29 99
Fax: 47 51 84 11
General Director:
M. François LE ROUX
Presses for the farming industry

Cambridge Energy Research
14, rue Duphot
75001 PARIS
Tel: 42 44 10 10
Fax: 40 15 05 22
Director: M. Joseph STANISLAW
Oil and gas research

Canon France
Z.I. Coudray
7, avenue Albert Einstein
93154 BLANC-MESNIL Cedex
Tel: 49 39 25 25
Fax: 48 67 52 50
Office automation equipment

Capsugel France
10, rue Timken
68000 COLMAR
Tel: (16) 89 20 57 09
Fax: (16) 89 41 48 11
President: M. Guido DRIESEN
Capsules for the pharmaceutics industry

Carborundum France
10, rue Lionel Terray
92500 RUEIL-MALMAISON
Tel: 47 16 94 00
Fax: 47 08 33 75

Cargill France
18-20, rue des Gaudines
B.P. 215
78108 ST-GERMAIN-EN-LAYE
Tel: 30 61 35 00
Fax: 30 61 35 35
President: M. François LOURY
Cereals, fodder for cattle, manure

Carrier
Route de Thil
B.P. 49
01120 MONTLUEL Cedex
Tel: (16) 72 25 21 21
Fax: (16) 72 25 22 51
President:
M. Géraud M.H. DARNIS
Air conditioning and refrigeration components

Cascade France
11, rue du Docteur Jean Charcot
B.P. 22
91421 MORANGIS Cedex
Tel: 64 54 75 00
Fax: 64 54 75 01
Co-Manager: M. Pierre FOURNIER
Hydraulic accessories for fork-lift trucks

Cascades S.A.
Les Mercuriales
40, rue Jean Jaurès
93176 BAGNOLET Cedex
Tel: 49 72 24 01
Fax: 43 60 69 69
Vice-President: M. Jean-Guy PEPIN
Cardboard manufacturer

Case Poclain S.A.
17, rue des Tournelles
60800 CREPY-EN-VALOIS
Tel: (16) 44 94 32 00
Fax: (16) 44 87 69 70

Caterpillar France S.A.
40, avenue Léon Blum
B.P. 55
38041 GRENOBLE Cedex 09
Tel: (16) 76 39 70 26
Fax: (16) 76 39 72 05
Managing Director: M. VITTECOQ
Earth-moving equipment

Celite France S.A.
9-11, rue du Colonel Rochebrune
92504 RUEIL-MALMAISON
Tel: 47 16 21 05
Fax: 47 16 21 39
Director: M. Bruno VAN HERPEN
Diatomite filter aids and fillers

Cenafrance
41, avenue Edouard Vaillant
92100 BOULOGNE
Tel: 46 20 44 66
Fax: 46 20 10 03
Raw materials for the paper-making industry

Chauveau J.H.
29, avenue Pierre Ier de Serbie
75116 PARIS
Tel: 47 20 85 60
Fax: 40 70 14 47
Director: M. J.H. CHAUVEAU
Import agents

Cheminées Sécurité
101, rue de Paris
Immeuble KHEOPS II
B.P. 97
77202 TORCY
Tel: 64 80 44 45
Fax: 64 80 04 70
Contact: M. Jean-Pierre JEGGE
Sell air shafts for fireplaces

Chevron Chemical
47, rue de Villiers
92527 NEUILLY-SUR-SEINE
Tel: 46 39 36 00
Fax: 46 39 37 80
Director: M. Jean MENARD
Manufactures and sells additives for motor oil

Chrysler Automotive Services
42, avenue de la Grande Armée
75017 PARIS
Tel: 45 72 93 40

Ciba Corning Diagnostics S.A.
Avenue du Gros Chêne
B.P. 109 - Eragny
95613 CERGY-PONTOISE Cedex
Tel: 34 40 40 00
Fax: 34 40 40 91
Director: M. Jean-Pierre ROUSSILLON

Ciba Vision Ophthalmics
B.P. 1129
31036 TOULOUSE Cedex
Tel: (16) 61 76 69 89
Fax: (16) 61 76 69 00

Cincinnati Milacron
12, rue Le Corbusier
Silic 246
Bâtiment Iéna
94568 RUNGIS Cedex
Tel: 41 80 11 30
Fax: 46 87 94 83
Sell machine tools

Cisco Systems Europe
16, avenue Québec
91940 LES ULIS
Tel: 69 18 61 00
Fax: 69 28 83 26
Vice-President: M. BRAWERMAN

Clarins
4, rue Berteaux Dumas
92200 NEUILLY
Tel: 47 38 12 12
Director: M. Christian COURTIN-CLARINS

Cobe France
37, Place de la Loire
94563 RUNGIS Cedex
Tel: 46 87 66 53
Fax: 46 87 97 24
Director: M. URBIN
Medical products

Cody Automation Corporation
10, avenue de l'Europe
78140 VELIZY-VILLACOUBLAY
Tel: 39 46 47 00
Fax: 30 70 65 01

Colgate Palmolive
55, Bd. de la Mission Marchand
92401 COURBEVOIE Cedex
Tel: 47 68 60 00
Fax: 47 68 63 03
Manufactures and distributes Colgate-Palmolive products

Compagnie Continentale Simmons
Le Mandinet II
Lognes
77437 MARNE-LA-VALLEE
Tel: 64 62 80 00
Fax: 60 37 86 22
Vice-President: M. Bernard MOREI
Bedding manufacturer (bedsteads and mattresses)

Compagnie Générale des Eaux
52, rue d'Anjou
75384 PARIS Cedex 08
Tel: 49 24 49 24
Fax: 49 24 69 99
Contact: M. Jean-Pierre TARDIEU

Compagnie Transair
Zone Nord Aéroport
B.P. 174
93352 LE BOURGET Cedex
Tel: 49 92 75 75
Fax: 49 92 75 00
Sales Assistant: Annie LEBARS
Airplane sales, assistance and maintenance

Continental Import Export Co.
9, rue Robert de Flers
75015 PARIS
Tel: 45 78 35 70
Fax: 45 77 24 64

Cooper Oil Tool France
19bis, Bd. d'Argenson
92200 NEUILLY-SUR-SEINE
Tel: 46 43 92 00
Fax: 46 43 92 02
Commercial Director:
M. JONVILLE
Manufactures oil-drilling equipment

Cooper Tools
4, avenue des Coquelicots
B.P. 63
94382 BONNEUIL-SUR-MARNE Cedex
Tel: 45 13 16 80
Fax: 43 77 94 24
General Manager:
M. A. MADRANGE
Hand tools: Weller, Nicholson, Lufkin

Cordis
Parc de Viry
5, rue de Ris
91178 VIRY-CHATILLON Cedex
Tel: 69 12 20 00
Fax: 69 05 58 22
Director: M. Michel BEAU
Medical equipment

Corning France
44, avenue de Valvins
77210 AVON
Tel: 64 69 75 00
Fax: 60 72 21 75
Director: M. Philippe DELLOYE
Technical glass-making

Corporate Printing Company International
116, avenue des Champs-Elysées
75008 PARIS
Tel: 44 21 82 80
Fax: 44 21 82 81
Director: M. Gregory GOOD

Coultronics France S.A.
29, avenue Georges Pompidou
95580 MARGENCY
Tel: 34 27 20 00
Fax: 34 16 12 23
Director: M. Jean-Pierre VAUGON
Scientific instruments

CPM Europe
34, avenue Albert Ier
B.P. 35
92502 RUEIL-MALMAISON
Tel: 47 49 29 99
Fax: 47 51 84 11
Director: M. François LE ROUX
Granule presses for the farming industry

Cristalleries de Baccarat
11, Place de la Madeleine
75008 PARIS
Tel: 42 65 36 26
Crystal manufacturer

Crompton & Knowles
Boulevard Dambourney
B.P. 4
76350 OISSEL
Tel: (16) 35 64 40 40
Fax: (16) 35 64 40 97
Director: M. Caste ALBERT
Chemicals and colouring agents

Crown Cork Company France
Z.I. La Marinière
7, rue Gutenberg
91919 BONDOUFLE Cedex
Tel: 60 86 46 40
Fax: 60 86 77 27
Crown cork caps and aerosol cans

Culligan France
4, avenue du Président Kennedy
78340 LES-CLAYES-SOUS-BOIS
Tel: 30 55 80 55
Fax: 30 55 56 23
Director: M. Christian OLIVIER
Water-processing technology

Cuno Europe
1, Bd. de l'Oise
95030 CERGY-PONTOISE Cedex
Tel: 30 73 16 15
Fax: 30 73 91 80
Filters

Curragh Tintawn
c/o GPI
32, Grande Rue
95510 VETHEUIL
Tel: 34 78 25 25
Fax: 34 78 25 00
President: M. Andrew HARTLEY
Carpet manufacturer

Danly France
Z.I. Pont Aspach
68520 BURNHAUPT-LE-HAUT
Tel: (16) 89 26 64 64
Fax: (16) 89 48 95 33
Director: M. Richard VOEGELIN
Tools for presses

Dart Europe S.A.
8, rue Lionel Terray
92500 RUEIL-MALMAISON
Tel: 47 32 02 34
Fax: 47 51 96 59
Director: Isabelle NOEL
Tupperware manufacturer

Dayco Europe S.A.R.L.
Rue Paul Langevin
B.P. 81
Z.I. rue Hellu-Lezennes
59260 HELLEMMES-LES-LILLES
Tel: (16) 20 33 26 16
Fax: (16) 20 04 06 60
Manager: M. John Lloyd PURDEN
Rubber traders

De Trey Dentsply, S.A.
72, rue du Général Leclerc
92270 BOIS-COLOMBES
Tel: 47 80 46 13
Fax: 47 84 96 51
Dental products and equipment

Delphi Automotive Systems
117, avenue des Nations
Z.A.C. Paris Nord II
B.P. 60059
95972 ROISSY CDG Cedex
Tel: 49 38 38 01
Fax: 49 38 39 80
President: M. Hans J. WEISER
Division of General Motors

Dennison France
8, rue Montgolfier
93115 ROSNY-SOUS-BOIS Cedex
Tel: 49 35 40 40
Fax: 48 94 88 73
Office furniture and automation systems

Deublin
B.P. 45
77423 MARNE-LA-VALLEE
Cedex 2
Tel: 64 61 61 61
Fax: 64 61 63 64
Manager: M. Jean-Louis TAIARIOL
Revolving joints

Dexter
14, rue Chanay
B.P. 51
71700 TOURNUS
Tel: (16) 85 40 45 45
Fax: (16) 85 32 19 06
President: M. Gérard MAZURE
Industrial lacquers and varnishes

Dickey John Europe
165, Bd. de Valmy
92706 COLOMBES
Tel: 41 19 21 80
Fax: 47 86 00 07
Electronic devices for farming machinery

Dionex
98, rue Albert Calmette
78350 JOUY-EN-JOSAS
Tel: 39 46 08 40
Fax: 30 70 69 16
Director: M. Christian TINET
Ion chromatography

Diversey France SA
18, avenue Maurice Chevalier
77831 OZOIR-LA-FERRIERE
Tel: 64 43 18 43
Fax: 64 43 18 11
Contact: M. Philippe FISCH
Cleaning products

DME France
P. A. de la Danne
B.P. 100
Eragny
95163 CERGY-PONTOISE
Tel: 34 48 31 60
Fax: 34 48 89 22
Manager: M. Bruno LAUREYS
Steel casts for injecting plastic

Dosage 2000
62-70, rue Yvan Tourguenieff
78380 BOUGIVAL
Tel: 30 82 68 69
Fax: 30 82 67 80
Commercial Director:
Susan STRAKER
Industrial fluid dispensers, valves and components

Dosapro Milton Roy
10, Grande Rue
B.P. 5
27360 PONT-ST-PIERRE
Tel: (16) 32 68 30 00
Fax: (16) 32 68 30 93
Director: M. Jean-Claude DEGREMONT
Measuring pumps

Dow Corning France
Le Britannia
20, Bd. Eugène Derwelle
69432 LYON Cedex 03
Tel: (16) 78 60 51 48
Fax: (16) 78 62 78 98
Commercial Director:
M. S. DELOBEL
Sells silicon

Dow France
17-21, rue St. Denis
B.P. 110
92106 BOULOGNE-BILLANCOURT Cedex
Tel: 49 09 78 78
Fax: 49 09 06 19
Director: M. Jean-Louis RAYNAUD
Chemicals

Dresser Produits Industriels
(Division Masoneilan)
107, avenue Charles de Gaulle
92521 NEUILLY-SUR-SEINE Cedex
Tel: 47 15 81 81
Fax: 46 24 77 68
Director: M. BUTZBERGER

Du Pont de Nemours France
137, rue de l'Université
75334 PARIS Cedex 07
Tel: 45 50 65 50
Fax: 47 53 09 65

Du Pont de Nemours Packaging
Boulevard Industriel
76580 LE TRAIT
Tel: (16) 35 37 93 58
Fax: (16) 35 37 91 47
President: M. Arsène SCHILTZ
Processes plastic film for food packaging

Dunlop France
62, rue Camille Desmoulins
B.P. 41
92133 ISSY-LES-MOULINEAUX Cedex
Tel: 40 93 12 34
Fax: 40 93 59 07
Commercial Director:
M. Didier LEDOUX

Duo-Fast France
Z.I. de la Petite Ile
B.P. 105
89300 JOIGNY
Tel: (16) 86 92 01 01
Fax: (16) 86 92 01 09
Manager: Mrs HAGNER

Dynatech Communications France
Bâtiment GAIA
9, Parc Ariane
78284 GUYANCOURT Cedex
Tel: 30 48 83 00
Fax: 30 48 83 10
Manager: M. Christopher JACKSON
Constructor and distributor of telecommunication equipments

Dynisco Instruments
466, rue Marché Rollay
94500 CHAMPIGNY-SUR-MARNE
Tel: 48 81 84 59
Fax: 48 81 83 34
President: M. Jean-Claude SOHIER
Pressure and heat sensors

ELDEC France
18, rue du 35ème
Régiment d'Aviation
Aztivwage Hall 30
69500 BRON
Tel: (16) 78 26 10 10
Fax: (16) 72 37 72 30
General Manager: M. Jacques IRLES
Develops, manufactures and sells goods for the aeronautics industry

Eldon-Rubbermaid
12-14, rue des Osiers
78310 COIGNIERES
Tel: 34 61 82 22
Fax: 34 61 17 11
General Director: M. Pierre FLEURY
Office technology, furniture and accessories

Elf Antar France
Tour Elf
Cedex 45
92078 PARIS LA DEFENSE
Tel: 47 44 45 46
Fax: 47 44 78 78
North American Division Director:
M. Yves SERRES (47 44 36 51)
Petroleum products

Elf Atochem Agri
1, rue des Frères Lumière
78370 PLAISIR
Tel: 30 81 73 00
Fax: 30 81 72 50
Financial Director:
M. DE LEPINEAU
Agri-chemicals

Elsag Bailey
100, rue de Paris
91342 MASSY Cedex
Tel: 64 47 20 00
Fax: 64 47 20 16

EMCO Wheaton S.A.
9, avenue du Canada
Parc Hightec
91966 LES ULIS Cedex
Tel: 64 46 27 26
Fax: 64 46 90 32
Director: M. Gabriel LEMIERE
Tank truck equipment and levers for loading goods

Endevco France
23, rue Baudin
93315 LE-PRE-ST-GERVAIS Cedex
Tel: 48 91 80 47
Fax: 48 43 45 26
Manager: M. Joachim RAMS
Measuring instruments

Enomfra S.A.
10, avenue Eiffel
77220 GRETZ-ARMAINVILLIERS
Tel: 64 06 47 76
Fax: 64 06 47 59
Deputy Director: M. Jean VASEUX
Geology

Epstein and Sons France Inc.
7-9, rue Barbette
75003 PARIS
Tel: 48 04 97 30
Fax: 48 04 31 81
Director: Perl NATHAN
Engineering and architecture

Esco
137, route d'Heyrieux
B.P. 229
69803 ST PRIEST Cedex
Tel: (16) 72 22 62 22
Fax: (16) 78 20 28 76
President: M. James E. SONGER
Public construction

Esso S.A.F.
2, rue des Martinets
92569 RUEIL-MALMAISON Cedex
Tel: 47 10 60 00
Fax: 47 10 66 03
Director: M. Jean VERRE

Ethnor
192, avenue Charles de Gaulle
92523 NEUILLY-SUR-SEINE Cedex
Tel: 46 41 59 90
Fax: 46 24 14 47
President: M. Jacques DUMONT
Medical equipment

Ets Paul Paulet
Z.I. de Pouldavid
B.P. 129
29177 DOUARNENEZ Cedex
Tel: (16) 98 74 40 00
Fax: (16) 98 74 40 40
President: M. Nick HARDING
Canned fish

Eur-Open
21, rue Fécamp
75012 PARIS
Tel: 42 71 70 47
Import-export consulting concerning Eastern European countries

Euramax Alumax
Avenue Beaunier
B.P. 25
42161 ANDREZIEUX-BOUTHEON
Tel: (16) 77 36 56 64
Fax: (16) 77 55 39 56
Director: M. Jean-Claude BONNARD
Aluminium processing

Euro Physical Acoustics
Leader Club n° 120
94373 SUCY-EN-BRIE Cedex
Tel: 49 82 60 40
Fax: 49 82 60 41
President: M. Jean-Claude LENAIN

Eurokafco
Z.I. Nord, Bâtiment 1
Allée du Plateau
77200 TORCY
Tel: 64 80 58 15
Fax: 60 05 43 56
President: M. Jean GUT
Equipment for processing meat and fish

Europate
1494, rue François Jacob
62806 LIEVIN Cedex
Tel: (16) 21 72 75 75
Fax: (16) 21 29 95 63
President: M. PATACZ

European Fiber Products
50, rue de Miromesnil
75008 PARIS
Tel: 42 66 31 08
Fax: 42 66 14 27

European Plastic Products Industry
12, rue Riquet
75019 PARIS
Tel: 40 35 44 66

Extraits Végétaux et Dérivés
Z.I. La Palun
13120 GARDANNE
Tel: (16) 42 58 37 62
Fax: (16) 42 58 31 42
President: M. Roger BOZZI
Licorice manufacturer

Exxon Chemical France
31, Place des Corolles
92098 PARIS LA DEFENSE 2
Tel: 49 03 50 00
Fax: 47 73 55 11
Director: M. Daniel MARIE
Petrochemicals

Fashion Fair
41, rue François Ier
75008 PARIS
Tel: 47 20 85 46
Fax: 47 20 85 45
Cosmetics for "femmes de couleur"

Fasim
8, rue G. Soufflot
Immeuble Le Sésame
78184 ST-QUENTIN-EN-YVELINES
Tel: 30 12 03 70
Fax: 30 48 08 08
President: M. GALABERT
Supplies automated equipment to teaching establishments

Fast Parallel Solutions
2, Place Gustave Eiffel
Silic 267
94578 RUNGIS Cedex
Tel: 46 87 25 22
Fax: 46 87 71 38
Director: M. TAUZIET
Distributes image-processing software and equipment

FCT
Rue de Sabanel
B.P. 7
81160 ST-JUERY
Tel: (16) 63 78 12 00
Fax: (16) 63 78 12 12
Director: M. ROSSI
Industrial faucets

Feeder S.A.
Bastide Blanche
RN 113
B.P.78-1
13742 VITROLLES
Tel: (16) 42 75 84 00
Fax: (16) 42 79 39 97
President: M. Louis ALOCCIO
Micro-computer wholesaler

Feralp Systems
Z.I. Richardets
51, rue de la Chapelle
93165 NOISY-LE-GRAND
Tel: 45 92 14 14
Fax: 45 92 30 10
President: M. ACCATENO
Fixed and mobile shelves

Ferro-France
43, rue Jeanne d'Arc
B.P. 23
52101 ST-DIZIER Cedex
Tel: (16) 25 07 33 33
Fax: (16) 25 56 36 06
Manager: M. Jean BONNAL

Finnigan Mat
Parc Club Orsay Université
2, rue Jacques Monod
91893 ORSAY Cedex
Tel: 69 41 98 00
Fax: 69 41 98 16

Fisher Controls
Rue Paul Baudry
B.P. 10
68700 CERNAY
Tel: (16) 89 37 64 00

Fleck Europe SNC
140, avenue Roland Garros
78532 BUC
Tel: 39 24 15 00
Fax: 39 56 03 90
Director: M. Jean FLECK
Control valves for water treatment

Floquet Monopole
B.P. 31
63, Bd. Robespierre
78301 POISSY Cedex
Tel: 30 65 27 00
Fax: 30 74 45 19
General Director: M. Robert RICHTER
Automobile equipment

Florasynth France S.A.
45, Bd. Marcel Pagnol
06130 LE PLAN DE GRASSE
Tel: (16) 93 09 33 50
Fax: (16) 93 09 33 99
Director: M. Jack N. FRIEDMAN
Raw materials for the perfume industry

FMC Europe
Route des Clérimois
B.P. 705
89107 SENS Cedex
Tel: (16) 86 95 87 00
Fax: (16) 86 95 19 16
General Secretary:
M. Henry KUFELD
Petroleum equipment

Foster Wheeler CEE
31, rue des Bourdonnais
75024 PARIS Cedex 01
Tel: 40 13 40 13
Fax: 42 33 81 98
President: M. Antoine O'NEILL
Refineries in the petrochemical world

Foxboro France
B.P. 741
95004 CERGY-PONTOISE Cedex
Tel: 30 37 88 55
Fax: 30 37 70 29
Director: M. Claude CONTRE
Process control

Fralsen Horlogerie
1, rue Denis Papin
25023 BESANCON Cedex 9
Tel: (16) 81 50 81 22
Fax: (16) 81 50 23 69
Director: M. Jean-Pierre CHAMBON
Timepieces

French Aerospace
3, rue Claude Pouillet
75017 PARIS
Tel: 44 40 00 41

Fruehauf France
2, avenue de l'Aunette
91130 RIS ORANGIS
Tel: 69 02 50 00

G.B.C. France
B.P. 79
93600 AULNAY-SOUS-BOIS
Tel: 48 69 96 07
Fax: 48 69 93 98
General Director: M. MEIER
Equipment for binding, coating with plastic and destroying documents

Gates Hydraulique
21, Bd. Monge
69330 MEYZIEU
Tel: (16) 72 45 12 12
Fax: (16) 72 02 81 08
Commercial Director:
M. Gérard BAAS
Hydraulic flexible tubing

Gaz de France (GDF)
2, rue Curnonsky
75017 PARIS
Tel: 47 54 24 32
Fax: 42 70 33 44
French Gas Board (International Delegation)

GEC Alsthom
38, avenue Kléber
75795 PARIS Cedex 16
Tel: 47 55 20 00
Fax: 47 55 266 14
Managing Director:
M. James CRONIN
Electrical manufacturer

General Electric Information
19, avenue Léon Gambetta
92000 MONTROUGE
Tel: 05 05 43 47

General Electric Plastics France
Z.I. de St. Guénault
B.P. 67
91002 EVRY Cedex
Tel: 60 79 69 00
Fax: 60 77 56 53
Director: M. Peter RENS

Genstar Container International
30, rue d'Orléans
92200 NEUILLY-SUR-SEINE
Tel: 47 45 98 00
Fax: 47 45 98 12
Fax: 47 45 98 13
Senior Vice-President:
M. François CALIMAS
Rental of containers

Gillette France
1, avenue Berthollet
74010 ANNECY Cedex
Tel: (16) 50 88 39 39
Fax: (16) 50 88 39 40
President: M. Alain CALVIERA

Gilson Medical Electronics France
72, rue Gambetta
B.P. 45
95400 VILLIERS-LE-BEL
Tel: 34 29 50 00
Fax: 34 29 50 80
Director: M. Eric MARTEAU D'AUTRY
Laboratory material

GL Specialty Chemicals
15, rue des Pas Perdus
B.P. 8338
St. Christophe
95804 CERGY Cedex
Tel: 34 25 44 41
Fax: 30 73 59 94
Director: M. LALANDE
Chemical products manufacturer

Glitsch France
Chemin des Moines
B.P. 76
13200 ARLES
Tel: (16) 90 18 48 00
Fax: (16) 90 18 48 07
Director: M. Ian SHEPHERD
Manufactures boilers

GM Powertrain
81, rue de la Rochelle
B.P. 33
67026 STRASBOURG Cedex
Tel: (16) 88 60 88 60
Fax: (16) 88 60 87 80
Plant Manager: M. Marc SCHIFF

Goodyear France
101, avenue de la Châtaigneraie
92500 RUEIL-MALMAISON
Tel: 47 16 23 00
Fax: 47 16 23 12
President: M. Sylvain VALENSI

Gould Instruments
57, rue St. Sauveur
Ballainvilliers
91165 LONGJUMEAU Cedex
Tel: 69 10 22 40
Fax: 69 34 20 73
Director: M. BRINBAL
Measuring instruments

Grace Industrial Chemicals
40, Bd. Henri Sellier
92156 SURESNES
Tel: 40 99 29 00
Manager: M. WERBE
Chemical products

Grace S.A.
23, rue St. Denis
B.P. 9
28231 EPERNON Cedex
Tel: (16) 37 28 91 00
Fax: (16) 37 28 91 91
Director: M. Patrick BRUN
Plastic packaging, glues, resins

Graco France
113, rue de Solets
Silic 141
94523 RUNGIS
Tel: 49 79 71 71
Fax: 46 86 65 39
Imports products for transferring liquids

Grand Metropolitan
6, rue Christophe Colomb
75008 PARIS
Tel: 49 52 40 00
Fax: 49 52 40 01
President: M. LOWES
Farming produce

Grumman International Inc.
23, rue Neuve Notre-Dame
78000 VERSAILLES
Tel: 30 21 20 40
Fax: 30 21 27 83
Director: M. Jacques POUS
French base of an American aeronautical group

Gulf European
90, avenue des Champs-Elysées
75008 PARIS
Tel: 44 95 06 60

H.F.T.
9, rue de Lens
92000 NANTERRE
Tel: 47 81 95 21
Fax: 47 84 12 40
Managing Director:
M. J.Y. LAUBIE
Steam boxes for the printing industry

Halliburton Company
Rue I. et F. Joliot Curie
B.P. 209 Lons
64142 BILLERE Cedex
Tel: (16) 59 32 14 46
Fax: (16) 59 62 18 62
Director: M. Francisco BA ROCHA
Oil-drilling services

Harborlite France S.A.
9-11, rue du Colonel Rochebrune
92504 RUEIL-MALMAISON
Tel: 47 16 21 15
Fax: 47 16 21 39
Director: M. Bruno VAN HERPEN
Derlite filter aids and fillers

Harman France
33, avenue du Maréchal de
Lattre de Tassigny
94127 FONTENAY-SOUS-BOIS Cedex
Tel: 45 14 47 80
Fax: 45 14 47 90
Director: M. Bruno BERTRAND
Importer of electronic equipment

Harmon/CFEM Façades
Zone Orlytech
18-20, avenue Louis Blériot
91781 WISSOUS Cedex
Tel: 49 75 53 30
Fax: 49 75 52 62
President: M. Gabriel SAHYOUN
Façades and glass-making

Harris Wilson Textiles
10, rue de la Grange Batelière
75009 PARIS
Tel: 42 46 80 10
Fax: 47 70 08 44

Hartley Business Services S.A.
115, rue de l'Abbé Groult
75011 PARIS
Tel: 47 27 33 20
Tel: 07 42 93 30
Fax: 47 27 34 84
Owner: Mr J. CHARLES
Wide range of fax and telephone products - free delivery and installation

Haynes International
B.P. 7110
95054 CERGY-PONTOISE Cedex
Tel: 34 48 31 00
Fax: 30 37 80 22
Contact: M. P. LIMOUSIN
Non-ferrous metals

Hayssen Europa
Le Portant- Grand Cap
152, Grande Rue de St. Clair
69731 CALUIRE ET CUIRE Cedex
Tel: (16) 78 08 90 81
Fax: (16) 78 08 65 18
Director: M. Alain CHICOUARD
Vertical and horizontal form-fill-seal machines, tissue overwrapping machines

Henkel Ecolab
8, rue Rouget de Lisle
92442 ISSY-LES-MOULINEAUX Cedex
Tel: 41 08 86 00
Fax: 41 08 02 24
Director: M. Jean GOURLET
Soap powder

Henkel Sanisol Floordress
3, avenue des Frenes
78180 MONTIGNY-LE-BRETONNEUX
Tel: 30 43 03 54
Fax: 30 57 10 18
President: M. Didier POUGET
Distributor of cleaning products

Hercules France
3, rue Eugène et Armand Peugeot
92508 RUEIL-MALMAISON
Tel: 47 10 24 00
President: M. Edouard DE CROUTTE
Chemicals for the paper industry

Herman Miller et Cie
37, avenue Pierre Ier de Serbie
75008 PARIS
Tel: 40 69 62 62
Fax: 40 70 15 15

Hexcel
3, avenue Condorcet
B.P. 1208
69608 VILLEURBANNE Cedex
Tel: (16) 72 44 40 00
Fax: (16) 78 89 72 30
Director: M. Claude GENIN
Industrial textile fibers

Honeycomb System
49, rue de la Sinne
68100 MULHOUSE
Tel: (16) 89 46 22 12
Fax: (16) 89 46 00 31
Unit Manager: M. STIMPFLING
Designs and sells machines for the non-woven textile industry

Hytorc Europe
2, square Mozart
75016 PARIS
Tel: 42 88 67 45
Fax: 42 88 66 96
Manager: M. Francis ROVER
Hydraulic torque wrenches

I.S.O. Roulements
15, rue de la Faisanderie
75016 PARIS
Tel: 44 05 86 86
Fax: 44 05 17 10
President: M. TOUBOL
Importer of ball and roller bearings

ICI France
196, rue Houdan
92330 SCEAUX
Tel: 41 13 32 32
Fax: 41 13 32 90
Contact: M. Jean-Marie DUCREUX

Ilco Unican
16, rue du Moulin des Bruyères
92400 COURBEVOIE
Tel: 47 89 11 96
Fax: 47 88 86 29
Director: M. Francis MORITZ
Electronic locks and mechanical push-button locks

Ilford Anitec
Parc Club de la Haute Maison
14, rue Galilée
Cité Descartes
77436 CHAMPS-SUR-MARNE
Tel: 64 61 96 03
Fax: 64 61 93 30
Marketing Director: M. Dominique LE FOULER (photo)
Marketing Director: M. Hervé MARANGE (graphics)
Photographic products and graphic arts

India Trading Company
4, Place Adolphe Chérioux
75015 PARIS
Tel: 48 56 28 94

Ingersoll-Rand
5-7, avenue Albert Einstein
Zone Industrielle
B.P. 113
78192 TRAPPES Cedex
Tel: 30 50 61 10
Fax: 30 50 02 18
President: M. Jean TORFS

Instron
11, Parc Ariane
78284 GUYANCOURT Cedex
Tel: 30 57 23 53
Fax: 30 64 67 11
Director: M. Steve BEEBE
Testing equipment

International Flavors Fragrances
47, rue Victor Hugo
92270 BOIS-COLOMBES
Tel: 46 49 60 60
Fax: 47 81 85 73
Vice-President: M. Harry VAN GELDER
Aromatic substances for the perfume and food industries

Intervascular
Athelia 1
13705 LA CIOTAT Cedex
Tel: (16) 42 08 46 46
Fax: (16) 42 08 13 49
President: M. Timothy HAINES
Vascular prostheses

Ircon
B.P. 57
77312 MARNE-LA-VALLEE Cedex 2
Tel: 60 06 78 67
Fax: 60 06 28 00
Manager: M. Guy LECLERC
Optical pyrometry

Isoconcept
12, avenue du Québec
Parc Evolic - Bâtiment I1
648 - Villebo
91965 LES ULIS
Tel: 69 28 05 52
Fax: 69 28 05 02
Director: M. Christian MORTESSAGNE
Medical and pharmaceutical equipment for hospitals

ISP France S.A.
Paris Nord II
B.P. 5007
95945 ROISSY CDG Cedex
Tel: 49 90 58 00
Fax: 49 90 58 05
Director: M. Gérard DEYBER
Chemicals and filters

ITW de France
305, chaussée Jules César
B.P. 17
95250 BEAUCHAMP
Tel: 30 40 40 40
Fax: 30 40 40 82
President: M. J.P. CORDOLA

ITW Surfaces et Finitions
163-171, avenue des Auréats
B.P. 1453
26014 VALENCE Cedex
Tel: (16) 75 75 27 00
Fax: (16) 75 75 27 49
Director: M. Michel MARIN
Spray gun manufacturer

John Deere
Rue du Paradis
B.P. 219
45140 ST-JEAN-DE-LA-RUELLE Cedex
Tel: (16) 38 72 30 00
Fax: (16) 38 74 86 65
President: M. J.P. FAVACHE

Johnson & Johnson
50, rue de Seine
92700 COLOMBES
Tel: 47 80 72 46
Fax: 47 69 11 03
President: M. Harry WALE

Johnson Controls France
357, rue Estienne d'Orves
92700 COLOMBES
Tel: 46 13 16 00
Fax: 47 80 93 83
President: M. Bruno NICOLAS
Air conditioning

Johnson Filtration Systems
Zone Industrielle
86530 AVAILLES-EN-CHATELLERAULT
Tel: (16) 49 02 16 00
Fax: (16) 49 02 16 16
President: M. Charles BACHY
Oil sump filters

Johnson Française
B.P. 606
95004 CERGY-PONTOISE Cedex
Tel: 34 21 21 21
Fax: 30 37 42 36
President: M. MARTIN
Domestic cleaning products

Johnson Matthey S.A.
B.P. 50240
Z.I. Paris Nord 11
13, rue de la Perdrix
95956 ROISSY CDG Cedex
Tel: 48 17 21 99
Fax: 48 63 27 02
Contact: M. HAUSLER
Specialty chemicals and metals

Jouets Ritvik France
13, rue des Réservoirs
95160 MONTMORENCY
Tel: 34 28 13 77
Fax: 34 28 03 85
Director: M. Joel RICHOUX
Toys

JP2 S.A.
15, rue Le Corbusier
Z.A. Europarc
94035 CRETEIL Cedex
Tel: 43 99 47 32
Fax: 43 99 07 58 5/9/95
President: M. Jean-Paul PARMENTIER
Retail trade of electronic equipment for cable television

K-Tron France
Z.I. de l'Abbaye
B.P. 60
38780 PONT-EVEQUE
Tel: (16) 74 85 94 25
Fax: (16) 74 57 66 25
Manager: M. Michel JAMEY
The leader in the field of machinery for electronic measuring and weighing

Keller Dorian Graveurs
10bis, rue St. Eusèbe
69425 LYON Cedex 3
Tel: (16) 78 53 10 57
Fax: (16) 78 53 37 58
Director: M. Georges DEBIEVRE
Industrial engraving

Kenner Parker France
Savoie Technolac
73382 LE-BOURGET-DU-LAC Cedex
Tel: (16) 79 96 47 47
Fax: (16) 79 96 47 99
Director: M. Paul AUDOUY
Games, toys

Kimberly Clark
12, rue de la Pierre Droite
77440 CONGIS-SUR-THEROUANNE
Tel: 64 35 46 93
Fax: 64 35 46 83
Pharmaceutical products

Kimberly-Clark Sopalin
26, rue Armengaud
92210 ST-CLOUD
Tel: 41 12 14 14
Fax: 41 12 15 15
President:
M. Anthony Brian HARRIS
Manufactures and sells products made from paper

Koch International S.A.R.L.
11, rue Guy Moquet
95100 ARGENTEUIL
Tel: 39 98 45 45
Fax: 34 11 15 28
Director: M. TORDGMAN
Burners, incinerators and flares

Kodak Pathé
26, rue Villiot
75012 PARIS
Tel: 40 01 35 55
Fax: 40 01 46 50
Director: M. JOFFRIN
Industrial imagery

Koni France
Le Logis de Bonneau
Route Nationale 7
B.P. 09
06271 VILLENEUVE-LOUBET Cedex
Tel: (16) 93 20 90 70
Fax: (16) 93 22 50 50
Director: B. DUGELAY
Shock absorbers

L'Oreal
41, rue Martre
92117 CLICHY
Tel: 47 56 70 00
Beauty care products, cosmetics, hair care

Laboratoires 3M Santé
3, rue Danton
92245 MALAKOFF Cedex
Tel: 49 65 51 51
Fax: 49 65 51 00
Director: M. Alain HARDY
Pharmaceutical laboratory

Laboratoires Allard
Les Collines de l'Arche
Cedex 24
92057 PARIS LA DEFENSE
Tel: 40 90 60 00
Fax: 49 00 14 51
President: M. Bernard HELAIN
Pharmaceutical products

Laboratoires Bristol-Myers Squibb
Les Collines de l'Arche
Cedex 24
92057 PARIS LA DEFENSE
Tel: 40 90 60 00
Fax: 40 90 91 80
President: M. Bernard HELAIN

Laboratoires C.R.P. Scherer
74, rue Principale
67930 BEINHEIM
Tel: (16) 88 63 31 31
Fax: (16) 88 86 24 28
Manager: M. ALTMANN
Pharmaceutical products

Laboratoires Merck Sharp & Dohme-Chibret
3, avenue Hoche
75008 PARIS
Tel: 47 54 87 25
Fax: 47 66 99 91
Managing Director: M. Alain BOUYSSET
Pharmaceutical products, medicine

Laboratoires Searle
52, rue Marcel Dassault
92514 BOULOGNE-BILLANCOURT Cedex
Tel: 47 61 78 00
Fax: 47 61 00 08
Director: Dr Jean-Pierre FATIGUE
Markets pharmaceutical and dietetic products

Laboratoires Smith, Kline & French
6, Esplanade Charles de Gaulle
92000 NANTERRE
Tel: 46 98 46 98
Fax: 46 98 49 00

Laboratoires St. Ives
2, rue Alfred de Vigny
78112 FOURQUEUX
Tel: 39 21 12 52
Fax: 39 21 11 24
Personal care products

Laboratoires Upjohn
Parc Industriel d'Incarville
B.P. 606
27106 VAL-DE-REUIL Cedex
Tel: (16) 32 25 70 70
Fax: (16) 32 25 70 26
Plant Manager: M. Gaston ROLAIN
Pharmaceutical laboratory

Laboratoires UPSA
128, rue Danton
92500 RUEIL-MALMAISON Cedex
Tel: 47 16 87 72
Chairman: M. Jacques DARDAUD
Pharmaceutical industry

Laboratoires Wyeth France
117, rue Château des Rentiers
75013 PARIS
Tel: 44 06 42 42
Pharmaceuticals

Lancôme International
188, rue Paul Hochart
94152 CHEVILLY-LARUE
Tel: 49 79 56 31
Fax: 49 79 51 94
Intl Director: M. SAJOT
Public Relations: Mme Claudine CLOT-DESMET

Lapeyre
15, rue André Karman
93300 AUBERVILLIERS
Tel: 48 11 74 00
Fax: 48 11 74 01
Marketing Manager: M. Stéphane CAMPION
Wooden Furniture, customized doors, windows and staircases

Leco France
22, rue des Morillons
Z.A. des Doucettes
95140 GARGES-LES-GONESSE
Tel: 39 93 98 00
Fax: 39 86 41 05
Manager: M. Robert TOUVENIN
Import/Export trader in measuring instruments

Lecroy
Avenue du Parana
B.P. 214
Z.A. de Courtaboeuf
91941 LES ULIS Cedex
Tel: 69 18 83 20
Fax: 69 07 40 42
Contact: M. Jean COUDEVILLE
Testing and measuring equipment

Leeds et Northrup France
1, rue Pavlov
78190 TRAPPES
Tel: 34 82 99 66
Fax: 34 82 99 60
Director: M. LAPEYRONIE
Sells measuring instruments

Leroy Somer
Route d'Heyrieux
B.P. 27
69360 ST-SYMPHORIEN-D'OZON
Tel: (16) 78 02 12 22
Fax: (16) 78 02 17 48
Contact: M. Bernard SORET
Electrical engines

Liard
Route Nationale 49
B.P. 69
59570 BAVAY
Tel: (16) 27 63 16 64
Fax: (16) 27 63 08 77
President: M. MARCHAND

Lilly France
203, Bureaux de la Colline
92213 ST-CLOUD
Tel: 49 11 34 34
Fax: 46 02 27 67
President: M. Frédéric CHAMPAVERE
Pharmaceutical laboratory

Liquid Paper/Paper Mate
4, rue Texel
75685 PARIS Cedex 14
Tel: 45 38 56 46

Lockheed Corporation International
4, rue de Penthièvre
75008 PARIS
Tel: 42 65 39 81
Fax: 42 65 39 79
Aeronautics

LTR Industries
7, avenue Ingres
75016 PARIS
Tel: 44 14 32 00
Fax: 44 14 32 49
Director: M. Jean-Pierre LE HETET
Reconstitution of tobacco waste

Lubrizol France
25, quai de France
B.P. 1062
76173 ROUEN Cedex
Tel: (16) 35 58 14 00
Fax: (16) 35 72 76 54
Director: M. Gérard ANGOUSTURES
Makes additives

Lucas
11, rue Lord Byron
75008 PARIS
Tel: 45 61 95 25
Fax: 45 61 10 97
Contact: M. J.C. MARTIN
Automobile and aeronautical manufacturer

Lyonnaise des Eaux
72, avenue de la Liberté
92753 NANTERRE Cedex
Tel: 46 95 50 00
Fax: 46 95 51 86
Communications Director:
M. Vincent DE LA VAISSIERE
Services related to energy, water, wastage, public building and cable TV

Machines Osborn
12, rue Marcelin Berthelot
Z.I. de la Grande Couture
95500 GONESSE
Tel: 39 85 79 66
Fax: 39 87 09 26
President: M. Jeannot FLICK
Equipment for foundries

Macy France
17, rue St. Florentin
75008 PARIS
Tel: 42 25 52 14
Fax: 45 61 48 06
Manager: Mme Kirsten WINTER

Marion Merrell Dow & Cie
16, rue d'Ankara
67080 STRASBOURG Cedex
Tel: (16) 88 41 45 01
Fax: (16) 88 45 90 75
Vice-President: Dr Guy TELL

Maréchal S.A.
5, avenue de Presles
94417 SAINT-MAURICE Cedex
Tel: 45 11 60 00
Fax: 45 11 60 60
Marketing Manager: M. Philippe NANTERMOZ
Industrial electrical equipment

Masoneilan
107, avenue Charles de Gaulle
92521 NEUILLY-SUR-SEINE Cedex
Tel: 47 15 81 81
Fax: 46 24 77 68
Marketing Director: M. Jacques CHEMOUL
Control valves

Massey Ferguson
29, quai de l'Industrie
91200 ATHIS MONS
Tel: 69 38 79 20
Fax: 69 38 99 90
President: M. Jean Bernard ROYEZ
Spare parts for tractors

Materials Research
66, Bd. de Thibaud
Z.I. de Thibaud
Batterie 307
31084 TOULOUSE Cedex
Tel: (16) 61 40 11 51
Fax: (16) 61 40 17 72
Director: M. René PERROT
PVD and CVD materials, equipment for the semi-conductor industry

Mather et Platt Wormald
29, avenue Georges Politzer
B.P. 122
78193 TRAPPES Cedex
Tel: 34 61 34 00
Fax: 30 51 80 05
President: M. THOUARD
Fire detection and protection

Mattel France S.A.
64-68, avenue de la Victoire
B.P 23
94310 ORLY
Tel: 48 92 23 33
Fax: 48 52 73 52
President: M. Robert GERSON
Toy manufacturer

Maxon
avenue du Parc
7, Le Campus
95033 CERGY-PONTOISE Cedex
Tel: 34 20 10 80
Fax: 34 20 10 88
Director: M. Jean-Pierre MARSAIS
Industrial burners

Mead Packaging Europe
5, allée du Bourbonnais
78312 MAUREPAS Cedex
Tel: 30 51 61 68
Fax: 30 51 16 27
President: M. Bertrand DUPRE

Mearl International France
96, rue St. Charles
75015 PARIS
Tel: 45 78 36 36
Fax: 45 78 36 38
Manager: M. Coert POLMAN
Pigments

Memorex Télex
3, rue Maurice Ravel
B.P. 141
92304 LEVALLOIS-PERRET
Tel: 45 60 89 00
Fax: 42 70 53 83

Mepps
B.P. 09
06390 CONTES
Tel: (16) 93 79 07 07
Fax: (16) 93 79 21 56
Fishing tackle

Merlin Médicale
1, avenue du 8 Mai 1945
B.P. 24
69672 BRON Cedex
Tel: (16) 72 15 56 56
Fax: (16) 72 15 56 50
Director: Mme Anne PAGES
Surgical instruments

Metal Improvement Company Inc.
Z.I. Amilly
45200 MONTARGIS
Tel: (16) 38 85 58 07
Fax: (16) 38 98 33 76
Director: M. Gilbert BEGUIAN

Micromeritics
181, rue Henri Bessemer
60100 CREIL
Tel: (16) 44 24 23 02
Fax: (16) 44 24 46 17
President: M. Raymond MALEY
Measuring instruments for laboratories

Midas France S.A.
108, avenue Jean Moulin
B.P. 53
78170 LA-CELLE-ST-CLOUD
Tel: 30 82 56 56
Fax: 30 82 62 31
Vice-President Europe:
M. Peter SCHALBURG
Exhaust pipes, silencers

Millipore
39, Route Industrielle de la Hardt
B.P. 116
67124 MOLSHEIM Cedex
Tel: (16) 88 38 90 00
Fax: (16) 88 38 91 90
Director: M. Dominique BALY
Filtering equipment for fluid purification

Minnesota Rubber Europe
14, rue du Fbg. St. Léger
B.P. 486
27004 EVREUX Cedex
Tel: (16) 32 29 52 29
Fax: (16) 32 33 07 59
Director: M. Hubert DE LA ROER

MKS Instruments France
43, rue du Commandant Rolland
93350 LE BOURGET
Tel: 48 35 39 39
Fax: 48 35 32 52
President: M. Bernard MARTIN
Sensors and gauges for measuring vacuum

Mobil Oil Française
Tour Septentrion
92976 PARIS LA DEFENSE Cedex
Tel: 41 45 42 41
Fax: 41 45 42 93
Director: M. Christian SCHNEEBELI
Distributor of oil by-products

Mod-Tap System Europe
15-17, rue des Tilleuls
Les Espaces du Verger
78960 VOISINS-LE-BRETONNEUX
Tel: 30 57 57 07
Fax: 30 43 12 98
Commercial Director:
M. Eric DUVAL
Cable systems for communications

Monroe Auto Equipement France
Z.I. des Béthunes
7, avenue du Fief
95310 ST-OUEN-L'AUMONE
Tel: 30 37 86 66
Fax: 34 64 09 29
Director: M. LONGRET

Monsanto
Immeuble Delalande
16-32, rue Aury Regnault
92411 COURBEVOIE Cedex
Tel: 41 16 43 00
Fax: 41 16 43 43
Director: M. Jean THOMAS
Chemical products

Moog S.A.R.L.
38, rue du Morvan
Silic 417
94573 RUNGIS Cedex
Tel: 45 60 70 00
Fax: 45 60 70 01
Manager: M. Bernard ALLAIN
Automation components and systems

MTS Systems France
6, rue Ste Claire Deville
77185 LOGNES
Tel: 60 17 13 51
Fax: 60 17 15 05
Manager: M. Werner ONGYERT
Makes and sells testing equipment

Nacanco
Z.I. des Huttes
Route des Vignots
59820 GRAVELINES
Tel: (16) 28 23 51 00
Fax: (16) 28 23 51 10
Contact: M. Jacques PIDOL
Metal boxes

Nalco France
14, rue Lavoisier
Z.I. de Coignières
B.P. 179
78310 MAUREPAS Cedex
Tel: 34 82 13 00
Fax: 30 62 68 06
Director: M. Jean-Pierre AMIOT
Water processing

National Starch & Chemical
B.P. 438
69655 VILLEFRANCHE-
SUR-SAONE
Tel: (16) 74 62 70 00
Fax: (16) 74 62 03 01
President: M. Maurice MARTIN
Glue manufacturer

Neutrogena France
5, rue de Logelbach
75017 PARIS
Tel: 44 15 35 35
Fax: 44 15 35 45
Director: M. Christian BARDIN
Products for the cosmetics and dermatology industries

Nordson France
L'Esplanade
Parc des Entreprises
2, rue Niels Boh
77462 LAGNY-SUR-MARNE Cedex
Tel: 64 12 14 00
Fax: 64 12 14 01
President: M. Patrice BOYER
Sells glue and paint applicators

Norton S.A.
Rue de l'Ambassadeur
B.P. 08
78702 CONFLANS
STE-HONORINE Cedex
Tel: 34 90 40 00
Fax: 39 19 89 56
Director: M. Claude DESLANDES

Ohmeda
Parc de Pissaloup
8, avenue Jean d'Alembert
78190 TRAPPES
Tel: 30 68 60 00
Fax: 30 68 60 01
President: M. Jean-François DOLLET
Sells medical equipment

OMC France
14, rue du Bois-du-Pont
Z.I. Les Béthunes
95310 ST-OUEN L'AUMONE
Tel: 34 40 30 30
Fax: 34 40 30 00
Director: M. André DAUXIN
Imports boats and boat engines

Omni Pac S.A.R.L.
64, rue de Miromesnil
75008 PARIS
Tel: 45 62 25 00
Fax: 45 61 13 61
Director: M. RICOUL
Packaging for foodstuffs

Ordo
Route de Nantes
85600 MONTAIGU
Tel: (16) 51 45 61 00
Fax: (16) 51 46 31 41
Managing Director:
M. Jean-Pierre OLIVREAU

Ortho Diagnostic Systems
69, rue de la Belle Etoile
Z.A.C. Nord II
95700 ROISSY-EN-FRANCE
Tel: 48 63 84 84
Fax: 48 63 2543
Managing Director:
M. Georges STOLERU
Subsidiary of Johnson & Johnson

Otis
4, Place Victor Hugo
92400 COURBEVOIE
Tel: 46 91 60 00
Fax: 47 68 95 97
President: M. Olivier ROBERT
Elevators, escalators

Owens Corning Fiberglass France
10, rue des Fers
95470 SURVILLIERS
Tel: 34 68 46 46
Fax: 34 68 61 28
President: M. VIDALIS
Fiberglass manufacturer

Oxygène Liquide
Tour Pleyel
93521 ST-DENIS
Tel: 48 09 75 00
Fax: 48 09 75 40
President: M. Bernard GUERINI
Industrial gas

Pacific Scientific
2, allée des Garays
Zone Industrielle
91124 PALAISEAU Cedex
Tel: 60 11 96 11
Fax: 60 11 93 76
Manager: M. VAN DER GUCHT
Sells particle counters

Packard Instrument
4-10, rue de la Grosse Pierre
Silic 159
94533 RUNGIS Cedex
Tel: 46 86 27 75
Fax: 46 86 37 94
Director: M. LE SAEC
Electronic, medical, scientific and nuclear instruments

Panduit
91, Bd. Alsace Lorraine
93110 ROSNY-SOUS-BOIS
Tel: 48 12 20 40
Fax: 48 94 06 72
Director: M. Marc MARTORELL
Cable ties, accessories, connectors

Papeteries de Cran S.A.
B.P. 15
74961 CRAN-GEVRIER Cedex
Tel: (16) 50 67 97 00
Director: M. Thomas LIVINGSTONE-LEARMONTH
Industrial and unusual types of paper

Parfums Christian Dior
33, avenue Hoche
75008 PARIS
Tel: 49 53 85 00
Fax: 49 53 85 01

Parfums Givenchy
74, rue Anatole France
92300 LEVALLOIS PERRET
Tel: 40 89 60 00
Fax: 40 89 60 91

Parfums Yves St-Laurent
28-34, Bd. du Parc
92521 NEUILLY-SUR-SEINE
Tel: 41 43 31 00
Fax: 41 43 30 38

Parke-Davis S.A.
11, avenue Dubonnet
92407 COURBEVOIE Cedex
Tel: 49 04 07 01
Fax: 49 04 07 44
President: M. Patrick
LAMORT DE GAIL
Pharmaceutical laboratory

Parker Hannifin Rak
Z.I. du Mont Blanc
B.P. 524
Ville La Grand
74112 ANNEMASSE Cedex
Tel: (16) 50 87 80 80
Fax: (16) 50 37 86 85

PCC France
Z.I. Peyrehitte
B.P. 11
64680 OGEU-LES-BAINS
Tel: (16) 59 34 94 55
Fax: (16) 59 34 93 55
President: M. Xavier CEYRAC
Foundry

Peerless France S.A.R.L.
P.A. Les Portes de la Forêt
5, allée Jean Monnet
77090 COLLEGIEN
Tel: 64 62 28 06
Contact: M. Jean-François GUERIF
Make and sell bathroom mats

Perkin Elmer Instruments
B.P. 304
78054 ST -QUENTIN-
EN-YVELINES Cedex
Tel: 30 85 63 63
Fax: 30 85 63 00
Director: G.M. PETRUCCI
Imports laboratory equipment

Permaswage
Z.I. des Dames
78340 LES-CLAYES-SOUS-BOIS
Tel: 30 55 01 20
Fax: 34 81 02 21
President: M. Robert M. CUMINS
Aeronautical connectors

Pfizer
86, rue de Paris
91407 ORSAY Cedex
Tel: 69 18 66 66
Fax: 69 07 75 38
Director: M. Jean-Raphaël
SOUCARET
Pharmaceutical laboratory

Philip Morris France
192, avenue Charles de Gaulle
92200 NEUILLY-SUR-SEINE
Tel: 46 43 73 00
Fax: 47 22 10 73
President: M. Alain FERNANDEZ
European Promotion

Phillips Petroleum
International France
13, rue Duphot
75001 PARIS
Radiophone: 21 22 52 97

Picky Poo Accessories Distribution
101, rue de Turenne
75003 PARIS
Tel: 42 72 39 23
Fax: 40 27 89 98
President: Giselle SIKSIK
Wholesaler

Pilkington France
191, avenue Aristide Briand
94230 CACHAN
Tel: 46 15 73 73
Fax: 46 15 73 70
General Director:
M. Christophe GUILLOT
Building materials and products

Pioneer Hi-Bred
Chemin de l'Enseigure
Borde Basse
31840 AUSSONNE
Tel: (16) 61 06 20 80
Deputy Director:
M. Jeffrey R. BEARD

Pitney Bowes France S.A.
Z.I. des Marais
1, avenue Louison Bobet
94124 FONTENAY-
SOUS-BOIS Cedex
Tel: 45 14 67 00
Fax: 48 76 52 41
Director: M. Cyril YOUSSOV
Mail processing

Plibrico Réfractaires
Z.I. du Coudray
6, avenue Albert Einstein
93150 LE BLANC-MESNIL
Tel: 48 67 18 52
Fax: 48 67 22 66
President: M. Pier Luigi GHIROTTI
Refractory, heat-resistant products

PMI Food Equipment
Group Europe
B.P. 306
8, rue Lionel Terray
92506 RUEIL-MALMAISON Cedex
Tel: 47 10 05 00
Fax: 47 51 39 83
President: M. Enzo DE BENEDETTI
Kitchen equipment for professional caterers

Polaroid France
B.P. 47
78391 BOIS D'ARCY Cedex
Tel: 30 85 60 60
Fax: 34 60 25 25
Managing Director: M. Gérard BOCQUENET

PPG Industries France
Chemin de Halage
B.P. 377
59307 VALENCIENNES Cedex
Tel: (16) 27 14 46 00
Fax: (16) 27 14 46 26
President: M. Fernand DEHANT
Paints, varnishes and resins

Praxair Industrial Gases
4, Place des Etats-Unis
Silic 218
94518 RUNGIS Cedex
Tel: 49 78 45 00
Fax: 46 75 94 61
President: M. Jacques BENOIT
Industrial gas, bottled gas

Prochimar
217, rue du Fbg. St. Honoré
75008 PARIS
Tel: 45 63 64 74
Fax: 45 63 85 09
Director: M. Jean-Claude HEUZE
Distributor of chemicals

Procter & Gamble S.A.
96, avenue Charles de Gaulle
92200 NEUILLY-SUR-SEINE
Tel: 40 88 55 11
Fax: 40 88 58 58
Director: M. J.P. VELTHUIZEN

Profroid Industries
178, rue du Fauge
Z.I. Les Paludes
B.P. 1152
13782 AUBAGNE Cedex
Tel: (16) 42 18 05 00
Fax: (16) 42 18 05 02
President: M. Jean-Pierre XIBERRAS
Refrigeration

Pulse Engineering
32, rue Jean Rostand
91893 ORSAY Cedex
Tel: 60 19 11 11
Fax: 60 19 09 10
President: M. David FLOWERS
Magnetic components

Rain Bird Europe
B.P. 72000
13792 AIX-EN-PROVENCE Cedex 3
Tel: (16) 42 24 44 61
Fax: (16) 42 24 24 72
Director: M. Daniel LEDERLIN
Manufactures and sells automatic watering equipment

Rank Xerox
7, rue Touzet Gaillard
93586 ST-OUEN Cedex
Tel: 49 48 47 46
Fax: 49 48 43 21
President: M. Franz SCHERER
Office equipment

Rans International Inc.
2, Villa Brimborion
92310 SEVRES
Tel: 45 34 77 74
Fax: 45 34 77 74
Contact:
M. Sevag KALAYDJIAN BA
International trade

Reckitt & Colman
15, rue Ampère
B.P. 83
91748 MASSY Cedex
Tel: 69 93 17 00
Fax: 69 93 19 99
Director: M. BEYELER
Cleaning products

Reynolds (R.J.) Tobacco France
35, rue des Abondances
92513 BOULOGNE-BILLANCOURT
Cedex
Tel: 46 99 46 00
Fax: 46 05 01 22
Director: M. Jacques LECLERC
Cigarettes: Winston, Camel...

Reynolds Aluminium France
1, rue du Ballon
Merxheim
68500 GUEBWILLER
Tel: (16) 89 74 46 00
Fax: (16) 89 74 46 01
President: M. James R. AITKEN

Reynolds European S.A.
17, rue des 2 Gares
92565 RUEIL-MALMAISON Cedex
Tel: 47 14 55 55
Fax: 47 14 55 15
Metals

Rhône Poulenc Rorer
20, avenue Raymond Aron
92165 ANTONY Cedex
Tel: 40 91 61 23
Fax: 47 02 50 14
Pharmaceutical products

Roberts
25, rue de la Gare
78370 PLAISIR
Tel: 30 55 68 91
Fax: 30 54 06 29
President: M. Wouter BAAN
Sells flooring equipment

Rockwell-Collins France
6, avenue Didier Daurat
B.P. 08
31701 BLAGNAC Cedex
Tel: (16) 61 71 77 00
Fax: (16) 61 71 51 69
President: M. Bernard LOTH
Aviation

Rohm and Haas France
La Tour de Lyon
185, rue de Bercy
75579 PARIS Cedex 12
Tel: 43 45 24 21
Fax: 43 45 28 19
Director: M. Hervé BELLEGO
Chemicals

Rohr Europe
22, chemin de la Crabe
31931 TOULOUSE
Tel: (16) 61 30 59 59
Fax: (16) 61 49 52 02
President: M. J.P. ROUZIERE

Rollin S.A.
B.P. 70
Steinbach
68702 CERNAY Cedex
Tel: (16) 89 38 43 43
Fax: (16) 89 75 78 89
President: M. Gérard LOEB
Industrial products made with elastomers

Rosemount
1, Place des Etats-Unis
Silic 265
94578 RUNGIS
Tel: 49 79 73 00
Fax: 49 79 73 99
Measuring instruments

Rothmans International France
10, rue Hamelin
75116 PARIS
Tel: 47 55 50 00
Fax: 47 55 51 20

S.G.E.
4, rue du Chemin de Fer
B.P. 50
94192 VILLENEUVE-
ST-GEORGES Cedex
Tel: 43 82 29 43
Fax: 43 82 42 68
Manager: M. Keith WRIGHT

S.P.E.
74370 PRINGY
Tel: (16) 50 27 20 03
Fax: (16) 50 27 25 75
President: M. F. GILLO
Accessories for the automobile industry

Sadaps Bardahl Corporation
Z.I. Roubaix-Est
59115 LEERS
Tel: (16) 20 83 03 97
Fax: (16) 20 82 97 87
President: M. Dominique LEPLAT
Makes and distributes additives, lubricants and cleaning agents for the automobile industry

Sames S.A.
13, chemin de Malacher
Zirst
38240 MEYLAN
Tel: (16) 76 41 60 60
Fax: (16) 76 41 60 90
Commercial Director: M. P. FABRE
Electrostatic paint equipment and installation

Samsonite France
504-520, Bd. Fernand Darchicourt
62110 HENIN-BEAUMONT
Tel: (16) 21 49 78 78
Fax: (16) 21 20 86 63
Director: M. Christian GUITTARD
Luggage

Sanger Paris S.A.
40, rue des Mathurins
75008 PARIS
Tel: 47 42 92 02
Fax: 42 66 28 94
President: M. Georges MUHLENHOFF
Imports meat and offal

Sangstat Atlantique
Institut de Biologie
9, quai Moncousu
44035 NANTES Cedex 01
Tel: (16) 40 48 79 81
Fax: (16) 40 48 26 89
President: M. Philippe POULETTY
Medicine, pharmaceuticals

Schering-Plough France
92, rue Baudin
92307 LEVALLOIS-PERRET Cedex
Tel: 41 06 35 00
Fax: 41 06 35 03
Pharmaceuticals for human and animal health care

Schlumberger
42, rue St. Dominique
75007 PARIS
Tel: 40 62 10 00
Fax: 40 62 10 30
Deputy General Counsel: M. Jim GUNDERSON
Petroleum products

Schrader
48, rue de Salins
B.P. 29
25301 PONTARLIER
Tel: (16) 81 38 56 56
Fax: (16) 81 46 41 42
President: M. A. BEARD
Valve manufacturer

Scott
66, route de Sartrouville
78230 LE PECQ
Tel: 34 80 41 41
Fax: 34 80 12 58
Manager: M. Antonio MARTINO
Paper for domestic use

Selas
Parc Technologique des Barbanniers
3-5, Place du Village
92632 GENNEVILLIERS Cedex
Tel: 46 13 99 99
Fax: 40 85 84 33
President: M. Christian BAILLIART
Oven manufacturer

Selkirk Manufacturing France
27, avenue des Trois Peuples
78180 MONTIGNY-LE-BRETONNEUX
Tel: 30 12 00 80
Fax: 30 48 00 27

Serpib Development Holding
14bis, rue Daru
75008 PARIS
Tel: 46 22 55 56
Fax: 47 63 53 76
President: M. Serge DE LANGSDORFF
Fire protection and asbestos decontamination

Servitech
8, rue Robert Schuman
94220 CHARENTON-LE-PONT
Tel: 45 18 19 05
Fax: 45 18 19 10
Manager: M. SEGUINET
Sells Black & Decker products

Shell France
89, Bd. Franklin Roosevelt
92564 RUEIL-MALMAISON Cedex
Tel: 47 14 71 00
Fax: 47 14 82 99

Shiseido France
79, rue Marcel Dassault
92100 BOULOGNE-BILLANCOURT
Tel: 46 94 10 00
Fax: 47 61 95 04
Cosmetics, beauty care products

SICOR S.A.
19, route de Meulan
78520 LIMAY
Tel: 34 78 87 87
Fax: 30 92 03 46
Director: M. Benoît-Joseph PONS
Fine chemicals for the pharmaceutics industry

Sierracin Corporation Europe
30bis, rue du Vieil Abrevoir
78100 ST-GERMAIN-EN-LAYE
Tel: 30 87 04 04
Fax: 30 87 03 84
Contact: M. Erich SCHOPS
Aeronautical components

Sifco Selective Plating
5, Bd. de Créteil
94107 ST-MAUR Cedex
Tel: 48 89 63 75
Fax: 42 83 14 73

Sigma Chimie
80, rue de Luzais
B.P. 701
38297 LA VERPILLIERE Cedex
Tel: (16) 74 82 28 00
Fax: (16) 74 95 68 08
Manager: M. Gilles FELLOUS
Chemicals

Singer
41, rue Pergolèse
75016 PARIS
Tel: 45 02 14 40
Fax: 45 01 92 14
Marketing Director: M. VIDAL
Sewing machines

Smart Products France
27, rue Jean de Beauvais
75005 PARIS
Tel: 43 25 88 72
Import and sell children's chairs for the catering industry

Smith International
B.P. 217
Lons
64142 BILLERE Cedex
Tel: (16) 59 92 35 50
Fax: (16) 59 92 35 98
Director: Mme Françoise KAES
Petroleum equipment

Smithkline Beecham
Laboratoires Pharmaceutiques
6, Esplanade Charles de Gaulle
92731 NANTERRE Cedex
Tel: 46 98 46 98
Fax: 46 98 49 00
Vice-President: M. Claude LAUFFET

Société Ara
140, rue de la Poudrette
B.P. 4052
69615 VILLEURBANNE Cedex
Tel: (16) 78 26 07 07
Fax: (16) 72 37 44 29
President: M. VALENTIN
Sells industrial sewing machines

Société de Prospection et d'Inventions Techniques
150, route de Lyon
26500 BOURG-LES -VALENCE
Tel: (16) 75 82 20 20
Fax: (16) 75 56 17 07
President: M. François LE FLOCH

Société des Céramiques Techniques
Route Oursbelille
B.P. 1
65460 BAZET
Tel: (16) 62 38 95 95
Fax: (16) 62 38 95 50
Telex: 520194
President: M. RIGAUX
Ceramics for filtering

Société Industrielle du Titane
45, rue de Courcelles
75008 PARIS
Tel: 53 83 93 60
Fax: 42 25 22 63
Chairman: M. Thomas CERNY
Distributor of titanium dioxide

Société Méditerrannénne du Froid
35, Bd. Capitaine Gèze
5F Parc Club des Aygalades
13014 MARSEILLE
Tel: (16) 91 11 62 30
Fax: (16) 91 63 05 80
Director: M. BIN MARCO
Industrial refrigeration

Sonoco France
Z.I. Les Alouettes
62800 LIEVIN
Tel: (16) 21 72 00 33
Fax: (16) 21 29 65 82

Spicer France
11, rue Georges Mangin
69400 VILLEFRANCHE-SUR-SAONE
Tel: (16) 74 62 69 69
Fax: (16) 74 62 38 85

Stanadyne Automotive
26-30, avenue des Frères Lumière
78190 TRAPPES
Tel: 34 82 24 24
General Director: M. Francis DEHAUSSY
Manufacturer of diesel engine equipment

Standard Wool France
157, rue de Roubaix
59200 TOURCOING
Tel: (16) 20 81 30 00
Fax: (16) 20 36 24 98
Contact: M. Pierre SIX

Stanley Mabo
24, rue Auguste Jouchoux
B.P. 1579
25009 BESANCON
Tel: (16) 81 66 36 36
Fax: (16) 81 88 21 71

Stanley Works Ltd France
Z.A. de l'Aqueduc
26, rue Georges Pompidou
78690 LES-ESSARTS-LE-ROI
Tel: 30 41 56 36
Fax: 30 88 90 45
President: Y. MARE
Automatic doors

Steelcase Strafor
56, rue Jean Giraudoux
B.P. 6K
67035 STRASBOURG Cedex
Tel: (16) 88 28 88 88
Fax: (16) 88 28 88 06
President: M. Jean-Charles PAUZE
Office furniture

Steiner France
18, avenue Ferdinand de Lesseps
91422 MORANGIS Cedex
Tel: 64 48 59 59
Fax: 64 48 41 59
Hygiene, sanitary products

Sterling International Group
235, rue du Fbg. St. Martin
75010 PARIS
Tel: 46 07 10 93

Stevens Security Systems
72, rue du Fbg. St. Honoré
75008 PARIS
Tel: 40 07 81 25
Fax: 40 07 80 40
Managing Director:
M. Howard W. RAYMOND
Equipment for printing bank notes

Sullair Europe
Chemin de Genas
B.P. 639
69805 ST PRIEST Cedex
Tel: (16) 72 23 24 25
Fax: (16) 78 90 71 68
President: M. Jim HYNCIK
Pneumatics and compressed air manufacturer

Sun Chemical S.A.
198-212, Route de Meaux
B.P. 24
93410 VAUJOURS
Tel: 49 63 73 02
Fax: 48 60 18 75
Executive Assistant:
M. Gérard GREVENT
Manufacturing of printing inks and varnishes

Sundstrand International
15, Bd. Eiffel
21604 LONGVIC Cedex
Tel: (16) 80 38 33 00
Fax: (16) 80 38 33 66
Tire manufacturer

Support Systems International
188, rue du Caducée
Parc Euromédecine
34195 MONTPELLIER Cedex 5
Tel: (16) 67 04 64 04
Fax: (16) 67 04 64 00
President: M. BONTRAGER
Mattresses, bedding

Swenson Process
7, Place de la Gare
B.P. 99
94210 LA-VARENNE-ST-HILAIRE
Tel: 48 85 90 41
Fax: 48 85 82 73

Tambrands France
B.P. 202
92212 ST-CLOUD Cedex
Tel: 47 11 24 24
Fax: 47 11 24 00
Tampons

TBI
72, rue du Fbg. St. Honoré
75008 PARIS
Tel: 40 07 86 98
Fax: 40 07 82 02

Techniparts/Dampers
37, rue Roger Salengro
69200 VENISSIEUX
Tel: (16) 78 78 46 90
Fax: (16) 78 75 83 61
Director: M. Anthony BEDFORD
Spare parts for industrial vehicles

Teledyne
738, rue Yves Kermen
92568 BOULOGNE Cedex
Tel: 47 61 08 08
Fax: 47 61 97 43
Director: M. Bernard DOLLE

Texaco France S.A.
5, rue Bellini
92806 PUTEAUX Cedex
Tel: 47 17 26 00
Fax: 47 76 30 50
Director: M. Des ESNARDS
Distributor of lubricants and oil products

Texas Instruments France
821, avenue Jack Kilby
B.P. 5
06271 VILLENEUVE-LOUBET Cedex
Tel: (16) 93 22 20 01
Fax: (16) 93 20 30 11
Chairman: M. Christian TORDO
Headquarters

Texas Instruments France
8, avenue Morane Saulnier
B.P. 67
78141 VELIZY
Tel: 30 70 10 01

Thermo Electric
26, rue Pasteur
94456 LIMEIL BREVANNES Cedex
Tel: 45 99 31 45
Fax: 45 99 25 96
Director: M. Jan JACOBS
Equipment for measuring temperatures

Thyssen Haniel
B.P. 10 439
95707 ROISSY CDG
Tel: 48 62 33 60
Fax: 48 62 46 11
Managing Director: M. Patrick BELLAPIANTA
Aircraft

Timken France
Avenue de l'Amazonie
Z.A. de Courtaboeuf
B.P. 107
91943 LES ULIS
Tel: 69 29 21 17
Fax: 69 29 21 23
Sales Manager:
M. Yves PEYRONNAUD
Tapered roller bearing manufacturer

Titeflex Europe
22, avenue Maurice Chevalier
Zone Industrielle
B.P. 73
77833-OZOIR-LA-FERRIERE Cedex
Tel: 64 40 06 08
Fax: 64 40 23 37
Director: Fabienne MAHIEU
Flexible hosing

Topflight France
21, avenue Europe
78400 CHATOU
Tel: 39 52 31 31
Fax: 39 52 35 21
Director: M. Pierre JOUANDON

Tracor France
1, allée de la Chartreuse
CE 1447
91020 EVRY Cedex
Tel: 60 91 42 49
Fax: 60 91 42 48
Manager: M. Yves DALLE
Computer peripherals

Trane
B.P. 6
88191 GOLBEY Cedex
Tel: (16) 29 31 75 00
Fax: (16) 29 31 12 29
General Director: M. Bruce ACHENBACH
Air conditioning equipments

Tremco
97, rue Mirabeau
94200 IVRY-SUR-SEINE
Tel: 49 60 57 22
Fax: 46 72 69 57
President: M. Joel MOREAU
Waterproofing products

Trinova
Z.I. La Vrillonnerie
B.P. 349
37173 CHAMBRAY-LES-TOURS Cedex
Tel: (16) 47 48 49 50
Fax: (16) 47 48 49 00
President: M. Alain BOUSSERT
Hydraulics

TRW Composants Moteurs Inc.
31, rue des Forges
67130 SCHIRMECK
Tel: (16) 88 49 60 60
Fax: (16) 88 97 14 55
Director: M. Christian CHILLES
Valves

TSI France Inc.
Parc Club Orsay Université
29, rue Jean Rostand
91893 ORSAY Cedex
Tel: 69 33 24 70
Director: M. KIRSCHSINK
Scientific instruments

Tuboscope Vetco France
Comble du Pré Plénard
59145 BERLAIMONT
Tel: (16) 27 67 62 39
Fax: (16) 27 67 28 75

UCAR
4, Place des Etats-Unis
Silic 214
94518 RUNGIS Cedex
Tel: 49 78 46 00
Fax: 46 86 52 62
Director: M. Maurice MARCELLIN
Graphite

Unicam France
98ter, Bd. Héloise
95100 ARGENTEUIL
Tel: 34 26 41 41
Fax: 39 47 85 66
President: M. Chris McINTYRE
Mass spectometry

Unilever France
157, Bd. Haussmann
75382 PARIS Cedex 08
Tel: 42 99 72 72
Fax: 42 99 73 33
Public Relations Director:
M. Max COPPOLANI
Foodstuffs, cosmetics, cleaning products

United Technologies Automotive Europe
72, rue du Colonel de Rochabruna
92380 GARCHES
Tel: 47 10 80 72
Fax: 47 01 24 68
President: M. Richard SLOAN
Electrical distribution system for cars

Univacier
24, avenue de l'Escouvrier
Parc Industriel #1
95205 SARCELLES Cedex
Tel: 39 92 40 00
Fax: 34 19 66 77
President: M. Guy LASSERE
Markets accessories for machine tools

UOP France
42, rue du Père Corentin
75014 PARIS
Tel: 45 41 60 03
Fax: 45 41 60 08
Director: M. Ken BLANE
Sells chemical and industrial products

Valenite Modco
B.P. 65
Z.I. Nord
42162 ANDREZIEUX- BOUTHEON Cedex
Tel: (16) 77 36 55 52
Fax: (16) 77 55 28 75
Plant Manager:
M. Alain PHILIPPE
Metallurgy

Valois
Le Prieuré
B.P. "G"
27110 LE NEUBOURG
Tel: (16) 32 24 84 84
Fax: (16) 32 35 29 14
Director: M. Pierre CHERU
Perfume industry

Varian
7, avenue des Tropiques
Z.I. de Courtaboeuf
91941 LES ULIS Cedex
Tel: 69 86 38 38
Fax: 69 28 23 08
Importer of scientific equipment

Veeco Instruments
Z.I. de la Gaudrée
11, rue Marie Poussepin
B.P. 42
91412 DOURDAN Cedex
Tel: 64 59 35 20
Fax: 64 59 72 22
Director: M. STEENBEKE
Measuring instruments

Veriphone
25, quai Panhard et Levassor
75644 PARIS Cedex 13
Tel: 45 85 44 77
Fax: 45 85 10 27
President: M. ROTTINGHUIS
Supply payment terminals

Videojet Cheshire
Parc Gutemberg
7, voie La Cardon
91126 PALAISEAU Cedex
Tel: 69 19 70 00
Fax: 69 32 01 45

Vishay Micromesures
98, Bd. Gabriel Péri
92240 MALAKOFF
Tel: 46 55 98 00
Fax: 42 53 67 94
Director: M. Jean-Luc LE GOER

Viskase
14, rue Riquet
75019 PARIS
Tel: 53 26 12 50
Fax: 53 26 12 60
Director: M. Craig BREESE
Director of Finance:
M. Jean-Luc TILLON
Commercial Manager France:
M. Jean-Charles MOHENG
Casings

W.L. Gore & Associés
4, rue Jean Mermoz
Z.I. St. Guénault
91031 EVRY Cedex
Tel: 60 79 60 79
Fax: 60 77 56 50
Director: M. Bernard GUEDON

Warner & Tourco
B.P. 95
49182 ST BARTHELEMY D'ANJOU Cedex
Tel: (16) 41 21 24 24
Fax: (16) 41 21 24 00
Manager M. Loic DU BESSET
Clutches, brakes

Waste Management
4, Rue d'Arsonval
95500 GONESSE
Tel: 39 85 00 10
Fax: 39 87 06 39
Manager: M. Stéphane RONTEIX
Recycling of industrial waste

Watlow France
16, rue Ampère
Z.I. Immeuble Somag
95307 CERGY-PONTOISE Cedex
Tel: 30 73 24 25
Fax: 30 73 28 75
Director: M. W. SCHAEFER
Heating elements

WCI-Ecoaudit
28, Bd. Kellermann
75013 PARIS
Tel: 45 81 30 40
Fax: 45 81 30 70
Director: M. Bernard WEIL
Engineering and science applied to the environment

Weatherford France S.A.
94, avenue Thimonnier
B.P. 119
64143 LONS Cedex
Tel: (16) 59 32 75 63
Fax: (16) 59 32 31 97
Contact: M. Claude JEUNOT
Provides services for the petroleum industry

Wemco Envirotech Pumpsystems France
19, rue du Colonel Moll
75017 PARIS
Tel: 45 74 97 00
Fax: 45 72 48 03
President: M. ALGARIN
Industrial pumps

Westinghouse Electrique France
3, Place Charles de Gaulle
B.P. 418
78055 ST-QUENTIN- EN- YVELINES Cedex
Tel: 30 57 05 05
Fax: 30 57 11 68
President: M. WAUTELET
French subsidiary

Whirlpool France
55, rue de Belfort
92400 COURBEVOIE
Tel: 47 89 43 25

Witco
20-22, rue de la Ville l'Evêque
75008 PARIS
Tel: 42 65 99 03
Fax: 42 65 67 61
President: M. Jean-Pierre CHARNAY
Chemicals for industry and agriculture

Worcester Controls France
Z.A. de Courtaboeuf
5, avenue de Scandinavie
B.P. 83
91943 LES ULIS Cedex
Tel: 69 18 87 30
Faucets and valves

Yves Rocher
3, allée de Grenelle
92444 ISSY-LES-MOULINEAUX
Tel: 41 08 55 00
Fax: 41 08 58 71
Vice-President: M. Daniel CAVIL
Beauty products

Zimmer
60, rue Gémeaux
94150 RUNGIS COMPLEXE
Tel: 41 80 71 71

Zodiac
58, Bd. Galliéni
92130 ISSY-LES-MOULINEAUX
Tel: 42 23 23 23

Abeille Assurances
52, rue de la Victoire
75009 PARIS
Tel: 42 80 75 75

Advantage Insurance Associates
57, rue du Fbg. Montmartre
75009 PARIS
Tel: 53 20 03 33
Fax: 44 63 00 97
Contact: Lauren PICKARD
English-speaking service-oriented firm specialized in health plans (see advertisement)

AGF
1, rue Louis Blanc
75496 PARIS Cedex 10
Tel: 40 03 40 00

AIG Europe
Tour American International
Cedex 46
92079 PARIS LA DEFENSE 2
Tel: 49 02 42 22
Fax: 47 73 71 42
President: M. Nicholas C. WALSH

Allianz Via Assurances
2-4, avenue du Général de Gaulle
94672 CHARENTON-LE-PONT
Cedex
Tel: 46 76 76 76
Fax: 46 76 76 13
Contact: Lucie WENGER
Damages insurance company (IARDT)

Anglo-French Underwriters
25, rue de Liège
75008 PARIS
Tel: 44 70 71 00
Fax: 42 93 47 42
Director: M. MARTINACHE

Athena Assurances
Immeuble PFA
Cedex 43
1, cours Michelet
92076 PARIS LA DEFENSE
Tel: 42 91 15 23
Fax: 42 91 12 20

Axa Assurances
La Grande Arche
Paroi Nord
92044 PARIS LA DEFENSE
Cedex 41
Tel: 49 01 16 00

Black Sea and Baltic General Insurance Co. Ltd
4, rue d'Argenson
75008 PARIS
Tel: 42 65 21 50
For insurance in Russia

British Continental and Overseas Agencies Assurances
9, rue de Clichy
75009 PARIS
Tel: 45 26 64 33
Fax: 40 16 03 39
Director: M. PAYNE

Cabinet Vasseur
79, route de la Reine
92100 BOULOGNE
Tel: 46 04 41 03
Fax: 46 03 11 26

Cerise Assurances
Sergine Frebourg
199-207, rue des Pyrénées
75020 PARIS
Tel: 47 97 64 80
Tel: 47 97 95 42
Contact: M. Reuben GILES
Anglo-American insurance broker in Paris

Chubb Insurance Company of Europe
16, avenue Matignon
75008 PARIS
Tel: 45 61 73 00
Fax: 45 61 98 51
Director: M. Keith DAVIES

Cigna International
14, rue Ballu
75009 PARIS
Tel: 44 53 63 63
Fax: 42 80 42 35

Commercial Union Association
125, rue du Président Wilson
92525 LEVALLOIS-PERRET
Tel: 49 68 90 00
Fax: 49 68 90 90
Director: M. DRAMARD

Continent
62, rue de Richelieu
75002 PARIS
Tel: 43 16 65 00

Continental Insurance Company
16, rue de Vienne
75008 PARIS
Tel: 40 08 09 04
Fax: 40 08 06 94

Contingency Insurance
48, rue de Châteaudun
75009 PARIS
Tel: 42 81 70 00
Fax: 42 81 71 75
Director: M. Bernard MILLEQUANT

Credit Insurance Association
35, rue Washington
75008 PARIS
Tel: 45 63 09 62
Fax: 53 75 06 76

Domestic & General Insurances Co. Ltd
14, rue Drouot
75009 PARIS
Tel: 44 83 80 30
Fax: 44 83 80 35

Eagle Star Vie S.A.
12, rue Torricelli
75017 PARIS
Tel: 44 09 44 09
Fax: 44 09 44 99
Director: M. Ghislain BEDUNEAU
Life insurance

European Credit Insurance and Collection Agency (ECICA)
67, rue de l'Assomption
75016 PARIS
Tel: 45 25 03 97
Fax: 45 24 59 44

Eclipse Combustion
6-8, avenue Salvador Allende
93804 EPINAY-SUR-SEINE Cedex
Tel: 48 21 39 83
Fax: 48 23 30 51
Manager: C. HAVELAAR
Industrial gas burners and mixed burners

Eurofil
3, rue Eugène et Armand Peugeot
92505 RUEIL-MALMAISON Cedex
Tel: 47 14 59 82
Fax: 47 14 59 32
President: M. Etienne SILHOL
Call for free guide, information service plus insurance for British residents in France

Europ Assistance
1, Promenade Bonnette
92633 GENNEVILLIERS Cedex
Tel: 41 85 85 85
Fax: 41 85 85 71
Assistance to persons and vehicles abroad

European Benefits Administrators
59, rue de Châteaudun
75009 PARIS
Tel: 42 81 97 00
Fax: 42 81 99 03
Director: M. Philip AUERBACH

F.A.C.
56, rue de Londres
75008 PARIS
Tel: 42 93 64 74
Fax: 42 93 44 93
Insurance specialist for foreigners

Factory Mutual International
Parc des Glaisins
B.P. 117
74941 ANNECY-LE-VIEUX Cedex
Tel: (16) 50 65 50 65
Fax: (16) 50 64 10 85
Contact: M. Michel VORONKOFF

Faugere & Jutheau
54, quai Michelet
92681 LEVALLOIS-PERRET
Tel: 41 34 50 00
Fax: 41 34 55 00
Manager: M. Hervé BLUMENTHAL

Gan Assurances
2, rue Pillet Will
75448 PARIS Cedex 09
Tel: 42 47 50 00
Tel: 42 47 77 99

General Accident and Life Insurance Corporation
84, rue Charles Michel
93206 ST DENIS Cedex
Tel: 49 33 12 00

GMF
4, rue Beaubourg
75004 PARIS
Tel: 47 26 75 75

Graham Miller France
26, rue Mogador
75009 PARIS
Tel: 42 80 37 81
Fax: 42 81 16 65
Director: M. Keith ALLEN

Groupama
24, rue de Charonne
75011 PARIS
Tel: 48 05 80 38
Fax: 43 57 84 23

Groupe Spinks
109, rue Victor Hugo
92532 LEVALLOIS-PERRET
Tel: 41 06 70 00
Fax: 41 06 70 90

Guardian France
20, rue Jacques Daguerre
92500 RUEIL-MALMAISON
Tel: 47 10 20 00
Fax: 47 10 20 10
Director: M. Robin G. MORLEY

Koa Fire Marine Insurance
90, avenue des Champs-Elysées
75008 PARIS
Tel: 45 61 01 08
Fax: 45 61 00 01

Lloyds of London
4, rue des Petits Pères
75002 PARIS
Tel: 42 60 43 43
Fax: 42 60 14 41

MAAF Assurances
10, Bd. Beaumarchais
75011 PARIS
Tel: 43 14 46 14
Fax: 43 14 46 00

Nieuw Rotterdam
18, rue de la Pépinière
75008 PARIS
Tel: 44 69 98 80
Fax: 44 69 98 89
Director: Mme Anne-Marie TOURMALIA

Nippon Insurance Company of Europe Ltd
21, rue des Pyramides
75001 PARIS
Tel: 42 96 84 58
Fax: 42 96 63 91

Norwich Union France
36, rue de Châteaudun
75009 PARIS
Tel: 40 23 40 23
Fax: 42 81 38 82
Commercial Director: M. DESIRY

Owa Insurance Services France
75, rue de Tocqueville
75017 PARIS
Tel: 44 15 57 70
Fax: 44 15 54 54

Paris-London Insurance
16, Place de la Madeleine
75008 PARIS
Tel: 47 42 33 92

Royal Insurance
47bis, avenue Hoche
75008 PARIS
Tel: 53 81 80 00

Sant and Co.
8, rue Halévy
75009 PARIS
Tel: 47 42 79 44
Fax: 42 66 95 05
Director: M. BEULLENS
International loss adjusters

Secco France S.A.
20, Bd. de Courcelles
75017 PARIS
Tel: 42 27 51 53
Fax: 43 80 14 10
Director: M. C.M. WILSON

Skandia International
4, rue Cambon
75001 PARIS
Tel: 42 61 51 45
Fax: 42 60 24 17
Reinsurance company

Société Générale de Courtage d'Assurances
7-9, rue de Belgrand
92309 LEVALLOIS
Tel: 47 56 60 60
Fax: 47 56 94 00
Chairman: M. Christian ROCHETEAU
Insurance brokers

Société Intercontinentale d'Assurances pour le Commerce et l'Industrie
46, rue Pierre Charron
75008 PARIS
Tel: 40 69 74 74
Fax: 47 20 47 18
Director: M. Daniel SACHS

Taylor-Sagassur
36, rue Laffitte
75009 PARIS
Tel: 44 79 04 04
Fax: 44 79 01 47
Contact: M. Philippe CONSOLI
Full range of short and long-term policies

Toplis et Harding
80, Bd. Haussmann
75008 PARIS
Tel: 43 87 40 16
Fax: 43 87 40 16
Director: M. OTTAWAY

Tyler and Co.
12, rue de la Paix
75002 PARIS
Tel: 42 61 63 31
Fax: 42 61 95 71
Director: M. B. ISITT

UAP Assurances
9, Place Vendôme
75001 PARIS
Tel: 42 86 71 71
Fax: 42 86 78 02

Vie Optimum S.A.
94, rue de Courcelles
75008 PARIS
Tel: 44 15 81 81
Fax: 47 54 04 98
Director: M. MERCIER

Winterthur
Tour Winterthur
Cedex 18
92085 PARIS LA DEFENSE
Tel: 49 03 87 87

Xaar Assurance
42, avenue Ste-Foy
92200 NEUILLY-SUR-SEINE
Tel: 46 43 88 00
Fax: 46 37 34 32

Yasuda Fire and Marine Insurance Co. Ltd
32, Bd. Haussmann
75009 PARIS
Tel: 48 24 15 14

13ème sans Frontières
16bis, rue E. et H. Rousselle
75013 PARIS
Tel: 45 89 52 00
French for foreigners

Accents of America
9, rue Casimir Delavigne
75006 PARIS
Tel: 44 07 05 05
Fax: 40 51 74 72
Director: Dr Sylvie SERIS

Accord
72, rue Rambuteau
75001 PARIS
Tel: 42 36 24 95
Fax: 42 21 17 91
French language and civilization courses

Accueil Franco-Nordique
7, rue de Surène
75008 PARIS
Tel: 42 66 53 02
Fax: 42 66 53 32
Contact: Carola STORBACKA
Specialized in French and Norwegian classes. Teachers specializing in FLE, preparation of DELF. Au-pair placement service

Alliance Française
101, Bd. Raspail
75006 PARIS
Tel: 45 44 38 28
Fax: 45 44 89 42
Contact: M. Marc BAILLY
French language studies at all levels

American Dream Center
163, rue de Charenton
75011 PARIS
Tel: 43 42 26 00
French & English classes, summer courses

American Language Institute
34, avenue de New York
75016 PARIS
Tel: 40 62 06 00
Fax: 47 20 45 64

American Lingo
4bis, avenue du Pavillon Sully
78230 LE PECQ
Tel: 39 73 00 88
Fax: 39 73 52 02
Contact: Barbara HANO
English business training and testing

An American in Paris
25, Bd. de Sébastopol
75001 PARIS
Tel: 40 26 22 90

Arc Langues System
38, quai Pelletan
92300 LEVALLOIS-PERRET
Tel: 47 39 58 29
Fax: 47 39 22 29
Director: M. Michel GUILLEMAT

Aspect
53, rue du Fbg. Poissonnière
75009 PARIS
Tel: 48 00 06 00
Fax: 48 00 05 94
Director: Mme BARTET

Bastille-Langues
5, rue Jean Beausire
75004 PARIS
Tel: 44 78 00 77
Fax: 44 78 07 42
French only

Berlitz France S.A.
15, rue Louis-le-Grand
75002 PARIS
Tel: 44 94 50 20
Fax: 44 94 50 22
Director: M. Patrick MOREL

British European Center
5, rue Richepanse
75008 PARIS
Tel: 42 60 35 57
Fax: 42 60 36 55
Director: Mme Elisabeth GUERRBAZ

British Institute in Paris
11, rue de Constantine
75007 PARIS
Tel: 45 55 71 99
Fax: 45 50 31 55
Director: M. Christophe CAMPOS
University courses in French, English and Translation

Business Talk France
134, Bd. Haussmann
75008 PARIS
Tel: 49 53 91 83
Fax: 49 53 91 83
High quality language training

Center for International Education
7, rue Berryer
75008 PARIS
Tel: 39 58 58 50
Fax: 39 58 58 50
Contact: G. Stephen RYER
Linguistic trips to the USA

Centre Culturel International
5, rue de Garches
92210 ST-CLOUD
Tel: 46 02 64 33
Tel: 47 71 61 03
Fax: 47 71 91 05
Contact: Mme BICKERT
French language courses. University qualified professors, private lessons à la carte. *Small groups - 3 to 6 hours a week*

Centre d'Echanges Internationaux
1, rue Gozlin
75006 PARIS
Tel: 45 49 26 25
Fax: 45 49 01 70
Director: M. DUFRENNE

Centre de Langue et Culture Italienne
4, rue des Prêtres St. Séverin
75005 PARIS
Tel: 46 34 27 00
Fax: 43 54 20 85
Italian classes, all levels, summer courses in Italy, cultural events

Centre International Linguistique Bouchereau
190, Bd. Haussmann
75008 PARIS
Tel: 42 56 14 96
Fax: 42 56 14 92
Director: Marie-Thérèse LOGEREAU
Language schools based in France, Canada and the USA

Cercle Performance
87, rue de Taitbout
75009 PARIS
Tel: 53 20 04 10
Fax: 53 20 04 12
French tuition

Clé International
27, rue de la Glacière
75013 PARIS
Tel: 45 87 44 00
Fax: 45 87 23 21

Cours de Civilisation Française de la Sorbonne
47, rue des Ecoles
75005 PARIS
Tel: 40 46 22 11
Director: M. BRUMEL

CPFP
20-22, rue Richer
75009 PARIS
Tel: 45 23 35 68
French courses for foreigners (free use of computer-assisted workshop)

DCR International
34-38, rue Camille Pelletan
92300 LEVALLOIS-PERRET
Tel: 47 39 58 29
Fax: 47 39 22 29
Director: M. GUILLEMAT

De Vraies Ecoles de Langues
36, rue de Chezy
92200 NEUILLY
Tel: 46 37 35 88
Fax: 47 47 84 61
Director: Mme N. HAIK
Language training

Ecola Language Express
111, avenue Victor Hugo
75016 PARIS
Tel: 45 53 76 97

Ecole de Langues de Neuilly
114, avenue Charles de Gaulle
92200 NEUILLY-SUR-SEINE
Tel: 46 37 56 41
Fax: 46 37 33 61
Director: G. HAIK
French and all major languages, private or group lessons, Resource Center

Ecole des 3 Ponts
Château de Matel
42300 ROANNE
Tel: (16) 77 71 53 00
Fax: (16) 77 70 80 01
Director: M. René DOREL
Study French language and cuisine in a superb château near Burgundy (see advertisement)

Ecole Nickerson
26, rue de la Tremoille
75008 PARIS
Tel: 47 23 36 03
Fax: 40 70 12 71
Director: Mme CHILTON

EF Institute
3, rue de Bassano
75016 PARIS
Tel: 42 96 57 46
Fax: 47 20 18 80
Minitel: 3616 EF
Director: M. Christophe BLONDEL
Intensive language courses for professionals

Elysées Business Langues
66, avenue des Champs-Elysées
Escalier C - 7ème étage
75008 PARIS
Tel: 46 22 54 83
Fax: 46 22 54 11
Director: Mme Monique ORSAT
Language courses for executives

English Communication International
84, rue St. Martin
75002 PARIS
Tel: 42 77 29 29
Fax: 42 77 41 41
Contact: Patricia ROGERS
English language training

English Home Holidays
30, rue Notre Dame des Victoires
75002 PARIS
Tel: 42 61 54 20
Fax: 42 61 03 65

Eurocentres
13, passage Dauphine
75006 PARIS
Tel: 43 25 81 40
Fax: 46 34 65 34
Public Relations: Mme Elisabeth ALBRECHT
French courses for adults in Paris, Amboise and La Rochelle. Cultural and leisure activities, family and hotel accommodation

Europa
1, Place d'Iéna
75116 PARIS
Tel: 47 23 57 22
Fax: 47 23 04 73
Organizes stays in American families

Executive Language Services
25, Bd. de Sébastopol
75001 PARIS
Tel: 42 36 32 32
Fax: 42 36 62 55
Director: Mme Dorothy POLLEY
English, French, German, Spanish and Russian courses as well as study abroad programs for adults in the USA, Canada, Russia, Europe, Australia, etc.

Executive Link
16, rue Christophe Colomb
75008 PARIS
Tel: 44 43 88 37
Fax: 44 43 88 10
Educational Advisor:
M. Anthony SHARP
Language and cross-cultural training for the corporate world

Expolangues
OIP
62, rue Miromesnil
75008 PARIS
Tel: 49 53 27 60
Fax: 49 53 27 88

Formalangues
106, Bd. Haussmann
75008 PARIS
Tel: 45 22 99 12
Fax: 45 22 08 25
Director: M. Philippe MAREC

Formavision Business and Educational Video
7, rue Cardinal Mercier
75009 PARIS
Tel: 45 26 87 00
Fax: 42 81 02 29
E-mail: 100600.2313 @ compuserve.com.
Director: M. DUNCAN-SMITH

Foyer Le Pont
86, rue de Gergovie
750014 PARIS
Tel: 45 42 51 21
Limited to six-month courses. Although financed by the German Government, open to other nationals

France Langue
2, rue de Sfax
75116 PARIS
Tel: 45 00 40 15
Fax: 45 00 53 41
Director: M. Bertrand PIOT
French lessons for foreigners

Groupe IPESUP
16, rue du Cloître Notre Dame
75004 PARIS
Tel: 48 04 81 06
Fax: 48 04 37 03
Intensive TOEFL and GMAT training

I.E.LP.
11, rue de Turbigo
75001 PARIS
Tel: 42 33 35 84
Fax: 42 21 04 66

Idefle
66, rue René Boulanger
75010 PARIS
Tel: 42 03 00 25
French classes for foreigners

IGS University
12, rue Alexandre Parodi
75010 PARIS
Tel: 40 03 15 04
Fax: 40 03 15 05
Director: M. DILLON
Undergraduate and graduate education

Inca Languages
17, rue de Turbigo
75002 PARIS
Tel: 40 26 35 32
Fax: 40 26 35 03

Inlingua Rive Gauche
109, rue de l'Université
75007 PARIS
Tel: 45 51 46 60

Institut Catholique de Paris
12, rue Cassette
75006 PARIS
Tel: 44 39 52 68
Fax: 44 39 52 09
Director: M. Jean-René ROUOUETTE
French language and civilisation courses

Institut de Langue Française
15, rue Arsène Houssaye
75008 PARIS
Tel: 42 27 14 77
Fax: 44 09 02 33
Director: M. Alain BOIS
English, French and German courses

Institut Parisien de Langue et de Civilisation Françaises
87, Bd. de Grenelle
75015 PARIS
Tel: 40 56 09 53
Fax: 43 06 46 30
Contact: Mme BLOSTIN
French courses for foreigners (see advertisement)

Institut Parisien de Langue et de Civilisation Françaises
2, rue Ducastel
78100 ST-GERMAIN-EN-LAYE
Tel: 39 73 27 55
Fax: 43 06 46 30
Contact: Mme BLOSTIN
French courses for foreigners

Institute of Applied Languages
41, rue de Turenne
75003 PARIS
Tel: 44 59 25 10
Fax: 44 59 25 15
Director: Tanya MENDOSA
Language training center of the Franco-British Chamber of Commerce

La Ferme
La Petite Eguille
17600 SAUJON
Tel: (16) 46 22 84 31
Fax: (16) 46 22 91 38
Residential language school on the Atlantic coast

Language & Communications Center
11, Place du Beffroi
95260 BEAUMONT-SUR-OISE
Tel: 34 70 38 38
Director: M. JACOBS

Language of International Insurance Institute
3, rue de l'Arrivée
B.P. 74
75749 PARIS Cedex 17
Tel: 43 21 20 23
Fax: 43 35 21 20

Language Studies International
350, rue St. Honoré
75001 PARIS
Tel: 42 60 53 70
Fax: 42 61 41 36
Director: Mme BOLLOTTE

Languages Plus Services
Le Luzard II
Bd. Salvador Allende
77186 NOISIEL
Tel: 60 17 60 14
Fax: 60 05 82 31
Director: M. William TOYNBEE
Language training

Langue et Culture Françaises
8, rue de Lota
75116 PARIS
Tel: 43 53 60 00 ext 8827
Intensive French courses (accommodation upon request)

Langue Onze
15, rue Gambey
75011 PARIS
Tel: 43 38 22 87
Director: Mme CLAUDIA
Intensive French tuition

Langues Plus
15, rue d'Hauteville
75010 PARIS
Tel: 48 00 06 93
Fax: 42 46 92 62
French courses

Lingua Club/Euro-Irish Summer School
7bis, rue Decrès
75014 PARIS
Tel: 45 39 28 28
Fax: 45 39 15 38
Director: Mrs Nadine BARBER
Private English tuition in Paris, Dublin and London

Loisirs Culturels à l'Etranger
89, avenue de Villiers
75017 PARIS
Tel: 42 67 75 75
Fax: 42 67 30 95
Language immersion in American families for 13-19 year-olds

MacDougall - English Language Study Group
8, rue Casimir Delavigne
75006 PARIS
Tel: 46 33 59 14
Fax: 40 46 81 39
Contact: M. John MACDOUGALL

Nanterre English Language Center
38, rue Salvador Allende
92000 NANTERRE
Tel: 41 37 06 89

New Directions for Teaching and Learning
21, rue Manin
75019 PARIS
Tel: 42 01 08 97
Director: Beatrice SOSS
English language classes - other languages on request

Oxford Intensive School of English
21, rue Théophile Renaud
75015 PARIS
Tel: 44 19 66 66
Fax: 44 19 66 80
Director: M. JINS

Paris Ecole des Roches Langues
8, rue Spinoza
75011 PARIS
Tel: 47 00 99 98
Fax: 43 57 14 46
French tuition

Paris Langues
FIAP
30, rue Cabanis
75014 PARIS
Tel: 45 65 05 28
Fax: 45 81 26 28
Offers a special "au pair" program

Patrick McCann
62, avenue de Wagram
75017 PARIS
Tel: 47 63 09 21
Fax: 47 63 09 18
Modern language training

Promolangue International
8, rue Blanche
75009 PARIS
Tel: 42 85 19 45
French and English courses

Quai d'Orsay Language Center
67, quai d'Orsay
75007 PARIS
Tel: 45 55 78 23
Fax: 45 51 87 14
Director: Barbara CURTIN
Language and intercultural training

Rapid English
30, rue St. Lazare
75009 PARIS
Tel: 42 80 64 85
Fax: 45 26 71 89

RHF
152bis, avenue Gabriel Péri
93400 ST-OUEN
Tel: 49 18 55 55
Fax: 40 12 02 84
Contact: Aline REILLY
English and French courses

Richard Organisation
O.S.F.B.
7, rue de l'Eperon
75006 PARIS
Tel: 43 29 76 31
Fax: 43 29 81 28
Director: M. LE CLERC

The American University of Paris
34, avenue de New York
75116 PARIS
Tel: 47 20 44 99
Fax: 47 53 88 03
Dean: Susan R. KINSEY
Preparation courses: TOEFL, GMAT, GRE, American language courses

The Open University
22, Place Georges Pompidou
Boîte 42
92300 LEVALLOIS-PERRET
Tel: 47 58 55 14
Fax: 47 58 55 25
Contact: Rosemary PEARSON
Britain's largest distance-teaching university

Transfer
20, rue Godot de Moroy
75009 PARIS
Tel: 42 66 14 11
Fax: 42 66 31 89

Télélangue Systèmes
Centre STS
6, avenue des Andes
Z.A. de Courtaboeuf
91952 LES ULIS
Tel: 64 46 05 77
Fax: 69 28 06 15
Contact: M. Joseph SCHOCK

Université de Paris Sorbonne
47, rue des Ecoles
75005 PARIS
Tel: 40 46 22 11
Fax: 40 46 32 29
French language and civilization courses (French baccalauréat level required)

USA Language Services
75, rue Claude Decaen
75012 PARIS
Tel: 43 47 30 42
Director: Shams SYED
Teaching American English and civilization

Virginia Language Center
12, rue Pavée
75004 PARIS
Tel: 42 72 15 95
Fax: 42 78 53 09
E-mail: phm@ellis.fdn.org,internet
Director: M. MASSART
Language school, negotiation seminars

Wall Street Institute
21, avenue Victor Hugo
75016 PARIS
Tel: 45 00 59 60
Fax: 45 01 22 64
Director: M. Peter WRIGHT

Miscellaneous
Divers

Assimil
11, rue des Pyramides
75001 PARIS
Tel: 45 76 87 37
Tel: 42 60 40 66 (store)
Fax: 40 20 02 17
Director of Communication:
Mme M. VANDENHENDE
Foreign language methods: books, tapes, software, self-taught French method

BBC Omnivox
8, rue de Berri
75008 PARIS
Tel: 45 62 44 24
Fax: 42 56 39 85

Bibliothèque Publique d'Information
Centre Georges Pompidou
19, rue Beaubourg
75004 PARIS
Tel: 44 78 44 45
Tel: 44 78 45 93
Free language laboratory

Chambre de Commerce et d'Industrie de Paris (C.C.I.P.)
2, rue Viarmes
75001 PARIS
Tel: 45 08 35 00
Language courses

Chambre de Commerce et d'Industrie de Paris (C.C.I.P.)
67, Bd. de Courcelles
75008 PARIS
Tel: 42 27 26 44
Language courses

Chambre de Commerce et d'Industrie de Paris (C.C.I.P.)
27, avenue de Friedland
75382 PARIS Cedex 8
Tel: 42 89 70 00
Fax: 42 89 78 68
Language courses

Fondation des Etats-Unis
Cité Universitaire
15, Bd. Jourdan
75690 PARIS
Admin: 45.89.35.77
Studies: 45.89.35.79
Director: M. Terence MURPHY
Residence and cultural center

I.L.C.F. Télélangue Systèmes
9, rue Thomas Ruphy
74000 ANNECY
Tel: (16) 50 66 25 84
Director: Mme Patricia NOBLE

Allen & Overy
1, avenue Franklin Roosevelt
75008 PARIS
Tel: 49 53 06 37
Fax: 49 53 91 52
Senior Partner:
M. David ST JOHN SUTTON

Archibald Andersen
Association d'Avocats
Tour Gan
Cedex 13
92082 PARIS LA DEFENSE 2
Tel: 42 91 07 00
Fax: 42 91 08 00
Contacts: MM. Thomas JAHN
& Patrick BIGNON

Baker & McKenzie
32, avenue Kléber
75116 PARIS
Tel: 44 17 53 00
Fax: 44 17 45 75
Senior Partner: Christine LAGARDE

Barker-Davies
1, rue Lincoln
75008 PARIS
Tel: 45 62 10 61
Fax: 45 63 34 77
Senior Partner: M. John Clive
BARKER-DAVIES

Berlioz & Co.
68, Bd. de Courcelles
75017 PARIS
Tel: 44 01 44 01
Fax: 42 67 04 43
Senior Partner: M. Georges BERLIOZ

Bureau Francis Lefebvre
3, Villa Emile Bergerat
92522 NEUILLY-SUR-SEINE
Tel: 47 38 55 00
Fax: 47 38 55 55
Contact: M. Robert BACONNIER
Legal advisers

Cabinet Benoît
16, rue Etienne Marcel
75002 PARIS
Tel: 42 33 49 96
Fax: 42 33 49 97
Senior Partner: Me Marc-Luc BENOIT

Cabinet Boquet
41, avenue Bosquet
75007 PARIS
Tel: 47 05 48 64
Fax: 47 05 17 74
Represents Louisiana businesses in France

Cabinet Catherine Kessedjian
72, Bd. St. Germain
75005 PARIS
Tel: 40 51 82 24
Fax: 44 07 20 51
Contact: Catherine KESSEDJIAN

Cabinet Lette et Associés
19, rue François Ier
75008 PARIS
Tel: 47 23 62 03

Cabinet Maître Dussans
1bis, avenue Foch
75016 PARIS
Tel: 45 00 46 77
Fax: 45 00 83 86

Cabinet Philippe Bouchet
1bis, Place de l'Alma
75116 PARIS
Tel: 47 23 73 70
Fax: 40 70 90 54

Cahill Gordon & Reindel
19, rue François Ier
75008 PARIS
Tel: 47 20 10 50
Fax: 47 23 06 38
Senior Partner: Me Freddy DRESSEN

Chaintrier Caillard & Associés
5, avenue George V
75008 PARIS
Tel: 47 23 00 09
Fax: 47 23 68 79
Senior Partner: Me Philippe
CHARHON

Cleary, Gottlieb,
Steen & Hamilton
41, avenue de Friedland
75008 PARIS
Tel: 40 74 68 00
Fax: 45 63 35 09

Clifford Chance
112, avenue Kléber
B.P. 163 Trocadéro
75770 PARIS Cedex 16
Tel: 44 05 52 52
Fax: 44 05 52 00
Contact: M. Brian CORDERY

Coudert Frères
52, avenue des Champs-Elysées
75008 PARIS
Tel: 43 59 01 60
Fax: 43 59 66 55
Senior Partner: M. Jacques BUHART

Curtis Mallet-Prévost Colt & Mosle
8, avenue Victor Hugo
75116 PARIS
Tel: 45 00 99 68
Fax: 45 00 84 06
Resident Partner: M. Peter WOLRICH

Daniel Laprès
3, rue de l'Arrivée
75015 PARIS
Tel: 45 38 67 07
Fax: 45 38 68 96

Davidson, Yann et Muriel
51, rue Vouille
75015 PARIS
Tel: 40 43 04 23
Fax: 40 43 04 60
Family law

Davis Polk & Wardwell
4, Place de la Concorde
75008 PARIS
Tel: 40 17 36 00
Fax: 42 65 22 34

Debevoise & Plimpton
21, avenue George V
75008 PARIS
Tel: 40 73 12 12
Fax: 47 20 50 82

Deprez, Degroux, Brugère, De Pingon
83, Bd. Haussmann
75008 PARIS
Tel: 42 65 70 81
Fax: 40 17 07 58
Partner: Me Michel McGUINTY

Donovan Leisure Newton & Irvine
130, rue du Fbg St. Honoré
75008 PARIS
Tel: 42 25 47 10
Fax: 42 56 08 06
Senoir Partner: Me. René DE MONSEIGNAT

Frere Cholmeley
42, avenue du Président Wilson
75116 PARIS
Tel: 44 34 71 00
Fax: 44 34 71 11
Senior Partner: M. Richard MEESE

Fried, Frank, Harris, Shriver & Jacobson
7, rue Royale
75008 PARIS
Tel: 40 17 04 04
Fax: 40 17 08 30

Goodman Freeman Phillips & Vineberg
83, Bd. Haussmann
75008 PARIS
Tel: 47 42 51 08
Canadian solicitors, commercial and industrial law

HSD Juridique et Fiscal
Tour Manhattan
6, Place de l'Iris
Cedex 21
92095 PARIS LA DEFENSE 2
Tel: 46 93 60 00
Fax: 47 67 01 06

Hughes Hubbard & Reed
47, avenue Georges Mandel
75116 PARIS
Tel: 44 05 80 00
Fax: 45 53 15 04
Managing Partner: M. Axel BAUM

J.P. Karsenty & Associates
24, Place du Général Catroux
75017 PARIS
Tel: 47 63 74 75
Fax: 46 22 33 27

Jean-Jacques Neuer
26, avenue Kléber
75116 PARIS
Tel: 45 01 82 13
Fax: 45 00 52 75

Joan Squires-Lind Law Offices
6, rue du Foin
75003 PARIS
Tel: 44 59 82 57
Fax: 44 59 82 69

John C. Fredenberger
109, avenue Henri Martin
75116 PARIS
Tel: 45 04 10 10
Fax: 45 04 49 67

Jones Day Reavis & Pogue
62, rue du Fbg. St. Honoré
75008 PARIS
Tel: 49 24 09 09
Fax: 49 24 04 71
Senior Partner: M. John CRAWFORD

Kimbrough & Associés
72, Bd. St. Germain
75005 PARIS
Tel: 43 25 15 05
Fax: 43 29 98 38
Senior Partner: M. Philip R. KIMBROUGH

KPMG Fidal Peat International
47, rue de Villiers
92200 NEUILLY-SUR-SEINE
Tel: 46 39 44 44
Fax: 47 59 71 38
Tax and legal consultants

Law Offices of Jacob & Polier
4, rue de Marignan
75008 PARIS
Tel: 47 23 41 51
Fax: 47 23 37 93

Levine & Okoshken
51, avenue Montaigne
75008 PARIS
Tel: 44 13 69 50
Fax: 45 63 24 96
Partner: M. Samuel OKOSHKEN
Income tax, wills and estate planning, corporate law, employment agreements, setting-up businesses

Mandel, Ngo et Associés
45, avenue Montaigne
75008 PARIS
Tel: 47 20 92 92
Fax: 47 23 53 21
Resident Partner: Me Martine-Claire BOURRY D'ANTIN

Maître Christiane Feral-Schuhl
50, avenue Victor Hugo
75016 PARIS
Tel: 44 17 46 90
Fax: 44 17 97 31

Meade & Nabias
85, rue de Courcelles
75017 PARIS
Tel: 42 67 14 89
Fax: 42 67 06 08
Director: M. Richard C. MEADE
Attorneys at law

Mitchell-Heggs & Associates
205, Bd. St. Germain
75007 PARIS
Tel: 44 39 29 19
Fax: 42 22 15 07

Moquet Borde Dieux Geens & Associés
30, avenue de Messine
75008 PARIS
Tel: 42 99 04 50
Fax: 46 63 91 49
Partner: Dominique BORDE, Esq.

Mudge Rose Guthrie Alexander & Ferdon
12, rue de la Paix
75002 PARIS
Tel: 42 61 57 71
Fax: 42 61 79 21

Osler Renault
4, rue Bayard
75008 PARIS
Tel: 42 89 00 54
Fax: 42 89 51 60
Partner: Me Serge GRAVEL

Patricia Chance-Duzant
Attorney-at-Law
6, avenue Théophile Gautier
75016 PARIS
Tel: 42 88 08 22
Fax: 45 20 12 67
General French and international law

Paul, Weiss, Rikfind, Wharton & Garrison
199, Bd. St. Germain
75007 PARIS
Tel: 45 49 33 85
Fax: 42 22 64 38
Resident Partner: M. Dominique FARGUE

Rogers & Wells
47, avenue Hoche
75008 PARIS
Tel: 44 09 46 00
Fax: 42 67 50 81
Fax: 44 09 46 01

Rosman Leonard Law Offices
40bis, rue Boissière
75116 PARIS
Tel: 47 55 44 73

Sagot & Maintrieu
9, rue d'Anjou
75008 PARIS
Tel: 42 66 48 20
Fax: 42 68 02 50
Senior Partners: M. Jacques SAGOT
& Mme Valérie MAINTRIEU

Sandra de Faultrier-Travers
51, rue de la Tour
75116 PARIS
Tel: 45 04 51 22
Fax: 45 04 51 41
Specializes in publishing

SCP Barsi, Doumith, Pavie
186, avenue Victor Hugo
75116 PARIS
Tel: 45 03 16 26
Fax: 45 03 07 86
Resident Partner: Me. Philippe PAVIE

SCP Frenot-Roquet
52, avenue Victor HUGO
75016 PARIS
Tel: 44 17 41 50
Fax: 44 17 41 60
Business law

Serra Michaud & Associés
2, rue de la Baume
75008 PARIS
Tel: 44 21 97 97
Fax: 42 89 57 90
Contact: M. James LEAVY
French and international law firm

Shearman & Sterling
12, rue d'Astorg
75008 PARIS
Tel: 44 71 17 17
Fax: 44 71 01 01

Slaughter and May
112, avenue Kléber
75116 PARIS
Tel: 44 05 60 00
Fax: 44 05 60 60
Senior Partner: M. Peter KETT
Solicitors and Avocats à la Cour

Société Juridique Internationale
39, rue François Ier
75008 PARIS
Tel: 40 73 82 00
Fax: 40 73 82 10
Resident Partner: Me Robert COUZIN

Stanley Chaney
29, avenue Hoche
75008 PARIS
Tel: 42 89 17 43
Fax: 45 63 70 73

Sullivan & Cromwell
8, Place Vendôme
75001 PARIS
Tel: 44 50 60 00
Fax: 44 50 60 60

Van Hagen
6, avenue George V
75008 PARIS
Tel: 47 20 00 64
Fax: 47 20 25 09
Senior Partner:
M. Anthony VAN HAGEN

White & Case
11, Bd. de la Madeleine
75001 PARIS
Tel: 42 60 34 05
Fax: 42 60 82 46
Senior Partner: M. John RIGGS, Jr.

Willkie Farr & Gallagher
6, avenue Vélasquez
75008 PARIS
Tel: 44 35 44 35
Fax: 42 89 87 01
Resident Partner: M. Jay F. LEARY

Withers
15, rue de Marignan
75008 PARIS
Tel: 49 53 06 66
Fax: 49 53 05 76
Senior Partner: M. Jonathan
EASTWOOD
English solicitors and French avocats

English-Language Libraries
Bibliothèques de Langue Anglaise

American Library in Paris
10, rue du Général Camou
75007 PARIS
Tel: 45 51 46 82
Fax: 45 50 25 83
Director: M. Robert GRATTAN
English-language lending library: books and periodicals, photocopy facilities, computerized periodicals research center. The largest collection of English language books in Paris

American University of Paris Library
9bis, rue Montessuy
75007 PARIS
Tel: 45 56 92 89

Benjamin Franklin Documentation Center
U.S. Consulate
2, rue St. Florentin
75042 PARIS Cedex 08
Tel: 42 96 33 10
9000 volumes in English, by appointment only

British Council Library
9-11, rue de Constantine
75007 PARIS
Tel: 49 55 73 00
Fax: 47 05 77 02
Head Librarian: Frances SALINIE
Lending and reference library, teaching resources section, English videos in VO

English Language Library for the Blind
35, rue Lemercier
75017 PARIS
Tel: 42 93 47 57
Director: Penelope TROUPE
Books on tape in English

Other Libraries
Autres Bibliothèques

Bibliothèque André Malraux
78, Bd. Raspail
75006 PARIS
Tel: 45 44 53 85
Specialized in the cinema

Bibliothèque Beaugrenelle
36-40, rue Emeriau
75015 PARIS
Tel: 45 77 63 40
Language teaching methods

Bibliothèque de Géographie
Université Paris I
Panthéon-Sorbonne
191, rue St. Jacques
75005 PARIS
Tel: 44 32 14 63

Bibliothèque de l'Opéra
Place Charles Garnier
75009 PARIS
Tel: 47 42 07 02
Fax: 42 65 10 16
Opera library

Bibliothèque des Arts
3, Place de l'Odéon
75006 PARIS
Tel: 46 33 18 18
Fax: 40 46 95 56

Bibliothèque Drouot
11, rue Drouot
75009 PARIS
Tel: 42 46 97 78
Art, auction sales

Bibliothèque du Louvre
Mairie Ier
4, Place du Louvre
75001 PARIS
Tel: 44 50 76 56

Bibliothèque Nationale (B.N.)
58, rue de Richelieu
75002 PARIS
Tel: 47 03 81 26
One of the world's most important and complete collections of books, periodicals, manuscripts and archives

Bibliothèque Marguerite Durand
79, rue Nationale
75013 PARIS
Tel: 45 70 80 30
Librarian: Mme DIZIER
Feminist library

Bibliothèque Picpus
70, rue de Picpus
75012 PARIS
Tel: 43 45 87 12
Specialized in music

Bibliothèque Publique d'Information
Centre Georges Pompidou
19, rue Beaubourg
75197 PARIS Cedex 04
Tel: 44 78 12 33
Minitel: 3615 BPI
Director: Mme BLANC-MONTMAYEUR
Excellent reference library, free access to all

Bibliothèque Ste-Geneviève
10, Place du Panthéon
75005 PARIS
Tel: 44 41 97 97
Fax: 44 41 97 96
Public interuniversity and encyclopaedic library

Bibliothèques et Discothèques de la Ville de Paris
31, rue des Francs-Bourgeois
75004 PARIS
Tel: 42 76 67 75
Main branch of the City of Paris' 55 municipal public libraries

Bibliothèque Trocadéro
6, rue du Commandant Schloesing
75016 PARIS
Tel: 47 04 70 85
Travel and tourism, teaching methods

Centre de Documentation
Chambre de Commerce et d'Industrie de Paris
16, rue Châteaubriand
75008 PARIS
Tel: 42 89 72 72
Reference library of the Chamber of Commerce and Industry

Cité Internationale Universitaire de Paris - Library
19, Bd. Jourdan
75014 PARIS
Tel: 44 16 65 20
Fax: 44 16 64 11

La Documentation Française
29, quai Voltaire
75007 PARIS
Tel: 40 15 70 00
Fax: 40 15 72 30

RL Documentation
8, rue du Trésor
75004 PARIS
Tel: 42 71 08 78
Fax: 53 81 60 21
Contact: Rebecca LEVIN
Audiovisual documentation

Université de la Sorbonne Nouvelle
Paris III
13, rue Santeuil
75005 PARIS
Tel: 45 87 40 00

Vidéothèque de Paris
Forum des Halles
2, Grande Galerie
75001 PARIS
Tel: 44 76 62 00
Video library with 4000+ films on Paris. Cinema with 4 films daily

36 28 00 61
American Embassy: list of US firms wishing to export to France

36 29 00 54
Automatic translation, specialized lexicons...

36 29 00 57 DATAPRESSE
Directory of journalists

36 68 09 66 ANGLOPHONE
Interactive information and contact service in English

3611 FUAJ
Information on French youth hostels

3614 G7
Taxi reservation service

3614 A LA CARTE
Everything on the USA: maps of states and cities, video guides, national parks...

3614 AFSUND
Tourist information provided by the South African Embassy

3614 AVIS
Rental of cars and professional vehicles

3614 BIBOP
Presents the portable city phone Bi-Bop

3614 DOC USA
Benjamin Franklin Documentation Center, US Embassy

3614 ED
French telephone directory (in English)

3614 EMS
Chronopost - fast mail service

3614 GMI
A choice of apartments and houses to rent in the Paris region

3614 IBMCATALOG
IBM catalog: price list, possibility to order goods directly

3614 MAIF
Information on MAIF insurance

3614 NATURISM
Information on "naturism" and naturist holiday centres (nudist colonies)

3614 NZKIWI
Economic and tourist information from the New Zealand Embassy

3614 ROUTE
Traffic conditions and highway information

3614 TELIB
Order books by Minitel

3615 50MILLIONS
Information and advice to consumers (practical tips, results of comparative surveys, legal and financial help)

3615 ABCDIVORCE
Information and advice about divorce in France

3615 ABCDOC
Directory of research departments and reference libraries in France

3615 ACTIONCV
Information on how to find a job: offers and requests, free classified ads

3615 ADEME
Agency for environmental protection

3615 AF
Air France information

3615 AFNOR
French and European standards

3615 AFP
News bulletins dispatched by Agence France Presse

3615 AIRFRANCE
Air France information

3615 AIRTEL
National and international airline schedules and fares

3615 ALOUER
Ads for renting and letting property in and around Paris (flats, houses, office premises)

3615 AMEX
American Express services and products

3615 AMNESTY

3615 APNEWS
World news bulletins by Associated Press

3615 APPLE
Service of Apple Company France: news, catalogs, ads, downloading

3615 ARGUS
Guide to secondhand car prices, updated weekly

3615 ARTE
Presentation of the Franco-German television channel Arte

3615 ARTS
One year of detailed listings of cultural events all over France

3615 ASTRO
This service tells you your Zodiac sign, your Chinese sign and your horoscope of the day or of the year

3615 ATTICA
Catalog of teaching manuals available from the Attica bookstore

3615 AUTO69
Classified ads for secondhand cars

3615 BASELINE
Cinematographic databank in English

3615 BASKETUSA
Information about US basketball: games, results (NBA, NCAA)

3615 BBC
British and international news in English by the BBC

3615 BBCVIDEO
Presents video English teaching methods Follow Me *and* Muzzi

3615 BBNEWS
Information by the French Baseball Federation

3615 BEBECAST
Casting opportunities for children

3615 BHV
Bargains, job offers, services of the Bazar de l'Hôtel de Ville

3615 BISONFUTE
Weather reports, traffic conditions

3615 BOOKSHOP
List of English books and tapes available on Minitel

3615 BR
British Rail

3615 BRITISH
Tourist information about Great Britain

3615 BUITONI
Information about Buitoni food products, recipes, games

3615 CADREMPLOI
Job listings for executive positions

3615 CANADA
Information released by the Canadian Embassy: tourism, formalities, travel, immigration

3615 CAP 2
Municipal libraries in Paris

3615 CAPITAL
One year of detailed listings of cultural events in Paris

3615 CBNEWS
Service offered by the advertising and communication weekly CB News

3615 CDROM
CD-Rom directory, publishers' catalog

3615 CEE
Legal and administrative facts concerning the European Economic Community

3615 CENTURY21
Century 21 real estate agency network in France

3615 CINEMA
Cinema news: current shoots, casting calls, reviews

3615 CLP
Poetry, writing and reading festival on Minitel

3615 CLUBMED
Club Méditérannée holidays: locations, prices, activities, bookings

3615 CNAP
Information on all events related to Plastic Arts

3615 CNIT
Information about the Centre des Nouvelles Industries et Technologies de Paris

3615 COCACOLA
Coca-Cola brand, sports news, booking service for concerts

3615 CORUS
Information on 150 mountain resorts

3615 COUNCIL
Council Travel Services agency: prices of regular and charter flights

3615 CVCURSUS
Advice for writing résumés (in 5 languages). Free postal delivery within 48 hours

3615 DEGRIFTOUR
Reduced travel tickets

3615 DICO
Dictionaries of spelling, synonyms, conjugations

3615 DISNEY
Information and games centered on the Disney world

3615 ELECTRE
Provides information on books and publishers

3615 EUROPCAR
Rental of cars and professional vehicles

3615 EUROTUNNEL
Information on the Channel tunnel

3615 FERRIES
Sea crossings and package tours available from Brittany Ferries

3615 FIGARO
News bulletins issued by Le Figaro

3615 FLORITEL
Flower delivery service for France

3615 FNAC
FNAC products and services (books, records, hi-fi equipment, photo)

3615 FOX
List of Fox-released films showing in Paris, video tapes of films available

3615 FRANCANADA
Provides addresses of student pen friends in Canada

3615 FRANCEANGL
Service to help find a student correspondent in England

3615 FRANCEUSA
Service to help find a student correspondent in the USA

3615 GAULT
Listing of 2500 selected Paris restaurants with Henri Gault's opinions on the best ones

3615 GBRETAGNE
Practical information on Great Britain

3615 GILLETTE
Presents the Gillette range

3615 GLISS
Ski-ing information

3615 GO
Discount rates for charters and regular flights

3615 GREENPEACE
Activities of the environmental organisation Greenpeace

3615 HERTZ
Rental of cars and professional vehicles

615 HOLLYWOOD
Promotional activities of the Hollywood brand. Games

3615 HOOVER
Hoover domestic appliances

3615 HORAV
Airport guide: flight departure and arrival times, hotels, car parks, services

3615 HOVER
Hoverspeed offers information about Channel crossings

3615 HUMA
Information about the day's edition of L'Humanité *- the official organ of the French Communist Party*

3615 ILFORD
Ilford photographic equipment and advice

3615 INC
Practical tips, advice and comparative surveys for consumers released by the Institut National de la Consommation

3615 INDE
Practical information on India

3615 INFOPARIS
Entertainment and home delivery services in and around Paris

3615 INPI
Guide issued by the Institut National de la Propriété Industrielle (INPI)

3615 INSEE
Data released by the polling institute INSEE

3615 INTERFLORA
Service for ordering flowers

3615 INTERNET
International English-language electronic mail network

3615 INVESTIR
The stock market live

3615 IRISHFERRI
Sea crossings and package tours available from Irish Ferries

3615 IRLANDE
Information on Ireland

3615 ITOUR
National directory of tourist offices by region, département *and town*

3615 JAP
Information on French studies

3615 JCREW
Minitel ordering service for products on the Jcrew catalog

3615 JOGGER
Information on running events and competitions

3615 KNORR
List of recipes using Knorr products

3615 LACENTRALE
Classified ads covering a wide range of themes

3615 LE15
Medical emergency information

3615 LEMONDE
Latest news and miscellaneous services (subscriptions, exam results) by the French daily Le Monde

3615 LESECHOS
News of the Stock Exchange world

3615 LETUDIANT
Service aimed at the student community (accommodation, studies, exams, jobs, courses)

3615 LEVIS
Presentation of the complete Levi-Strauss range

3615 LIBE
American and international news in English direct from USA Today

3615 LIONS
Lions Club: the association and its major events

3615 LIRE
Information about the current issue of Lire, *a monthly literary magazine*

3615 LOCAT
Looking for an apartment? Find one through classified ads and agencies on the Minitel

3615 LOTO
Results and earnings of the National Lottery and related games (Keno, sports lottery)

3615 MANIF
Information about forthcoming strikes and demonstrations

3615 MARITEL
Administrative and practical information for future brides and grooms

3615 MEDIALAND
Information about advertising media for the written press

3615 METEO
Regular update on the weather situation in France

3615 MICHELIN
Road itineraries in France and Europe, information on tires, hotels and restaurants

3615 MINIKID
Babysitting service

3615 MINITELUSA
English-language service housing several servers

3615 MONEY
Direct link to the Paris and New York stock markets

3615 NETWORK
English-language interactive contact and information service for anglophone residents and visitors to Paris. Offers a host of practical tips, ads and advice on living in the French capital (see advertisement)

3615 NEWBALANCE
Presents the New Balance sports shoe range

3615 NEWS
Comprehensive coverage of French and international news: politics, weather reports, Stock Exchange, strikes

3615 ORC
Hotel booking service for EEC countries

3615 OT CAN
Tourist Office, Canadian Embassy

3615 PARIS
Information and services concerning the French capital

3615 PARISCOPE
Weekly guide to entertainment and cultural events in the Paris region (comes out on Wednesday)

3615 PARKER
List of Parker board games, as well as interactive on-screen games

3615 PARTYLINE
Information about night clubs and private parties in Paris

3615 PAT
Tourist and medical information on thermal resorts

3615 PCMAG
Specialized in PC news and ads

3615 PEPSI
Pepsi-Cola: information, games

3615 PIO
Information and advice on living in the French capital

3615 PLCINE
Cinema information, times and locations

3615 POLAROID
Polaroid products: cameras, film, photographic accessories, video tapes

3615 RADIONOVA
Radio Nova: programs, games

3615 RANDO
Guide to walking trips in France

3615 RATP
This connection is helpful in determining the best means of transport to use (RER, métro, bus) and how long it will take you

3615 RESIST
National listing of lost or stolen checks

3615 ROCKINFO
Information on rock music performances all over France: concerts, festivals, tickets

3615 ROTARY
Presents the Rotary Club: directory of clubs in France

3615 ROUTARD
International travel information for small budgets

3615 SCOTCHBEEF
Professional addresses of the Scotch Beef Club members

3615 SEALINK
Times and prices for ferries to England and Ireland

3615 SICI
Professional information for the arts world delivered by the Ministry of Culture

3615 SNCF
French National Railway information. Train times, reservations, sleeping facilities, etc.

3615 SQUASH
French Squash Federation: results, clubs, events

3615 STATES
Provides information about the United States (studies, entertainment, associations, museums, sport, etc.)

3615 STU
Information exchange network on modeling

3615 SVM
Service offered by the magazine Science et Vie Micro

3615 TELERAMA
Cultural weekly review: radio and TV programs, subscriptions, films

3615 TEXMEX
Information about Texan and Latin American cuisine

3615 TIMBERLAND
Information about Timberland shoes

3615 TMK
This service allows you to order your groceries via Minitel, delivered to your door the same day. Make sure to order the catalog, or you will spend most of your costly time browsing the selection on the screen

3615 TORAH
Information on the French Jewish community

3615 TRESOR06
French Treasury Department service for checking bank accounts

3615 ULYSSE
List of classified ads issued by the National Employment Agency

3615 UR75
Information released by URSSAF concerning social security contributions and unemployment benefits for French workers

3615 VATEL
Cooking recipes in English and French

3615 VILLETTE
Information on the program at La Villette Science Center

3615 VIRGIN
Virgin Records bulletin: list of concerts, new releases, fan clubs

3615 VOYAGEL
Practical information for trouble-free holidays

3615 VROUM
Sale of secondhand vehicles and spare parts

3615 WARNER
New Warner Bros releases, games, boutique

3615 WILSON
Presents the range of Wilson France sports articles (tennis, golf...)

3615 WORLD
American news flashes, information on visas for the USA

3615 WWF
Presents the activities of the World Wildlife Fund

3615 YOGA
French Hatha Yoga Federation

3616 ALTERN
Access to the international Internet network

3616 AMEXTC
Limited service for ordering American Express traveler's checks

3616 ANDERSEN
Presents the Arthur Andersen Informatics Company

3616 ASSOS
Directory of various associations and organisations with list of events

3616 AUDIOTEL
Presents Audiotel with list of numbers

3616 BDFINFO
Corporate information from the Banque de France

3616 BUSINESS
Advertisements for business opportunities in France and abroad

3616 DIGITAL
Digital Equipment France catalog

3616 DINERSCLUB
Facilities extended to the members of Diner's Club International

3616 FREE CALL
List of subscribers belonging to the Free Call network

3616 HFSP
Biological research (in English)

3616 HIGHTECH
Mac Graw Hill Publishers: scientific books and magazines

3616 IBM
Presents the whole IBM range: software, PS/1, PS/2, AS/400

3616 MICROSOFT
Presents Microsoft services and products

3616 NMPP
Weekly statistics on newspaper and magazine sales in Paris

3616 SALONS
International fairs and expos

3617 ABCADOPT
Information and practical advice about adoption in France

3617 ABCJUSTICE
General information on legal matters, standard letters for official correspondence

3617 ALLOCAST
Ads by casting agencies to find models, actors, extras

3617 ASS
News, ads, lists of addresses for aspiring actors and actresses. See also 3617 CINETEL

3617 AUTOSANTE
Medical encyclopaedia including up-to-date information on AIDS

3617 BIL
Legal information about the corporate world

3617 CCN
List of existing publications

3617 CEE
Information on the European Economic Community

3617 CHARTS
Information and advice on the Stock Exchange market

3617 COMPU
Databank and downloading of information on the USA

3617 ED
English-language listing of all French telephone subscribers

3617 EMAIL
Software downloading, access to the Usernet system

3617 EUROPAGES
European directory of businesses

3617 FAX
Send faxes by Minitel

3617 FISK
Assessment of income tax, Stock Exchange news

3617 FOR SALE
The largest choice of real estate ads in and around Paris

3617 INFOBREVET
French and European patents

3617 IPSOS
Results of opinion polls

3617 JANNONCE
More than 10000 classified ads

3617 LES1000
Listing of the 1000 largest companies in France

3617 PLPA
Classified ads from Le Parisien: *real estate, automobiles...*

3617 ROQUE
If you are a chess fanatic this will interest you. Not only can you play chess with the computer, but with many other players at the same time

3617 SALAIR
Salary assessment service

3617 SIRENE
National listing of registered companies in France

3617 SPRINT
Associated Press: world news in French and English

3617 TARIF MEDIA
Guide to advertising rates in the written press

3617 TASS
News from the Russian press agency Tass in French. Section on business opportunities in Russia and CEI countries

3617 TIMES
Provides a facsimile of the newspaper published on your date of birth (from 1880 up to today)

3617 TO LET
The largest choice of real estate ads in and around Paris

3617 USACCESS
Yellow pages directory of New York and New England

3617 VAE
List of exhibits presented at auction sales

3617 VERIF
Information on the corporate world: turnover, staff, debt, profit, etc.

3619 BILLPAY
Teleservice for paying American bills (limited access)

3619 CALIFORNIA
English-speaking access to the Californian videotex network

3619 GB1
Access to télématique *services in Britain*

3619 PCFLOWERS
English-speaking service for ordering flowers in Canada and the USA

3619 USA1
English-speaking access to the north American videotex network

3619 USA2
Quote (Canada): Stock Exchange data on foreign markets

A.D.A.G.P.
11, rue Berryer
75008 PARIS
Tel: 43 59 09 79
Fax: 45 63 44 89
Deputy Director: Mrs Christiane RAMONBORDES

ADAMI
10A, rue de la Paix
75001 PARIS
Tel: 40 15 10 00
Fax: 40 15 10 30
General Director: M. Christian JAMES

Addition
57, rue du Fbg. Montmartre
75009 PARIS
Tel: 42 81 44 13
Fax: 45 26 28 54
Production Director: M. Thomas LEPINE

Agence France Presse (AFP)
11-15, Place de la Bourse
75002 PARIS
Tel: 40 41 46 46
Fax: 40 41 47 5
Publishing: Mme Christine POUGET

Agence Michelle Lapautre
6, rue Jean Carriès
75007 PARIS
Tel: 47 34 82 41
Fax: 47 34 00 90
Director: Mlle Michelle LAPAUTRE

ALP/Marshall Cavendish
81, rue d'Amsterdam
75008 PARIS
Tel: 44 53 95 00
Fax: 44 53 91 76
General Director: M. Christian LAGRANGE

American Media Services Intl
10, rue Poussin
75016 PARIS
Tel: 45 20 79 72
Fax: 45 27 17 23
Business Development Director: M. Richard MOSENTHAL

Apple Computer Europe, Inc.
15, av. EdouardBelin
92566 RUEIL-MALMAISON
Tel: 47 14 64 00
Fax: 47 14 12 26
New Media Manager: M. Jim COOK

ARTE/La Sept Editions
39-43, quai André Citroën
75739 PARIS Cedex 15
Tel: 44 14 81 00
Fax: 44 14 80 00
Manager: Mlle Anne SCHUCHMAN

Banque Worms
Le Voltaire
1, Place des Degrés
92059 PARIS LA DEFENSE Cedex 58
Tel: 49 07 56 02
Fax: 49 07 53 14
Director: M. Pierre BIOSSE DUPLAN

Bayard Presse
3-5, rue Bayard
75008 PARIS
Tel: 44 35 60 60
Fax: 44 35 60 41
Rights Manager: Mme Anne-Claire BEURTHEY

Bibliothèque Nationale de France
1, Place Valhubert
75013 PARIS
Tel: 44 06 31 86
Fax: 45 83 84 36
Audiovisual Production: Mme Elisa KIREMITDJIAN

Broad Romero International
236, Bd. St. Germain
75007 PARIS
Tel: 45 49 14 84
Fax: 45 49 09 12
Managing Director: M. Philippe BROAD

Bull Multimédia
Rue Jean Jaurès
78340 LES-CLAYES-SOUS-BOIS
Tel: 30 80 77 34
Fax: 30 80 75 50
Marketing Director: M. Roger CROCOMBE

Business Week Paris
128, rue du Fbg. St. Honoré
75008 PARIS
Tel: 40 75 25 01
Fax: 42 89 04 00
Journalist: Mme Gail EDMONDSON

Canal +
85-89, quai André Citroën
75711 PARIS Cedex 15
Tel: 44 25 10 00
Fax: 44 25 12 34
Intl Public Relations:
Mme Laurence GALLOT

CD-RAMA
45bis, Route des Gardes
92190 MEUDON
Tel: 46 29 00 81
Fax: 46 23 96 46
Director/Editor-in-Chief:
M. Michel ROUSSEAU

Centre National de Documentation Pédagogique (CNDP)
29, rue d'Ulm
75230 PARIS Cedex 05
Tel: 46 34 92 97
Fax: 40 46 96 57
General Director: M. Pierre TRINCAL

Clifford Chance
112, avenue Kléber
B.P. 163 Trocadéro
75770 PARIS Cedex 16
Tel: 44 05 52 52
Fax: 44 05 52 00
Head of Computer Technology:
M. Jean-Luc LEVY

Club d'Investissement Média Europe
4, avenue de l'Europe
94366 BRY SUR MARNE Cedex
Tel: 49 83 28 63
Fax: 49 83 26 26
President: M. Arie SMIT

Communication CB News
175-177, rue d'Aguesseau
92100 BOULOGNE
Tel: 46 04 12 12
Fax: 46 04 38 52
Director: M. Christian BLACHAS

Computergram International
Passage d'Enfer
75014 PARIS
Tel: 40 47 03 18
Fax: 40 47 85 69
Journalist: Mme Marsha JOHNSTON

Confluence Multimedia Publishing
33, avenue de la République
75011 PARIS
Tel: 40 21 12 52
Fax: 40 21 75 78
Director: M. Georges GUILLOT

Danimage Multimedia
32, chemin de Saint Laurent
06800 CAGNES-SUR-MER
Tel: (16) 93 14 41 03
Fax: (16) 93 14 42 54
General Manager: M. Patrick WETTERWALD

Digital TV International
Edicom
21, rue Tournefort
75005 PARIS
Tel: 47 07 29 29
Fax: 47 07 30 66
Editor-in-Chief: M. Olivier BELLIN

Direction des Musées de France
6, rue des Pyramides
75041 PARIS Cedex 01
Tel: 40 15 73 00
Fax: 40 15 34 10
Director: Mme Françoise CACHIN

Disney Consumer Products
10, Allée Bienvenue
93885 NOISY-LE-GRAND
Tel: 49 31 10 93
Fax: 49 31 10 99
Publications Director:
Mme Jennifer CAMPBELL

Disney Hachette Edition
44, avenue des Champs-Elysées
75008 PARIS
Tel: 44 20 55 69
Fax: 42 89 33 69
Director: Mme Catherine TEISSANDER

Disney Interactive Europe, Middle East and Africa
44, avenue des Champs-Elysées
75008 PARIS
Tel: 44 20 55 19
Fax: 42 56 03 56
Manager: M. Marc BIDOU

ECCSI Newsletter
3, rue Camille Saint Saens
92400 COURBEVOIE
Tel: 46 67 39 29
Fax: 47 89 48 10
Chief Editor: M. Jean-Didier GRATON

Editions Atlas
89, rue La Boétie
75004 PARIS
Tel: 40 74 38 83
General Director: M. Bernard CANETTI

Editions Bordas
17, rue Rémy Dumoncel
75014 PARIS
Tel: 42 79 62 00
Fax: 43 22 85 18
President: M. Jean LISSARRAGUE

Editions du Seuil
27, rue Jacob
75006 PARIS
Tel: 40 46 50 50
Fax: 43 26 50 84
Audiovisual & Intl Rights Dpt:
Mme Marie-France FONTAINE

Editions Gallimard
5, rue Sébastien Bottin
75007 PARIS
Tel: 49 54 42 00
Fax: 45 44 39 46
Head Audiovisual Rights Dpt:
Mme Isabelle GALLIMARD

Editions Nathan
9, rue Méchain
75014 PARIS
Tel: 45 87 50 00
Fax: 43 31 21 69
President: M. Bertrand EVENO

Edusoft
132, Bd. Camélinat
92247 MALAKOFF Cedex
Tel: 46 73 05 55
Fax: 46 73 05 65
Export Manager: Mlle Catherine BALL

Electre Multimédia
35, rue Grégoire de Tours
75005 PARIS
Tel: 44 21 28 00
Fax: 44 41 28 95
Head Multimedia Dpt:
M. Olivier CADOU

Electricité de France
2, rue Louis Murat
75008 PARIS
Tel: 40 42 55 63
Fax: 40 42 72 20
Head Audiovisual Communications Director:
Mme Isabelle WATTEAUX-SUDOL

Encyclopaedia Universalis S.A.
10, rue Vercingétorix
75014 PARIS
Tel: 43 21 41 10
Fax: 43 21 62 89
General Director: M. Jacques BERSANI

Flammarion
26, rue Racine
75006 PARIS
Tel: 40 51 31 00
Fax: 43 29 21 48
General Director:
M. Jean-Pierre ARBON
Nouvelles Technologies:
Chloé BENAROYA
& M. Bruno de SA MOREIRA

FNAC
148, rue Anatole France
92596 LEVALLOIS-PERRET Cedex
Tel: 49 64 35 33
Fax: 49 64 25 25
Commercial Director: M. Jacques MARGULES

France 2
22, avenue Montaigne
75008 PARIS
Tel: 44 21 42 42
Communications Director:
Mme Brigitte SCHMIT

France 3
116, avenue du Président Kennedy
75016 PARIS
Tel: 42 30 22 22
Fax: 42 24 63 66
Communications Director:
M. Charles GREBER

France Télécom Multimédia
103, rue de Grenelle
75007 PARIS
Tel: 44 14 18 03
Tel: 44 14 18 04
Fax: 44 14 18 10
President: M. Gérard EYMERY

France Télévision
42, avenue d'Iéna
75116 PARIS
Tel: 44 31 60 00
Communications Adviser:
M. Jean-Claude LEMAIGNEN

Globe Trotter Network S.A.
5, rue d'Artois
75008 PARIS
Tel: 42 80 56 54
Fax: 48 78 04 23
President: M. Stéphane DYKMAN

Groupe Schneider - Schneider Electric S.A.
Site SZE, avenue des Jeux Olympiques
Communication BTT
38050 GRENOBLE Cedex
Tel: (16) 76 39 46 87
Fax: (16) 76 39 87 52
Contact: M. Pierre LAMARCA

Gyoza Media
44, rue Vieille du Temple
75004 PARIS
Tel: 40 29 03 96
Fax: 40 29 03 34
E-mail: 100272.257@compuserve.com
Contact: M. Cory McCLOUD
CD-ROM & Web development and consulting

Hachette Filipacchi Presse
145-149, rue Anatole France
92300 LEVALLOIS-PERRET
Tel: 41 34 60 00
Fax: 41 34 69 99
Deputy Director: M. Hervé DIGNE

Hachette Livre
24, Bd. St. Germain
75288 PARIS Cedex 06
Tel: 46 34 86 34
Fax: 46 34 65 45
President: M. Jean-Louis LISIMACHIO

Havas S.A.
136, avenue Charles de Gaulle
92522 NEUILLY-SUR-SEINE Cedex
Tel: 47 47 30 00
Telex: F 611 860
Head Development: Mme Anne LALOU

Home Shopping Service
11, rue de Téhéran
75008 PARIS
Tel: 44 13 91 75
Fax: 44 13 91 96
General Director: M. Roland KLUGER

Hyptique
55, rue Traversière
75012 PARIS
Tel: 44 67 02 30
Fax: 44 67 02 32
Director: M. Pierre LAVOIE

Hérisson, Fox and Company
11, rue Lacépède
75005 PARIS
Tel: 44 08 76 40
Fax: 45 87 04 97
President: M. Javier ERGUETA

IBM
IBM Coordination
Tour Pascal - Service 7260
22, Rte Demi-Lune
92075 PARIS LA DEFENSE
Tel: 47 67 60 00
Fax: 47 67 65 00
Electronic Publishing Program Manager: M. Yvor DRACS

Infogrames Entertainment
84, rue du Ier Mars 1943
69628 VILLEURBANNE Cedex
Tel: (16) 72 65 50 00
Fax: (16) 72 65 50 01
General Director: M. Christophe SAPET

Institut National de l'Audiovisuel
4, avenue de l'Europe
94366 BRY-SUR-MARNE Cedex
Tel: 49 83 20 00
Fax: 49 83 31 95
President: M. Jean-Pierre TEYSSIER

Interactive Fiction
3, rue Decrès
75014 PARIS
Tel: 43 95 05 05
Fax: 43 95 03 64
Editorial Director: M. Louis MESPLE

Joystick/Joypad
10, rue Thierry Le Luron
92592 LEVALLOIS Cedex
Tel: 41 34 85 00
Fax: 41 34 87 99
Editor-in-Chief: M. Claude LUCAS

Kodak Images Services/ Laboratoire Micro-Images
Z.A.C. Charles de Gaulle
25, rue Farman
93297 TREMBLAY-EN-FRANCE
Tel: 49 63 41 23
Fax: 49 63 41 31
President: M. Jean-François BORDIER

Kodak Pathé
26, rue Villiot
75594 PARIS Cedex 12
Tel: 40 01 40 33
Fax: 40 01 47 35
Public Relations: Mme Alexandra AUDIBERT

Larousse S.A.
Export Service
17, rue du Montparnasse
75298 PARIS Cedex 6
Tel: 44 39 44 10
Fax: 44 39 41 07
President: M. Patrice MAUBOURGUET

Le Monde Informatique
2, Place des Vosges
Immeuble Lafayette
Cedex 65
92051 PARIS LA DEFENSE 5
Tel: 49 04 79 00
Fax: 49 04 78 00
Journalist: Mme Anne-Marie ROUZERE

Les Echos
46, rue La Boétie
75381 PARIS Cedex 08
Tel: 49 53 65 65
Fax: 45 61 48 92
Journalist: M. P. DE GASQUET

Libération
11, rue Béranger
75154 PARIS Cedex 03
Tel: 42 76 17 89
Fax: 42 72 33 17
Director: M. Serge JULY

Livredis
11-15, rue Pierre Rigaud
94855 IVRY-SUR-SEINE
Tel: 49 59 60 01
Fax: 46 58 00 43
President: M. Dominique MAILLOTTE

Locatel Alcatel Alsthom
Technoparc
2-10, rue Charles Edouard Jeanneret
78306 POISSY
Tel: 39 11 13 13
Fax: 30 65 50 98

Matra Hachette Multimédia
131, avenue Charles de Gaulle
92200 NEUILLY-SUR-SEINE
Tel: 47 45 94 45
Fax: 47 45 94 60
President: M. Arnaud LAGARDERE

Mediaplay International
75, avenue Niel
75017 PARIS
Tel: 47 54 05 65
Fax: 46 22 22 76
President: Mme Ferhan COOK

Micro Kid's Multimedia
Productions Richard Joffo
30, rue Eugène Carrière
75018 PARIS
Tel: 42 55 29 10
Fax: 42 55 08 48
Producer: Mme Marianne LANGLOIS

Microsoft
18, avenue du Québec
Z.A. de Courtaboeuf 1
91957 LES ULIS Cedex
Tel: 69 86 46 46
Fax: 64 46 06 60
Microsoft Europe: M. Gérard BAZ

Ministère de la Culture
3, rue de Valois
75001 PARIS
Tel: 40 15 80 00
Fax: 40 15 81 72
Communications Director:
Mme Catherine SIMON

MPO (Moulages Plastiques de l'Ouest)
77, rue de Paris
92100 BOULOGNE-BILLANCOURT
Tel: 41 10 51 51
Fax: 41 10 51 52
General Directors: MM. Loic & Serge DE POIX

ODA
7, avenue de la Cristallerie
92317 SEVRES Cedex
Tel: 46 23 32 58
Fax: 46 23 32 59
Multimedia Projects Manager:
M. Christophe HADAMAR

Pacific Press Service
38, Domaine de la Tuilerie
78590 NOISY-LE-ROI
Tel: 34 62 66 40
Fax: 34 62 95 07
Director Europe: M. Russel MELCHER

Pathé Interactive
5, Bd. Malesherbes
75401 PARIS Cedex 08
Tel: 49 24 43 33
Fax: 49 24 43 50
President: Mme Janine LANGLOIS-GLANDIER

Philips Interactive Media France
64, rue Carnot
B.P. 306
92156 SURESNES Cedex
Tel: 47 28 93 00
Fax: 47 28 56 55
President: M. Jean-Claude LARUE

Polygram S.A.
20, rue des Fossés St. Jacques
75235 PARIS Cedex 5
Tel: 44 41 91 91
Fax: 44 41 91 90
President: M. Alfredo GANGOTENA

Publisher's Weekly
B.P. 214
75264 PARIS Cedex 06
Tel: 43 21 77 82
Fax: 43 35 02 31
Correspondent Europe:
M. Herbert LOTTMAN

Quartier Latin Group
37, rue Froidevaux
75014 PARIS
Tel: 43 22 45 46
Fax: 43 35 35 80
President: M. Michel NOLL

Reed Midem Organization
179, avenue Victor Hugo
75016 PARIS
Tel: 44 34 44 44
Fax: 44 34 44 00
Chief Executive: M. Xavier ROY

Reuters
8, rue du Sentier
75002 PARIS
Tel: 42 21 54 52
Fax: 42 36 10 72
Correspondent: M. Marcel MICHELSON

SACD
11bis, rue Ballu
75009 PARIS
Tel: 40 23 45 60
Fax: 40 23 46 69
President: M. YOURI
Société des Auteurs et Compositeurs Dramatiques

SACEM
225, avenue Charles de Gaulle
92200 NEUILLY
Tel: 47 15 47 15
Fax: 47 15 47 86
President: M. Jacques DEMARNY
Société des Auteurs, Compositeurs et Editeurs de Musique

SCAM
38, rue du Fbg. St. Jacques
75014 PARIS
Tel: 40 51 33 00
Fax: 43 54 92 99
Communications Director:
M. Stéphane JOSEPH
Société Civile des Auteurs Multimédia

Software Publishers Association Europe
57, rue Pierre Charron
75008 PARIS
Tel: 45 63 02 02
Fax: 45 63 02 31
Managing Director: M. Gérard GABELLA

Sonovision
1, avenue Edouard Belin
92856 RUEIL-MALMAISON
Tel: 41 29 97 63
Fax: 41 29 97 91
Advertising Director: Mme Sophie JOFFO

Sony Software
131, avenue de Wagram
75838 PARIS Cedex 17
Tel: 44 40 65 13
Fax: 44 40 65 31
Fax: 44 40 66 66
Telex: 219045F
Director: M. Pierre-Antoine ULLMO

SVM/Excelsior Publications
1, rue du Colonel Pierre Avia
75015 PARIS
Tel: 46 48 47 67
Fax: 46 48 47 93
Advertising Director: M. Bertrand CLAVIERES

Sygma S.A.
74bis, rue Lauriston
75116 PARIS
Tel: 47 27 70 30
Fax: 47 27 23 59
President: M. Hubert HENROTTE

Technology Investment Partners
196, avenue Victor Hugo
75116 PARIS
Tel: 45 03 04 15
Fax: 45 04 83 99
Managing Director: M. Jacques BERNARD

TF1 Enterprises
305, avenue Le Jour se Lève
92656 BOULOGNE
Tel: 41 41 27 69
Fax: 41 41 29 29
President: M. Patrick LE LAY

Télérama/Télérama Junior
129, Bd. Malesherbes
75017 PARIS
Tel: 48 88 48 88
Fax: 47 64 02 04
Editor-in-Chief: M. MANTOY

Time Warner Interactive
49, avenue Kléber
75016 PARIS
Tel: 53 67 71 40
Fax: 40 70 12 55

Ubi Soft
28, rue Armand Carrel
93108 MONTREUIL Cedex
Tel: 48 18 50 00
Fax: 48 18 50 38
President: M. Yves GUILLEMOT

Variety
64, rue Jean-Pierre Timbaud
75011 PARIS
Tel: 43 55 07 43
Fax: 43 55 06 99
Correspondent: M. Mike WILLIAMS

Virgin France S.A.
11, Place des Vosges
75004 PARIS
Tel: 44 54 64 74
Fax: 44 54 64 67
Head Multimedia Dpt:
M. Gérard BEULLAC

Virgin Interactive Entertainment
233, rue de la Croix Nivert
75015 PARIS
Tel: 53 68 10 10
Fax: 53 68 10 30
General Director: M. Thierry BRAILLE

Warner Chapell Music France
12, rue de Penthièvre
75008 PARIS
Tel: 42 66 40 42
Fax: 42 66 29 17
President: M. Jean DAVOUST

Warner Home Video
B.P. 656
75826 PARIS Cedex 17
Tel: 44 01 49 99
Fax: 40 54 71 79
Director of Special Programming:
Mlle Caroline LANG

Warner Interactive Entertainment
26, Bd. Malesherbes
75008 PARIS
Tel: 43 12 31 00
Fax: 43 12 31 19
Distributor of CD-Rom interactive video games

Welcome Communication & Distribution
Immeuble Canal Plus Horizons
101, rue Leblanc
75015 PARIS
Tel: 53 78 01 00
Fax: 53 78 01 01
President: M. Michel POULAIN

On-line Services
En Réseau

Anglo Communication Europe
16, rue Kléber
92130 ISSY-LES-MOULINEAUX
Tel: 46 43 09 87
On-line services

Bertelsmann Information Professionnelle
8, rue Armand Moisant
75015 PARIS
Tel: 40 64 71 90
Fax: 43 20 70 38
Expanding America On Line in Europe

CalvaCom
8-10, rue Nieuport
78140 VELIZY
Tel: 34 63 19 19
Fax: 34 63 19 48
Internet access

CompuServe
Centre Atria Rueil 2000
21, avenue Edouard Belin
92566 RUEIL-MALMAISON
Tel: 36 63 81 22
Tel: 36 63 81 31
Fax: 47 14 21 51
Director: M. Bernard USUNIER
Communications Director:
Florence DUCLOS (47 14 21 50)

DDB en Réseau
41, rue Prony
75017 PARIS
Tel: 47 66 01 01

Digital Online
11, rue Clouet
75015 PARIS
Tel: 42 19 93 31
Fax: 42 19 93 32
Director: M. Albert NAHMANY

EUNET France
52, avenue de la Grande Armée
75017 PARIS
Tel: 53 81 60 60
Fax: 45 74 52 79
Director: M. Eric LAURENT-RICARD
Internet access provider

Filenet
Vélizy Plus
1bis, rue du Petit Clamart
78140 VELIZY
Tel: 40 83 06 06
Fax: 40 94 00 75
Marketing Assistant:
Marie-Laure ROCHER

FranceNet
28, rue Desaix
75015 PARIS
Tel: 43 92 14 49
Fax: 43 92 14 45
E-mail: http://www.FranceNet.fr/.
Hot Line: 43.92.14.48
Monday-Friday 10h00-22h00
Minitel: 3615 FRANCENET

Institut Formation Internet
11, Villa Bellevue
75019 PARIS
Tel: 42 45 42 71

Jouve Systèmes d'Information
B.P. 2734
75027 PARIS Cedex 01
Tel: 44 76 86 00
Fax: 44 76 86 10
Director: M. Guy COQUARD

Matra Hachette Multimédia Online
131, avenue Charles de Gaulle
92200 NEUILLY-SUR-SEINE
Tel: 47 45 96 07
Fax: 47 45 96 09
General Director: M. Grégoire SENTILHES

http://www.paris-anglo.com
http://www.paris-anglo.com
http://www.paris-anglo.com
http://www.paris-anglo.com
http://www.paris-anglo.com
http://www.paris-anglo.com
http://www.paris-anglo.com
http://www.paris-anglo.com

see.you. ~~there~~. here.soon

http://www.paris-anglo.com
http://www.paris-anglo.com
http://www.paris-anglo.com
http://www.paris-anglo.com
http://www.paris-anglo.com
http://www.paris-anglo.com
http://www.paris-anglo.com
http://www.paris-anglo.com
http://www.paris-anglo.com
http://www.paris-an m

http://www.paris-c om
http://www.paris-an .com
http://www.paris-anglo.com
http://www.paris-anglo.com

Mosaique
47, rue de Maubeuge
75009 PARIS
Tel: 49 95 03 26
Fax: 49 95 02 31
Commercial Director: M. Christian PINEAU

Sipa Press
101, Bd. Murat
75016 PARIS
Tel: 47 43 47 43
Fax: 47 43 47 44
Intl Editor-in-Chief:
M. Jean-Louis BERSUDER

Uplift Technology
20, rue Fessant
75019 PARIS
Tel: 42 06 79 17
Fax: 42 06 79 18
Internet service

World On Line
158, rue de Grenelle
75007 PARIS
Tel: 44 18 72 72
Fax: 44 18 72 73
Marketing Manager:
M. Michel BLOCH

Worldnet
SCT
B.P. 141
Les Coudreaux
77649 CHELLES
Tel: 60 20 85 14
Fax: 64 21 65 35

Ziff Davis France
14, Place Marie-Jeanne Bassot
92300 LEVALLOIS-PERRET
Tel: 46 39 55 00
Fax: 46 39 02 06
Contact: M. Pascal RIVIERE

Arc de Triomphe
Rond-Point des Champs-Elysées
Place Charles de Gaulle
75017 PARIS
Tel: 43 80 31 31

Ateliers des Beaux-Arts
15, rue Jean Lantier
75001 PARIS
Tel: 42 36 06 68

Basilique du Sacré Cœur
35, rue du Chevalier de la Barre
75018 PARIS
Tel: 42 51 17 02

Catacombes
1, Place Denfert Rochereau
75014 PARIS
Tel: 43 22 47 63

Centre National de la Photographie
11, rue Berryer
75008 PARIS
Tel: 53 76 12 32
Fax: 53 76 12 33

Château de Fontainebleau
Place Général de Gaulle
77300 FONTAINEBLEAU
Tel: 60 71 50 70
Fax: 60 71 50 71

Château de Vincennes
Avenue de Paris
94300 VINCENNES
Tel: 43 28 15 48

Cimetière Montparnasse
3, Bd. Edgar Quinet
75014 PARIS
Tel: 44 10 86 50
Home to many poets, artists and writers

Cimitière du Père Lachaise
Bd. de Ménilmontant
75020 PARIS
Tel: 43 70 70 33
Labyrinthine cemetary with many famous graves

Cité des Sciences et de l'Industrie
Parc de la Villette
30, avenue Corentin Cariou
75019 PARIS
Tel: 40 05 70 00
Minitel: 3615 VILLETTE
The world of Science and Technology presented in an original manner with many interactive video games

Conciergerie
1, quai de l'Horloge
75001 PARIS
Tel: 43 54 30 06
France's oldest prison

Disneyland Paris
B.P. 100
77777 MARNE-LA-VALLEE
Admin: 64 74 40 00
Res: 64 74 60 65
Info: 60 30 60 30
Minitel: 3615 EURO DISNEY
Director: M. Philippe BOURGUIGNON
Disney theme park 32 km. east of Paris

Ecole Nationale Supérieure des Beaux-Arts
17, quai Malaquais
75006 PARIS
Tel: 47 03 50 00
Fax: 47 03 50 80

Eglise de la Madeleine
Place de la Madeleine
75008 PARIS
Tel: 44 51 69 00

Eglise Saint-Sulpice
Place Saint-Sulpice
75006 PARIS
Tel: 46 33 21 78
Monumental church with frescoes by Delacroix

Eiffel Tower
Champ de Mars
75007 PARIS
Tel: 44 11 23 23

Espace Montmartre Salvador Dali
11, rue Poulbot
75018 PARIS
Tel: 42 64 40 10
Permanent exhibition of 330 works

Galerie Nationale du Jeu de Paume
Place de la Concorde
75001 PARIS
Tel: 47 03 12 50
Commercial Director:
M. Jean-Philippe ARNOULD

Galeries Nationales du Grand Palais
Avenue du Général Eisenhower
75008 PARIS
Tel: 44 13 17 17

Hôtel de Ville
4, Place de l'Hôtel de Ville
75003 PARIS
Tel: 42 76 40 40
Paris' recently-restored Town Hall

Institut Océanographique
195, rue St. Jacques
75005 PARIS
Tel: 43 25 63 10

Les Egouts de Paris
93, quai d'Orsay
75007 PARIS
Tel: 47 05 10 29
Sewers of Paris

Maison de Balzac
47, rue Raynouard
75016 PARIS
Tel: 42 24 56 38
Museum, visits, conferences and library

Maison de Victor Hugo
Hôtel de Rohan-Guéménée
6, Place des Vosges
75004 PARIS
Tel: 42 72 10 16

Musée Antoine Bourdelle
16-18, rue Antoine Bourdelle
75015 PARIS
Tel: 45 48 67 27

Musée Bouchard
25, rue de l'Yvette
75016 PARIS
Tel: 46 47 63 46
Figurative sculpture

Musée Carnavalet
23, rue de Sévigné
75003 PARIS
Tel: 42 72 21 13

Musée Cernuschi
7, avenue Velasquez
75008 PARIS
Tel: 45 63 50 75
Ancient Chinese art

Musée du Cinéma Henri Langlois
Palais de Chaillot
75016 PARIS
Tel: 45 53 74 39
The history of the film industry

Musée du Cristal
30bis, rue de Paradis
75010 PARIS
Tel: 47 70 64 30

Musée du Louvre
Rue de Rivoli
75001 PARIS
Tel: 40 20 50 50
Minitel: 3615 LOUVRE

Musée du Petit Palais
Avenue Winston Churchill
75008 PARIS
Tel: 42 65 12 73
Fax: 42 65 24 60
Public Relations: Martine CARRICHON

Musée du Vin
5-7, square Charles Dickens
75016 PARIS
Tel: 45 25 63 26
The Art of Oenology

Musée d'Art Juif
42, rue des Saules
75018 PARIS
Tel: 42 57 84 15
Fax: 42 57 26 30
Museum of Jewish art and culture

Musée d'Art Moderne de la Ville de Paris
11, avenue du Président Wilson
75016 PARIS
Tel: 53 67 40 00

Musée d'Orsay
162, rue de Lille
75007 PARIS
Info: 45 49 11 11
Admin: 40 49 48 14
Splendid Impressionist and Art Déco collections in a beautifully-converted train station

Musée d'Art Américain
99, rue Claude Monet
27620 GIVERNY
Tel: (16) 32 51 94 65
Fax: (16) 32 51 94 67
Contact: Mme Mayalène CROSSLEY
Showcases American art

Musée de l'Air et de l'Espace
Aéroport du Bourget
B.P. 173
93350 LE BOURGET
Tel: 49 92 71 71
Air and Space Museum

Musée de l'Armée
Hôtel National des Invalides
51, Bd. La Tour Maubourg
75007 PARIS
Tel: 44 42 37 67
Military history museum

Musée de l'Affiche et de la Publicité
107, rue de Rivoli
75001 PARIS
Tel: 42 60 26 60
Advertising and Poster Museum. Temporary exhibitions only (call for information)

Musée de l'Histoire de France
Hôtel de Soubise
60, rue des Francs Bourgeois
75003 PARIS
Tel: 40 27 60 96

Musée de l'Holographie
Forum des Halles
Niveau -1
75001 PARIS
Tel: 40 39 96 83

Musée de l'Homme
Palais de Chaillot
17, Place du Trocadéro
75016 PARIS
Tel: 44 05 72 72

Musée de l'Institut du Monde Arabe
1, rue des Fossés St. Bernard
75005 PARIS
Tel: 40 51 38 38

Musée de la Chasse et de la Nature
Hôtel Guénégaud
60, rue des Archives
75004 PARIS
Tel: 42 72 86 43
Hunting Museum

Musée de la Marine
Palais de Chaillot
Place du Trocadéro
75116 PARIS
Tel: 45 53 31 70
Fax: 47 27 49 67
Public Relations Director:
Mme FEREY DE ROSENGATH

Musée de la Mode et du Costume
10, avenue Pierre Ier de Serbie
75016 PARIS
Tel: 47 20 85 23

Musée de la Mode et du Textile
109, rue de Rivoli
75001 PARIS
Tel: 44 55 58 86
Fashion and textile museum

Musée de la Monnaie
11, quai de Conti
75006 PARIS
Tel: 40 46 55 35
Director: Mme COHEN

Musée de la Parfumerie Fragonard
9, rue Scribe
75009 PARIS
Tel: 47 42 04 56
The story of perfume through the ages

Musée de la Poste
34, bd de Vaugirard
75015 PARIS
Tel: 42 79 23 00
Post Office Museum (amusing gift store)

Musée de la Poupée
Impasse Berthaud
75003 PARIS
Tel: 42 72 55 90
Doll Museum

Musée de la Serrure
1, rue de la Perle
75003 PARIS
Tel: 42 77 79 62
Keys and locks

Musée de la Vie Romantique
16, rue Chaptal
75009 PARIS
Tel: 48 74 95 38

Musée de Montmartre
12, rue Cortot
75018 PARIS
Tel: 46 06 61 11

Musée des Arts Africains et Océaniens
293, avenue Daumesnil
75012 PARIS
Tel: 43 46 51 61
Fax: 43 43 27 53

Musée des Arts Décoratifs
Palais du Louvre
107, rue de Rivoli
75001 PARIS
Tel: 44 55 57 50
Contact: Pascale DE SEZE

Musée des Arts et Métiers
292, rue St. Martin
75003 PARIS
Tel: 40 27 22 20
Fax: 40 27 26 62
Museum of corporate trades and guilds

Musée des Arts et Traditions Populaires
6, avenue du Mahatma Gandhi
75116 PARIS
Tel: 44 17 60 00

Musée des Lunettes et Lorgnettes
380, rue St. Honoré
75001 PARIS
Tel: 40 20 06 98
Spectacles, Monocle and Binocular Museum

Musée en Herbe
Jardin d'Acclimatation
Bois de Boulogne
Tel: 40 67 97 66
Children's museum

Musée Eugène Delacroix
6, rue de Furstemberg
75006 PARIS
Tel: 43 54 04 87

Musée Grévin
10, Bd. Montmartre
75002 PARIS
Tel: 42 46 13 26
Museum of wax figures

Musée Maillol
Fondation Dina Vierny
59-61, rue de Grenelle
75007 PARIS
Tel: 42 22 59 58

Musée Marmottan
2, rue Louis Boilly
75016 PARIS
Tel: 42 24 07 02
Impressionist works

Musée National d'Art Moderne
Centre Georges Pompidou
Place Beaubourg
75004 PARIS
Tel: 44 78 12 33

Musée National de l'Orangerie
Place de la Concorde
75001 PARIS
Tel: 42 97 48 16

Musée National de la Coopération Franco-Américaine
Château de Blérancourt
02300 BLERANCOURT
Tel: (16) 23 39 60 16
Fax: (16) 23 39 62 85
Museum and library

Musée National des Arts Asiatiques
6, place d'Iena
75016 PARIS
Tel: 47 23 61 65
Asian art and archaeology

Musée National des Monuments Français
1, Place de Trocadéro
75116 PARIS
Tel: 44 05 39 10

Musée National du Moyen Age
Thermes de Cluny
6, Place Paul Painlevé
75005 PARIS
Tel: 43 25 62 00
Commercial Director: M. Michel MAUNIER
Medieval works of art, poetry and music, shows

Musée Picasso
5, rue de Thorigny
75003 PARIS
Tel: 42 71 25 21
Greatest single collection of Picasso's work

Musée Robert Keyaerts
Château de Planchoury
37130 ST-MICHEL-SUR-LOIRE-LANGEAIS
Tel: (16) 47 96 81 52
Fax: (16) 47 96 51 98
More than 50 Cadillac models on show, brought together by the collector Robert Keyaerts

Musée Rodin
Hôtel Biron
77, rue de Varenne
75007 PARIS
Tel: 47 05 01 34
Museum and sculpture garden

Musée Zadkine
100bis, rue d'Assas
75006 PARIS
Tel: 43 26 91 90

Musée-Galerie de la Seita et du Tabac
12, rue Surcouf
75007 PARIS
Tel: 45 56 60 17
The history of tobacco. Nice collections of snuff boxes

Muséum National d'Histoire Naturelle
Jardin des Plantes
57, rue Cuvier
75005 PARIS
Tel: 43 36 54 26
Public Relations Director:
Mme GENEVIEVE
Public galleries, temporary exhibitions, greenhouses, zoological garden, library, research laboratories

Notre-Dame de Paris
Place du Parvis de Notre-Dame
75004 PARIS
Tel: 42 34 56 10
Tel: 43 29 83 51 (crypt)

Palais de Chaillot
Place du Trocadéro
75016 PARIS
Designed for the 1889 World Fair

Palais de la Découverte
Avenue Franklin Roosevelt
75008 PARIS
Tel: 40 74 81 82
Minitel: 3615 DECOUVERTE

Panthéon
Place du Panthéon
75005 PARIS
Tel: 43 54 34 51
Monument and tomb for many great French personalities

Pavillon des Arts
101, rue Rambuteau
75001 PARIS
Tel: 42 33 82 50

Tour Montparnasse
Rue de l'Arrivée
75015 PARIS
Tel: 45 38 52 56
Splendid view of Paris

American Graffiti
10, rue Douai
75009 PARIS
Tel: 48 74 22 79
Acoustic guitars and accessories

Barclay
16, rue des Fossés St. Jacques
75005 PARIS
Tel: 44 41 95 95
Record company

Blue Line
5, rue Léon Giraud
75019 PARIS
Tel: 48 03 33 99
Fax: 48 03 24 50
Commercial Director:
M. Christian BOURGAUT
Organizes jazz concerts

By Unlimited Art
85, Bd. Henri Sellier
92150 SURESNES
Tel: 42 04 33 04
Managers: MM. Philippe
& Louis-Pierre YSCHARD
Recording studio

Chez Gègène
Allée des Guinguettes
162bis, quai Polangis
94340 JOINVILLE-LE-PONT
Tel: 48 83 29 43
Open-air dance restaurant on the banks of the Marne

FNAC Musique
24, Bd. des Italiens
75009 PARIS
Tel: 48 01 02 03
CD records, tapes, books on music

Gray Matters
14, rue de Birague
75004 PARIS
Tel: 42 77 03 03
Fax: 42 77 82 36
Director: Alexandra GRAY
Artist management

Groove Music School
54, Bd. Clichy
75018 PARIS
Tel: 42 55 17 53

GTR Communication
112, Route de Fourqueux
78100 ST-GERMAIN-EN-LAYE
Tel: 34 51 44 70
Fax: 44 76 39 61
President: Mrs Jee JACQUET
Vice-President: M. Jean-Luc
RAYMOND
Specialized in AOR and West Coast music

Laser Karaoke Agent
32, Bd. Ménilmontant
75020 PARIS
Tel: 47 97 49 11

Librairie Musicale de Paris
68bis, rue Réaumur
75003 PARIS
Tel: 42 72 30 72
700 square meters of sheet music

O'CD
26, rue des Ecoles
75005 PARIS
Tel: 43 25 23 27
Fax: 43 25 26 74
Good selection of CD records

Panasonic AEI
27, rue Raymond Losserand
75014 PARIS
Tel: 43 35 44 00

Pioneer AEI
178, Bd. Pereire
75017 PARIS
Tel: 45 74 97 28

SACEM
211, avenue Jean Jaurès
75019 PARIS
Tel: 47 15 47 15
Society of Music Authors, Composers and Publishers

Warner Music
94, rue de la Fontaine
75016 PARIS
Tel: 45 25 51 31
Fax: 45 27 39 07
Director: Mme Anne-Laure WARNER

Record Labels/Publishers
Labels/Editeurs

Arcade
33, avenue Mozart
75016 PARIS
Tel: 44 96 50 60

Arion
36, avenue Hoche
75008 PARIS
Tel: 45 63 76 70
Fax: 45 63 79 54

Artistes et Producteurs Associés
39, rue Jean Goujon
75008 PARIS
Tel: 42 25 46 52
Fax: 40 74 01 93
Director: M. Christian DE RONSERAY
Music publisher and producer

Baby Records
29, rue Marignan
75008 PARIS
Tel: 42 25 23 99
Fax: 40 74 04 19

BMG Music Publishing
10, rue Duphot
75001 PARIS
Fax: 42 86 98 98

Budde Music France
5, rue Denis Poisson
75017 PARIS
Tel: 45 74 43 72
Fax: 45 74 52 33

Delabel Editions
24, Place des Vosges
75003 PARIS
Tel: 42 74 58 06
Fax: 42 74 59 86
Director: M. Emmanuel DE BURTEL

Do It Music
47, rue Erlanger
75016 PARIS
Tel: 40 71 82 19
Fax: 46 51 67 03

Elliot Music
45, rue Vauvenargues
75018 PARIS
Tel: 42 26 16 15
Fax: 46 27 79 99

EMI France
43, rue Camille Desmoulins
92130 ISSY-LES-MOULINEAUX
Tel: 46 29 20 20
Fax: 46 29 21 21
President: M. Gilbert OHAYON

Firstars
4, rue Chapon
75003 PARIS
Tel: 42 77 58 03
Fax: 42 77 50 15
Director: M. Henry PADOVANI
Music label, artistic management, publishers

FNAC Productions
99, rue du Cherche Midi
75006 PARIS
Tel: 44 39 50 00
Fax: 44 39 50 30

Harmonia Mundi
31, rue Vandrezanne
75013 PARIS
Tel: 53 80 02 22
Fax: 53 80 02 25

Jazz Black Market Records
7, rue Henri Monnier
75009 PARIS
Tel: 40 16 05 66

MCA Caravelle Music France
35, Bd. Malesherbes
75008 PARIS
Tel: 42 65 08 73
Fax: 42 65 11 34

Music Marketing Europe
33, avenue Mozart
75016 PARIS
Tel: 44 96 50 60
Fax: 44 96 50 61

One World Music
53, rue de l'Amiral Mouchez
75013 PARIS
Fax: 45 80 30 34

Peterson
42, rue du Fer à Moulin
75005 PARIS
Tel: 45 35 41 71
Fax: 43 37 15 33
Music publishers

Polygram Musique
20, rue des Fossés St. Jacques
75235 PARIS Cedex 5
Tel: 44 41 94 94

Sony Music Entertainment
131, avenue de Wagram
75017 PARIS
Tel: 44 40 60 60
Fax: 44 40 66 66
CBS France

Top Records
17, avenue du Président Wilson
75116 PARIS
Tel: 47 23 79 19
Fax: 47 23 00 27

Virgin France
11, Place des Vosges
75004 PARIS
Tel: 44 54 64 74
Fax: 44 54 64 96
President: M. Patrick ZELNIK

Warner Chapell Music France
20, rue Ville de l'Evêque
75008 PARIS
Tel: 42 66 40 42
Fax: 42 66 29 17

WEA Music
100, avenue du Président Kennedy
75016 PARIS
Tel: 44 30 40 00
Fax: 44 30 40 50

Caveau de la Huchette
5, rue de la Huchette
75005 PARIS
Tel: 43 26 65 05
Legendary Parisian jazz club

Crazy Horse Saloon
12, avenue George V
75008 PARIS
Tel: 47 23 32 32

Folies Bergères
32, rue Richer
75009 PARIS
Tel: 44 79 98 98

Jazz Club Lionel Hampton
81, rue Gouvion-St.-Cyr
75017 PARIS
Tel: 40 68 30 42
Manager: M. Philippe MAROIS

La Chapelle des Lombards
19, rue de Lappe
75011 PARIS
Tel: 47 70 81 47

La Locomotive
9, Bd. de Clichy
75018 PARIS
Tel: 42 57 37 37

La Villa
29, rue Jacob
75006 PARIS
Tel: 43 26 60 60

Lapin Agile
22, rue des Saules
75018 PARIS
Tel: 46 06 85 87

Le Balajo
9, rue de Lappe
75011 PARIS
Tel: 47 00 07 87

Le Bataclan
50, Bd. Voltaire
75011 PARIS
Tel: 47 00 39 21

Le Duc des Lombards
42, rue des Lombards
75001 PARIS
Tel: 42 33 22 88

Le Lido de Paris
116 bis, avenue des
Champs-Elysées
75008 PARIS
Tel: 40 76 56 10
Commercial Director: M. C. MURY
Cabaret, restaurant

Le Palace
8, rue du Fbg. Montmartre
75009 PARIS
Tel: 42 46 10 87
Trendy discotheque

Le Sunset
60, rue des Lombards
75001 PARIS
Tel: 40 26 46 60

Le Tango
15, rue Jules Lamant et Fils
93330 NEUILLY-SUR-MARNE
Tel: 43 08 20 49

Les Bains Douches
7, rue du Bourg l'Abbé
75003 PARIS
Tel: 48 87 01 80
The "in" place for the film and fashion crowd

Manhattan Jazz Club
New York Hotel
Disneyland Paris
B.P. 100
77777 MARNE-LA-VALLEE
Tel: 60 45 75 13

Moulin Rouge
82, Bd. de Clichy
75018 PARIS
Tel: 46 06 00 19

New Morning
7-9, rue des Petites Ecuries
75010 PARIS
Tel: 45 23 51 41
Concert club featuring jazz, salsa, Brazilian, African and world music

Paradis Latin
28, rue du Cardinal Lemoine
75005 PARIS
Res: 43 25 28 28

Passage du Nord-Ouest
13, rue du Fbg. Montmartre
75009 PARIS
Tel: 36 68 03 32

Whisky à Gogo
57, rue de Seine
75006 PARIS
Tel: 43 29 60 01

AAAA
62, rue Claude Bernard
75005 PARIS
Tel: 45 35 37 27

AABBC
20, rue Godot de Mauroy
75009 PARIS
Tel: 42 66 14 11
Fax: 42 66 31 89
Anglo-American Business and Culture Center. Located in Paris and Evry

Accueil d'Irlande
18, rue Neuve des Boulets
75011 PARIS
Tel: 43 48 08 60

AFL-CIO
23, rue de Rome
75008 PARIS
Tel: 43 87 74 57
Fax: 43 87 74 60
President: M. Lane KIRKLAND
European offices of the American Federation of Labour - Congress of Industrial Organizations

Africa Regional Services
USIS
2, rue St. Florentin
75001 PARIS
Tel: 43 12 46 80
Director: Mme Yolande VERON-SULLIVAN
Program Director: M. Thavanh SVENGSOUK
Cultural Affairs: M. Dominique NICOLAS

African Development
86, rue Ranelagh
75016 PARIS
Tel: 42 24 59 62
Fax: 40 50 03 87

AFS/VSF
46, avenue Jean Duhail
94372 FONTENAY-SOUS-BOIS Cedex
Tel: 43 94 11 88
Long-term stays in America, Australia, Canada, etc. for 15-18 year-olds

American Battle Monuments Commission
68, rue du 19 Janvier
92380 GARCHES
Tel: 47 01 19 76
Fax: 47 41 19 79
Director: Colonel Merlin PUGH
Upkeeps WWI and WWI cemeteries in Europe

American Business Forum
3, rue Washington
75008 PARIS
Tel: 53 75 20 71
Fax: 53 75 20 59

American Cathedral Junior Guild
23, avenue George V
75008 PARIS
Tel: 47 20 17 92
Chairman: Rebecca LECAUCHOIS

American Catholic Women's Group
St. Joseph's Church
50, avenue Hoche
75008 PARIS
Tel: 42 27 28 56
Contact: Anita MALLICK

American Club
The Mona Bismarck Foundation
34, avenue de New York
75016 PARIS
Tel: 47 23 64 36
Fax: 47 23 66 01

American Friends of Blérancourt
The Mona Bismarck Foundation
4, avenue de New York
75016 PARIS
Tel: 47 20 22 28
Promotion and renovation of the French National Museum of Franco-American Cooperation at Blérancourt

American Joint Distribution Committee
33, rue Miromesnil
75008 PARIS
Tel: 44 51 64 00
Fax: 44 51 64 10
Relief aid to foreign countries

American Language in Context
2, rue des Gravilliers
75003 PARIS
Tel: 42 77 29 12
Contact: M. John DAVIDSON
For business executives wanting to learn English in America

American Memorial Day Association
The Mona Bismarck Foundation
34, avenue de New York
75016 PARIS
Tel: 47 23 38 88

American Overseas Memorial Day Association
34, avenue de New York
75016 PARIS
Tel: 42 61 55 77

American Women's Group in Paris
22bis, rue Pétrarque
75116 PARIS
Tel: 47 55 87 50

Amherst College Alumni Association
c/o Hughes Hubbard & Reed
47, avenue George Mandel
75116 PARIS
Tel: 44 05 80 00
Fax: 45 53 15 04
Contact: M. Axel BAUM

Amis du Jardin Shakespeare du Pré Catelan
1, Place de Wagram
75017 PARIS
Tel: 42 27 39 54
Chairman: M. L. HEMPHILL

Amnesty International
4, rue de la Pierre Levée
75011 PARIS
Tel: 49 23 11 11
Fax: 43 38 26 15
Minitel: 3615 AMNESTY

Anglo-American Business and Culture Center
20, rue Godot de Mauroy
75009 PARIS
Tel: 42 66 14 11

Armée du Salut
National Headquarters
76, rue de Rome
75008 PARIS
Tel: 44 60 89 95
Salvation Army

Art Musique Echange
17, rue Maître Albert
75005 PARIS
Tel: 43 29 65 91
Contact: Linda DE NAZELLE
Concerts and cultural events in private homes to foster greater Franco-American understanding

Asia Business Center
73, Bd. Ménilmontant
75011 PARIS
Tel: 49 29 03 06
Fax: 49 29 04 71

Association de la Presse Etrangère
35, rue des Francs Bourgeois
75004 PARIS
Tel: 42 78 11 90
Fax: 42 78 08 78
Contact: Anne-Marie BOUCHAERT
Foreign Press Association

Association Franco-Ecossaise
5, rue de l'Alboni
75016 PARIS
Tel: 42 22 30 78
President: M. Georges DICKSON

Association Frank
32, rue Edouard Vaillant
93100 MONTREUIL
Tel: 48 59 66 58
Fax: 48 59 66 68
E-mail:
100265.1435@compuserve.com
Director: M. David APPLEFIELD
Publishes the literary journal Frank, Paris-Anglophone, and the Paris-Anglophone web site

Association Linguistique et Culturelle
Franco-Britannique
5, Place de l'Etape
78200 MANTES LA JOLIE
Tel: 30 92 72 00
Fax: 30 92 35 28

Association of American Wives of Europeans (AAWE)
B.P. 127
92154 SURESNES Cedex
Tel: 47 28 46 39
Activities for members and their children, publishes AAWE Guide to Education

Association of Americans Resident Overseas (AARO)
B.P. 127
92154 SURESNES Cedex
Tel: 42 04 09 38
Contact: Barbara STERN

Association of Irish Women in France (AIWF)
24, rue de Grenelle
75007 PARIS
President: Patricia BLACK
Promoting social and cultural contacts and providing friendly and professional help to Irish women in France

B'nai Brith Youth Organization
5bis, rue de Rochechouart
75009 PARIS
Tel: 40 82 95 75

B.I.A.C.
13, chausée de la Muette
75016 PARIS
Tel: 42 30 09 60
Fax: 45 24 66 20
Business & Industry Advisory Committee

Bloom Where You Are Planted
Women of the American Church
65, quai d'Orsay
75007 PARIS
Tel: 47 05 07 99
Newcomer orientation series in October

Blue Note Studio
19, avenue de St. Cloud
78000 VERSAILLES
Tel: 39 50 27 46
Artistic Director: Denise REVE
Organizes shows combining poetry, dance, music, mime and theater

Boy Scouts of America
c/o American Embassy
2, avenue Gabriel
75382 PARIS Cedex 8
Tel: 43 12 20 55
Contact: M. Don TERRY

British & Commonwealth Women's Association
7, rue Auguste Vacquerie
75116 PARIS
Tel: 47 20 01 36
President: Valerie CHEMAMA
A club for holders of British and Commonwealth passports offering cultural visits, entertainment, talks, social occasions plus a comprehensive English library and monthly newsletter

British Diplomatic Spouses Association
British Embassy
33, rue du Fbg. St. Honoré
75008 PARIS
Contact: M. Arthur PLAXY

British European Center
5, rue Richepanse
75008 PARIS
Tel: 42 60 40 97
Fax: 42 60 36 55

British Legion
8, rue Boudreau
75009 PARIS
Tel: 47 42 19 26

British Overseas Trade Board
c/o Ambassade de Grande-Bretagne
35, rue du Fbg. St. Honoré
75008 PARIS
Tel: 42 66 91 42
Contact: M. Brian WEST

Business Connexions
10, Jardins Boieldieu
92800 PUTEAUX
Tel: 46 96 09 95
Fax: 43 20 47 02
Organizes theme-oriented business luncheons

Business Development Network International
4, avenue des Jonchères
78121 CRESPIERES
Tel: 30 54 94 66
Fax: 30 54 94 67
Contact: Mme E. DE VULPILLIERES
Finds new clients at business card exchanges in Paris. Stages seminars and individual sessions "How to Make Your Small Business Prosperous". Low cost for tight budgets. In French and English

Business Group Center
114bis, rue Michel-Ange
75016 PARIS
Tel: 40 71 28 85

Canadian Women's Association
5, rue de Constantine
75007 PARIS
Tel: 44 05 01 66
President: Nadine SAMMON

Centrale Franco-Britannique
19, rue Saulnier
75009 PARIS
Tel: 48 01 25 77
Fax: 48 01 25 90

Centre d'Echanges Internationaux
1, rue Gozlin
75006 PARIS
Tel: 45 49 26 25
Language study abroad for children, teenagers and adults

Cercle de Jazz Traditionnel et de Musique Classique
16, rue des Sycomores
34080 MONTPELLIER
Tel: (16) 67 61 18 99
Fax: (16) 67 61 18 99
Contact: M. Arthur FELL
Association aimed at promoting traditional jazz and classical music

CGT
263, rue de Paris
93100 MONTREUIL
Tel: 48 18 80 00
Labor union

Children's Academy on Tour
66, avenue des
Champs-Elysées, no. 74
75008 PARIS
Tel: 44 95 14 31
Contact: Sabrina SCOTT
A children's organization for cultural awareness

Club Culturel Franco-Americain
13, avenue du Maréchal Leclerc
92360 MEUDON-LA-FORET
Tel: 46 30 71 37
Fax: 46 31 46 80
Contact: Catherine AUBIN
Discovery of the private France

CNC
12, rue de Lubeck
75016 PARIS
Tel: 44 34 34 40
Fax: 47 55 04 91
National Film Office

Columbia Business Club France-Amérique
9, avenue Franklin Roosevelt
75008 PARIS
Tel: 42 24 62 62
Fax: 45 20 70 06
Columbia University Business School Alumni Association
2nd address: c/o OCMI, 10, rue Chardin, 75016, Paris

Commission Franco-Américaine d'Echanges Universitaires
9, rue Chardin
75016 PARIS
Tel: 45 20 46 54
Fax: 42 88 04 79

Community Liaison Office
Embassy of the United States
2, avenue Gabriel
75008 PARIS
Tel: 43 12 22 15
Contact: Suellen VITTITOW

Community Liaison Office
Australian Embassy
4, rue Jean Rey
75015 PARIS
Tel: 40 59 35 61
Fax: 40 59 33 10

Community Liaison Office
British Embassy
35, rue du Fbg. St. Honoré
75383 PARIS Cedex 08
Tel: 42 66 91 42 ext 3510

Conseil National du Patronat Français
31, avenue Pierre Ier de Serbie
75016 PARIS
Tel: 40 69 44 44
Fax: 47 23 47 32
President: M. Jean GANDOIS
French National Employers Association

Conseillers du Commerce Extérieur
22, avenue Franklin Roosevelt
75008 PARIS
Tel: 43 59 66 24
Fax: 42 25 29 87
Contact: Mme Veronique PEYRELONGUE

Contact B
c/o Terrell
10, rue Rodier
75009 PARIS
Tel: 45 26 81 34
Contact: Bridget TERRELL
Helps young people to find jobs

Cornell Club of France
85, rue de Courcelles
75017 PARIS
Tel: 42 67 14 89
Fax: 42 67 06 08
E-mail:
100451.3613@compuserve.com
President: Me Richard MEADE
Meetings among alumni and with alumni of other schools

Daughters of the American Revolution
c/o Mrs. Alain MAITROT
118, avenue Félix Faure
75015 PARIS
Tel: 45 54 64 19

Democrats Abroad (France)
30, rue des Rosiers
75004 PARIS
Tel: 48 04 51 75
Fax: 48 04 51 17
Contact: M. Allin SEWARD

Duke University Club
5, rue Bargue
75015 PARIS
Tel: 45 66 49 05
Contact: M. J. SMALLHOOVER

Echange France-Amérique du Nord (EFAN)
20, rue Louis David
75116 PARIS
Tel: 45 03 12 77
Fax: 40 72 62 49
E-mail:
100536,2241@compuserve.com
Contact: Monique CARLIER
Exchanges between French and American Senior High Schools

EFFS
9, rue Duphot
75001 PARIS
Tel: 42 86 81 94
Educational Foundation for Foreign Study

English Juniors' Club
3, rue Faustin Hélie
75116 PARIS
Tel: 42 03 66 87
Contact: Monique IFERGAN
English courses for young kids

English Speaking Union France
21, rue Michel Ange
75016 PARIS
Tel: 46 51 55 24
President: Mme Beatrix DE MONTGERMONT-KEIL
Promoting understanding and friendship worldwide

European Strategy and Lobbying
123, avenue des Champs-Elysées
75008 PARIS
Tel: 40 73 14 00

European Trading Union
22, Bd. Gouvion St. Cyr
75017 PARIS
Tel: 45 72 31 87

European Working Group on Human Gene Transfer and Therapy
1, avenue Claude Vellefaux
75010 PARIS
Tel: 42 06 92 14

Eurosynergy Network
7, rue Leroux
75016 PARIS
Tel: 45 00 37 77
Fax: 45 00 83 47
Contact: Valerie SCHUMAN
Networking, developing links between towns or municipalities and small and medium-sized companies. Operates in conjunction with OCEAN

Fondation Cartier pour l'Art Contemporain
261, Bd. Raspail
75014 PARIS
Tel: 42 18 56 50

Fondation Maréchal Foch
Pavillon Balsan
40, rue Worth
92151 SURESNES
Tel: 45 06 29 24
Fax: 46 97 04 39
Contact: Corinne DENIS
Medical aid to those in need

Fondation Soros (Paris)
38, Bd. Beaumarchais
75011 PARIS
Tel: 48 05 24 74
Fax: 40 21 65 41
E-mail: sorosparis@gn.apc.org
Contact: Annette LABOREY

France Louisiane-Franco Américaine
28, Bd. de Strasbourg
75010 PARIS
Tel: 42 40 68 78
Fax: 42 40 68 80
Develops cultural and economic relations between France and Louisiana

France-Amérique
9, avenue Franklin Roosevelt
75008 PARIS
Tel: 43 59 51 00
Fax: 40 75 00 97
President: M. André ROSS
Fosters cultural and economic relations

France-Canada
5, rue de Constantine
75007 PARIS
Tel: 45 55 83 65

France-Etats-Unis
6, Bd. de Grenelle
75015 PARIS
Tel: 45 77 48 92
President: M. J. MAISONROUGE

France-Ontario
Allée de Clotomont
77183 CROISSY-BEAUBOURG
Tel: 60 06 44 50
Fax: 60 05 03 45
President: Christine SCARANO

France-Québec
24, rue Modigliani
75015 PARIS
Tel: 45 54 35 37
Fax: 45 57 69 44
President: M. Georges POIRIER

French Board for Foreign Trade
10, avenue d'Iéna
75016 PARIS
Tel: 40 73 30 00
Fax: 40 73 39 79
President: M. DOUBIN

French-American Center
10, montée de la Tour
30400 VILLENEUVE-LES-AVIGNON
Tel: (16) 90 25 93 23
Fax: (16) 90 25 93 24
Director: M. Jerôme Henry RUDES
An educational and cultural center in the south of France

Friends of Vieilles Maisons Françaises
91, rue du Fbg. St. Honoré
75370 PARIS Cedex 08
Tel: 42 66 00 12
Fax: 49 24 95 99
Contact: Suzanne ESTABLIE
US non-profit cultural organization

Georgetown University Club
24bis, rue Greuze
75016 PARIS
Tel: 47 27 48 43

Groupe d'Amitié France - Etats Unis
126, rue de l'Université
75007 PARIS
Tel: 40 63 86 26
Fax: 40 63 86 80
Intl Affairs Director:
Mme GIBEL-DEBURGE
Exchanges between Members of Parliament

Groupe d'Amitié France-Etats Unis du Sénat
Palais du Luxembourg
75291 PARIS Cedex 06
Tel: 42 34 27 73
Fax: 42 34 21 69
Contact: M. Pierre DE FLEURIEU
Maintains relations with US Senate and House of Representatives

Harvard Business School Club of France
9, avenue Franklin Roosevelt
75008 PARIS
Tel: 42 56 20 98
Fax: 45 62 39 08

Indian Women's Association
11, rue Ste Anne
75001 PARIS
Tel: 47 49 28 25
President: Mrs Iyer RUGMINI

Interalliée Club
33, rue du Fbg. St. Honoré
75008 PARIS
Tel: 42 65 96 00
Private club with restaurant

International Business Service
120, avenue des Champs-Elysées
75008 PARIS
Tel: 43 59 12 07

International League for the Protection of Horses
3, rue de Lyon
75012 PARIS
Tel: 44 67 95 76
Fax: 44 67 00 57

International Student & Au Pair Bureau
38, rue Daumesnil
75012 PARIS
Tel: 43 46 04 67

IOP - Organisations, Idées et Promotion
62, rue Miromesnil
75008 PARIS
Tel: 49 53 27 60
Fax: 49 53 27 88
Minitel: 3616 SALONS
Contact: Mme Christine FRICHET
Organises world fairs and conferences (e.g. Expolangues)

International Council of Scientific Unions
51, Bd. Montmorency
75008 PARIS
Tel: 45 25 03 29
Fax: 42 88 94 31

Jamaican Group
19, rue du Docteur Blanche
75016 PARIS
Tel: 42 88 85 37
Contact: Paula THOMAS

Junior Service League of Paris
34, avenue de New York
75016 PARIS
Tel: 45 77 09 78
President: Caroline ROBERT
Aiming to improve the community through trained volunteers in areas such as health, the arts and child welfare

L'Europe des Arts
75, rue du Fbg. St. Honoré
75008 PARIS
Tel: 47 42 27 79
Fax: 47 42 55 48
President: Janet GREENBERG
Cultural club of European executives

La Léche League France
7, allée des Bruyères
78620 L'ETANG LA VILLE
Tel: 39 58 45 84
Information and advice on breastfeeding

Laboratoire International de Pansémiotique Moderne
182, avenue Jean Lolive
93500 PANTIN
Tel: 48 40 53 57
Contact: M. Christophe MIELLE

Le Méridien Hotel Business Center
19, rue du Commandant Mouchotte
75014 PARIS
Tel: 44 36 49 08

Lions Club International
295, rue St. Jacques
75005 PARIS
Tel: 46 34 14 10
Fax: 46 33 92 41

Maison de l'Amérique Latine
217, Bd. St. Germain
75007 PARIS
Tel: 49 54 75 00
South American cultural center

Maison des Provinces de France
CIUP-chambre 204
55, Bd. Jourdan
75014 PARIS
Tel: 44 16 01 32
Contact: Kisok ROH
Student hostel

Maxim's Business Club
5, rue Royale
75008 PARIS
Tel: 42 65 34 41
Fax: 40 07 00 46

MIT Club of France
9, avenue Franklin Roosevelt
75008 PARIS
Tel: 43 59 01 39
Fax: 45 61 06 41

Nigerian Women in Paris
40, Bd. Gabriel Péri
92240 MALAKOFF
Contact: Buki KOGBE

OECD
2, rue André Pascal
75016 PARIS Cedex 16
Tel: 45 24 82 00
Fax: 45 24 85 00
Secretary General:
M. Jean-Claude PAYE
Organization for Economic Cooperation and Development

OECD British Delegation
19, rue de Franqueville
75016 PARIS
Tel: 45 24 98 28

OECD Canadian Delegation
15bis, rue de Franqueville
75016 PARIS
Tel: 44 43 20 90

Office National Irlandais du Bétail et de la Viande
33, rue de Miromesnil
75008 PARIS
Tel: 42 66 22 93
Fax: 42 66 22 88
Director: M. James O'DONNELL
Irish National Cattle and Meat Association

Office of American Services
2, rue St. Florentin
75382 PARIS Cedex 08
Tel: 43 12 22 22

Organisations, Idées et Promotion (OIP)
62, rue de Miromesnil
75008 PARIS
Tel: 49 53 27 60
Fax: 49 53 27 88

Paris Alumnae/i Network P.A.N.
4bis, avenue du Pavillon Sully
78230 LE PECQ
Tel: 39 73 00 88
Fax: 39 73 52 02
Contact: Barbara HANO
Graduates of US colleges and universities

Paris American Academy
7, rue Berthollet
75005 PARIS
Tel: 44 08 99 69

Paris American AIDS Committee
1, Bd. du Temple
75001 PARIS
Tel: 42 27 45 75
Fax: 42 27 45 75
Contact: M. David SELIKOWITZ

Paris Welsh Society
10, rue de l'Armée d'Orient
75018 PARIS
Tel: 46 06 76 13
President: Nesta PIERRY
Monthly meetings, lunch or dinner

Paris Writers' Workshop
WICE
20, Bd. Montparnasse
75015 PARIS
Tel: 45 66 75 50
Fax: 40 65 96 53

Point de Vue Canada
5, rue Pecquay
75004 PARIS
Tel: 40 27 91 36
Fax: 42 77 76 69
Director: Mme Lynda CADIEUX
Promotes tourism to Canada

Princeton Paris Research Corporation
5, rue Lincoln
75008 PARIS
Tel: 45 63 4018

Péril - Europe
4, rue de la Monnaie
30400 VILLENEUVE-LES-AVIGNON
Tel: (16) 90 25 43 77
Contact: M. Alexandre ROUSSET
Solves problems of language hegemony

Reid Hall Film Committee
4, rue de Chevreuse
75006 PARIS
Tel: 43 20 64 65

Republicans Abroad (France)
c/o Mme Habourdin
87, avenue Mozart
75016 PARIS
Tel: 42 88 77 78
President: Ms. Phyllis MORGAN

Retired Officers' Association
The Mona Bismarck Foundation
34, avenue de New York
75016 PARIS
Tel: 47 23 38 88

Rotary Club of Paris
40, Bd. Emile Augier
75116 PARIS
Tel: 45 04 14 44
Fax: 45 04 93 98

Réunion des Musées Nationaux (RMN)
49, rue Etienne Marcel
75001 PARIS
Tel: 40 13 48 00
Fax: 40 13 48 61
Association of French National Museums

Société des Cincinnati de France
2bis, rue Rabelais
75008 PARIS
Tel: 45 61 45 40
Fax: 45 61 45 40

Société Protectrice des Animaux
39, Bd. Berthier
75017 PARIS
Tel: 43 80 40 66
Fax: 47 63 74 76
Animal protection

Sons of the American Revolution
52, avenue des Champs-Elysées
75008 PARIS
Tel: 43 59 10 31
President: M. Helie DE NOAILLES

SPADEM
15, rue St. Nicholas
75012 PARIS
Tel: 43 34 58 58
Fax: 43 44 84 54
Association for visual artists' rights

Swedish Women's Educational Association
70, rue Pasteur
91330 YERRES
Tel: 69 48 03 09
Fax: 69 49 22 13
President: Aivi PERTEL-TORRES

The Mona Bismarck Foundation
34, avenue de New York
75016 PARIS
Tel: 47 23 38 88
Fax: 42 86 94 07
Director: Mme DUNHAM
Promotes French-American culture & art

The Travellers Club
25, avenue des Champs-Elysées
75008 PARIS
Tel: 43 59 75 00
Fax: 45 62 95 16

TOC'H Association
14, avenue de Joinville
94130 NOGENT-SUR-MARNE
Tel: 48 73 48 37
Contact: Doris LECK
Charity association for English-speaking senior citizens

Trinity College Dublin Association France
c/o 22, rue de Navarin
75009 PARIS
Tel: 48 74 09 71
Fax: 30 53 26 21
Hon. Secretary: Denise PHELAN
University of Dublin Graduates' Association

"Un Enfant par la Main"
6, rue Paul Cézanne
93364 NEUILLY PLAISANCE
Tel: 49 44 66 33
Contact: Marguerite GUYOT
Helps underprivileged children

UNESCO
7, Place de Fontenoy
75700 PARIS Cedex 07
Tel: 45 68 10 00
Fax: 45 67 16 90
Director: M. Federico MAYOR-ZARAGOZA

Union Chrétienne de Jeunes Filles (YWCA)
22, rue de Naples
75008 PARIS
Tel: 45 22 23 49
Fax: 42 94 81 24
Director: Mme Anne-Marie BONEU
Residential foyers for young women

Union Routière de France
10, rue Clément Marot
75008 PARIS
Tel: 40 70 05 45
Fax: 47 23 77 57
Communications Director:
Mlle Christine BURRONI
French Transport Union

United Service Organization Inc.
20, rue de la Tremoille
75008 PARIS
Tel: 40 70 99 68
Fax: 40 70 99 53
Director: Mme Beverley CERCHIO

Volunteers of the American Hospital of Paris
63, Bd. Victor Hugo
92200 NEUILLY-SUR-SEINE
Tel: 46 41 25 48
Services, library for patients, sale of "Le Cookbook" to aid hospital

Wine Business Club
16, rue St. Petersbourg
75008 PARIS
Tel: 42 93 10 43
Fax: 42 93 10 08
President: M. Alain MARTY

World Federation of Americans Abroad
B.P. 27
92154 SURESNES
Tel: 42 04 05 24
Fax: 42 04 09 12
President: M. Gregory GOOD

World Monuments Fund
The Mona Bismarck Foundation
34, avenue de New York
75116 PARIS
Tel: 47 20 71 99
Fax: 47 20 71 27

World Trade Center Paris CCIP
2, Place de la Défense
CNIT B.P. 460
92053 PARIS LA DEFENSE
Tel: 46 12 25 80
Fax: 47 73 60 04
Contact: Mme Geneviève FOURNIER

Yale Club of Paris
30, rue des Rosiers
75004 PARIS
Tel: 48 04 51 75
Fax: 48 04 51 17
President: M. Allin SEWARD

YMCA/YWCA
5, Place de Vénétie
75013 PARIS
Tel: 45 83 62 63
Fax: 45 86 64 92

Youth for Understanding
30, Place St. Georges
75009 PARIS
Tel: 45 26 37 38
Fax: 45 26 35 25
Contact: Luce MARTEL
One-year study trips to the USA

English-Language Newpapers
Journaux de Langue Anglaise

Asia Times
108, rue Montmartre
75002 PARIS
Tel: 42 21 09 47

Bureau of National Affairs, Washington
78, rue des Archives
75003 PARIS
Tel: 42 72 92 52
Fax: 40 27 83 00
Correspondent: Mme Barbara CASASSUS

Chicago Tribune
1, rue Delambre
75014 PARIS
Tel: 43 20 55 50
Fax: 43 20 87 88
Correspondent: Sharon WAXMAN

Daily Express
11, rue de Vaugirard
75006 PARIS
Tel: 43 54 42 00
Fax: 43 29 86 47
Correspondent: M. Jack GEE

Daily Mail
36, rue du Sentier
75002 PARIS
Tel: 45 08 48 41
Tel: 42 00 76 69
Fax: 45 08 48 43
Correspondent: M. Peter SHARD

Daily Telegraph/ Sunday Telegraph
242, rue de Rivoli
75001 PARIS
Tel: 42 60 38 85
Fax: 42 61 52 91
Correspondent: Mrs Suzanne LOWRY

Evening Standard/ Sunday Express
47, avenue de Sorraines
78110 LE VESINET
Tel: 39 76 88 88
Correspondent: M. Peter DEWHIRST

Hearst Newspapers
162, rue du Fbg. St. Honoré
75008 PARIS
Tel: 45 63 13 28
Fax: 45 53 66 75
Correspondent Europe:
M. Bernard KAPLAN

International Herald Tribune
181, avenue Charles de Gaulle
92521 NEUILLY Cedex
Tel: 41 43 93 00
Fax: 41.43.93.38 (editorial)
Executive Editor: M. John VINOCUR
Daily newspaper written and compiled by local staff with The New York Times and The Washington Post, catering primarily to the international business community

Los Angeles Times
10, Bd. Malesherbes
75008 PARIS
Tel: 49 24 96 65
Fax: 40 07 03 95
Bureau Chief: Scott KRAFT

New York Times Syndication
Sales Corporation
3, rue Scribe
75009 PARIS
Tel: 47 42 17 11
Fax: 47 42 18 81

Saint Petersbourg Times
162, rue du Fbg. St. Honoré
75008 PARIS
Tel: 42 56 29 74
Fax: 42 56 44 05
Correspondent: M. Wilbur LANDREY

The European
44, rue de la Bienfaisance
75008 PARIS
Tel: 45 63 03 62
Fax: 45 62 98 34
Bureau Chief: Anne-Elisabeth MOUTET
The weekly newspaper for Europe

The Financial Times
168, rue de Rivoli
75001 PARIS
Tel: 42 97 06 26
Fax: 42 97 06 29
Bureau Chief: M. David BUCHAN
(see advertisement)

The Guardian
26, rue de la Pépinière
75008 PARIS
Tel: 30 54 41 51

The Herald
39, rue Jean Jaurès
92300 LEVALLOIS-PERRET
Tel: 45 74 28 17
Correspondent: M. Nicholas POWELL

The Independent
38, avenue Gabriel
75008 PARIS
Tel: 53 75 24 39
Fax: 53 75 24 39
Correspondent: Mary DEJEVSKY

The New York Times
3, rue Scribe
75009 PARIS
Tel: 42 66 37 49
Fax: 47 42 88 21
Manager: Daphné ANGLES

The Times/The Sunday Times
8, rue Halévy
75441 PARIS Cedex 09
Tel: 47 42 73 21
Fax: 47 42 72 96
Times Correspondent:
M. Charles BREMNER
Sunday Times Correspondent:
M. Tony ALLEN-MILLS

The Washington Post
1, rue Delambre
75014 PARIS
Tel: 43 20 55 50
Fax: 43 20 87 88
Correspondent: Sharon WAXMAN

The Washington Post
181, avenue Charles de Gaulle
92521 NEUILLY-SUR-SEINE
Tel: 41 43 92 22
Fax: 41 43 92 23
Correspondent: Sharon WAXMAN

USA Today International
17, rue Tronchet
75008 PARIS
Tel: 42 66 08 61
Fax: 42 66 08 74
(see advertisement)

Variety
64, rue Jean-Pierre Timbaud
75011 PARIS
Tel: 43 55 07 43
Fax: 43 55 06 99
Correspondent: M. Mike WILLIAMS
Legendary weekly for music and entertainment

Vocable
4, rue de Cérisoles
75008 PARIS
Tel: 47 20 74 16
Fax: 47 23 49 80
Geared towards French readers wanting to maintain and improve their foreign language skills. English edition available at kiosks and bookstores

Wall Street Journal
3, rue du Fbg. St. Honoré
75008 PARIS
Tel: 47 42 08 06
Fax: 47 42 90 98
Bureau Chief: M. Thomas KAMM

English-Language Magazines
Revues de Langue Anglaise

Across the Board
16, rue Spontini
75116 PARIS
Tel: 45 53 36 32
Fax: 45 53 36 32
Correspondent: M. Judson GOODING

Art International
77, rue des Archives
75003 PARIS
Tel: 48 04 84 54
Fax: 48 04 82 00
Editors: Michael PEPPIATT
& Jill LLOYD
Quarterly in English on all aspects of art

Arts Magazine
54, avenue d'Italie
75013 PARIS
Tel: 45 89 23 05
Fax: 45 88 57 22
Correspondent: Diana HOROWITZ
American contemporary art magazine (Paris office)

Boulevard Magazine
68, rue des Archives
75003 PARIS
Tel: 44 78 82 82
Publisher: Fiona LAZAREFF
Advertising Director:
Susan MORROW
(see advertisement)

Fairchild Publications
9, rue Royale
75008 PARIS
Tel: 44 51 13 00
Fax: 42 68 16 41
Publishes Women's Wear Daily, Sport Style, Children's Business, Fashion Business Europe...

Fashion Guide Publications
20, rue Danielle Casanova
75002 PARIS
Tel: 42 60 54 45
Fax: 42 60 59 91

First-Class à Paris
31, avenue des Champs-Elysées
75008 PARIS
Tel: 42 25 26 25
Fax: 43 60 08 08
Director: M. Laurent MIMOUN
Editions M.J.M.

France - Why and Where
c/o Mediatime France
68, rue des Archives
75003 PARIS
Tel: 44 78 82 82
Fax: 44 78 82 83
Editor: Mme Christine HOHENADEL
An indispensable guide for business relocation

Hearst Publications
42, avenue Montaigne
75008 PARIS
Tel: 47 23 63 44
Fax: 47 20 10 29
European Executive Editor:
Jane CATTANI
Publishes Harper's Bazaar, Marie-Claire USA *and* Town and Country

International Fund Investment
181, avenue Charles de Gaulle
92200 NEUILLY-SUR-SEINE
Tel: 46 37 93 11
Fax: 46 37 21 33
Editor: M. BAKER
World investment magazine

Life Magazine
14, rue de Marignan
75008 PARIS
Tel: 44 95 70 31

Macmillan Magazines
3-5, rue Joseph Sansboeuf
75008 PARIS
Tel: 43 87 42 17
Fax: 43 87 42 15
Correspondent: M. D. BUTLER

National Oilwell
122, rue du Fbg. St. Honoré
75008 PARIS
Tel: 42 25 22 79
Fax: 45 62 86 64

New York Magazine
127, rue Ranelagh
75016 PARIS
Tel: 46 47 90 23

Newsweek
162, rue du Fbg. St. Honoré
75008 PARIS
Tel: 42 56 06 81
Tel: 42 89 45 70
Editor-in-Chief: M. Christopher DICKEY

Time Out Paris
100, rue du Fbg. St. Antoine
75012 PARIS
Tel: 44 87 00 45
Fax: 44 73 90 60
Managing Director: Karen ALBRECHT
Selection of the city's best shows and entertainment in English. Published in Pariscope

Publisher's Weekly
B.P. 214
75264 PARIS Cedex 06
Tel: 43 21 77 82
Correspondent Europe:
M. Herbert LOTTMAN

The Economist
26, rue de la Pépinière
75008 PARIS
Tel: 42 94 21 76
Fax: 42 94 22 17
Correspondent: M. Edward CARR

The Traveler
73, rue de Vaugirard
75006 PARIS
Tel: 53 71 10 00

Time Magazine
14, rue de Marignan
75008 PARIS
Tel: 44 95 00 30
Subscriptions: 05 90 59 86

Time-Life International
67, avenue de Wagram
75017 PARIS
Tel: 44 01 49 99
Fax: 44 01 49 29
President: M. Jeb SIDER

Vanity Fair Magazine
127, rue du Ranelagh
75016 PARIS
Tel: 46 47 90 23

Vintage International Magazine
20, rue Friant
75014 PARIS
Tel: 45 43 37 26
Editor-in-Chief: M. Jacques SALLE
Quarterly consumer-oriented magazine about wine and spirits

Where Paris
5, rue La Boétie
75008 PARIS
Tel: 44 56 31 96
Fax: 42 66 49 11
Senior Editor: Alexandra D'EPREMESNIL
*English-language magazine about living it up in Paris, available from **** hotels*

French Newspapers
Journaux Français

France-Soir
37, rue du Louvre
75002 PARIS
Tel: 44 82 87 00

InfoMatin
32, rue René Boulanger
75472 PARIS Cedex 10
Tel: 44 84 70 00
Fax: 44 84 70 70
Editor-in-Chief: M. JEZEGABEL
A bird's-eye view of French news

L'Humanité
32, rue Jean Jaurès
93528 ST DENIS Cedex
Tel: 49 22 72 72
Fax: 49 22 72 51
Editor-in-Chief: M. Claude CABANES
Official organ of the French Communist Party

L'Equipe
4, rue Rouget de Lisle
92137 ISSY-LES-MOULINEAUX
Tel: 40 93 20 20
Editor-in-Chief: M. Jérôme BUREAU
Daily newspaper on sport

La Centrale des Particuliers
11, avenue Dubonnet
92416 COURBEVOIE Cedex
Tel: 41 16 60 01
Fax: 41 16 60 09
President: M. Marc DUALE
Newspaper specialized in classified ads

Le Canard Enchaîné
173, rue St. Honoré
75001 PARIS
Tel: 42 60 31 36
Editor-in-Chief: M. Claude ANGELI
Satirical news and commentary

Le Figaro
37, rue du Louvre
75002 PARIS
Tel: 42 21 62 00
Fax: 42 21 64 05
Editor-in-Chief: M. Antoine Pierre MARIANO
Conservative French daily

Le Monde
15, rue Falguière
75501 PARIS Cedex 15
Tel: 40 65 25 25
Fax: 40 65 25 99
Editor-in-Chief: M. Jean-Noel BERGEROUX
Comprehensive evening newspaper with a liberal outlook

Le Parisien
25, avenue Michelet
93408 ST-OUEN Cedex
Tel: 40 10 30 30
Fax: 40 12 90 90
Editor-in-Chief: M. Gilbert CHALEIL

Les Echos
46, rue La Boétie
75381 PARIS Cedex 08
Tel: 49 53 65 65
Fax: 45 61 48 92
Editor-in-Chief: M. Nicolas BEYTOUT
Financial daily

Libération
11, rue Béranger
75003 PARIS
Tel: 42 76 17 89
Fax: 42 72 94 93
Director: M. Serge JULY
Daily newspaper

VSD
15, rue Cassette
75280 PARIS Cedex 6
Tel: 45 49 55 55
Fax: 45 49 41 66
President: M. François SIEGEL
Weekend tabloid

French Magazines
Revues Françaises

Cahiers du Cinéma
9, passage de la Boule Blanche
75012 PARIS
Tel: 43 43 92 20
Fax: 43 43 95 04
Editor-in-Chief: M. Thierry JOUSSE
Monthly magazine devoted to all aspects of the film industry

Capital
15, rue Galvani
75017 PARIS
Tel: 40 55 48 50
French monthly devoted to economic matters

CB News
175-177, rue d'Aguesseau
92100 BOULOGNE
Tel: 46 04 12 12
Fax: 46 04 38 52
Director: M. Christian BLACHAS
French advertising and media weekly

Condé Nast Publications
73, rue de Vaugirard
75006 PARIS
Tel: 53 71 10 00
Tel: 05 23 82 80
Fax: 53 71 11 44 (Intl)

Elle
149-151, rue Anatole France
92534 LEVALLOIS-PERRET Cedex
Tel: 41 34 60 00
Fax: 41 34 74 92
Editor-in-Chief: M. Jean Dominique BAUBY

Globe Hebdo
73, rue Pascal
75013 PARIS
Tel: 47 07 04 07

Groupe Hachette Filipacchi
149-151, rue Anatole France
92534 LEVALLOIS-PERRET Cedex
Tel: 40 74 70 00
Fax: 40 74 31 25
Publishes Paris-Match, Télé-7-Jours, Elle

Groupe Novapress
33, rue du Fbg. St. Antoine
75011 PARIS
Tel: 53 33 33 00
Fax: 43 44 48 16

L'Etudiant
27, rue du Chemin Vert
75543 PARIS Cedex 11
Tel: 48 07 41 41
Fax: 47 00 79 80
A comprehensive magazine for the student community

L'Evénement du Jeudi
2, rue Christine
75006 PARIS
Tel: 43 54 84 80
Fax: 46 34 69 36
Editor-in-Chief:
M. Jean-François KAHN
Weekly magazine (politics, economy, arts)

L'Express
61, avenue Hoche
75008 PARIS
Tel: 40 54 30 00
Fax: 40 54 34 40
Editor-in-Chief:
Christine OCKRENT

L'Officiel des Spectacles
1, rue Berri
75008 PARIS
Tel: 42 25 57 84
Fax: 45 61 04 00
Entertainment weekly

Le Nouvel Observateur
10-12, Place de la Bourse
75002 PARIS
Tel: 44 88 34 34
Fax: 44 88 34 28
Executive Assistant:
Mme Sonia LE NORCY

Le Point
140, rue de Rennes
75006 PARIS
Tel: 49 54 10 10

Lire
61, avenue Hoche
75380 PARIS Cedex 8
Tel: 40 54 30 00
Fax: 45 63 48 14
Literary monthly

Livres Hebdo
30, rue Dauphine
75006 PARIS
Tel: 44 41 28 00
Fax: 43 29 77 85

Magazine Littéraire
40, rue des Saints Pères
75007 PARIS
Tel: 45 44 14 51
Fax: 45 48 86 36

Marie-Claire
10, Bd. des Frères Voisin
Cedex 9
92792 ISSY-LES-MOULINEAUX
Tel: 41 46 88 88
Fax: 41 46 86 86
President: Mme Evelyne PROUVOST-BERRY

NMPP
52, rue Jacques Hillairet
75012 PARIS
Tel: 49 28 70 00
National Press Distributors

Positif
156, rue Oberkampf
75011 PARIS
Tel: 43 38 19 66
Fax: 43 38 63 10
Film monthly

SEPCOM
5-7, rue de l'Amiral Courbet
94160 ST MANDE
Tel: 43 98 22 22
Fax: 43 28 72 12
Director: M. Jean KAMINSKY
French press group publishing computer mags

Nova Magazine
33, rue du Fbg. St. Antoine
75012 PARIS
Tel: 53 33 33 35
Fax: 43 44 48 16
Editor-in-Chief: M. Patrick ZERBIB
New magazine for trendy Parisians (city life, films, cultural events, portraits, smart tips)

Télérama/Télérama Junior
129, Bd. Malesherbes
75017 PARIS
Tel: 48 88 48 88
Fax: 47 64 02 04
Director: M. Claude SALES
Weekly TV/Radio magazine

Vogue Décoration/
Maisons et Jardins
73, rue de Vaugirard
75006 PARIS
Tel: 53 71 10 00
Fax: 53 71 11 88

Vogue Glamour
73, rue de Vaugirard
75006 PARIS
Tel: 53 71 10 00
Fax: 53 71 10 55

Vogue Hommes
73, rue de Vaugirard
75006 PARIS
Tel: 53 71 10 00
Fax: 53 71 11 00

Journals/Newsletters
Périodiques/Bulletins

Commerce in France
21, avenue George V
75008 PARIS
Tel: 47 23 80 26
Fax: 47 20 18 62
Editor: M. John DAVIDSON
Published by the American Chamber of Commerce

Courrier International
4, rue Raoul Dufy
75020 PARIS
Tel: 43 58 49 49
Fax: 43 58 49 00
Weekly newsletter with the essential of the world's press in French

Crosstown Paris
2, rue de Paradis
75010 PARIS
Tel: 48 00 96 84
Fax: 42 47 12 34
Editor: Bonnie WOOLLEY
Monthly newsletter in English

Entrevue
IMEC
25, rue de Lille
75007 PARIS
Tel: 42 61 29 29
Fax: 49 27 03 15
Director: M. Olivier CORPET

European Sponsorship Report
65, Bd. de Grenelle
75015 PARIS
Tel: 45 79 04 14

France-USA Contacts (FUSAC)
3, rue Larochelle
75014 PARIS
Tel: 45 38 56 57
Fax: 45 38 98 94
Editors: John & Lisa VAN DEN BOS
Fortnightly circular with useful tips as well as housing and employment ads

Frank: An International Journal of Contemporary Writing & Art
32, rue Edouard Vaillant
93100 MONTREUIL
Tel: 49 59 66 58
Fax: 48 59 66 68
E-mail:
100265.1435@compuserve.com
Editor: M. David APPLEFIELD
Journal of fiction, poetry, literary interviews and contemporary art since 1983

Mediatime France
68, rue des Archives
75003 PARIS
Tel: 44 78 82 82
Fax: 44 78 82 83
Publications Director:
Fiona LAZAREFF
Bi-monthly English-language magazine on French art de vivre *and culture*

Média Sid
19, rue de Constantine
75340 PARIS Cedex 7
Tel: 42 75 76 85
Fax: 42 75 76 67
Contact: M. Daniel IELLI
Directory of press and multimedia companies

Paris Free Voice
American Church
65, quai d'Orsay
75007 PARIS
Tel: 47 53 77 23
Fax: 45 50 36 96
Editor/Publisher: M. Bob BISHOP
Arts, entertainment and community-oriented free newspaper reaching 75000 readers

Paris Transcontinental
Sorbonne Nouvelle
5, rue de l'Ecole de Médecine
75006 PARIS
Tel: 69 01 86 35
Editor-in-Chief: Claire LARRIERE
A magazine of original short stories in English

Raw Vision
22, rue de Turin
75008 PARIS
Tel: 43 87 55 08
Fax: 42 93 86 25
Paris Editor: Sandra KWOCK SILVE
Periodical specialising in Art Brut and Primitive art from around the world, published in London

The New Recorder
La Presse Orange E.U.R.L.
Place des Arcades
47120 MONTLANQUIN
Tel: (16) 53 36 47 67
Fax: (16) 53 36 53 75
Publisher: M. R. FINN
English-language monthly review

Today in English - Bayard Presse
3-5, rue Bayard
75008 PARIS
Tel: 44 35 60 60
Fax: 44 35 60 47
Editor: Barbara OUDIZ
Monthly news magazine devoted to the anglophone world (see advertisement)

Trim International
94, rue St. Lazare
75442 PARIS Cedex 09
Tel: 48 78 38 32
Fax: 45 26 07 00
President: M. Thierry AUMONIER
Publishes Media Relations Worldletter

U.S. News & World Report
8, rue de Choiseul
75002 PARIS
Tel: 42 60 21 72
Fax: 42 60 22 61

Ziff Davis France
14, Place Marie-Jeanne Bassot
92300 LEVALLOIS-PERRET
Tel: 46 39 55 00
Fax: 46 39 02 06
Minitel: 3615 P C EXPERT
Contact: M. Pascal RIVIERE
Newsletters, microcomputing publisher

English-Language Television
Télévision de Langue Anglaise

ABC News
Immeuble CIT
3, rue de l'Arrivée
75749 PARIS Cedex 15
Tel: 40 47 80 81
Fax: 40 47 66 58
Correspondent: M. Jim BITTERMAN

British Broadcasting Corporation (BBC)
155, rue du Fbg. St.Honoré
75008 PARIS
Tel: 45 63 15 88
Fax: 45 63 67 12
Minitel: 3614 BBC
Correspondent: M. Kevin CONNOLLY

Cable News Network (CNN)
25, rue de Ponthieu
75008 PARIS
Tel: 42 89 23 31
Fax: 42 89 23 02
Bureau Chief: M. Peter HUMI

Canadian Broadcasting Corporation
17, avenue Matignon
75008 PARIS
Tel: 44 21 15 15
Fax: 44 21 15 14

CBS News
37, rue Marbeuf
75008 PARIS
Tel: 53 83 80 90
Fax: 45 61 49 76
Manager: M. Bob ALBERTSON

MTV Europe
12, rue Florence
75008 PARIS
Tel: 40 08 05 26

New Zealand Television
31, Bd. Edgar Quinet
75014 PARIS
Tel: 43 35 51 21
Fax: 43 35 51 21
Contact: M. Ian BORTHWICK

Tokyo Broadcasting Systems
20, rue du Fbg. St. Honoré
75008 PARIS
Tel: 42 66 66 00
Fax: 42 66 66 01

French Television
Télévision Française

Canal +
85-89, quai André Citroën
75711 PARIS Cedex 15
Tel: 44 25 10 00
Fax: 44 25 12 34
Intl Public Relations:
Mme Laurence GALLOT
Pay channel with emphasis on film and sport

France 2
22, avenue Montaigne
75008 PARIS
Tel: 44 21 42 42
Fax: 44 21 51 45
Communications Director:
Mme Brigitte SCHMIT

France 3
116, avenue du Président Kennedy
75016 PARIS
Tel: 42 30 22 22
Fax: 42 24 49 33
Communications Director:
M. Charles GREBER

France Télévision
42, avenue d'Iéna
75116 PARIS
Tel: 44 31 60 00
Communications Adviser:
M. Jean-Claude LEMAIGNEN
Public TV network, consisting of France 2 and France 3

La Sept/ARTE
50, avenue Théophile Gautier
75016 PARIS
Tel: 44 14 77 77
Fax: 44 14 77 00
President: M. Jérôme CLEMENT
High-brow Franco-German TV channel with an emphasis on culture and the arts

M6
16, cours Albert Ier
75008 PARIS
Tel: 45 63 17 17
Fax: 45 63 78 52
President: M. Jean DRUCKER

Paris TV Cable
4-6, Villa Thoreton
75015 PARIS
Tel: 44 25 80 00
Connects French viewers to cable network

Pariscope
151, rue Anatole France
92534 LEVALLOIS-PERRET Cedex
Tel: 41 34 73 47
Entertainment weekly (films, exhibitions, plays, concerts)

RTL Télévision
22, rue Bayard
75008 PARIS
Tel: 40 70 40 70
Fax: 40 70 41 04

TF1
1, quai du Point du Jour
92656 BOULOGNE Cedex
Tel: 41 41 12 34
Fax: 41 41 34 00
President: M. Patrice LE LAY
France's main private TV network

Radio

Stations de Radio

British Broadcasting Corporation (BBC)
155, rue du Fbg. St.Honoré
75008 PARIS
Tel: 45 63 15 88
Fax: 45 63 67 12
Minitel: 3614 BBC
Correspondent: M. Kevin CONNOLLY

Europe 1
26bis, rue François Ier
75008 PARIS
Tel: 42 32 90 00
Fax: 47 23 17 10

FIP
Maison de Radio-France
116, avenue du Président Kennedy
75786 PARIS Cedex 16
Tel: 42 20 12 34
Fax: 42 30 45 69
Music and traffic information

France Culture
116, avenue du Président Kennedy
75786 PARIS Cedex 16
Tel: 42 30 22 22

France Info
Maison de Radio-France
116, avenue du Président Kennedy
75786 PARIS Cedex 16
Tel: 42 30 22 22

France Inter
Maison de Radio-France
116, avenue du Président Kennedy
75786 PARIS Cedex 16
Tel: 42 30 22 22

Fun Radio
143, avenue Charles de Gaulle
92200 NEUILLY
Tel: 46 40 48 48
For the younger generation

NRJ
39, avenue d'Iéna
75016 PARIS
Tel: 47 20 06 06
Fax: 47 23 32 87

Ofredia/Partenaire Radio
33, rue du Fbg. St. Antoine
75010 PARIS
Tel: 53 33 80 80
Fax: 53 33 80 81
President: M. Jean-Michel BROSSEAU
Production of radio programs

Radio Bleue
Maison de Radio-France
116, avenue du Président Kennedy
75786 PARIS Cedex 16
Tel: 42 30 22 22

Radio Canada CBC
17, avenue Matignon
75008 PARIS
Tel: 44 21 15 15

Radio France Internationale
116, avenue du Président Kennedy
75786 PARIS Cedex 16
Tel: 42 30 30 62
Fax: 42 30 40 37
Editor-in-Chief English Service: M. Simson NAJOVITS
English and French language radio transmissions

Radio Monte Carlo (RMC)
12, rue Magellan
75008 PARIS 40 69 88 00
Fax: 40 69 88 44

Radio Nova
33, rue du Fbg. St. Antoine
75011 PARIS
Tel: 53 33 33 15
Fax: 43 47 33 39
World Music

Riviera Radio
16, Bd. Princesse Charlotte
98000 MONACO
Tel: (16) 93 25 49 06
Fax: (16) 93 30 42 45
English-language radio broadcast along the Riviera coast (news, talk shows, music, advertising)

RTL Radio
22, rue Bayard
75008 PARIS
Tel: 40 70 40 70
Fax: 40 70 41 04

Skyrock
6, rue Pierre Lescot
75001 PARIS
Tel: 42 36 96 96

News Agencies
Agences de Presse

Agence France-Presse (AFP)
13, Place de la Bourse
75002 PARIS
Tel: 40 41 46 46
Fax: 40 41 47 43
President: M. Lionel FLEURY

Agence Reuter
8, rue Sentier
75002 PARIS
Tel: 42 21 50 00

AP Dow Jones News Service
162, rue du Fbg. St. Honoré
75008 PARIS
Tel: 42 56 09 72
Fax: 42 25 87 36

Associated Press (AP)
162, rue du Fbg St. Honoré
75008 PARIS
Tel: 43 59 86 76
Fax: 40 74 00 45
Bureau Chief: M. Harry DUNPHY

Association de la Presse Etrangère à Paris
35, rue des Francs Bourgeois
75004 PARIS
Tel: 42 78 11 90
Fax: 42 78 08 78
President: Mme Evelyn WESQUIDA

Bloomberg
8, avenue Kléber
75116 PARIS
TeL 44 17 35 53
Financial news agency

Gamma
70, rue Jean Bleuzen
92170 VANVES
Tel: 41 23 77 00
Fax: 44 32 12 00
Press photo agency

Knight-Ridder Financial News
115, rue Réaumur
75002 PARIS
Tel: 44 88 44 50
Fax: 40 13 05 40
Bureau Chief: M. Brian CHILDS
Financial news agency

Magnum Photos
5, passage Piver
75011 PARIS
Tel: 43 55 15 55
Fax: 43 55 21 04
Photographic news agency

Middle East News Agency
6, rue de la Michodière
75002 PARIS
Tel: 47 42 16 03

Reporters sans Frontières
5, rue Geoffroy Marie
75009 PARIS
Tel: 44 83 84 84
Fax: 45 23 11 51

Reuters
19-21, rue Poissonnière
75083 PARIS Cedex 02
Tel: 42 21 50 00
Fax: 42 36 10 72
Director: M. François DURIAUD

United Press International (UPI)
8, rue de Choiseul
75002 PARIS
Tel: 42 60 30 87
Fax: 42 60 30 98

World Press Freedom Committee
9, Place du Président Mithouard
75007 PARIS
Tel: 47 83 39 88
Fax: 45 66 83 02
European Representative:
M. Ronald KOVEN
Defends and promotes independent media

Worldwide Television News
43, rue de Richelieu
75001 PARIS
Tel: 42 60 52 43
Fax: 42 60 49 44
Television press agency

Printing Services
Imprimeurs

3M France
Bd. de l'Oise
95006 CERGY-PONTOISE Cedex
Tel: 30 31 61 61
Fax: 30 31 74 26

A.M. International S.A.
60, rue Berthelot
92402 COURBEVOIE
Tel: 43 34 31 21
Fax: 43 34 96 80

Compo Rive Gauche
26, rue Monsieur le Prince
75006 PARIS
Tel: 43 25 33 43
Fax: 44 07 10 38
Numéris: 44 10 71 35
Director: Mme Monique LEPRINCE
Flashage (Linotronic imaging from Macintosh & P.C.), electronic photo-engraving

Docuprint, Inc.
14, rue Francoeur
75018 PARIS
Tel: 42 51 39 93
Fax: 42 62 55 20
Contact: Victor
To make a great IMPRESSION! American printer in Paris can print your reports, newsletters, brochures in Paris or New York hassle-free, European or American paper sizes

Ets. Caramanos
2, rue Robert Giraudineau
94300 VINCENNES
Tel: 43 28 63 81
Fax: 43 28 20 81
Discount photocopies & offset with a smile

Groupe Fecomme
38, rue Gabriel Prolongée
77410 CLAYE-SOUILLY
Tel: 60 26 67 00
Fax: 60 26 70 16

Imprimerie Bussière
23, rue Jean de Beauvais
75005 PARIS
Tel: 43 26 01 22
Fax: 46 34 58 87
Export Manager: M. Pierre-Jean DOUILLARD

Moore France
22, rue de Sèvres
92102 BOULOGNE-BILLANCOURT Cedex
Tel: 49 09 41 11
Fax: 46 03 05 14
President: M. Olivier JUTEAU

Print International France
22, rue Coysevox
75018 PARIS
Tel: 42 63 97 47
Fax: 42 63 97 48
Director: M. David NASH
Graphic services and printing

Prorata Services
27, rue Linné
75005 PARIS
Tel: 45 35 94 14
Fax: 45 35 19 13
Laser printing, scan, design, layout, Mac and PC by the hour

Graphic Design
Arts Graphiques

Artech Creation
55, rue de Rivoli
75001 PARIS
Tel: 42 33 09 28
Fax: 44 88 26 55

Astra Dessin
47, rue des Archives
75003 PARIS
Tel: 42 78 08 56
Fax: 42 71 81 48
Supplies for drawing and painting

Barbara Torgoff Desktop Publishing
98, rue Vieille du Temple
75003 PARIS
E-mail:
100350.1663@compuserve.com
Tel: 48 87 09 56
Fax: 42 77 33 77

Brigitte Gleizes Design
46, rue de Clichy
75009 PARIS
Tel: 40 23 92 25
Fax: 48 74 66 38
Director: Brigitte GLEIZES
Graphic design, visual communication, corporate identity, interior architecture

Design Principals
26, Bd. Raspail
75007 PARIS
Tel: 45 49 29 11
Fax: 45 49 14 39
Contacts: Carole MOY
& Karen SHECKLER-WILSON

Designworks
32, rue Eugène Sue
75018 PARIS
Tel: 42 59 39 58

Graphics Group/France
67, rue Croulebarbe
75013 PARIS
Tel: 43 36 79 00
Fax: 43 36 35 57
Director: M. Larry LARSON
Visual aids, graphics, desktop publishing

Graphigro Créa
157-159, rue Lecourbe
75015 PARIS
Tel: 42 50 45 49
Fax: 48 56 01 65
Contact: M. Philippe MARCELIN
Supplies for the graphics industry

Graphiques Lafayette
10, rue Notre-Dame-de-Lorette
75009 PARIS
Tel: 42 80 32 23
Fax: 48 74 92 65
Contact: Nicolas PAGNIER

Gyoza Media
44, rue Vieille du Temple
75004 PARIS
Tel: 40 29 03 96
Fax: 40 29 03 34
E-mail: 100272.257@compuserve.com
Contact: M. Cory McCLOUD
Interactive media design for screen & print

Image & Fonction
94, rue St. Honoré
75001 PARIS
Tel: 40 26 01 73
Fax: 40 26 03 22
Contact: Pamela WESSON
Graphic design, communications

Letraset France
13, rue Marceau
93104 MONTREUIL
Tel: 48 70 33 50
Fax: 48 70 33 65
Drawing and graphics arts products

Linotype France S.A.
13, rue Charles Cros
93294 TREMBLAY-EN-FRANCE
Tel: 49 63 68 95
Fax: 49 63 68 00

Pages
41-43bis, rue de Cronstadt
75015 PARIS
Tel: 45 30 25 83
E-mail: 100257.715@compuserve.com
Director: Connie NICHOLSON
Graphic design, Macintosh lessons

Peggy King
78, rue Marcadet
75018 PARIS
Tel: 42 55 81 19
Fax: 42 55 06 33
Design and photography

Polychrome Chemco
8, avenue François Arago
Z.I. B.P. 116
92164 ANTONY Cedex
Tel: 40 96 56 56
Fax: 46 68 72 79
Director: M. Patrick BERARD

Studio 44
44, rue Legendre
75017 PARIS
Tel: 42 67 21 11
Fax: 47 64 45 11

WB Associés
171, avenue du Général Leclerc
91330 YERRES
Tel: 69 48 35 35
Fax: 69 48 42 12
Director: M. Martine WINTER
Publication design/Communications

A.B.M. Rent a Flat
12, rue Valentin Hauy
75015 PARIS
Tel: 45 67 04 04
Fax: 45 67 90 15
Contact: M. Gerald DE CONCLOIS
Short-term rental of furnished flats

Agenda Immobilier
7, rue des Quatre Vents
75006 PARIS
Tel: 40 51 79 56
Contact: M. BOUBEL

Allô Logement Temporaire
4, Place de la Chapelle
75018 PARIS
Tel: 42 09 00 07
Fax: 46 07 14 41
Contact: M. Georg RIEDIGER
Furnished private accommodation

Apalachee Bay Residential Property
58, rue Galilée
75008 PARIS
Tel: 40 21 39 67
Fax: 48 07 14 34
An extensive range of carefully-selected apartments within the city limits

As You Like It
International Home Hunters
207, rue de Picquenard
78630 ORGEVAL
Tel: 39 75 43 49
Fax: 39 75 94 81
Rentals and sales in the western suburbs

ASLOM Company
75, avenue Parmentier
75011 PARIS
Tel: 43 49 67 79
Fax: 47 86 11 11
High class furnished apartments

At Home in Paris
25, avenue Hoche
75008 PARIS
Tel: 45 63 25 60
Furnished flats

At Home in Paris
16, rue Médéric
75017 PARIS
Tel: 42 12 40 40
Fax: 42 12 40 48
Real estate agency

Auguste-Thouard-Binswanger
24, rue Jacques Ibert
92300 LEVALLOIS-PERRET
Tel: 47 59 20 00
Fax: 47 59 22 69
President: M. Claude HEURTEUX

B.H. International
6, rue de Solférino
75007 PARIS
Tel: 47 53 03 00
Fax: 45 55 71 36

Best Nest
33, rue Vivienne
75002 PARIS
Tel: 42 50 96 22
Fax: 42 50 96 22

Castle & Cottage Vacations in Europe
19, rue du Colonel Moll
75017 PARIS
Tel: 40 68 77 37
Fax: 40 68 92 06
Contact: D.S. JOOST
Country Home Rentals and Bed & Breakfasts

Cattalan Johnson Immobilier
17, rue de la Baume
75008 PARIS
Tel: 45 74 87 77
Fax: 45 74 87 80
French-American agency specialized in residential rental property

Century 21 France
Rue des Cévennes, Bâtiment 4
Petite Montagne Sud, C.E. 1701
91017 EVRY Cedex LISSES
Tel: 69 11 12 21
Fax: 60 86 90 07

Chadwyck Healey
50, rue de Paradis
75010 PARIS
Tel: 44 83 81 81
Fax: 44 83 81 83
Director: M. Jean-Pierre SAKOUN

Citadines Prestige Haussmann
131, Bd. Haussmann
75008 PARIS
Tel: 53 77 07 07
Fax: 45 63 46 64
Furnished studios and apartments

Citadines Trocadéro
29bis, rue St. Didier
75116 PARIS
Tel: 44 34 73 73
Fax: 47 04 50 07
Furnished studios and apartments

COREPI
20, rue Bicentenaire
de la Révolution
92120 PLESSIS-PATE
Tel: 60 84 40 92
Fax: 40 50 10 69
Contact: Frances DRAXL
Furnished apartment rentals

De Circourt Associates
170, rue de Grenelle
75007 PARIS
Tel: 47 53 86 38
Fax: 45 51 75 77
Director: Claire DE CIRCOURT
Short and long-term rental of high standard furnished apartments in and around Paris
(see advertisement)

Embassy Service
43, avenue Marceau
75116 PARIS
Tel: 47 20 30 05
Fax: 47 20 34 04

Entrée into Paris
184, avenue Charles de Gaullle
92200 NEUILLY-SUR-SEINE
Tel: 40 88 39 40
Fax: 46 37 22 09

Euro Service Immobilier
155, rue de Courcelles
75017 PARIS
Tel: 47 66 43 93
Fax: 47 66 13 10
Directeur: M. Robert DANA
Rental of furnished flats

Fayrouz
55, rue d'Orsel
75018 PARIS
Tel: 42 58 72 56
Fax: 42 58 72 56
Manager: Amel FOUHANE
Rental of office premises

France Lodge
5, rue du Fbg. Montmartre
75009 PARIS
Tel: 48 01 02 17
Fax: 42 46 65 61
Bed and breakfast and rental of furnished apartments in Paris

G.E.F.I.C.
8-10, Place de l'Europe
94220 CHARENTON-LE-PONT
Tel: 45 18 34 18
Fax: 48 93 56 16
President: M. Stéphane LECAT
Real estate promotion, consulting and management

Gerancia
34, avenue des Champs-Elysées
75008 PARIS
Tel: 43 59 65 81
Furnished rentals off the Champs-Elysées, no agency fee

Healey & Baker
5, rue Royale
75008 PARIS
Tel: 42 65 01 13
Fax: 42 65 02 47
Director: M. Robert LIPSCOMB

Higgs & Hill France
4, rue de Marignan
75008 PARIS
Tel: 40 70 00 17
Fax: 40 70 16 87

Home Rental
116, avenue des Champs-Elysées
75008 PARIS
Tel: 44 21 81 16
Fax: 44 21 81 38
Director: M. Claude CHOPARD-LALLIER
Furnished home rentals in Paris

International Home Service
14, Domaine de Montvoisin
GOMMETZ-LAVILLE
Tel: 60 12 57 67
Fax: 60 12 57 67
Contact: Mme NOUHAUT

Intervac
230, Bd. Voltaire
75011 PARIS
Tel: 43 70 21 22
Fax: 43 70 73 35
Director: M. Lucien MAZIK
Exchange of lodging in over 40 countries

John Arthur & Tiffen
174, Bd. Haussmann
75008 PARIS
Tel: 44 21 11 44

John Taylor
86, avenue Victor Hugo
75008 PARIS
Tel: 45 53 25 25
Fax: 47 55 63 97
Real estate consultants

Jones Lang Wootton S.A.
49, avenue Hoche
75008 PARIS
Tel: 40 55 15 15
Fax: 46 22 28 28
Director: M. Robert WATERLAND
European Partner: M. Thierry LAROUE-PONT
International consulting on business property

Kaufman & Broad
44, rue Washington
75008 PARIS
Tel: 45 61 70 00
Fax: 53 75 30 10
President: M. Guy NAFILYAN
Builder/Promoter

KHS Immo S.A.R.L.
B.P. 318-16
75767 PARIS Cedex 16
Tel: 42 15 04 57
Fax: 42 30 53 76
Furnished rentals and prestige flats for sale

Lamy S.A.
142, rue de Rivoli
75001 PARIS
Tel: 44 07 19 57
Chartered surveyor

Locaflat
63, avenue La Motte-Picquet
75015 PARIS
Tel: 43 06 78 79
Fax: 40 56 99 69
Short term apartment renting

M. et Mme Z. Szabo
7, rue Charles V
75004 PARIS
Tel: 42 72 49 02
Fax: 42 78 73 63
Short-term furnished housing

Multiburo
17, rue de Galilée
75016 PARIS
Tel: 47 23 47 47
Fax: 47 23 06 59
Office rentals

P.A.A. Housing Service
9, rue des Ursulines
75005 PARIS
Tel: 43 25 35 09
Fax: 43 54 57 98

Ray Lampard
International Media
6, rue Bertin Poirée
75001 PARIS
Tel: 40 28 01 19
Tel: 42 21 13 31
Fax: 40 26 34 33
Director: M. Ray LAMPARD
Short and long-term apartment rentals

Résidence Champ de Mars
26, rue de l'Exposition
75007 PARIS
Tel: 44 18 62 44
Fax: 45 51 70 22
Newly-renovated fully-equipped apartments for long and short term leases

Richard Ellis
37, rue la Bienfaisance
75008 PARIS
Tel: 45 63 08 08
Fax: 45 63 64 64
President: M. Gérard ROBERT

Servissimo
18, rue Bude
75004 PARIS
Tel: 43 29 03 23
Fax: 43 29 53 43
Contact: Catherine GODET
Short-term rentals on the Ile-St-Louis

Studios Dauphine
13, rue Dauphine
75006 PARIS
Tel: 40 46 93 13
Furnished rooms and studios in Paris

Alastair Sawday Publishing
36, rue de Chabrol
75010 PARIS
Tel: 48 00 96 11
Fax: 48 00 96 11
Editing and Translating:
Ann COOKE YARBOROUGH
New tours, guides and translations

Alyscamps Press
35, rue de l'Espérance
75013 PARIS
Tel: 45 81 15 24
Fax: 45 81 15 24
Fax: 43 36 35 57
Publisher: M. Karl OREND
Publishes literary criticism, fiction, biography, poetry, translations. No unsolicited manuscripts. Authors include Henry Miller, D.H. Lawrence, Mistral, Aldington, Campbell, Lorca, Powys, Graves...

Association Calder
28, rue du Général Delorme
93100 MONTREUIL
Tel: 49 88 75 12
Director: M. John CALDER
The French office of Calder Publications

Association Frank
32, rue Edouard Vaillant
93100 MONTREUIL
Tel: 48 59 66 58
Fax: 48 59 66 68
E-mail:
100265.1435@compuserve.com
Director: M. David APPLEFIELD
Publishes Paris-Anglophone *and the literary journal* Frank

Association Les Amis de la Fonderie
32, rue Edouard Vaillant
93100 MONTREUIL
Tel: 48 59 66 58

BBC English
8, rue de Berri
75008 PARIS
Tel: 43 59 80 05
Fax: 42 56 39 85

Bookking International
60, rue St. André des Arts
75006 PARIS
Tel: 44 41 65 30
Fax: 43 25 64 92
Quality remainders

British Council
9-11, rue de Constantine
75007 PARIS
Tel: 49 55 73 00
Fax: 47 05 77 02
Public Relations: M. Duncan JACKMAN

Business Editing
89, rue du Fbg. St. Martin
75010 PARIS
Tel: 42 06 66 15
Fax: 42 06 69 02

Business News
3, rue de l'Arrivée
75015 PARIS
Tel: 43 20 02 44
Publishes newsletters for the corporate community

Christian Science Monitor
48, rue de la Clef
75005 PARIS
Tel: 43 31 22 90

Data Research Publications
6, rue Mignard
75116 PARIS
Tel: 45 03 02 72
Fax: 45 03 02 96

Dow Jones Publishing Company
42, rue Damrémont
75018 PARIS
Tel: 42 55 54 22
Fax: 42 23 96 13
Circulation Manager: M. Stanley HERTZBERG

EBSCO Subscription Services
55bis, avenue Jean Jaurès
B.P. 48
78580 MAULE
Tel: 30 90 62 26
Fax: 30 90 62 32
Manager: M. GUET
Subscription agency and C.D. vendor

Editions Business News
56, Bd. Voltaire
75011 PARIS
Tel: 48 06 55 80
Fax: 48 06 76 38
Monthly publications on commercial affairs and marketing strategies in Poland and Czechoslovakia

Elliott Klein
47, rue St. André des Arts
75006 PARIS
Tel: 43 29 62 68
Fax: 43 26 52 36
Publishes scholarly works and translations

Encyclopaedia Britannica
2, rue du Pont Colbert
78023 VERSAILLES
Tel: 39 24 45 45
Fax: 39 24 45 00

Entertainment
1bis, rue St. Augustin
75002 PARIS
Tel: 42 86 86 34
Fax: 42 86 86 30
Manager: Jeannine FENSTER
Commercial Director: Rose ELBAZ
Paris guide offering interesting rebates. Publishers of the international coupon book (see advertisement)

Est-Ouest Internationale
140, rue de Belleville
75020 PARIS
Tel: 44 62 73 84
Fax: 40 09 03 79
Editor: M. Georges FERENCZI

Europages
3, avenue de Friedland
75008 PARIS
Tel: 53 77 54 00
Fax: 42 89 34 73
Communication Assistant: Karoline RAETS

Handshake Editions
83, rue de la Tombe-Issoire
Atelier A2
75014 PARIS
Tel: 43 27 17 67
Fax: 43 20 41 95
Director: M. Jim HAYNES
A kitchen-table folly - come for tea!

Harwood Academic Publishers
12, cour St. Eloi
75012 PARIS
Tel: 49 28 91 00
Fax: 43 43 18 10

International Children's Guide
44, rue Eugène Carrière
75018 PARIS
Tel: 42 23 40 14

International Masters Publishers
100, avenue de Suffren
75015 PARIS
Tel: 44 49 19 00
Fax: 44 49 19 01

Jackson Publishing
35, rue de l'Espérance
75013 PARIS
Tel: 45 81 15 24
Fax: 45 81 15 24
Literary Researcher: M. Karl OREND

John Libbey Eurotext
127, avenue de la République
92120 MONTROUGE
Tel: 46 73 06 60
Fax: 40 84 09 99
Directors: M. Gilles CAHN & Martine KRIEF
Medical and scientific publications

Lonely Planet
71bis, rue Cardinal Lemoine
75005 PARIS
Tel: 46 34 00 58

McGraw Hill Publications
128, rue du Fbg. St. Honoré
75008 PARIS
Tel: 40 75 25 00
Fax: 42 89 04 00
Vice-President: M. Bruno HERMANN

Média Sid
19, rue de Constantine
75340 PARIS Cedex 7
Tel: 42 75 76 85
Fax: 42 75 76 67
Contact: M. Daniel IELLI
Directory of press and multimedia companies

National Geographic Magazine
90, avenue des Champs-Elysées
75008 PARIS
Tel: 43 59 25 06
Fax: 45 63 79 65
Director: M. Michel A. BOUTIN

OECD Publishing
33, rue Octave Feuillet
75016 PARIS
Tel: 45 24 82 00
Fax: 45 24 85 00
General Secretary:
M. Jean-Claude PAYE

Overseas Publishers Association
12, cour St. Eloi
75012 PARIS
Tel: 49 28 91 00
Fax: 43 43 18 10

Paris-Anglophone
Association Frank
32, rue Edouard Vaillant
93100 MONTREUIL
Tel: 48 59 66 58
Fax: 48 59 66 68
E-mail:
100265.1435@compuserve.com
Editor: M. David APPLEFIELD
The complete directory of English-speaking Paris, published in book form and on-line

Professional Photography Directory
11, rue Tronchet
75008 PARIS
Tel: 05 25 92 04

Reed Business Publishing
15bis, rue Ernest Renan
92130 ISSY-LES-MOULINEAUX
Tel: 46 29 46 29
Fax: 40 93 03 37
Director: M. MUSSARD

Show Business Guide
24, rue Vieille du Temple
75004 PARIS
Tel: 48 87 34 34
Minitel: 3617 GSB
40000 show business addresses

Software Publishers' Association Europe
57, rue Pierre Charron
75008 PARIS
Tel: 45 63 02 02
Fax: 45 63 68 03

Speakeasy Publications/Nathan
9, rue Méchain
75014 PARIS
Tel: 45 87 50 31
Director: Mme Michelle SOMMERS
Publication of English-language learning products

UNESCO Presses/Publications
7, Place de Fontenoy
75700 PARIS Cedex 07
Tel: 45 68 10 00
Courrier Editor (English):
M. MALKIN

Who's Who in European Commerce in Industry
10, rue du Mont Doré
75017 PARIS
Tel: 43 87 04 93
Fax: 43 87 12 81

Other Publishers
Autres Editeurs

Actes Sud
18, rue Savoie
75006 PARIS
Tel: 43 54 70 61
Fax: 40 51 79 77
Publishes international literary works in translation

Art F.M.R. - Franco Maria Ricci
Britannica France
Tour Maine Montparnasse
33, avenue du Maine
75755 PARIS Cedex 15
Tel: 43 27 94 17

Assimil
11, rue des Pyramides
75001 PARIS
Tel: 45 76 87 37
Tel: 42 60 40 66 (store)
Fax: 40 20 02 17
Communications Director:
Mme Magdeleine VANDENHENDE
Foreign language methods: books, tapes, software self-taught French method

Autrement
17, rue du Louvre
75001 PARIS
Tel: 40 26 06 06
Fax: 47 70 97 52
City guides

Bertelsmann
44, rue de la Bienfaisance
75008 PARIS
Tel: 45 63 67 07
Fax: 43 59 66 73

Bordas, Dunod, Gauthier, Villars
17, rue Rémy Dumoncel
75014 PARIS
Tel: 42 79 62 00
Fax: 43 22 85 18
Practical books in French

Centre National de Documentation Pédagogique
29, rue d'Ulm
75230 PARIS Cedex 5
Tel: 46 34 90 00
Fax: 46 34 55 44

Charles Letts & Co. Ltd
46bis, rue Roger Salengro
94126 FONTENAY-SOUS-BOIS Cedex
Tel: 43 94 04 70
Fax: 48 77 69 28
Sales Manager: R.M. FRANCHI
Calendars, pocket and desk agendas

Christian Bourgois Editeur
12, avenue d'Italie
75013 PARIS
Tel: 45 44 09 13
Fax: 45 44 87 86
Director: M. Christian BOURGOIS
Publishes American fiction in translation

Dictionnaires Le Robert
27, rue de la Glacière
75013 PARIS
Tel: 45 87 43 00
Fax: 45 35 76 06

Editions Albin Michel
22, rue Huyghens
75680 PARIS Cedex 14
Tel: 42 79 10 00
Fax: 43 27 21 58

Editions d'Annabelle
8, rue d'Anjou
75008 PARIS
Tel: 47 42 01 61
Fax: 47 42 42 14
Director: Mme ROLLAND
Children's publisher

Editions Denöel
9, rue du Cherche-Midi
75006 PARIS
Tel: 44 39 73 73
Fax: 44 39 73 90

Editions des Femmes
6, rue de Mézières
75006 PARIS
Tel: 42 22 60 74
Fax: 42 22 62 73
Women's literature

Editions Didier
13, rue de l'Odéon
75006 PARIS
Tel: 44 41 31 31
School books, teaching material

Editions du Centre Pompidou
75191 PARIS Cedex 4
Tel: 44 78 12 33
Fax: 44 78 12 05
Manager: M Ph. BIDAINE

Editions du Seuil
27, rue Jacob
75006 PARIS
Tel: 40 46 50 50
Fax: 43 29 08 29
Marketing & Sales Manager:
M. Denis BOEHRINGER
Literary publishing

Editions Franco-Britanniques
10, rue de l'Echiquier
75010 PARIS
Tel: 40 22 93 43

Editions Gallimard
5, rue Sébastien Bottin
75007 PARIS
Tel: 49 54 42 00
Fax: 45 44 39 46
Director: M. Antoine GALLIMARD
Literary titles and translations

Editions Grasset
61, rue des Saints Pères
75006 PARIS
Tel: 44 39 22 00
Fax: 42 22 64 18

Editions Jean-Michel Place
12, rue Pierre et Marie Curie
75005 PARIS
Tel: 46 33 05 11
Fax: 46 34 52 65
Publisher of literary titles, journals and selected guides

Editions Larousse
5, square Max Hymans
75015 PARIS
Tel: 44 39 44 00
French dictionaries & encyclopaedias

Editions Odile Jacob
15, rue Soufflot
75005 PARIS
Tel: 44 41 64 84
Fax: 43 29 88 77
Political and economic analysis

Editions Robert Laffont
24, avenue Marceau
75008 PARIS
Tel: 53 67 14 00
Fax: 53 67 14 14

Editions Sauret
7, quai Voltaire
75007 PARIS
Tel: 49 27 00 33
Director: M. Raymond LEVY
Books on contemporary art

Editions Scientifiques Elsevier
141, rue de Javel
75747 PARIS Cedex 15
Tel: 45 58 90 57
Fax: 45 58 94 19

Fixot Editions
24, avenue Marceau
75381 PARIS Cedex 08
Tel: 53 67 14 00

Flammarion
26, rue Racine
75006 PARIS
Tel: 40 51 31 00
Fax: 43 29 76 44
Director: M. FLAMMARION

Hachette Littérature Générale
79, Bd. St. Germain
75006 PARIS
Tel: 46 34 85 93
Fax: 46 34 65 45
Specializes in guide books

IMEC - Institut Mémoire de l'Edition Contemporaine
25, rue de Lille
75007 PARIS
Tel: 42 61 29 29
Fax: 49 27 03 15
Director: M. Olivier CORPET

Julliard Editions
20, rue des Grands Augustins
75006 PARIS
Tel: 44 41 73 80
Fax: 44 41 73 81

L'Harmattan
7, rue de l'Ecole Polytechnique
75005 PARIS
Tel: 43 54 79 10
Fax: 43 25 82 03
Director: M. PRYEN

Le Groupe COBB
14, Place Marie-Jeanne Bassot
92593 LEVALLOIS-PERRET Cedex
Tel: 46 39 56 38
Fax: 46 39 00 69
E-mail:
djamet.notes@mail.zd.ziff.com
Chief Editor: M. Denis JAMET
Publishers of technical newsletters

Les Presses de la Cité
12, avenue d'Italie
75013 PARIS
Tel: 44 16 05 00
Fax: 44 16 05 11

Michelin Green Guides
46, avenue de Breteuil
75007 PARIS
Tel: 45 66 12 34
Fax: 45 66 11 63

Noblet-Franklin France
1-3, Bd. Charles de Gaulle
92707 COLOMBES Cedex
Tel: 47 60 40 40
Fax: 47 60 40 30
The world's first French-English speaking dictionary

Nouveaux Horizons/USIS
2, rue St. Florentin
75382 PARIS Cedex 08
Tel: 43 12 22 22
Fax: 43 12 46 57
Director: Mme VERON-SULLIVAN

Parigramme
59, rue Beaubourg
75003 PARIS
Tel: 44 54 24 24
Fax: 44 54 24 20
Director: M. François BESSE
Publishes books on Paris

Pen Club France
6, rue François Miron
75004 PARIS
Tel: 42 77 37 87
Fax: 42 78 64 87
President: M. Jean ORIZET

Reed Editions France
32, rue de la Bienfaisance
75008 PARIS
Tel: 42 94 25 96

Salon du Livre
O.I.P.
62, rue de Miromesnil
75008 PARIS
Tel: 49 53 27 00
Fax: 49 53 27 86
Annual book/publishing fair

Sélection du Reader's Digest
1-7, avenue Louis Pasteur
B.P. 101
92220 BAGNEUX Cedex
Tel: 46 74 84 84
Fax: 46 74 85 80
President: Mme Bénédicte BARRE

Literary Agents
Agents Littéraires

Agence Hoffman
77, Bd. St. Michel
75005 PARIS
Tel: 43 26 56 94
Fax: 43 26 34 07
Directors: MM. Boris
& Georges HOFFMAN

Dawson France
Rue de la Prairie
91149 VILLEBON
Tel: 69 10 47 00
Fax: 64 54 83 26
Subscription agent and international bookseller

Frédérique Porretta
70, rue d'Assas
75006 PARIS
Tel: 45 44 88 68
Fax: 45 44 69 36

La Nouvelle Agence
7, rue de Corneille
75006 PARIS
Tel: 43 25 85 60
Fax: 43 25 47 98
Director: Mme Mary KLING

Lora Fountain Agency
127, Bd. Voltaire
75011 PARIS
Tel: 43 56 21 96
Fax: 43 48 22 72
Selling translation rights for English-language publishers and agencies

Adath Shalom
22 bis, rue des Belles Feuilles
75116 PARIS
Tel: 45 53 84 09
Fax: 45 53 45 02
Jewish conservative congregation

American Cathedral
23, avenue George V
75008 PARIS
Tel: 47 20 17 92
Dean: Rev. E. HUNT
Episcopalian and Anglican Pro-Cathedral Church of the Holy Trinity

American Church in Paris
65, quai d'Orsay
75007 PARIS
Tel: 47 05 07 99
Fax: 45 50 36 96
Pastor: Dr. Larry KALAJAINEN
Associate Pastor: Dr Richard SOMMERS
Religious service for all Protestant denominations

Christian Science Church
36, Bd. St. Jacques
75014 PARIS
Tel: 47 07 26 60

Church of Christ
4, rue Déodat-de-Severac
75017 PARIS
Tel: 42 27 50 86

Church of Jesus Christ of Latterday Saints
23, rue du 11 Novembre
78110 LE VESINET
Tel: 39 76 68 84
Leader: M. Charles E. JONES

Consistoire Israélite de Paris
17, rue St. Georges
75009 PARIS
Tel: 40 82 26 26
Synagogue

Emmanuel Baptist Church of Paris
56, rue des Bons Raisins
92500 RUEIL-MALMAISON
Tel: 47 51 29 63
Fax: 47 14 02 31
Pastor: Dr. Bill Clark THOMAS

Great Synagogue
44, rue de la Victoire
75009 PARIS
Tel: 45 26 95 36

Holy Trinity Church (Anglican)
15, avenue Camot
78600 MAISONS-LAFITTE
Tel: 39 62 34 97
Contact: Rev. Ben EATON

Hope International Church of Paris at La Chapelle Evangélique
8, Bd. de Neuilly
92800 PARIS LA DEFENSE
Tel: 47 73 53 54
Reverend: M. Henry A. PAASONEN
Christian workshop and fellowship, service in English Sundays, 9h45

La Mosquée
Place du Puits de l'Ermite
75005 PARIS
Tel: 45 35 97 33
Fax: 45 35 16 23
Moslem mosque

Lutheran Church
16, rue Chauchat
75009 PARIS
Tel: 47 70 80 30

R.P. Andrew Phillips
26, rue de Sartrouville
95240 CORMEILLES-EN-PARISIS
Tel: 39 78 71 54
Orthodox Priest

Reformed Church of France
47, rue de Clichy
75009 PARIS
Tel: 48 74 90 92

Religious Society of Friends (Quakers)
114bis, rue de Vaugirard
75006 PARIS
Tel: 45 48 74 23

Scots Kirk - Church of Scotland
17, rue Bayard
75008 PARIS
Tel: 48 78 47 94
Contact: Rev. Bill REID
English-speaking worship, Sunday service at 10h30

St. George's Anglican Church
7, rue Auguste Vacquerie
75116 PARIS
Tel: 47 20 22 51
Chaplain: Rev. Martin DRAPER

St. Joseph's Roman Catholic Church
50, avenue Hoche
75008 PARIS
Tel: 42 27 28 56
Fax: 42 27 86 49
Contact: Fr. Paul Francis SPENCER

St. Mark's Church
31, rue du Pont Colbert
78000 VERSAILLES
Tel: 39 02 79 45
Fax: 39 50 97 29
President Chaplain:
Rev. David MARSHALL
Sunday services, housegroups

St. Michael's Anglican Church
5, rue d'Aguesseau
75008 PARIS
Tel: 47 42 70 88
Fax: 47 42 70 11
Contact: Rev. Andrew WARBURTON
Sunday services in English (10.30 am and 6.30 pm)

Temple of the Annunciation
19, rue de Cortambert
75016 PARIS
Tel: 45 03 43 10

Union Libérale Israélite de France
24, rue Copernic
75116 PARIS
Tel: 47 04 37 27
Contact: Rabbi Michael WILLIAMS
Services on Fridays at 18h00 and Saturdays at 10h30

Unitarian Universalist Fellowship of Paris
7, rue Geoffroy l'Angevin
75004 PARIS
Tel: 42 77 96 77
Monthly services in English, religious education for children, discussion groups, social activities

Women of the American Church
American Church of Paris
65, quai d'Orsay
75007 PARIS
Tel: 47 05 07 99
Tel: 44 19 77 48
Contact: Meribeth WITHROW
Neighborhood coffee meetings, monthly programs

"Homefinders" Relocation Service
2, rue Raymond Poincaré
92380 GARCHES
Tel: 47 41 22 67
Fax: 47 41 48 96
Manager: Mrs Domini MUDARRES
Established 1989 in Paris and in the western suburbs. Personalized homefinding service

Andrew Speirs
42, rue d'Orléans
78580 MAULE
Tel: 34 75 17 33
Fax: 34 75 17 36
English relocation consultants: administrative formalities, schools, housing

At Home Abroad
28, rue Basfroi
75011 PARIS
Tel: 40 09 08 37
Fax: 40 09 98 16
Director: Susan ORSONI
Relocation service

Corporate Relocations France
15, rue Croix Castel
78600 MAISONS-LAFFITTE
Tel: 39 12 00 60
Fax: 39 12 36 00
Managing Director:
Mme Annabel GREEN
Relocation management firm working with Human Resources to help their international personnel move into France: on site assistance, administrative formalities, cross-cultural training

Cosmopolitan Services Unlimited
50, rue de l'Assomption
75016 PARIS
Tel: 45 27 84 30
Fax: 45 20 23 07
Relocation specialists

Culture Crossings Ltd
51, rue de Bellechasse
75007 PARIS
Tel: 45 56 04 62
Fax: 45 55 91 86
Director: Polly PLATT
Cultural adaptation seminars for foreign executives and their spouses

Executive Relocations
3, rue Berryer
75008 PARIS
Tel: 40 74 00 02
Fax: 42 56 19 29
Managing Director: Judy BRAHAM
Full relocation and setting-in services. Founding member of the Global Relocation Partnership worldwide

France Welcome
Chemin du Radium
91190 GIF-SUR-YVETTE
Tel: 69 41 28 79
President: Mme LAPEYRE
To help newcomers learn French language and customs

International Relocation Assistance
2, rue Georges Saché
75014 PARIS
Tel: 45 45 58 38
Fax: 45 45 58 41
Director: Marie-Christine BAUCHE
Relocation services

International Welcome to Paris
119, rue de Longchamp
B.P. 232
92205 NEUILLY-SUR-SEINE Cedex
Tel: 47 47 40 45
Tel: 47 22 77 55
Fax: 47 22 31 60
Fax: 47 22 45 02
Directors: Mme D. AMELINE
& Mme F. DE CREMIERS
Helps anglophones feel at home in Paris

NDH Conseil
17, Place de la Résistance
92130 ISSY-LES-MOULINEAUX
Tel: 46 45 78 00
Fax: 46 45 99 03
International relocation service

Paris Welcome Service
16, Rue Vézelay
75008 PARIS
Tel: 43 59 70 40
Fax: 43 59 70 39
Director: Mme A. LENCLUD

Relocation Service
17, rue du Colisée
75008 PARIS
Tel: 42 89 09 15

Shippers
Agents Maritimes

Air Express International France
Aérogare des Agents de Fret
B.P. 10406
95707 ROISSY CDG
Tel: 49 19 68 68
Fax: 48 62 49 94
International air freight forwarder

Air Freight Parcel Service
Fret Nord - Bâtiment Administratif
Aéroport Charles de Gaulle
95700 ROISSY-EN-FRANCE
Tel: 48 62 16 28

Airship Services
14, rue du Théâtre
75014 PARIS
Tel: 49 66 71 94

Ashland Shipping Company
88, avenue Foch
75008 PARIS
Tel: 45 00 32 62

Bansard International
11, rue Léon Jouhaux
75010 PARIS
Tel: 42 39 12 60
Fax: 42 41 19 09
Tel: 47 03 48 13 (air)
International freight forwarding

Canada Maritime Agencies France
90, avenue Ledru Rollin
75011 PARIS
Tel: 47 00 56 91
Fax: 43 44 84 52
Director: M. Eric GUERROUANI

Compagnie d'Affrètement et de Transport
82, rue du Point du Jour
921007 BOULOGNE Cedex
Tel: 41 03 74 44
Fax: 41 03 71 09
Commercial Director: M. JULIAN

Daher America, Inc.
Zone de Fret 4
Rue du Chapelier
95707 ROISSY CDG Cedex
Tel: 48 62 74 44
Fax: 48 62 55 58
Director: M. Gerald WHITE
Commercial Contact:
M. Tim CAMPBELL
Air/ocean freight, customs broker, packing, forwarding

Emery Worldwide
B.P. 10408
95707 ROISSY CDG
Tel: 48 62 36 40
Fax: 48 62 50 75
Director: M. Roger POTIN-VESPERAS
International air freight

Excess Baggage Company
34-56B, rue de la Belle Borne
2, avenue Fret n° 4
95723 ROISSY CDG Cedex
Tel: 48 62 73 05
Fax: 48 62 73 01
Contact: Angélique LHOTEL

Federal Express
30-32, rue des Voyelles
95705 ROISSY
Tel: 48 64 83 00
Fax: 48 62 32 30
Express air courier

French Freight Professionals
10, rue des Deux Cèdres
95700 ROISSY-EN-FRANCE
Tel: 48 62 49 65

G.T.S.E.
Orly Fret
B.P. 829
Entrepôts Juliette BT 132D
94549 ORLY AEROGARE
Tel: 49 75 32 88
Fax: 49 75 33 86
Director: M. ABDESSELAM
Export/Import shipping service

Garonor
B.P 780
93614 AULNAY-SOUS-BOIS Cedex
Tel: 48 65 42 84
Fax: 48 65 30 40
Director: M. CRESSENT
Logistics parks: storage and distribution

Heppner Paris International
Z.I. de Coudray
5, avenue Armand-Esders
93150 LE BLANC-MESNIL
Tel: 49 39 39 39
Fax: 48 67 69 29
Sales manager: M. CANTAIS

International Art Transport
60, rue Pierre Charron
75008 PARIS
Tel: 42 56 43 00
Fax: 45 61 91 05

Johnson Henry Sons
5, rue Jacques Kable
75018 PARIS
Tel: 46 07 94 39
Fax: 46 07 52 83
Commercial Director: M. GILLES
Customs and shipping agent

Jules Roy S.A.
Groupe Schenker
B.P. 10216
95703 ROISSY CDG
Tel: 48 62 34 44
Fax: 48 62 33 10
Commercial Director:
M. Alexandre CUVELIER

Lloyd's Register of Shipping
32, rue Caumartin
75009 PARIS
Tel: 47 42 60 30
Fax: 42 66 99 10
Fax: 47 42 10 58
Director: M. J.P. PAGE
Industrial checks, shipping classification

Logistic Air/Sea France
4, rue du TE Bâtiment 3450C
95706 ROISSY CDG
Tel: 48 62 80 42
Fax: 48 62 80 44
Specialize in excess baggage

Oceanlink
49, Route Principale du Port
92230 GENNEVILLIERS
Tel: 42 81 18 81
Fax: 47 94 28 04
Trans-European logistic services

United Parcel Service France
87, avenue de l'Aérodrome
B.P. 39
94310 ORLY VILLE
Tel: 48 92 50 00
Fax: 48 92 51 07
Free call: 05 01 70 17
Express air and road transport

Urschel International Ltd
Orly Fret 747
94398 ORLY AEROGARE Cedex
Tel: 48 52 75 75
Fax: 46 86 00 45
Commercial Director:
M. Alain PENSEC

World Freight
4, Chemin Dime
95700 ROISSY-EN-FRANCE
Tel: 34 29 00 44
Fax: 34 29 92 44

Movers
Déménageurs

Access
221, Bd. Macdonald
75019 PARIS
Tel: 44 65 88 88
Fax: 44 65 88 87
Marketing Director: Corinne SACERDOTE
Self-storage, self-stockage
Two new locations:
33, avenue Maréchal de Lattre de Tassigny
94120 FONTENAY-SOUS-BOIS
Tel: 48 77 71 71
Fax: 48 77 50 51

73, rue Noël Pons
92000 NANTERRE
Tel: 46 49 32 32
Fax: 47 82 45 59

AGS
9-11, Bd. Galliéni
92230 GENNEVILLIERS
Tel: 40 80 20 20
Sea packing, storage facilities, dismantling. Attends to all customs and administrative formalities

American Worldwide
201, avenue Jean Lolive
Bâtiment F
93500 PANTIN
Tel: 48 46 00 72
Fax: 48 43 97 32

Arthur Pierre
Z.I. du Petit Parc
78920 ECQUEVILLY
Tel: 34 75 92 92
Fax: 34 75 56 26
Sales Manager: M. Philippe MIRAULT
International customs brokers, storage

Delahaye Moving
Z.I. des Amandiers
165, rue de Bezance
78420 CARRIERE-SUR-SEINE
Tel: 39 13 46 82
Fax: 39 13 48 55

Desbordes International
14, rue Véga
75012 PARIS
Tel: 44 73 84 84
Fax: 43 42 51 48
President: M. PIRIOU

Ecotrans
33, rue du Professeur Calmette
94400 VITRY-SUR-SEINE
Tel: 46 70 76 36
Fax: 49 60 60 29
Contact: Mme SASSI
Removals, errands 7 days a week

European Cedars Service
38, rue de Berri
75008 PARIS
Tel: 46 97 77 03
Fax: 45 06 51 11
Bi-Bop: 07 01 51 84
Contact: M. Joseph BECHARA
Moving and shipping, car rentals with drivers
2nd location:
18, avenue Georges Pompidou
92800 PUTEAUX

Excelmove
50, avenue du Général de Gaulle
92130 ISSY-LES-MOULINEAUX
Tel: 46 45 72 72
Fax: 46 45 58 43

France Transport Express
43, Bd. Auguste Blanqui
75013 PARIS
Tel: 44 62 78 78
Fax: 44 62 78 79
Contact: M. Dominique CHARLES
For all your transport and moving needs

Global International B.V.
Tour Litwin
10, rue Jean Jaurès
92800 PUTEAUX
Tel: 47 76 44 44
Fax: 47 76 35 90
E-mail: 76041.115@compuserve.com
Director: M. Andrew SMITH
International removals. An American company operating overseas

Grospiron International
15, rue Danielle Casanova
93300 AUBERVILLIERS
Tel: 48 11 71 71
Fax: 48 11 71 70

Homeship
62, rue St. Lazare
75009 PARIS
Tel: 42 81 18 81
Fax: 48 74 37 94
Director: M. Charles FUCHS
International (vehicles, luggage)

Interdean
515, rue Hélène Boucher
78530 Z.I. BUC
Tel: 39 56 90 00
Fax: 39 56 30 28

Neer Service
2, rue Désiré Lemoine
93300 AUBERVILLIERS
Tel: 48 35 47 00
International moving specialists

Trans Euro Worldwide
22, rue du Gros Murger, B.P. 210
95614 CERGY-PONTOISE Cedex
Tel: 34 48 97 97
Fax: 34 48 93 22

Transpaq International
116bis, avenue des Champs-Elysées
75008 PARIS
Tel: 45 63 43 00
Fax: 45 63 03 42
Contact: M. DEBBAS
Overseas removals

Fashion
Mode

Agnès B.
6, rue du Jour
75001 PARIS
Tel: 45 08 56 56

Amatchi
13, rue du Roi de Sicile
75004 PARIS
Tel: 40 29 97 14
Lingerie and swimwear for men and women

Ann Taylor
102, rue Réaumur
75002 PARIS
Tel: 42 33 72 42
Women's clothes

Au Coton
120, rue Rambuteau
75003 PARIS
Tel: 42 33 60 44
Cotton clothing for women

Barneys of New York
33-35, rue de Valois
75001 PARIS
Tel: 47 03 41 30
Fax: 42 96 20 45
Managers: Sandra CHOLLET & Jessica BRATT

Bata
99, rue St. Lazare
92806 PARIS
Tel: 45 96 04 63
Shoes and leather goods

Borsalino
368, rue St. Honoré
75001 PARIS
Tel: 49 26 00 75
Hatter

Boutique Lacoste
95, avenue des Champs-Elysées
75008 PARIS
Tel: 47 23 76 00

British House
162, rue du Fbg. St. Honoré
75008 PARIS
Tel: 42 56 37 42
Prêt-à-Porter

British Shoes
8, rue de Prague
75012 PARIS
Tel: 43 41 98 18

Burberry's of London
8, Bd. Malesherbes
75008 PARIS
Tel: 42 66 13 01
Fax: 40 07 77 48
Contact: M. Pierre MANTOIS

Burton of London
14, Bd. Poissonnière
75009 PARIS
Tel: 47 70 55 19

Calvin Klein
176, avenue Charles de Gaulle
92522 NEUILLY-SUR-SEINE
Tel: 47 45 93 00

Caroline Rohmer
14, avenue Victor Hugo
75116 PARIS
Tel: 45 01 24 95

Cerruti 1881
48, rue Pierre Charron
75008 PARIS
Tel: 40 70 18 81
For men

Chanel
135, avenue Charles de Gaulle
92521 NEUILLY-SUR-SEINE Cedex
Tel: 46 43 40 00
Fax: 47 47 60 34

Chantal Thomass
1, rue Vivienne
75001 PARIS
Tel: 40 15 02 36
Designer clothes and lingerie

Chaussures Bally
4, rue du Havre
75009 PARIS
Tel: 44 53 75 75

Chaussures Eram
12, rue de Rivoli
75004 PARIS
Tel: 40 27 99 20

Chaussures Heyraud
23, Bd. des Capucines
75002 PARIS
Tel: 42 60 50 91

Chevignon
49, rue Etienne Marcel
75002 PARIS
Tel: 40 28 05 77
Fax: 40 28 04 67

Christian Dior
30, avenue Montaigne
75008 PARIS
Tel: 40 73 54 44

Church's
4, rue des Petits Pères
75002 PARIS
Tel: 40 20 94 67
Fax: 47 05 14 73
Commercial Director: M. DEBAIG

Clarence
104, avenue des Champs-Elysées
75008 PARIS
Tel: 45 62 75 19
Shoes, handbags, luggage

Claude Montana Boutique
31, rue de Grenelle
75007 PARIS
Tel: 42 22 69 56

Cordonnerie Anglaise
28, rue des Archives
75004 PARIS
Tel: 48 87 11 43
Fax: 48 87 14 47
Director: M. BONNET
Sells Goodyear shoes and accessories, shoe repairs

Courrèges
10, avenue Victor Hugo
75116 PARIS
Tel: 45 01 70 18

Cowboy Dream
21, rue de Turbigo
75002 PARIS
Tel: 42 36 30 05
American gear

Daniel Hechter
146, Bd. St. Germain
75006 PARIS
Tel: 43 26 96 36
Director: M. Charles JACOB

Devernois
70, rue St. Dominique
75007 PARIS
Tel: 47 05 69 28

Dorothée Bis
33, rue de Sèvres
75006 PARIS
Tel: 42 22 00 45

Finsbury
17, rue des Petits-Champs
75001 PARIS
Tel: 40 15 92 99
The smart shoes

Gérard Pasquier
8, avenue Victor Hugo
75016 PARIS
Tel: 45 00 91 29

Givenchy
3, avenue George V
75008 PARIS
Tel: 44 31 50 23

Gucci
2, rue du Fbg. St. Honoré
75008 PARIS
Tel: 42 96 83 27
Fax: 42 97 41 88
Director: M. PRIOU

Guy Laroche
29, avenue Montaigne
75008 PARIS
Tel: 40 69 69 00
Fax: 40 70 04 51

Handsome
54, rue de Richelieu
75001 PARIS
Tel: 40 20 03 21
Fashion wear for men

Harley-Davidson
48, rue de la Chapelle
75018 PARIS
Tel: 46 07 83 21
Harley fashion and collectibles

Harry Winston of New York
29, avenue Montaigne
75008 PARIS
Tel: 47 20 03 09
Fax: 47 23 92 97
Director: M. Philippe SCHAEFFER

Hermès
24, rue du Fbg. St. Honoré
75008 PARIS
Tel: 40 17 47 17
Fax: 40 17 47 18
Deputy Director: M. THOMAS

Hugo Boss
12-14, Rond-Point des Champs-Elysées
75008 PARIS
Tel: 53 67 81 10

Infinitif
78, avenue des Champs-Elysées
75008 PARIS
Tel: 45 62 27 26
Fax: 45 62 54 90

Island
Place des Victoires
75002 PARIS
Tel: 42 61 77 77

Jean-Louis Scherrer
51, avenue Montaigne
75008 PARIS
Tel: 42 99 05 79

Jean-Paul Gaultier
6, rue Vivienne
75002 PARIS
Tel: 42 86 05 05
Fax: 42 83 06 89

Jocelyn Chausseurs
76-78, avenue des Champs-Elysées
75008 PARIS
Tel: 45 62 36 33

Jockey Club
240bis, Bd. St. Germain
75007 PARIS
Tel: 45 48 28 77

John Baillie Real Scotch Tailor
1, rue Auber
75009 PARIS
Tel: 47 42 49 17

Kenzo
3, Place des Victoires
75001 PARIS
Tel: 40 39 72 00

Lanvin
15, rue du Fbg. St. Honoré
75008 PARIS
Tel: 44 71 33 33

Laura Ashley
94, rue de Rennes
75006 PARIS
Tel: 44 39 20 69
Fax: 44 39 20 79
Commercial Director: M. DELORT

Lee Cooper Paris
18-20, rue Pierre Lescot
75001 PARIS
Tel: 45 08 04 83

Levi Strauss
7-9, rue Pierre Lescot
75001 PARIS
Tel: 45 08 18 19

Louis Féraud
88, rue du Fbg. St. Honoré
75008 PARIS
Tel: 42 65 27 29
Fax: 40 07 01 16
President: Mme BOIVIN

Madame Zaza of Marseille
18, rue Ste-Croix-de-la-Bretonnerie
75004 PARIS
Tel: 48 04 76 03

Magic Retour
36, rue de la Sablière
75014 PARIS
Tel: 45 43 67 61
Owner: Olivier
Women's clothes and accessories ranging from the twenties to the sixties

Manfield
94, rue du Bac
75007 PARIS
Tel: 42 84 32 61

Mariella Burani
412, rue St. Honoré
75008 PARIS
Tel: 42 60 36 50

Maximilien
93-95, avenue des Champs-Elysées
75008 PARIS
Tel: 47 23 68 37

Menkes
12, rue Rambuteau
75004 PARIS
Tel: 40 27 91 81
Fax: 40 27 98 61
Tailor-made dancing shoes. Specialized in accessories for Flamenco performers

Mephisto
101, rue de la Convention
75015 PARIS
Tel: 40 60 10 57
Fax: 40 60 10 57
Long-lasting air cushion-sole shoes

Minelli
61, rue Caumartin
75009 PARIS
Tel: 40 16 11 71
Elegant shoes for women

Old America
48, rue des Francs Bourgeois
75003 PARIS
Tel: 42 74 79 54
Fax: 42 74 79 55
Women's clothing

Old English Tailors
18, rue Godot de Mauroy
75009 PARIS
Tel: 42 65 27 05

Paco Rabanne
7, rue du Cherche-Midi
75006 PARIS
Tel: 40 49 08 53

Parallax
10, rue du Four
75006 PARIS
Tel: 43 26 12 58

Peter Hadley
6bis, Place des Petits Pères
75002 PARIS
Tel: 42 86 83 73

Pierre Balmain
44, rue François Ier
75008 PARIS
Tel: 47 20 35 34

Pierre Cardin
82, rue du Fbg. St. Honoré
75008 PARIS
Tel: 42 65 26 88
Fax: 42 66 04 51

Polo Ralph Lauren
2, Place de la Madeleine
75008 PARIS
Tel: 44 77 53 50
Fax: 47 03 38 37

Repetto
22, rue de la Paix
75002 PARIS
Tel: 44 71 83 00
Clothing for dance and gym enthusiasts

Rodier
35, rue de Sèvres
75006 PARIS
Tel: 45 48 49 15

Sabbia Rosa
73, rue des Saints Pères
75006 PARIS
Tel: 45 48 88 37
Lingerie

Seraphina
22, rue du Vieux Colombier
75006 PARIS
Tel: 45 48 16 62
Lingerie

Ted Lapidus
35, rue François Ier
75008 PARIS
Tel: 44 43 49 90
Fax: 47 23 06 41
Manager: M. Olivier KLEIN

Tehen
5bis, rue des Rosiers
75004 PARIS
Tel: 40 27 97 37
Soft, comfortable knitwear for women

Ton Sur Ton
84, avenue des Champs-Elysées
75008 PARIS
Tel: 43 59 19 59
Ladies' fashion

Vuitton Louis
54, avenue Montaigne
75008 PARIS
Tel: 45 62 47 00

Yves Saint-Laurent
38, rue du Fbg. St. Honoré
75008 PARIS
Tel: 42 65 74 59

Jewelry/Cosmetics
Bijoux/Cosmétiques

Boucheron
26, Place Vendôme
75001 PARIS
Tel: 42 61 58 16
Fax: 40 20 95 39
Fine jewelry

Cartier
13, rue de la Paix
75002 PARIS
Tel: 42 61 58 56
Fax: 42 18 53 75

Centre Franco-Américain Parfumerie
49, rue d'Aboukir
75002 PARIS
Tel: 42 36 77 46
Director: Mme ANDRE
Duty-free and discount perfume

Chaumet
12, Place Vendôme
75001 PARIS
Tel: 44 77 24 00
Fax: 44 77 29 89
Fine jewelry

Cie des Comptoirs de la Banquise
45, rue des Archives
75003 PARIS
Tel: 42 71 47 87
Fax: 42 71 47 88
Chunky jewelry and accessories

Crabtree & Evelyn
177, Bd. St. Germain
75006 PARIS
Tel: 45 44 68 76
Fax: 40 49 00 67
Cosmetics and gastronomic delicacies

France Tax Free Shopping
4, Place de l'Opéra
75002 PARIS
Tel: 42 66 24 14
Fax: 42 66 24 41

Galerie Thibaudet
8, rue du Bac
75007 PARIS
Tel: 45 48 93 54
Fax: 42 61 22 56
Secondhand jewelry and silverware at half-price

Guerlain
2, Place Vendôme
75001 PARIS
Tel: 42 60 68 61

Marley
19, rue de la Paix
75002 PARIS
Tel: 42 65 68 71
Fax: 49 24 04 69
Jewelry store

Mauboussin
20, Place Vendôme
75001 PARIS
Tel: 44 55 10 10
Fine jewelry since 1827

Mellerio
9, rue de la Paix
75002 PARIS
Tel: 42 61 57 53
Fax: 49 27 04 90
Jewelry store

Michel Swiss Perfumes & Cosmetics
16, rue de la Paix
75002 PARIS
Tel: 42 61 61 11
Fax: 49 27 94 47
Director: M. Philippe REIN

Parfums Nina Ricci
17, rue François Ier
75008 PARIS
Tel: 49 52 56 00

Parfums Ralph Lauren
16, Place Vendôme
75001 PARIS
Tel: 42 86 94 46

Parfums Rochas
33, rue François Ier
75008 PARIS
Tel: 47 23 54 56
Fax: 47 20 16 46

Puiforcat
2, avenue Matignon
75008 PARIS
Tel: 45 63 10 10
Fax: 42 56 27 15
Jewelry store

René Boivin
49, avenue Montaigne
75008 PARIS
Tel: 47 20 82 64
Fax: 47 20 82 62
Marketing Director:
Mlle Agnès MORIN
Fine jeweler

Shiseido
Salons du Palais Royal
142, Galerie de Valois
25, rue de Valois
75001 PARIS
Tel: 49 27 09 09
Excellent Japanese cosmetics and beauty care products with elegant packaging

The Body Shop
150, rue de Rivoli
75001 PARIS
Tel: 40 15 05 04
Fax: 40 15 04 60
Environmentally-conscious beauty products

Van Cleef & Arpels
22, Place Vendôme
75001 PARIS
Tel: 42 61 58 58
Fax: 47 03 93 57

Home Decoration/Furniture
Decoration Intérieure/Mobilier

Artis Flora
75, rue Vieille du Temple
75003 PARIS
Tel: 48 87 76 18
Fax: 48 87 98 60
Master-weavers, replicas of famous tapestries

Bains-Plus
51, rue des Francs Bourgeois
75004 PARIS
Tel: 48 87 83 07
Fax: 48 87 19 12
Clothing, accessories, and scented soaps and salts for the bathroom

Barry Lindon
15, Bd. St. Germain
75005 PARIS
Tel: 43 26 88 85
Antiques

Bouchara
54, Bd. Haussmann
75009 PARIS
Tel: 42 80 66 95
All types of material for fashion and interior decoration

Boutique Descamps
4, rue Donizetti
75016 PARIS
Tel: 42 88 14 19
Towelling bathrobes and house linen

Christofle
9, rue Royale
75008 PARIS
Tel: 49 33 43 00
Fax: 49 33 43 08
Quality silverware for the table

Classic Concept
8, rue du Mail
75002 PARIS
Tel: 47 03 96 60
Modern furniture

Contrecourant
4, rue des Ecoles
75005 PARIS
Tel: 43 54 95 49
Fax: 44 07 11 91
Casual house garments and accessories

Darty
Place de la Madeleine
75008 PARIS
Tel: 42 65 84 71
Fax: 40 07 05 62
TV and hi-fi equipment, household appliances

Electrorama - La Quincaillerie
11, Bd. St. Germain
75005 PARIS
Tel: 43 29 31 30
Fax: 40 46 80 46
Lamps in all shapes, sizes and styles

Habitat
Forum des Halles, Niveau -2
Porte Rambuteau
75001 PARIS
Tel: 40 39 91 06
Fax: 42 21 46 36
Furniture, decorative objects

Herolia
75, rue Vieille du Temple
75003 PARIS
Tel: 48 87 66 93
Wooden and wrought-iron decorative objects for the home

IKEA
202, rue Henri Barbusse
78370 PLAISIR
Tel: 30 79 21 21
Fax: 30 79 21 11
Furniture for tight budgets

La Chaise Longue
8, rue Princesse
75006 PARIS
Tel: 43 29 62 39
Fax: 43 29 62 39
Fun objects for the home

La Compagnie du Lit
91, Bd. Raspail
75006 PARIS
Tel: 42 22 51 51
Fax: 45 44 96 71
The bedding specialist

Lalique
11, rue Royale
75008 PARIS
Tel: 42 66 52 40
Fax: 42 65 59 06

Le Loft
17bis, rue Pavée
75004 PARIS
Tel: 48 87 46 50
Fax: 48 04 92 88
English and Scandinavian antique pine furniture

Les Toiles de Mayenne
74, rue Linois
75015 PARIS
Tel: 45 75 56 02
Interior decoration, fabrics

Linge des Vosges
94, rue St. Antoine
75004 PARIS
Tel: 42 72 38 26
House linen

Manuel Canovas
7, rue de Furstenberg
75006 PARIS
Tel: 43 25 75 98
Interior decoration, fabrics

Martin Bolton
48, rue des Archives
75004 PARIS
Tel: 42 72 27 19
English antiques, china, silverware

Mondo
85, Bd. Beaumarchais
75003 PARIS
Tel: 48 04 04 02
The Japanese mattress specialist

Pier Import
40, avenue des Champs-Elysées
75008 PARIS
Tel: 45 61 23 71
Exotic furniture, printed fabric, decorative objects for the home

Rotinrama
81, rue Lecourbe
75015 PARIS
Tel: 47 83 71 44
Fax: 43 06 16 75
Rattan furniture at rock-bottom prices

SOF
38, Bd. Richard Lenoir
75011 PARIS
Tel: 49 23 42 02
Fax: 49 23 04 92
Japanese mattresses, frames and covers

Stephany's House
7, rue Montenotte
75017 PARIS
Tel: 44 09 72 23
Fax: 44 09 73 37
English-style furniture, decoration

Taïr Mercier
7, Bd. St. Germain
75005 PARIS
Tel: 43 54 19 97
Fax: 43 25 57 22
Unusual dinner services, table mats, glasses

The Curtain Shop
23, rue Davioud
75016 PARIS
Tel: 45 25 36 26
New and secondhand curtains

Villa Marais
40, rue des Francs-Bourgeois
75003 PARIS
Tel: 42 78 42 40
Fax: 42 78 42 65
Unusual objets d'art *for the home*

Gift Shops
Boutiques de Cadeaux

Axis Boutique
13, rue de Charonne
75011 PARIS
Tel: 48 06 79 10
Fax: 46 78 54 19
Original stationery, gadgets & tableware

Diptyque
34, Bd. St. Germain
75005 PARIS
Tel: 43 26 45 27
Fax: 43 54 27 01
Gift shop

H. G. Thomas
36, Bd. St. Germain
75005 PARIS
Tel: 46 33 57 50
Gift shop for men

Heureka
25, rue Rambuteau
75004 PARIS
Tel: 42 72 06 27
Watches for all tastes

Homme Sweet Homme
45, rue Vieille du Temple
75004 PARIS
Tel: 48 04 94 99
Gifts and accessories for men

Le Chat Huant
50-52, rue Galande
75005 PARIS
Tel: 46 33 67 56
Fax: 46 33 76 22

Le Comptoir Irlandais
153, Bd. Voltaire
75011 PARIS
Tel: 43 71 25 81
Irish clothing and gifts

Le Jardin Moghol
53, rue Vieille du Temple
75004 PARIS
Tel: 48 87 41 32
Fax: 48 87 44 45
Indian crafts

Les Montres
7, rue de Castiglione
75001 PARIS
Tel: 42 60 65 88
Watches

Les Toquées d'à Côté
8, rue du Bourg-Tibourg
75004 PARIS
Tel: 42 77 23 35
Decorative creations in glass and wood

Maréchal
232, rue de Rivoli
75001 PARIS
Tel: 42 60 71 83
Fax: 42 60 33 76
Hand-painted miniature boxes in Limoges porcelain

Namaste
52, rue des Francs Bourgeois
75003 PARIS
Tel: 42 77 76 35
Indian and Nepalese crafts (jewelry, clothes, incense, ritual accessories)

Nysà
28bis, rue Cardinal Lemoine
75005 PARIS
Tel: 46 33 71 36
Ancient craftwork from India and Nepal

Sac et Sac
5, rue du Sabot
75006 PARIS
Tel: 42 22 90 84
Fax: 42 22 91 87
Leather goods and accessories

Seiko Boutique
49, avenue de l'Opéra
75002 PARIS
Tel: 42 61 54 61

The Disney Store
44, avenue des Champs-Elysées
75008 PARIS
Tel: 45 61 45 25

Tumbleweed
19, rue de Turenne
75004 PARIS
Tel: 42 78 06 10
Contemporary American craftwork: wooden toys, gadgets, puzzles and boxes

Specialty Foods
Spécialités Gastronomiques

Androuet
41, rue d'Amsterdam
75008 PARIS
Tel: 48 74 26 90
Master cheesemaker

Authentic American Donut
20, rue Bouvier
75011 PARIS
Tel: 44 93 58 58

Berthillon
31, rue St-Louis-en-l'Ile
75004 PARIS
Tel: 43 54 31 61
The ice cream specialist

Bread and Best
10, rue St. Marc
75002 PARIS
Tel: 40 26 56 66
Fax: 40 26 58 06
E-mail: 73631.1672.compuserve.com
Contact: M. David BEST
High-quality English sandwich and salad restaurant (home/office delivery)

British Corner
153, rue de Grenelle
75007 PARIS
Tel: 47 53 88 01
Fine foods

Casa Bini
36, rue Grégoire de Tours
75006 PARIS
Tel: 46 34 05 60
Manager: Mme LAURENT
Fine Italian foods

Cookie Connexion
160, avenue Ledru Rollin
75011 PARIS
Tel: 43 79 16 79
Sale of fresh American pastries

Cookie Délice
26, avenue Jean Moulin
75014 PARIS
Tel: 45 45 41 02

Cynthia's Bake Shop
31, rue Pétion
75011 PARIS
Tel: 43 48 06 84
Chocolate brownies, cheesecake, fresh bagels, scones

Dalloyau
99, rue du Fbg. St. Honoré
75008 PARIS
Tel: 43 59 18 10
Fax: 45 63 82 92
Delicious pastries

Debauve & Gallais
30, rue des Saints Pères
75007 PARIS
Tel: 45 48 54 67
Fine chocolates

Fauchon
26, Place de la Madeleine
75008 PARIS
Tel: 47 42 60 11
Rare and unusual delicacies

FLO Prestige Traiteur
60, rue La Boétie
75008 PARIS
Tel: 45 63 03 03
Quality delicatessen

Gérard Mulot
76, rue de Seine
75006 PARIS
Tel: 43 26 85 77
Fine chocolates, pastries and prepared dishes

Grande Epicerie de Paris
142, rue du Bac
75007 PARIS
Tel: 44 39 81 00
Gastronomic specialties: exotic fruit, preserves, confectionery, teas, spirits, etc.

Hédiard
21, Place de la Madeleine
75008 PARIS
Tel: 43 12 88 88
Fax: 42 66 31 97
Sweet and savory gastronomic delicacies

Jadis et Gourmande
27, rue Boissy d'Anglas
75008 PARIS
Tel: 42 65 23 23
Delicious homemade chocolate and sweets

Jeff de Bruges
66, Bd. St. Germain
75005 PARIS
Tel: 43 54 49 00
Belgian chocolates, ice cream

L'Epicerie du Monde
43, rue Monge
75005 PARIS
Tel: 40 46 07 50
Manager: M. Patrick ELOUARGHI
Groceries from all over the world

L'Epicerie Verte
5, rue Saussier Leroy
75017 PARIS
Tel: 47 64 19 68
Delicatessen for natural biological food (take-away service)

La Maison des Colonies
47, rue Vieille du Temple
75004 PARIS
Tel: 48 87 98 59
Fine selection of teas and freshly-roasted coffees

Laura Todd Cookies
2, rue Pierre Lescot
75001 PARIS
Tel: 42 36 15 87
Contact: M. Thierry HONORE
Cookies, brownies, muffins, ice cream

Le Comptoir Irlandais
153, Bd. Voltaire
75011 PARIS
Tel: 43 71 25 81
Genuine Irish food and whiskey

Le Stübli
10 and 11, rue Poncelet
75017 PARIS
Tel: 42 27 81 86
Fax: 42 67 61 69
German and Austrian delicatessen

Mariage Frères
30-32, rue du Bourg Tibourg
75004 PARIS
Tel: 42 72 28 11
Delightfully old-fashioned tea room and boutique

Mexi & Co.
10, rue Dante
75005 PARIS
Tel: 46 34 14 12
Director: Mme Claudia ORREGO
Mexican and American food products

Natura-Diet
15, rue Rambuteau
75004 PARIS
Tel: 42 71 08 13
Owner: Mme VIDET
Health food store

Naturalia
52, rue St. Antoine
75004 PARIS
Tel: 48 87 87 50
A wide selection of natural and organic food products. Also sells supplements for athletes and restricted diets

Nectar des Bourbons Fine Wines
37, rue de Turenne
75003 PARIS
Tel: 40 27 99 12
Fax: 40 27 99 12
Manager: M. Alain DECHY
Specialized in Burgundy. Organises wine tastings

Oldies but Goodies
16, rue du Bourg Tibourg
75004 PARIS
Tel: 48 87 14 37
Food store

Patrick Lesec Selections
46, rue St. Placide
75006 PARIS
Tel: 42 84 38 20
Fax: 42 84 38 22
Manager: M. Patrick LESEC
Fine wines from France and Italy

Petrossian
18, Bd. de la Tour Maubourg
75007 PARIS
Tel: 45 51 38 74
Tel: 42 65 18 45 (PR) 44 11 32 35
Caviar and East European specialties

Phineas
99, rue de l'Ouest
75014 PARIS
Tel: 45 41 33 50
Sweet and savoury pies to eat there or to take away

Pickwick's
8, rue Mandar
75002 PARIS
Tel: 40 26 06 58
Fax: 40 20 98 72
Owners: Richard & Neil
Food and drink straight from the British Isles. Good selection of products, warm welcome

Richart Chocolatiers
258, Bd. St. Germain
75007 PARIS
Tel: 45 55 66 00
Manager: Mme ALEXANDRAKIS
Exquisitely-presented fine chocolates

Ryst-Dupeyron
79, rue du Bac
75007 PARIS
Tel: 45 48 80 93
Wine store

San Francisco Muffin Company
35, rue du Dragon
75006 PARIS
Tel: 45 79 09 09
Fax: 45 79 03 50
Director: Mme Lisa KOBLENTZ
American bakery

Saumon Fumé d'Irlande
13, rue Eugène Varlin
75010 PARIS
Tel: 42 09 63 73
Irish smoked salmon

Saveurs d'Irlande
5, cité Vauxhall
75010 PARIS
Tel: 42 00 36 20
Fax: 42 00 33 12
Irish products

SDV - Le Marché des Amériques
20, rue Jean Daudin
75020 PARIS
Tel: 53 69 63 50
Fax: 53 69 63 51
Contact: Jacques
Sells Mexican and American food and beverages

Thanksgiving
20, rue St. Paul
75004 PARIS
Tel: 42 77 68 29
Director: Judith BLUYSEN
American groceries and restaurant

The General Store
82, rue de Grenelle
75007 PARIS
Tel: 45 48 63 16
American groceries and wines

The Original Cookie Company
Centre Commercial Galaxie
30, avenue d'Italie
75013 PARIS
Tel: 45 88 86 92

The Real McCoy
194, rue de Grenelle
75007 PARIS
Tel: 45 56 98 82
American groceries and take-out service

Miscellaneous
Divers

Christian Tortu
6, carrefour de l'Odéon
75006 PARIS
Tel: 43 26 02 56
Fax: 43 29 71 99
Exquisite flower shop

Dadi's House of Guitar
7, rue Douai
75009 PARIS
Tel: 45 26 55 10
Sells musical instruments

Electrica for Sony
11-24, rue des Halles
75001 PARIS
Tel: 42 21 11 11
Everything for Sony lovers, parts and repairs on "Sony Street"

Hanimex France
18, rue Ampère
B.P. 91
95500 GONESSE
Tel: 39 85 96 33
Photographic and video equipment

Ikebana Deco
70-72, Bd. St. Germain
75005 PARIS
Tel: 43 26 69 56
Miniature plant and flower arrangements, bonzaï

Les Mille Feuilles
2, rue Rambuteau
75003 PARIS
Tel: 42 78 32 93
Splendid bric-à-brac flower shop (books, vases, pots)

Les Tissus Reine
5, Place St. Pierre
75018 PARIS
Tel: 46 06 02 31
Wide choice of textiles for fashion and decoration

The FiloFax: Center
32, rue des Francs Bourgeois
75003 PARIS
Tel: 42 78 67 87

Thorp of London
8, avenue Villars
75007 PARIS
Tel: 47 53 76 37
Fax: 45 55 97 81
Fabrics

Toys-R-Us
Centre Commercial "Les Quatre Temps"
92092 PARIS LA DEFENSE
Tel: 47 76 29 78
Toy store

"Le Joigny"
Place du Marché
89300 JOIGNY
Tel: (16) 86 62 18 78
Fax: (16) 86 91 42 91
Contact: M. Peter HEUMANN
One-day cruises, bar and restaurant on board

A Carnaval et Fêtes
22, avenue Ledru Rollin
75011 PARIS
Tel: 43 47 06 08
Costume rental for special occasions

Agence Vintage
Tel: 44 94 40 24
50 vintage models dating back to the 1920s (with chauffeur)

Alkor
1, rue Grévin
94100 ST-MAUR-DES-FOSSES
Tel: 43 97 22 80
Fax: 48 89 18 75
Director: M. Frank CARROLL
Specialized in purchasing antiques and works of art for international clients

Alliance Conseils
32, rue Etienne Marcel
75002 PARIS
Tel: 42 36 27 07
Fax: 42 21 40 59
Contact: Annie WAGNER
Revamp your image with a Paris fashion specialist!

Allôstop
84, passage Brady
75010 PARIS
Tel: 42 46 00 66
Hitchhiking service

Always Agency
149, avenue Victor Hugo
75116 PARIS
Tel: 47 55 77 64
Fax: 47 55 77 07
Prestige host/hostess service

Angels et Bermans
196, Bd. Voltaire
75011 PARIS
Tel: 43 67 16 16
Fax: 43 67 16 16
Costume makers

Anim'
116, rue de Charenton
75012 PARIS
Tel: 43 38 29 70
Fax: 47 00 54 40
Director: M. Peter BLAKE
Domestic electric appliances for rent

Antar
42, rue Beaubourg
75003 PARIS
Tel: 42 78 49 16
Gas station open all night

Assemblée Permanente des Chambres d'Agriculture
9, avenue George V
75008 PARIS
Tel: 47 23 55 40
Fax: 47 23 84 97
Director: Mlle BRINBAUM
Arranges lodging on farms

Atelier d'INK
1, passage Rauch
75011 PARIS
Tel: 43 79 96 04
Contact: Nalitt KAPLAN
Personalized greetings cards

Atelier F.R.
Tel: 45 00 57 89
Fabrics, wallpapers, furnishings and bath fixtures at reduced prices (home delivery)

Atom
90, rue de l'Ourcq
75019 PARIS
Tel: 40 34 29 50
Fax: 40 34 08 45
Car repairs

Au Clown de la République
11, Bd. St. Martin
75003 PARIS
Tel: 42 72 73 73
Costume rental for special occasions

Au Nom de la Rose
Tel: 46 34 10 64
Compose bouquets of roses

Barbara Romer
27, allée du Valois
60500 CHANTILLY
Tel: 44 57 30 48
Fax: 44 57 30 48
Make-up for special occasions (fashion, weddings, photography)

Baxter's Press Agency
15, rue Hegesippe Moreau
75018 PARIS
Tel: 42 93 34 19
Fax: 42 93 34 19
Contact: A.M. BAXTER
24-hour photographic services

Bedford
Tel: 42 65 08 57
Professional shoe care and repairs

Bio Art Theatre Laboratories New York/Paris
66, rue du Château des Rentiers
75013 PARIS
Tel: 45 85 03 38
Fax: 44 23 71 60
Founding Director US/Europe:
Mme M.A. BARCHEVSKA
Life enhancement skills

Bombard Balloon Adventures
Château de Laborde
Laborde au Château
21200 BEAUNE
Tel: (16) 80 26 63 30
Fax: (16) 80 26 69 20
Res: 47 30 04 49
President: M. Buddy BOMBARD
Hot air balloon visits of the Loire region

Boulangerie de l'Ancienne Comédie
10, rue de l'Ancienne Comédie
75006 PARIS
Tel: 43 26 89 72
Fax: 43 29 07 40
Director: M. Jean-Michel GALEK
24-hour bakery

British Accent
34, Bd. Haussmann
75009 PARIS
Res: 48 01 48 52
Admin: 48 01 48 87
Fax: 48 01 48 18
Director: M. James MAYOR
British lifestyle by mail order

British Import Antiques
2, Place du Palais Royal
75002 PARIS
Tel: 42 60 19 12

Camps de Luca
11, Place de la Madeleine
75008 PARIS
Tel: 42 65 42 15
Fax: 42 65 40 03
Tailor

Carlota
Tel: 47 47 12 12
Manicure and pedicure home visits

Chaz Foxton
Tel: 45 25 21 17
Carpentry, electrical and tile work

CHEP France
51, rue Pierre
92110 CLICHY
Tel: 49 68 77 77
Rental of wooden pallets for transport

Chevalier Conservation
64, Bd. de la Mission-Marchand
92400 COURBEVOIE
Tel: 47 88 41 41
Fax: 43 34 08 99
Directors: Pierre & Dominique CHEVALIER
Cleaning and restoring carpets and rugs

Château de Lesvault
58370 ONLAY
Tel: (16) 86 84 32 91
Fax: (16) 86 84 35 78
Director: Bibbi LEE

Continental Waterways
9, rue Jean-Renaud
21000 DIJON
Tel: 80 30 49 20
Fax: 80 30 27 01
Director: M. Guy BARDET
Barge trips in Burgundy

Courtney Kolar
50, rue Godefroy Cavaignac
75011 PARIS
Tel: 44 64 78 18
Freelance photographer and photojournalist

Crown Heights in Paris
28, rue de l'Ourcq
75019 PARIS
Tel: 40 36 55 93
Fax: 40 36 55 94

Dad
Tel: 69 03 20 48
Pet food and litter home delivery service

Deco 64
40, rue des Blancs-Manteaux
75004 PARIS
Tel: 43 74 65 43
Fax: 43 98 90 81
Painting and other renovation services

Delta Services Organizations
127, rue Amelot
75011 PARIS
Tel: 48 44 96 67
Dinners, galas, hostesses, etc.

Domino's Pizza
65, rue St. Dominique
75007 PARIS
Tel: 47 05 73 73
Recording: 36 67 21 21
Home delivery service

Edwards & Edwards
Tel: 42 65 39 21
Booking service for shows in Paris, London, New York and Berlin

Ellinas Phone Rentals
Tel: 48 67 55 55
Fax: 48 67 39 89
Supplies portable phones in France

Enterprise B.M.
Tel: 42 41 86 10
Fax: 42 01 25 52
Repairs, interior decorating

Entreprise Murray
38, rue Servan
75011 PARIS
Tel: 43 44 34 47
Fax: 43 44 42 47
E-mail:
100063.1044@compuserve.com
Director: M. Christopher MURRAY
British general contractor: all renovations

Espace Wagram
39, avenue Wagram
75017 PARIS
Tel: 43 80 30 03
Rental service of conference rooms

Esso
338, rue St. Honoré
75001 PARIS
Tel: 42 60 49 37
Gas station open all night

Fehrenbach Driving School
53, Bd. Henri Sellier
92150 SURESNES
Tel: 45 06 31 17
Fax: 47 28 81 89
Director: M. Michel FEHRENBACH
New highway code book in English

Fleurilège
Place de l'Eglise
78290 CROISSY-SUR-SEINE
Tel: 39 76 80 08
Fax: 39 76 21 42
Plants, real and fake flowers, floral arrangements for special events

France Montgolfières
76, rue Balard
75015 PARIS
Tel: 40 60 11 23
Fax: 45 58 60 73
Contact: M. David LA BEAUME
Hot air balloon trips, canoeing weekends

Franco-Americain du Froid
183, avenue du Maine
75014 PARIS
Tel: 45 40 94 10
Fax: 45 39 38 33
Director: M. PICARD
American appliances

Frédéric Chaubin
8, rue des Fossés St. Jacques
75005 PARIS
Tel: 43 29 39 46
Photographer

Garage Parking Saint-Honoré
336, rue St. Honoré
75001 PARIS
Tel: 42 61 50 60
Fax: 42 61 53 91
Car park management

Gardienes Tortonesi
Tel: 42 24 80 64
Learn haute couture with a seasoned specialist (French, English, Spanish)

Helen Hygreckos
15, avenue Porte d'Asnières
75017 PARIS
Tel: 43 80 50 08
Paints portraits and restores paintings

Herbier du Diois
Le Perrier
26150 DIE
Tel: (16) 75 22 12 07
Fax: (16) 75 22 18 60
Contact: Ton VINK
Sells herbs

Home Shopping Service
31, rue Henri Rochefort
75017 PARIS
Tel: 44 29 13 13
Fax: 47 66 22 22

Intea
37, avenue Junot
75018 PARIS
Tel: 46 06 68 01
Fax: 46 06 35 36
Manager: Corinne LELARGE
Designs all types of packaging (aluminium, cardboard, plastic)

Interflora
45, rue Vivienne
75002 PARIS
Tel: 44 82 28 21
Fax: 44 82 28 57
Worldwide flower service

International French Business
73, Bd. Clichy
75009 PARIS
Tel: 49 70 08 08
Fax: 49 70 00 04

La Redoute
Tel: (16) 20 69 86 00
Mail-order catalog for clothes and accessories

Le Médaillier Franklin
4, avenue de l' Escouvrier
95200 SARCELLES
Tel: 39 33 29 00
Fax: 34 19 72 10
President: Irène BABANY
Mail-order sales for decorative objects and medals

Le Tattoo Parlour
Tel: 45 41 29 57
Contact: M. Jimmy COQUELLE
Traditional Tribal and Celtic artwork - call for an appointment

Leichner L.J.C. Laukrom
11bis, rue du Colisée
75008 PARIS
Tel: 42 25 05 41
Theatrical make-up for parties and carnivals

Liselott Nissen
7, rue de Thorigny
75003 PARIS
Tel: 42 77 76 89
Reporter and portrait photographer

Magon Home Improvements
12, rue Corneille
78220 VIROFLAY
Tel: 30 24 74 68
Contact: Jasi MAGON
Interior decoration and renovation work

Mail Boxes Etc.
208, rue de la Convention
75015 PARIS
Tel: 44 19 60 20
Fax: 44 19 60 29
Handles all your postal, business and communications needs

Metropolitan Languages
151, rue Billancourt
92100 BOULOGNE-BILLANCOURT
Tel: 46 04 57 32

Michael Lo Sardo
10, rue du Croissant
75002 PARIS
Tel: 40 41 92 50
Piano tuning and repairs

Mille Break-First
7-9, passage Abel Leblanc
75012 PARIS
Tel: 43 45 76 53
Fax: 43 07 59 71
Contact: Valérie
The only company in France specializing in breakfast home delivery. Special prices for companies

Nelson et Entreprises
Ile de la Cité
11, rue d'Arcole
75004 PARIS
Tel: 40 46 85 14
Fax: 46 34 75 04
Director: Brenda NELSON
Shopping, workshops, perfume gift service, high fashion shows for visitors

Northrop and Johnson
13, rue Pasteur
06400 CANNES
Tel: (16) 93 94 20 08
Fax: (16) 93 94 42 29
President: M. Cornelis VAN VLIET
Sale and rental of luxury boats

Officers Group Security
12, rue Dugommier
75012 PARIS
Tel: 43 44 61 07
Fax: 43 42 39 50
Surveillance, protection

Olivier Laederich
28, rue Barque
75015 PARIS
Tel: 43 06 72 62
Fax: 45 67 99 68
Interior design

Otis
4, Place Victor Hugo
92400 COURBEVOIE
Tel: 46 91 60 00
Tel: 05 24 24 07
24h service for elevator installations

P.E.P. Action Business Center
16, rue Christophe Colomb
75008 PARIS
Tel: 44 43 88 00
Fax: 44 43 88 10
Answering service, secretarial assistance, conference rooms

Palace Mobile
Tel: 43 31 94 53
Hire a professional DJ for your party!

Paris Contact
26, rue des Trois Frères
75018 PARIS
Tel: 42 51 08 40
Fax: 42 51 08 40
Contact: Jill DANEELS
Personalized guided tours in English

Paris International
65, rue Pascal
75013 PARIS
Tel: 43 31 81 69
Fax: 43 37 11 46
Director: M. SINGH
Guides, personal services, interpreters

Peter & Oriel Caine
10, rue Samson
93200 SAINT-DENIS
Tel: 48 09 21 40
Fax: 42 43 75 51
Contacts: Peter & Oriel CAINE
Paris walking tours

Promenades de Style
52, rue du Fbg. Poissonnière
75010 PARIS
Tel: 47 70 08 28
Fax: 48 24 05 60
Anglophone Chauffeur: Edward
1964 Lincoln convertible - Tours and events

Rainbow International
40, rue Galilée
77380 COMBS-LA-VILLE
Tel: 60 60 18 16
The cleaning specialist for carpets, rugs and upholstery

Rebecca Brite
21, rue Lauriston
75116 PARIS
Tel: 45 53 27 31
Editing services

Shadow
Tel: 46 57 33 33
Treat yourself to a ride in a Rolls-Royce

Sharjeel Assad Mufti
18, avenue Victor Cresson
92130 ISSY-LES-MOULINEAUX
Tel: 46 42 51 20
Fax: 46 42 51 20
Indian astrology, palmistry and counseling

Shell
6, Bd. Raspail
75007 PARIS
Tel: 45 48 43 12
Gas station open all night

Soleil Plus
5, rue Brey
75017 PARIS
Tel: 45 72 46 48
Sun-tanning center, cheap rates - 30F a session

Stanhome
10, rue Jean Jaurès
92807 PUTEAUX Cedex
Tel: 41 26 01 01
Cleaning products sold privately

Studio B. Esclapez
1, rue Gutenberg
75015 PARIS
Tel: 45 75 21 01
Fax: 45 77 23 99
Agent: M. T. SMITH
Commercial photographer

Sylvia Toh
262, rue St. Honoré
75001 PARIS
Tel: 42 97 45 92
Fax: 40 20 97 52
Photo-journalism aimed at the Singapore/Malaysian press

Taylor Home Service
Tel: 47 47 55 82
Tailor-made suits and shirts for men

Teinturerie Saint James
Tel: 45 00 67 83
Cleaning and ironing service for delicate fabrics

Tennessee
16, rue d'Athènes
75009 PARIS
Tel: 45 26 50 57
Fax: 45 26 50 85

The Art of Picasso
67, Bd. Soult
75012 PARIS
Tel: 40 01 01 30

The Magic Touch
Tel: 45 20 60 02
Carpet cleaning specialist

The Three Ducks Hostel
6, Place Etienne Pernet
75015 PARIS
Tel: 48 42 04 05
Youth hostel for foreign students

Theatrix
Custom Picture Framing/
Specialty Painting
Tel: 45 21 41 53
Fax: 45 21 41 53
Designers: Denis & Lynda GUERET
By appointment only

Théatre à la Carte
83, rue Charles Frérot
94250 GENTILLY
Tel: 45 47 16 16
Fax: 45 47 46 60
Manager M. Christian POISSONNEAU
Organises theater performances for companies

Tom Craig Photography
17, rue Mayet
75006 PARIS
Tel: 45 66 62 66
Fax: 45 66 62 66
Contact: M. Tom CRAIG
Press photographer

Top Boy
35, Bd. de Strasbourg
75010 PARIS
Tel: 47 70 40 78
Fax: 42 46 43 90
Director: Sophie GLASMAN
Costume and wig rental

Top Retouches
8, rue Gramme
75015 PARIS
Tel: 48 42 55 05
Alterations

Tosca
17, avenue Gambetta
75020 PARIS
Tel: 43 58 43 17
Fax: 43 58 79 95
Interior decorating services

Trois Suisses
Tel: 36 67 36 36
Clothing for the whole family by mail-order

Up with People
60, rue Pergolèse
75016 PARIS
Tel: 45 00 32 08
Fax: 45 00 32 15
Entertainment organization

Associations

Fédérations

America's Cup in France
8, rue Georges Leclanché
75015 PARIS
Tel: 43 22 75 15
Fax: 43 22 52 02

American Golf
14, rue du Regard
75006 PARIS
Tel: 45 49 12 52
Commercial Director:
M. BERNADET

Association SooBahkDo France
19, rue d'Aligre
75012 PARIS
Tel: 44 67 75 27
Fax: 44 67 75 27
Contact: Master Eui-Jeong CHOI
Traditional Korean martial art

Baseball Club de France
29, rue la Quintinie
75015 PARIS
Tel: 42 50 50 01

CNOSF
1, avenue Pierre de Coubertin
75013 PARIS
Tel: 40 78 28 00
Fax: 40 78 29 51
French representation of the International Olympic Committee

Comité de l'Ile de France de Rugby
56, avenue de St. Mandé
75012 PARIS
Tel: 43 42 51 51
Information on amateur clubs and organizations

Fédération Française de Rugby
7, Cité d'Antin
75009 PARIS
Tel: 48 74 84 75
Fax: 45 26 19 19

Fédération Française des Sports de Glace
35, rue Félicien David
75016 PARIS
Tel: 45 27 75 75
Fax: 45 27 39 59
Ice Sports Federation

Fédération Française d'Escrime
14, rue Moncey
75009 PARIS
Tel: 44 53 27 50
National Fencing Federation

Fédération Française de Boxe
25, Bd. des Italiens
75002 PARIS
Tel: 47 42 82 27
Fax: 42 66 00 78

Fédération Française de Football Américain
13bis, avenue Général Galliéni
92000 NANTERRE
Tel: 47 29 22 03

Fédération Française de Golf
69, avenue Victor Hugo
75116 PARIS
Tel: 44 17 63 00
Fax: 44 17 63 63
General Director: M. Hubert CHESNEAU

Fédération Française de Tennis
2, avenue Gordon Bennett
75016 PARIS
Tel: 47 43 48 00

Fédération Française de Voile
55, avenue Kléber
75016 PARIS
Tel: 44 05 81 00
National Sailing Federation

Paris Université Club (PUC)
3, avenue Pierre de Coubertin
75013 PARIS
Tel: 44 16 62 62

Racing Club de France
5, rue Eblé
75007 PARIS
Tel: 45 67 55 86

Health Clubs/Classes
Clubs & Centres Sportifs

Aerobics, American-Style
65, quai d'Orsay
75007 PARIS
Tel: 47 05 07 99
Contact: Alison BENNEY
Paris fitness professionals offer hi/lo, step, body sculpting and funk classes

Club Quartier Latin
19, rue de Pontoise
75005 PARIS
Tel: 43 54 82 45

Espace Vit'Halles
48, rue Rambuteau
75003 PARIS
Tel: 42 77 21 71
Fully-equipped American style health club

Forest Hill
4, rue Louis Armand
75015 PARIS
Tel: 40 60 10 00

Gymnase Club Champs-Elysées
26, rue de Berri
75008 PARIS
Tel: 43 59 04 58
Fax: 42 56 76 28
Health club

Gymnase Club Denfert Rochereau
28, avenue du Général Leclerc
75014 PARIS
Tel: 45 42 50 57
Fax: 45 42 17 92
Health club

Gymnase Club Vaugirard
208, rue de Vaugirard
75015 PARIS
Tel: 47 83 99 45
Fax: 40 61 04 48
Health club

Rendez-Vous de la Nature
96, rue Mouffetard
75005 PARIS
Tel: 43 36 59 34
Health club

Ritz Health Club
Hôtel Ritz
15, Place Vendôme
75041 PARIS Cedex 01
Tel: 43 16 30 60

Shape and Physical Condition
(Private Training in Gym or at Home)
8, rue Edouard Manet
94000 CRETEIL 43 99 27 14
Trainer: Tatiana DUPRES
Weight work-out, gym, stretching

Sporting Goods/Sportswear
Equipements/Vêtements de Sport

Adidas
3, rue du Louvre
75001 PARIS
Tel: 42 60 34 83
Free call: 05 01 10 01
Fax: 42 86 98 05

Adidas
Route de Saessolsheim
B.P. 67
67702 SAVERNE Cedex
Tel: (16) 88 57 88 00
Minitel: 3615 ADIDAS
Headquarters

Athlete's Foot
30, avenue d'Italie
75013 PARIS
Tel: 45 81 38 33

Au Vieux Campeur
48, rue des Ecoles
75005 PARIS
Tel: 43 29 12 32
Everything for camping, hiking and climbing enthusiasts

Boxter Import USA
40, rue St. Antoine
75004 PARIS
Tel: 42 72 38 61
Fax: 42 77 89 99

Chattanooga Surf Skateboard Shop
53, avenue Bosquet
75007 PARIS
Tel: 45 51 76 65
Fax: 47 53 01 50

City Sport
28, Bd. Poissonnière
75009 PARIS
Tel: 42 46 56 03
Fax: 42 46 56 38

Comptoir du Golf
22, avenue de la Grande Armée
75017 PARIS
Tel: 43 80 15 00
Fax: 47 63 89 91

Decathlon
26, avenue de Wagram
75008 PARIS
Tel: 45 72 66 88
Fax: 45 72 44 88

Decathlon S.A.
4, rue Louis Armand
75015 PARIS
Tel: 45 58 60 45
Sporting equipment - Headquarters

Everlast
17, rue Beaurepaire
75010 PARIS
Tel: 42 08 44 00
Fax: 42 08 45 00

Foot Locker France
22, avenue du Général Leclerc
75014 PARIS
Tel: 40 44 99 01
Sporting footwear by Nike, Reebok, etc.

Football Shop
20, rue Abel
75012 PARIS
Tel: 44 74 01 22

France Archerie
7, rue Fernand Foureau
75012 PARIS
Tel: 43 44 00 24
Fax: 43 41 04 08
For adepts of archery

Friendship Sport
6, rue Moulinet
75013 PARIS
Tel: 45 80 90 55
Table tennis furniture and accessories

Go Sport
Nouveau Forum des Halles
Place Carrée
75001 PARIS
Tel: 40 26 40 52

Hockey Corner
140, avenue du Maine
75014 PARIS
Tel: 43 20 82 27

Nike France
Fief Z.I. Béthunes
95310 ST-OUEN L'AUMONE
Tel: 34 30 10 00
Fax: 34 30 11 99
General Director: M. Philippe SANDT
Sporting clothes and footwear

O'Neill Irish International Sports Co. Ltd
B.P. 136
13252 MARSEILLE Cedex 06
Tel: (16) 91 37 88 14
Fax: (16) 91 81 39 00
Contact: M. Patrick FABRE
Manufactures and sells rugby tops

Pierre Christian
14, rue Beaugrenelle
75015 PARIS
Tel: 45 75 37 00
Fax: 45 77 20 98
American baseball and football equipment

Pins'Up Sporting Goods
11bis, rue Baliat
92400 COURBEVOIE
Tel: 47 68 50 54
Fax: 43 34 18 24
Personalized sportswear (T-shirts, caps, coach jackets, rubgy sweaters)

Reebok
14, rue du Théâtre
75015 PARIS
Tel: 45 78 00 28

San Diego Locals
164, avenue Parmentier
75010 PARIS
Tel: 42 01 16 17
Surfing equipment

Sport USA
40, rue de la Croix Nivert
75015 PARIS
Tel: 45 67 59 16
Specializes in Amerian sporting equipment and clothes - NFL, NBA, NHL, MLB, NCAA

Western House
23, rue des Canettes
75006 PARIS
Tel: 43 54 71 17
Sports clothes and footwear for athletes

Stadiums/Pools/Etc.
Stades/Piscines/Etc.

Aqua Boulevard
4, rue Louis Armand
75015 PARIS
Tel: 40 60 10 00
Water sports center

Aqualand
GIF-SUR-YVETTE
Tel: 60 12 25 90
Outdoor pool with waves

Bayard UCPA
Centre Equestre
Bois de Vincennes
75012 PARIS
Tel: 43 65 46 87
Fax: 43 65 85 94
Horseback riding

Bowling de Paris
Jardin d'Acclimatation
Bois de Boulogne
75116 PARIS
Tel: 40 67 94 00
Fax: 40 67 10 92
Restaurant, 24 bowling alleys, billiards...

Bowling Montparnasse
27, rue du Commandant Mouchotte
75014 PARIS
Tel: 43 21 61 32
Bowling, billiards, games room

Bowling Mouffetard
73, rue Mouffetard
75005 PARIS
Tel: 43 31 09 35
Bowling, billiards, snack-bar

Camping Bois de Boulogne
Allée Bord de l'Eau
75016 PARIS
Tel: 45 24 30 00
Fax: 42 24 42 95

Centre Hippique du Touring Club
Route de la Muette à Neuilly
75016 PARIS
Tel: 45 01 20 88
Fax: 40 67 71 02

Golf des Yvelines
Château de la Couharde
78940 LA-QUEUE-LEZ-YVELINES
Tel: 34 86 48 89
Fax: 34 86 50 31
Director: M. Jean-René MANGE
Golf course

Gymnase Club Rennes
149, rue de Rennes
75006 PARIS
Tel: 45 44 24 35
Features 6 squash courts

Hippodrome d'Auteuil
Route d'Auteuil aux Lacs
75016 PARIS
Tel: 45 27 12 25
Steeplechase competitions only

Hippodrome de Longchamp
Bois de Boulogne
75016 PARIS
Tel: 44 30 75 00
Venue for flat racing events, including the Prix de l'Arc de Triomphe

Hippodrome de Vincennes
2, Route de la Ferme
75012 PARIS
Tel: 49 77 17 17
For trotting races only

International Tennis Club
136, Bd. Brune
75014 PARIS
Tel: 45 40 94 23

La Main Jaune
Place de la Porte de Champerret
75017 PARIS
Tel: 47 63 26 47
Fax: 47 63 15 03
Indoor roller skating rink and dance hall

Patinoire Pailleron
30, rue Edouard Pailleron
75019 PARIS
Tel: 42 39 86 10
Skating rink with bar

Piscine Butte aux Cailles
5, Place Paul Verlaine
75013 PARIS
Tel: 45 89 60 05

Piscine de Pontoise
19, rue de Pontoise
75005 PARIS
Tel: 43 54 82 45
Water aerobics, swimming instruction for all ages

Roland Garros
2, avenue Gordon Bennett
75016 PARIS
Tel: 47 43 48 00
French Tennis Open and Paris Open

Squash Club des Corolles
48, Square des Corolles
Défense 2, 908
92 PARIS LA DEFENSE
Tel: 49 00 13 90

Squash Front de Seine
21, rue Gaston de Caillavet
75015 PARIS
Tel: 45 75 35 37

Stade du Parc des Princes
24, rue du Commandant Guilbaud
75016 PARIS
Tel: 42 88 02 76
Paris' legendary football arena

Stade Olympique de Paris
49, rue Nationale
75013 PARIS
Tel: 45 84 05 05
Football stadium

Stadium Squash Club
66, avenue d'Ivry
75013 PARIS
Tel: 45 85 39 06

Standard Athletic Club
Route Forestière du
Pavé de Meudon
92360 MEUDON-LA-FORET
Tel: 46 26 16 09
Cricket, squash, tennis, football, rugby, hockey, snooker, bridge

Tennis de Longchamp
19, Bd. Anatole France
92100 BOULOGNE
Tel: 46 03 84 49

Bike Rentals
Location de Vélos

Bicyclub de France
8, Place de la Porte de Champerret
75017 PARIS
Tel: 47 66 55 92
Fax: 43 80 35 68
Bicycle rentals and tours

Maison du Vélo
11, rue Fénelon
75010 PARIS
Tel: 42 81 24 72
Bicycle sales and repairs center with a wide range of spare parts and accessories

Mountain Bike Folie's
246, rue Grande
77300 FONTAINEBLEAU
Tel: 64 23 43 07
Bike rentals

Paris Bike
83, rue Daguerre
75014 PARIS
Tel: 45 38 58 58
Fax: 43 20 71 93
Director: M. Thierry VINH MAU
Bicycle tours of Paris, bike rentals

Paris by Cycle
78, rue de l'Ouest
75014 PARIS
Tel: 40 47 08 04
Bicycle rentals

Paris Vélo
2, rue du Fer à Moulin
75005 PARIS
Tel: 43 37 59 22
Fax: 47 07 67 45
Director: M. Olivier CATHALA
Bicycle rentals

English-Language Theater
Compagnies de Langue Anglaise

ACT
84, rue Pixérécourt
75020 PARIS
Tel: 40 33 64 02
Fax: 40 33 64 03
Contacts: Anne & Andrew WILSON
Professional English theater

Acting International
148, rue du Temple
75003 PARIS
Tel: 42 71 08 98
Contact: Lesley CHATTERLEY
Bilingual acting programs

Actor's Institute
42, rue du Fbg. St. Denis
75010 PARIS
Tel: 42 46 66 66
Fax: 42 46 69 97
Creativity courses and workshops in self-expression

Actorat
16, rue des Grands Augustins
75006 PARIS
Tel: 43 25 46 63
Fax: 43 25 43 32
Bilingual drama classes

Compagnie du Horlà
21, rue Henri Regnault
92210 ST-CLOUD
Tel: 47 71 23 46
Director: Dana Burns WESTBERG
Versatile company performing the work of American playwrights in French

Company Oz
4, rue Georges Saché
75014 PARIS
Tel: 45 43 05 26
Contact: Mme Michèle MATHIEU
English-speaking theatre company

Dear Conjunction Theatre Company
6, rue Arthur Rozier
75019 PARIS
Tel: 42 41 69 65
Fax: 42 06 26 94
Contact: Patricia KESSLER
Bilingual theater touring company

Franco-Américaine de Cinéma et Théâtre (FACT)
16, rue de Clichy
75009 PARIS
Tel: 48 78 84 63
Professional acting workshops in French and English

International Players
3, rue de la Mascotte
78290 CROISSY-SUR-SEINE
Tel: 39 76 98 43
Contact: Mrs Alex AEBISCHER
Amateur company performing plays in English

On Stage
27, rue de la Beaune
93100 MONTREUIL
Tel: 48 59 41 50
Contact: M. Nick CALDERBANK
Performs Anglophone plays in V.O.

Sweeney Irish Pub
18, rue Laplace
75005 PARIS
Tel: 46 33 36 37
Stages one act plays in its cellar

French Theaters
Théâtres Français

Atelier Bastille
76, rue du Fbg. St. Antoine
75011 PARIS
Tel: 44 74 98 26

Athénée Louis Jouvet
4, square de l'Opéra
75009 PARIS
Tel: 47 42 67 27

Bouffes du Nord
37bis, Bd. de la Chapelle
75010 PARIS
Tel: 46 07 34 50

Comédie de Paris
42, rue Fontaine
75009 PARIS
Tel: 42 81 00 11

Comédie Française
2, rue de Richelieu
75001 PARIS
Tel: 40 15 00 15
Prestigious national theater with classical repertoire

Espace Cardin
1-3, avenue Gabriel
75008 PARIS
Tel: 42 66 17 30

Huchette
23, rue de la Huchette
75005 PARIS
Tel: 43 26 38 99

La Compagnie de Théâtre Européen d'Argo
27, rue de Verneuil
75007 PARIS
Tel: 40 20 98 67
Fax: 43 06 07 07
Contact: Carole CHICHET

Lucernaire Forum
53, rue Notre-Dame-des-Champs
75006 PARIS
Tel: 45 44 57 34

Madeleine
19, rue de Surène
75008 PARIS
Tel: 42 65 07 09

Marigny
Carré Marigny
75008 PARIS
Tel: 42 56 04 41

Mathurins
36, rue des Mathurins
75008 PARIS
Tel: 42 65 90 00

Montparnasse
31, rue de la Gaïté
75014 PARIS
Tel: 43 22 77 74

Palais des Glaces
37, rue Fbg. du Temple
75010 PARIS
Tel: 42 02 27 17

Palais-Royal
38, rue Montpensier
75001 PARIS
Tel: 42 97 59 81
Classical plays

Paris Villette
211, avenue Jean Jaurès
75019 PARIS
Tel: 42 02 02 68

Petit Théâtre de Paris
15, rue Blanche
75009 PARIS
Tel: 42 80 01 81

St. Georges
51, rue St. Georges
75009 PARIS
Tel: 48 78 63 47

Théâtre de l'Aquarium
"Cartoucherie"
Bois de Vincennes
75012 PARIS
Tel: 43 74 72 74

Théâtre de l'Epée de Bois
"Cartoucherie"
Bois de Vincennes
75012 PARIS
Tel: 48 08 39 74

Théâtre de l'Est Parisien
159, avenue Gambetta
75020 PARIS
Tel: 43 64 80 80

Théâtre de l'Odéon
Place de l'Odéon
75006 PARIS
Tel: 44 41 36 36

Théâtre de la Bastille
76, rue de la Roquette
75011 PARIS
Tel: 43 57 42 14

Théâtre de la Main d'Or
15, passage de la Main d'Or
75011 PARIS
Tel: 48 05 67 89

Théâtre de la Tempête
"Cartoucherie"
Bois de Vincennes
75012 PARIS
Tel: 43 74 94 07

Théâtre de la Ville
2, Place du Châtelet
75004 PARIS
Tel: 42 74 22 77

Théâtre de Nesle
8, rue de Nesle
75006 PARIS
Res: 46 34 61 04

Théâtre des Amandiers
7, avenue Pablo Picasso
92000 NANTERRE
Tel: 46 14 70 00

Théâtre des Champs-Elysées
15, avenue Montaigne
75008 PARIS
Tel: 49 52 50 50

Théâtre du Chaudron
"Cartoucherie"
Bois de Vincennes
75012 PARIS
Tel: 43 28 97 04

Théâtre du Gymnase Marie-Bell
38, Bd. Bonne Nouvelle
75010 PARIS
Tel: 42 46 79 79

Théâtre du Rond-Point
2bis, avenue Franklin Roosevelt
75008 PARIS
Tel: 44 95 98 00

Théâtre du Soleil
"Cartoucherie"
Bois de Vincennes
75012 PARIS
Tel: 43 74 24 08

Théâtre du Vieux Colombier
21, rue du Vieux Colombier
75006 PARIS
Tel: 44 39 87 00

Théâtre Essaïon
6, rue Pierre au Lard
75004 PARIS
Tel: 42 78 46 42
Fax: 42 74 04 54
Director: Mme Alida LATESSA
Theater workshops

Théâtre Grévin
10, Bd. Montmartre
75009 PARIS
Tel: 42 46 84 47

Théâtre National de Chaillot
Place du Trocadéro
75016 PARIS
Tel: 47 27 81 15

Théâtre National de la Colline
15, rue Malte Brun
75020 PARIS
Tel: 44 62 52 52

Théâtre Silvia Montfort
106, rue Brancion
75015 PARIS
Tel: 45 31 10 96

Théâtre Tristan Bernard
64, rue du Rocher
75008 PARIS
Tel: 42 93 65 36

Theatrical Agents
Production Théâtrale

Cindy Brace
31, rue Milton
75009 PARIS
Tel: 45 26 33 49
Fax: 48 74 51 42
Artistic agent

D.P.I.
80, rue de Lagny
75020 PARIS
Tel: 43 79 81 46
Fax: 43 79 81 46
E-mail: 100416.573@compuserve.com
Contact: Dominic PEISSEL
Bilingual production management

Dance
Danse

Aidohouedo, l'Arc-en-Ciel
127, rue d'Avron
75020 PARIS
Tel: 43 56 75 80
Fax: 43 56 27 83
President: M. Jean-Fortuné
DE SOUZA
African dance workshops

Body Sparks
6, rue St. Anastase
75003 PARIS
Tel: 42 71 03 46
Fax: 43 46 57 17
Director: Mme Suzanne SPARKS
Dance, Salsa, Latin America

Cours de Dance
Etiennette Morgan
Salle Pleyel
Studio 617
252, rue du Fbg. St. Honoré
75008 PARIS
Tel: 45 63 32 90
English-speaking dance classes: ballet, jazz, limbering, ballroom dancing

K-Danse
14, Bd. Raspail
75007 PARIS
Tel: 46 33 93 43
Contact: Mme GODEBSKI
Classical and contemporary dance lessons (jazz, rock)
2nd address: 13, rue Valette, 75005, Paris

Studio Aline Roux
92bis, Bd. Montparnasse
75014 PARIS
Tel: 43 20 44 39
Administrator: Mme Jacqueline
DE PERCEVAL
Dance instruction for children and adults (classical, modern, jazz)

A'BTI - Agence Bilis Traduction Interprètes
24, rue Laffitte
75009 PARIS
Tel: 47 70 50 80
Fax: 42 46 37 43
Director: M. Jean D'ANTHONAY
Translation, interpreting, visa legalisations

Agence Volker Marek
361, rue Lecourbe
75015 PARIS
Tel: 45 57 16 76
Fax: 45 57 49 45
Managing Director:
M. Volker MAREK
Translations - All languages

Arc Langues
38, rue Camille Pelletan
92300 LEVALLOIS-PERRET
Tel: 47 39 58 29
Fax: 47 39 22 29
Director: M. Michel GUILLEMAT

Astradul
B.P. 225 07
75327 PARIS Cedex 07
Tel: 39 83 66 63
Tel: 69 00 22 87
Association of qualified translators from London University. French and English translators

Berlitz Traduction
63, rue Aristide Briand
92300 LEVALLOIS-PERRET
Tel: 47 57 71 71
Fax: 47 57 29 92
Director: Mme Aurélie SALMON-LOGIEZ
Translation

Bernard Varlet
24, rue de la Libération
77230 DAMMARTIN-EN-GOELE
(near Roissy Airport)
Tel: 60 03 41 75
Translator, interpreter, French teacher for foreigners and experienced English teacher. All levels, children and adults (Bachelor of Arts & Master of Arts). Has lived in the USA

Cabinet de la Hanse
44, rue La Boétie
75008 PARIS
Tel: 45 63 81 18
Fax: 42 25 45 26
Director: M. Cornelis DE PREST

CG Traduction
8, rue Rameau
B.P. 235
78002 VERSAILLES Cedex
Tel: 30 21 86 37
Fax: 39 02 00 64
Director: Mme Catherine GRANELL

Communications Européennes
8, rue de Surène
75008 PARIS
Tel: 42 66 43 30
Fax: 42 66 28 20

Courtney McConnel
11, rue Alphonse Penaud
75020 PARIS
Tel: 40 30 20 45
Fax: 40 30 20 45
Qualified translator in English/French/Spanish

Dataid
48, avenue Raymond Poincaré
75016 PARIS
Tel: 45 53 47 26
Fax: 47 55 19 16

Eileen Osmand Savdié
4, rue Descombes
75017 PARIS
Tel: 43 80 80 75
Fax: 40 54 80 48
Translation service: official documents, technical, scientific, economic and literary

Europublica
21, rue St. Fiacre
75002 PARIS
Tel: 40 26 44 77
Fax: 45 08 44 25

EuroTexte
73, Bd. de Sébastopol
75002 PARIS
Tel: 42 21 14 00
Fax: 42 21 14 17
Director: Lori THICKE
Technical, commercial and legal translations

Extratext
19, rue Le Brun
75013 PARIS
Tel: 43 31 93 92
Fax: 43 31 96 33
Director: M. Kevin HARRIGAN
Copywriting, translation, PAO

ICC
3, rue des Batignolles
75017 PARIS
Tel: 43 87 29 29
Fax: 45 22 49 13
Director: M. Barton REICHERT
Corporate and financial translation

Julia Delille-Gomory
31, rue Franklin
91704 STE-GENEVIEVE-DES-BOIS
Cedex
Tel: 60 16 08 88 (home)
Tel: 45 44 22 52 (office)
Fax: 69 51 01 93
Bilingual Conference Interpreter (AIIC)

Kane Traduction
10, rue Paul Vaillant Couturier
92300 LEVALLOIS-PERRET
Tel: 40 89 08 16
Director: M. Franklin KANE
Technical, commercial translation

Linguacom International
83, rue Michel Ange
75016 PARIS
Tel: 46 51 29 77
Fax: 47 43 18 94
Director: M. Asamanja GHOSE
Complete range of language and translating services

Nagpal International Translation Services
65, rue Pascal
75013 PARIS
Tel: 47 07 55 28
Fax: 43 37 11 46
Director: D.C. NAGPAL
General and scientific translations

Tanya Leslie
29, rue au Maire
75003 PARIS
Tel: 42 77 39 44
Translating and interpreting services in French, English, Italian and Spanish (advertising, fiction, travel, film)

Titra-Film
1, quai Gabriel Péri
94340 JOINVILLE-LE-PONT
Tel: 48 89 19 89
French subtitles for foreign films

Tony Frank Paschall
19, allée Marc Chagall
75013 PARIS
Tel: 45 86 03 28
Fax: 45 86 05 24
TV, film, press, publishing

Traductor S.A.R.L.
120, avenue des Champs-Elysées
75008 PARIS
Tel: 45 62 50 41
Fax: 42 25 03 74
Director: Mme Marie-France THUREL

Translantic
170, rue du Fbg. St. Antoine
75012 PARIS
Tel: 40 09 89 62
Fax: 40 09 92 66
E-mail:
100016.3311@compuserve.com
Translation, computer consulting

Ursula Grüber Communication Internationale
83, rue St. Honoré
75001 PARIS
Tel: 42 33 57 61
Fax: 42 21 41 14
President: Ursula GRUBER
Copywriting, adaptation of advertising texts

Voices
13, rue Chambéry
75015 PARIS
Tel: 45 31 65 48
Director: Michèle MARSHALL
Translation, commentary and dubbing by a team of professional English and American actors. All other languages accepted

WordPower
4bis, rue St. Sabin
75011 PARIS
Tel: 47 00 46 10
Fax: 47 00 54 40
Editor/Agent: Gina DOGGETT
Translator, editor, literary agent

Aéroports de Paris
291, Bd. Raspail
75675 PARIS Cedex 14
Tel: 43 35 70 00
Administration of airport authorities

British Rail International
19, rue des Mathurins
75009 PARIS
Tel: 44 51 06 11
Fax: 42 66 40 43
Contact: M. Michael CHESWORTH

Bâteaux Mouches
Port Conférence
75008 PARIS
Tel: 42 25 96 10
Fax: 42 25 02 28

Bâteaux Parisiens
Port La Bourdonnais
75007 PARIS
Tel: 44 11 33 44

Canadian National Railway
1, rue Scribe
75009 PARIS
Tel: 47 42 76 50
Fax: 47 42 24 39
Canadian railroad

Compagnie Transair
Zone Nord Aéroport
B.P. 174
93352 LE BOURGET Cedex
Tel: 49 92 75 75
Fax: 49 92 75 00
Sales Assistant: Annie LEBARS
Airplane sales and and maintenance

Deutsche Bahn
13, rue d'Alsace
75010 PARIS
Tel: 46 07 13 40
Fax: 40 37 26 64
German Railway

Eurolines
28, avenue du Général de Gaulle
93170 BAGNOLET
Tel: 49 72 51 51
Fax: 49 72 51 61
International bus and coach station

Eurostar
Tel: 42 66 40 43
Fax: 44 51 06 02
High-speed passenger train linking Paris to London via the Channel Tunnel

Eurotunnel
112, avenue Kléber
B.P. 166
75770 PARIS Cedex 16
Tel: 44 05 62 00
Fax: 44 05 62 90
Communications Director:
Mme Dominique MAIRE

Eurotunnel
B.P. 69
62231 COQUELLES
Admin: (16) 21 00 60 00
Info: (16) 21 00 69 14
Calais headquarters

Fédération Nationale Transports Routiers
6, rue Paul Valéry
75016 PARIS
Tel: 45 53 92 88
Fax: 45 53 11 39
Defends and promotes road transport

HeliFrance
4, avenue de la Porte de Sèvres
75015 PARIS
Tel: 45 54 95 11
Fax: 45 54 18 81
Public helicopter transport and tourist trips

Hoverspeed
165, avenue de Clichy
75017 PARIS
Tel: 40 25 22 00
Hydrofoil to the UK

Irish Ferries
32, rue du Quatre Septembre
75002 PARIS
Tel: 42 66 90 90
Fax: 42 66 15 80

P & O European Ferries
Maison de Grande-Bretagne
19, rue des Mathurins
75009 PARIS
Tel: 44 51 00 51

RATP
52, quai de la Rapée
75012 PARIS
Tel: 44 68 20 20
Minitel: 3615 RATP
Route Info: 36 68 77 14
Parisian Transport Association
(see advertisement)

Union Routière de France
10, rue Clément Marot
75008 PARIS
Tel: 40 70 05 45
Fax: 47 23 77 57
Communications Director:
Mlle Christine BURRONI
French Transport Union

Sealink Voyages
23, rue Louis le Grand
75002 PARIS
Tel: 44 94 40 40
Fax: 42 65 10 17

SNCF Train Info.
16, Bd. des Capucines
75002 PARIS
Info: 45 82 50 50
Res: 3615 SNCF

Vedettes de Paris
Port de Suffren
75007 PARIS
Tel: 47 05 71 29
Fax: 47 05 74 53
Tourist boat tours and rentals

Vedettes Pont-Neuf
Square du Vert Galant
75001 PARIS
Tel: 46 33 98 38

Venise Simplon Orient Express
75, avenue des Champs-Elysées
75008 PARIS
Tel: 45 62 00 69

Travel Agencies
Agences de Voyage

Access Voyages
6, rue Pierre Lescot
75001 PARIS
Tel: 40 13 02 02
Te: 42 21 46 94
Minitel: 3615 ACCESSVOYAGE

Aclat Multitour
202, rue de Rivoli
75001 PARIS
Tel: 42 60 82 09
Fax: 40 20 90 70

African Safari Club
13, rue des Pyramides
75001 PARIS
Tel: 42 86 53 55

Agence Airliner
14, rue Crussol
75011 PARIS
Tel: 43 38 34 34
Fax: 43 38 01 65

Agence Solari
111, avenue Victor Hugo
75016 PARIS
Tel: 47 04 93 93
Fax: 47 27 48 54

Air Promotion Group
66, avenue des Champs-Elysées
75008 PARIS
Tel: 40 74 00 74
Fax: 40 74 05 51

Any Way
46, rue des Lombards
75001 PARIS
Tel: 40 28 00 74
Fax: 42 36 11 41

Australie Tours
129, rue Lauriston
75016 PARIS
Tel: 45 53 58 39
Fax: 47 55 95 93

Blue Marble Travel
2, rue Dussoubs
75002 PARIS
Tel: 42 36 02 34
Fax: 42 21 14 77
Director: M. Nicolas CLIFFORD
Bike trips for adults (20-5). Specialist in long-distance European train tickets

Canada Welcome
24, Bd. Port Royal
75005 PARIS
Tel: 43 37 43 96

Canadien National
1, rue Scribe
75009 PARIS
Tel: 47 42 76 50
Fax: 47 42 24 39
Director: M. Pierre BRICOUT

Carlson Wagonlit Travel
168, rue du Fbg. St. Honoré
75008 PARIS
Tel: 53 77 26 80
Fax: 42 56 41 98

Cash & Go
54, rue Taitbout
75009 PARIS
Tel: 44 53 49 49
Fax: 42 82 94 24
High quality travel service at competitive prices

CIT
3, Bd. des Capucines
75002 PARIS
Tel: 44 51 39 51
Fax: 42 66 54 57

Club Méditerranée
25, rue Vivienne
75002 PARIS
Tel: 42 86 40 00
Fax: 42 61 40 59
Director: M. TRIGANO

Council Travel
66, avenue des Champs-Elysées
75008 PARIS
Tel: 40 75 95 10 (Europe)
Fax: 42 56 65 27
Headquarters

Council Travel Services
22, rue des Pyramides
75001 PARIS
Tel: 44 55 55 65
Minitel: 3615 COUNCIL

CTS Voyages
20, rue des Carmes
75005 PARIS
Tel: 43 25 00 76
Fax: 43 54 48 98

Finch Travel Service
France - The French Way
13, rue Linné
75005 PARIS
Tel: 45 87 25 03
Fax: 45 87 24 96
Director: M. Geoffrey FINCH
The travel specialist for France, offering a wide range of in-depth regional tours (Hotel Barges, Private Gardens and Châteaux,Wine and Gastronomic Tours)

Forum Voyages
11, avenue de l'Opéra
75001 PARIS
Tel: 42 61 20 20
Fax: 42 61 39 12

Fram Voyages
120, rue de Rivoli
75001 PARIS
Tel: 40 26 30 31
Fax: 40 26 30 32

Frantour
7, rue Pablo Neruda
92532 LEVALLOIS-PERRET Cedex
Tel: 45 19 12 00

Go Voyages
36, rue du Chemin Vert
75011 PARIS
Tel: 49 23 26 86
Fax: 49 23 27 38

Groupe Voyages Québec
20, rue du Château
95320 ST-LEU-LA-FORET
Tel: 34 18 18 18
Fax: 34 18 18 00
Director: M. René POITRAS

Gulliver's Travel Agency
80, avenue Marceau
75008 PARIS
Tel: 47 23 53 03
Fax: 47 23 53 55

Havas Voyages
26, avenue de l'Opéra
75001 PARIS
Tel: 42 61 80 56
Fax: 47 03 32 13

Holt Paris Welcome Service
12, rue Helder
75009 PARIS
Tel: 45 23 08 14
Fax: 42 47 19 89
Directors: Susan & Alan HOLT
Take care of travel arrangements for English and American visitors to France as well as accommodation, cultural tours, sporting events...

Intairline
28, rue Delambre
75014 PARIS
Tel: 43 20 90 46
Light air fares on major scheduled airlines

Jet Set
41-45, rue de Galilée
75116 PARIS
Tel: 53 67 13 00
Fax: 53 67 13 29
Tour operator specializing in the US and Canada

Jet Tours
19, avenue de Tourville
75007 PARIS
Tel: 47 05 01 95
Fax: 47 05 98 55

La Balade du Monde
10, rue St. Claude
75003 PARIS
Tel: 40 27 86 87
Contact: M. WIGELMAN
Special fares in business, economy and first class

La Balade du Monde
99, rue de Sèvres
75006 PARIS
Tel: 45 49 47 49
Contact: M. WIGELMAN
English-speaking travel agency offering promotions and special fares in business, first and economy class

Look Voyages
6, rue Marbeuf
75008 PARIS
Tel: 44 31 84 22
Fax: 44 31 84 41
Minitel: 3615 LOOK

Maison des Amériques
4, rue Chapon
75003 PARIS
Tel: 42 77 50 50
Fax: 42 77 50 60
Regular flights to major US cities

Non Stop USA
7, rue Berryer
75008 PARIS
Tel: 45 62 02 06
Fax: 45 62 02 10
Director: M. Mario CASSUTO
Business and leisure travel

Nouveau Monde
8, rue Mabillon
75006 PARIS
Tel: 43 29 40 40
Fax: 46 34 19 67

Nouvelles Frontières
66, Bd. St. Michel
75006 PARIS
Tel: 46 34 55 30
Fax: 46 33 76 65
Minitel: 3615 NF
Agency

Nouvelles Frontières
87, Bd. de Grenelle
75015 PARIS
Tel: 41 41 58 58
Fax: 44 61 84 18
Administrative offices

Octopus Voyages
63, rue Cambronne
75015 PARIS
Tel: 40 61 00 04
Major chain hotel discounts ("Room Service") and "Discount Air System". Seminars and Conferences

Pacific Holidays
34, avenue du Général Leclerc
75014 PARIS
Tel: 45 41 52 58
Fax: 45 39 49 06

Sabre Travel Information Network
77, rue La Boétie
75008 PARIS
Tel: 42 89 03 58
Fax: 45 61 90 60
Sells computerized booking systems to travel agencies

Sally Huet Travel Consultants
6D, avenue Francis Chaveton
92210 ST-CLOUD
Tel: 46 02 96 97
Fax: 47 71 85 20
Free holiday planning, worldwide travel

Sidon Travel France
34, avenue des Champs-Elysées
75008 PARIS
Tel: 42 56 40 30
Fax: 42 25 41 21

Tips on Trips and Camps
Conseils Loisirs Culturels USA
15, rue Georges Lafenestre
92340 BOURG-LA-REINE
Tel: 46 83 04 66
Fax: 46 83 04 66
Contact: Suzanne ANTEBY
Summer camps and youth travel

Tourism Consulting Group
34, avenue Général Leclerc
75014 PARIS
Tel: 45 39 61 10

Tours 33
85, Bd St. Michel
75005 PARIS
Tel: 43 29 69 50
Fax: 43 25 29 85
Communications Director:
Véronique THEVENARD
Travel agency specializing in Australia, New Zealand and the Pacific

Travelstore
14, Bd. de la Madeleine
75009 PARIS
Tel: 53 30 50 00
Fax: 53 30 50 10
President: M. Denis POLLET
Huge multi-storey travel center: agencies, documentation, guides, booking services

Usit Voyages
12, rue Vivienne
75002 PARIS
Tel: 44 55 32 60
Fax: 44 55 32 61
Contact: Jane WHIBLEY
Anglophone travel agency, worldwide air fares

Vacances Air Canada
10, rue de la Paix
75002 PARIS
Tel: 40 15 15 15
Fax: 42 61 68 81
President: M. Bernard DESANLIS
Tour operator

Verseau l'Espace Vacances
8, rue Oberkampf
75011 PARIS
Tel: 43 55 57 62
Fax: 48 05 14 97
Package tours

Via Voyages
26, rue de la Pépinière
75008 PARIS
Tel: 44 70 03 61
Fax: 43 87 50 94

Voyageurs aux USA/ Voyageurs au Canada
55, rue Ste Anne
75002 PARIS
Tel: 42 86 17 30
Admin: 42 86 16 61
Voyageurs en Australie: 42 86 16 99
Voyageurs en Inde: 42 86 16 90
Fax: 42 60 35 44
Tour operator specializing in the USA and Canada

Wagonlit Travel
50, rue de Londres
75008 PARIS
Tel: 44 90 33 33
Fax: 44 90 33 15

Wingate Travel
19bis, rue du Mont Thabor
75001 PARIS
Tel: 44 77 30 16
Fax: 40 20 94 55
Director: M. Eric SAVOURNIN
Operator of American tours

English-Language Tourist Offices
Offices de Tourisme Anglophones

South African Tourist Board
61, rue La Boétie
75008 PARIS
Tel: 45 61 01 97
Fax: 45 61 01 96

Australian Tourist Commission
4, rue Jean Rey
75015 PARIS
Tel: 45 79 42 77
Fax: 45 79 19 07
Tourist information on Australia

Bahamas Tourist Office
60, rue St. Lazare
75009 PARIS
Tel: 45 26 62 62
Fax: 48 74 06 05

Bureau d'Information de Boston and Massachusetts Massport
5bis, rue du Louvre
75001 PARIS
Tel: 44 77 88 07
Information center

Bureau d'Information New Orleans et Puerto Rico
5bis, rue du Louvre
75001 PARIS
Tel: 44 77 88 06
Information center

Canada
35, avenue Montaigne
75008 PARIS
Tel: 44 43 29 00
Visas: 44 43 29 16
Fax: 44 43 29 99
Minitel: 3615 OTCAN

Centre d'Information de l'Ile de Jersey
Tel: 48 04 86 06
Tel: (16) 88 94 10 20
Tourist information about Jersey

Hong Kong Tourist Association
53, rue François Ier
75008 PARIS
Tel: 47 20 39 54
Fax: 47 23 09 65
Closed to the public - please call, write or fax

Irish Tourist Board
33, rue Miromesnil
75008 PARIS
Tel: 47 42 03 36
Fax: 47 42 01 64
Director: Mme ADES
Promotion of tourism to Ireland

Irish Trade Board
33, rue Miromesnil
75008 PARIS
Tel: 42 65 98 05
Fax: 47 42 84 76
Marketing Adviser:
Mlle Mary GORMAN

Northern Ireland Tourist Office
3, rue de Pontoise
78100 ST-GERMAIN-EN-LAYE
Tel: 39 21 93 80

Office du Tourisme et des Congrès de Paris
127, avenue des Champs-Elysées
75008 PARIS
Tel: 49 52 53 54
Fax: 49 52 53 00
English Recording: 49 52 53 56
Press: 49 52 53 66

Office du Tourisme Indien
8, Bd. de la Madeleine
75009 PARIS
Tel: 42 65 83 86
Fax: 42 65 01 16

Tourist Office of Great Britain
19, rue des Mathurins
75009 PARIS
Tel: 44 51 56 22
Fax: 44 51 56 21
Minitel: 3615 BRITISH
Director: M. Bruce TAYLOR

Tourist Office of the United States
4, avenue Gabriel
75382 PARIS Cedex 08
Tel: 42 60 00 66
Fax: 40 15 08 74
Director of Communication:
Marianne CORRIEZ

Other Tourist Offices
Autres Offices de Tourisme

Austria
58, rue de Monceau
75008 PARIS
Tel: 53 83 95 20
Fax: 45 61 97 67
Minitel: 3615 AUTRICHE

Belgium
21, Bd. des Capucines
75002 PARIS
Tel: 47 42 41 18
Fax: 47 42 71 83

Cyprus
15, rue de la Paix
75002 PARIS
Tel: 42 61 42 49
Fax: 42 61 65 13

Czech Republic
32, avenue de l'Opéra
75002 PARIS
Tel: 47 42 74 87

Federal Republic of Germany
9, Bd. de la Madeleine
75001 PARIS
Tel: 40 20 01 88
Fax: 40 20 17 00

Finland
13, rue Auber
75009 PARIS
Tel: 42 66 40 13
Fax: 47 42 87 22

Greece
3, avenue de l'Opéra
75001 PARIS
Tel: 42 60 65 75
Fax: 42 60 10 28

Israel
22, rue des Capucines
75008 PARIS
Tel: 42 61 01 97

Italy
23, rue de la Paix
75002 PARIS
Tel: 42 66 03 96
Fax: 47 42 19 74

Latvia
14, Bd. Montmartre
75009 PARIS
Tel: 48 01 00 44
Fax: 48 01 03 71

Morocco
161, rue St. Honoré
75001 PARIS
Tel: 42 60 63 50
Fax: 40 15 97 34

Norway
88, avenue Charles de Gaulle
92523 NEUILLY-SUR-SEINE
Tel: 46 41 49 00

Poland
49, avenue de l'Opéra
75002 PARIS
Tel: 47 42 07 42 ??
Fax: 49 24 94 36 ??

Portugal
7, rue Scribe
75009 PARIS
Tel: 47 42 55 57
Fax: 42 66 06 89

Saint Lucia
53, rue François Ier
75008 PARIS
Tel: 47 20 34 66
Fax: 47 23 09 65

Spain
43ter, avenue Pierre Ier de Serbie
75008 PARIS
Tel: 47 23 65 61
Fax: 47 23 63 15

Sweden
11, rue Payenne
75003 PARIS
Tel: 42 72 58 77
Fax: 42 72 58 49

Switzerland
11bis, rue Scribe
75009 PARIS
Tel: 44 51 65 51

Singapore
2, Place du Palais Royal
75001 PARIS
Tel: 42 97 16 16

The Netherlands
31, avenue des Champs-Elysées
75008 PARIS
Tel: 42 25 41 25

Tunisia
32, avenue de l'Opéra
75002 PARIS
Tel: 47 42 72 67
Fax: 47 42 52 68

Turkey
102, avenue des Champs-Elysées
75008 PARIS
Tel: 45 62 78 68
Fax: 45 63 81 05

Universities
Universités

Alma College
c/o Alliance Française
101, Bd. Raspail
75006 PARIS
Tel: 45 49 08 16
Director: Mme BOUNOURE

American Business School
120, rue Danton
92303 LEVALLOIS-PERRET Cedex
Tel: 47 59 90 43
Fax: 40 67 96 96
BS/BA and MBA programs

Architecture Program Jan-June
4, rue de Jarente
75004 PARIS
Tel: 42 78 53 44

Boston University - Paris
Tour CIT - Bureau 309
3, rue de l'Arrivée
B.P. 43
75749 PARIS Cedex 15
Tel: 43 35 00 60
Fax: 40 47 85 14
Contact: Mme Karlene WALLACE
Master of Arts in international relations, internship program

Center for University Programs Abroad
19-21, rue Cassette
75006 PARIS
Tel: 42 22 87 50
Fax: 45 48 23 24
Director: Mme Elliot CHATELIN
Junior year abroad program

Central College (Iowa)
214, Bd. Raspail
75014 PARIS
Tel: 43 20 76 09
Director: Mme Inge DRAPPIER

Chicago Overseas Program
15, Bd. Jourdan
75014 PARIS
Tel: 43 49 58 29

Columbia University
Reid Hall
4, rue de Chevreuse
75006 PARIS
Tel: 43 20 24 83
Director of Studies: Mme Danielle HASSE-DUBOSC

Ecole des Hautes Etudes en Sciences Sociales
14, rue Corvisart
75013 PARIS
Tel: 44 08 51 70
Fax: 44 08 51 71

Ecole Nationale Supérieure des Arts Décoratifs
31, rue d'Ulm
75005 PARIS
Tel: 42 34 97 00
National School of Decorative Arts

Ecole Nationale Supérieure des Beaux-Arts
14, rue Bonaparte
75006 PARIS
Tel: 47 03 50 00
Fax: 47 03 50 80
Director: M. Yves MICHAUD
Painting, sculpture, engraving, drawing classes, art exhibits, publishing

EDUCO/Duke/Cornell
23, rue du Montparnasse
75006 PARIS
Tel: 42 22 34 66
Fax: 45 48 24 86
E-mail: jcody@elias.ens.fr
Director: Mme Shelby OCANA

Europe Business School
27, Bd. Ney
75018 PARIS
Tel: 40 36 92 93

European School of Management
6, avenue de la Porte de Champerret
75017 PARIS
Tel: 44 09 33 00
Director: M. Xavier CORNU
European Masters in Intl. Business

European University
137, avenue Jean Jaurès
92140 CLAMART
Tel: 46 44 39 39
Fax: 46 44 59 00
President: M. Xavier NIEBERDING

European University of America
17-25, rue de Chaillot
75016 PARIS
Tel: 40 70 11 71

Georgia Institute of Technology
144, avenue de Flandre
75019 PARIS
Tel: 40 36 32 57

Gordon France
22, rue Royale
75008 PARIS
Tel: 42 60 16 24
Fax: 40 15 09 38
Private school for management training

Graduate Research Institute
4, rue de Chevreuse
75006 PARIS
Tel: 43 35 56 96

Graham School of Management
St Xavier University
20, rue St. Petersbourg
75008 PARIS
Tel: 42 93 13 87
Fax: 45 22 12 65

Hamilton College
Reid Hall
4, rue de la Chevreuse
75006 PARIS
Tel: 43 20 77 77
Fax: 42 79 07 76
Junior Year in France

Hollins College
4, Place de l'Odéon
75006 PARIS
Tel: 46 34 59 85

IMHI - Cornell University/ Groupe ESSEC
B.P. 105
Avenue Bernard Hirsch
95021 CERGY-PONTOISE Cedex
Tel: 34 43 30 00
Fax: 34 43 17 01
E-mail: richez@ped.essec.fr
Deputy Director: M. NOWLIS
Graduate studies in international hotel management (Master's level)

Indiana University School of Journalism
The Paris Reporting Project
74, Bd. Voltaire
75011 PARIS
Tel: 43 38 14 26
Fax: 48 06 62 03
Contact: Dr ARALYNN McMANE
6-week summer journalism study abroad program

INSEAD
Bd. de Constance
77305 FONTAINEBLEAU Cedex
Tel: 60 72 40 00
Fax: 60 72 42 42
Dean: M. Antonio BORGES
Ten-month graduate MBA program

Institut Franco-Américain de Management
19, rue Cépré
75015 PARIS
Tel: 47 34 38 23
Fax: 47 83 31 72
Director: Mme JOSEPH
Associated with Hartford, Northeastern, Boston and Pace Universities

Institute for American Universities
27, Place de l'Université
13625 AIX-EN-PROVENCE
Cedex 1
Tel: (16) 42 23 39 35
Fax: (16) 42 21 11 38

Institute of European Studies
77, rue Daguerre
75014 PARIS
Tel: 43 22 64 13

International University of America
17, rue de Chaillot
75016 PARIS
Tel: 40 70 11 71
Fax: 40 70 10 10
Contact: M. FORGET
One-year MBA program in San Francisco

ISG International School of Business
4, 6, 8, rue de Lota
75116 PARIS
Tel: 53 70 82 22
Fax: 47 55 96 31

James Madison University
26, rue Auguste Comte
92170 VANVES
Tel: 46 44 57 51

Les Ateliers - Ecole Nationale Supérieure de Création Industrielle
48, rue St. Sabin
75011 PARIS
Tel: 49 23 12 12
Fax: 43 38 51 36

Lincoln International Business School
65, rue du Théâtre
75015 PARIS
Tel: 45 77 11 61
Fax: 40 58 12 77

MBA Institute
38, rue des Blancs Manteaux
75004 PARIS
Tel: 42 78 95 45
Fax: 48 04 37 03
Director: M. Philippe GAILLOCHET
Courses in international management

MICEFA Student Exchange
Centre St. Jacques
26, rue du Fbg. St. Jacques
75014 PARIS
Tel: 40 51 76 96
Fax: 44 07 18 10
Director: Mme Nancy MERRITT
CUNY, Berkeley, U. of Texas-Austin, U. of Denver Florida Intl, Waterloo, Cal. State, New Jersey, Indiana, Illinois, Puerto Rico, Waterloo (Canada)

Middlebury College
Reid Hall
4, rue de Chevreuse
75006 PARIS
Tel: 43 20 70 57

New York University
56, rue de Passy
75016 PARIS
Tel: 42 88 52 84
Fax: 42 24 03 73
Director: Prof. Maud S. WALTHER

Paris Center for Critical Studies
1, Place de l'Odéon
75006 PARIS
Tel: 46 33 85 33
Fax: 43 26 97 45
Director: M. Dana POLAN
Undergraduate and graduate level courses

Parsons School of Design, Paris
14, rue Letellier
75015 PARIS
Tel: 45 77 39 66
Fax: 45 77 10 44
Admissions: Holly WARNER
BFA in Fine Arts, Fashion and Visual Communication. BBA in Design Marketing. Extensive summer programs

Reid Hall
4, rue de Chevreuse
75006 PARIS
Tel: 43 20 33 07
Center for American universities

Saint Xavier University
20, rue de St. Petersbourg
75008 PARIS
Tel: 42 93 13 87
Fax: 45 22 12 65
Dean: M. Joe GOLDIAMOND
Executive MBA

Sarah Lawrence College
Reid Hall
4, rue de Chevreuse
75006 PARIS
Tel: 43 22 14 36
Fax: 43 22 69 26
Director: Prof. Monique MIDDLETON
Academic Year in Paris

Schiller International University
32, Bd. de Vaugirard
75015 PARIS
Tel: 45 38 56 01
Fax: 45 38 54 30
Director: Heidi MILLER
Accredited American University with international programs created in 1964 (see advertisement)

Scripps in France
78, rue du Cherche Midi
75006 PARIS
Tel: 45 48 77 50
Fax: 45 48 77 54
Director: Mathilde SITBON
Higher education

SCHILLER INTERNATIONAL UNIVERSITY : PIONEER IN MULTICULTURAL LEARNING

Founded in 1964 by Dr. Walter Leibrecht, Schiller International University has taken a global approach to education. It attracts students from over 100 countries, offering a truly international education that prepares them for a global marketplace and a global future. Schiller International University has ten campuses in six countries (USA, France, Germany, Great-Britain, Spain, Switzerland). The university offers degrees in internationl business, international relations and diplomacy and international hotel and tourism management.

The Paris campus, opened in 1968, is located in the Montparnasse area. Students can get undergraduate and graduate degrees in the fields of business administration and international relations. The faculty features successful teacher-practitioners with a wide range of international experience. Special programs are designed for working professionals. The educational process puts particular emphasis on developing international and cross-cultural competencies through foreign language acquisition, inter-campus transfer and intense interaction among people with diverse backgrounds.

Skidmore College
Programs in Paris
142, rue de Rivoli
75001 PARIS
Tel: 42 36 02 55
Fax: 45 08 42 87
Director: Dr. Norman STOKLE

Smith College
4, rue de Chevreuse
Reid Hall
75006 PARIS
Tel: 43 21 65 54
Junior Year in Paris

Southern Methodist University
Reid Hall
4, rue de Chevreuse
75006 PARIS
Tel: 43 20 04 86

SUNY Brockport/SUNY Oswego
Centre Franco-Américain
1, Place de l'Odéon
75006 PARIS
Tel: 46 34 16 10
Tel: 47 05 01 96

Sweetbriar College Junior
Year in France
c/o Alliance Française
101, Bd. Raspail
75006 PARIS
Tel: 45 48 79 30
Fax: 45 49 27 52
Director: M. Emile LANGLOIS

The American University of Paris
34, avenue de New York
75116 PARIS
Tel: 47 20 44 99
Fax: 47 20 45 64
Dean: Mme Susan R. KINSEY
Division of Continuing Education - offers English-language courses, professional certificates, professional and executive seminar tours for visiting Americans

The American University of Paris
31, avenue Bosquet
75007 PARIS
Tel: 40 62 07 20
Fax: 47 05 34 32
President: M. Lee HUEBNER
Admissions Director: Kathy NANCE

The Center for Global Business
Studies in Association with
Hartford University
8, Terrasse Bellini
92807 PARIS LA DEFENSE 11
Tel: 49 00 19 61
Fax: 47 76 45 13
Executive Director:
Pamela D. MEADE
12-month intensive American MBA program (see advertisement)

Tufts University
2, rue des Taillandiers
75011 PARIS
Tel: 43 38 14 18
Director: Mme Virginia REMMERS

Tulane University
Reid Hall
4, rue de Chevreuse
75006 PARIS
Tel: 43 21 35 85
Director: Mme Madeleine
BEAUFORT

University of Southern Europe
2, avenue Prince Héréditaire Albert
MC 98000 MONACO
Tel: (16) 92 05 70 57
Fax: (16) 92 05 28 30
E-mail: use@monaco.mc
Contact: Dorota KOWALSKA
BSBA and MBA studies in Monaco

Université de Paris IV
Sorbonne - Faculté d'Anglais
1, rue Victor Cousin
75230 PARIS Cedex 05
Tel: 40 46 25 99
Director: M. ROUGE
Contact: Pr François GALLIX
Advanced diplomas in international management

Université de Paris VII
UFR d'Etudes Anglophones
10, rue Charles V
75004 PARIS
Tel: 44 78 34 99
Fax: 44 78 34 80
Institut d'Anglais Charles V

Wesleyan University
Program in Paris
Reid Hall
4, rue de Chevreuse
75006 PARIS
Tel: 43 22 12 47
Fax: 40 47 83 28
Study abroad programs for US students

Schools
Ecoles

"L'Ecole Aujourd'hui -
School for Today"
24, Bd. Edgar Quinet
75014 PARIS
Tel: 43 20 61 24
Coordinator: P. KOHEN
Bilingual primary education

A.I.M. Hotel Administration
31, quai de Grenelle
75015 PARIS
Tel: 45 75 65 75
Fax: 40 59 03 02
International hotel management school

American Boarding Foundation
45, rue des Dames
75017 PARIS
Tel: 45 22 20 24
Fax: 44 70 05 37
Association representing 40 American boarding schools in Paris

American Institute
for Foreign Study
10, rue du Docteur Blanche
75016 PARIS
Tel: 46 47 92 74

American School
Harriet Bonelli
1, rue Crébillon
75006 PARIS
Tel: 46 34 78 05
English tuition for 3 to 14 year-olds

American School
of Modern Music
117, rue de la Croix Nivert
75015 PARIS
Tel: 45 31 16 07

American School of Paris
41, rue Pasteur
92210 ST-CLOUD
Tel: 46 02 54 43
Fax: 46 02 23 90
Director ASP Extension Program:
Laurence FENIOU-SALIM
English lessons, all levels, all ages

American Section - Lycée
International de St. Germain-en-Laye
Rue du Fer-à-Cheval
B.P. 230
78104 ST-GERMAIN-EN-LAYE Cedex
Tel: 34 51 74 85
Fax: 30 87 00 49
Director: M. D. Michael VEITH
Bilingual English/French schooling

Art School
7, rue d'Hautpoul
75019 PARIS
Tel: 42 49 32 03

Bilingual Montessori
School of Paris
65, quai d'Orsay
75007 PARIS
Tel: 45 55 13 27
Directress: Barbara PORTER
Bilingual Montessori for children aged 3 to 6

Bilingual Nursery School
125, rue d'avron
75020 PARIS
Tel: 43 70 33 45

British School of Paris
38, quai de l'Ecluse
78290 CROISSY-SUR-SEINE
Tel: 34 80 45 90
Fax: 39 76 12 69
Principal: M. HONOUR

CEMHI
52, rue St. Lazare
75009 PARIS
Tel: 45 26 59 28
Fax: 45 26 59 29
European Center for Hotel Management

Collège Franco-Britannique
9B, Bd. Jourdan
75014 PARIS
Tel: 44 16 24 06

Collège International de Fontainebleau-Sec
48, rue Guérin
77300 FONTAINEBLEAU
Tel: 64 22 11 77

Collège Lycée Marcel Roby
6, rue Giraud Teulon
78100 ST.-GERMAIN-EN-LAYE
Tel: 34 51 00 96

E.I.C.A.
16, rue des Grands Augustins
75006 PARIS
Tel: 43 25 43 63
Fax: 43 25 43 32
For aspiring directors, journalists, screenwriters, film editors and TV anchormen

Ecole Active Bilingue
52, avenue Victor Hugo
75116 PARIS
Tel: 45 00 11 57
Fax: 45 01 75 79
Director: Mme CONCHARD
Secondary education - American and British section

Ecole Active Bilingue
6, avenue Van Dyck
75008 PARIS
Tel: 46 22 14 24
Fax: 47 66 58 93
Director: Mrs DHERS
Primary and secondary education

Ecole Active Bilingue
24bis, rue de Berri
75008 PARIS
Tel: 45 63 30 73
Fax: 45 62 36 05

Ecole Active Bilingue
Relations Extérieures
117, Bd. Malesherbes
75008 PARIS
Tel: 45 63 47 00
Tel: 45 63 62 22
Fax: 45 63 62 23
Public Relations: Mrs Nicole HOURCADE-REDING
(see advertisement)

Ecole Active Bilingue Jeannine Manuel
418bis, rue Albert Bailly
59700 MARCQ-EN-BAROEUL
Tel: (16) 20 65 90 50
Fax: (16) 20 98 06 41
Director: Mme LUX
Day School/Boarding School from 6ème to Terminale + international Bac

Ecole du Louvre
34, quai du Louvre
75041 PARIS Cedex 01
Tel: 40 20 56 14
Tel: 40 20 56 15
Fax: 42 60 40 36

Institut Catholique de Paris
21, rue d'Assas
75006 PARIS
Tel: 44 39 52 00

Institut de Gestion Sociale
25, rue François Ier
75008 PARIS
Tel: 53 67 84 00
Fax: 40 70 10 74
Bilingual management training and consulting

International School of Paris
6, rue Beethoven
75016 PARIS
Tel: 42 24 09 54
Fax: 45 27 15 93
Director: M. Nigel PRENTKI
High school

Jardin d'Enfants Montessori d'Auteuil
53, rue Erlanger
75016 PARIS
Tel: 45 55 13 27

Le Petit Cours
104, rue Ordener
75018 PARIS
Tel: 46 06 80 33
Fax: 46 06 94 09
Director: M. Daniel MATUL
Bilingual pre-school and primary education for children. Recreational activities open to all on Wednesday afternoons

Lennen Bilingual School
65, quai d'Orsay
75007 PARIS
Tel: 47 05 66 55

Lycée de Sèvres - Section Internationale
21, rue du Dr Lederman
92310 SEVRES
Tel: 46 26 60 10

Marymount School
72, Bd. de la Saussaye
92200 NEUILLY-SUR-SEINE
Tel: 46 24 10 51
Headmistress: Sister Genevieve MURPHY

Maxim's
52, rue St. Lazare
75009 PARIS
Tel: 45 26 59 28
Fax: 45 26 59 29
Tourism and hotel management school (bilingual program)

Paris American Academy
9, rue des Ursulines
75005 PARIS
Tel: 43 25 08 91
Director: M. Richard ROY
School of Fine Art, Fashion and Interior Design

Spéos
8, rue Jules Vallès
75011 PARIS
Tel: 40 09 18 58
Fax: 40 09 84 97
Director: M. Pierre-Yves MAHE
Photography school

The American Section
Lycée Franco-Américain
Marcel Roby
6, rue Giraud Teulon
B.P. 143
78100 ST-GERMAIN-EN-LAYE
Tel: 34 51 00 96
Fax: 34 51 95 70
Director: M. Don ANDERSON
Bilingual-bicultural education

Thomas Jefferson School
13, rue de la Clef
75005 PARIS
Tel: 43 37 93 31

United Nations Nursery School
40, rue Pierre Guérin
75016 PARIS
Tel: 45 27 20 24
International bilingual school for children aged 2 to 6. Summer school in July, English and dance lessons on Wednesday

Educational Programs
Stages/Séjours Linguistiques

Academic Year Abroad
4, rue de Chevreuse
75006 PARIS
Tel: 43 20 91 92
Director: Mme Paule SCHNEERSOHN

Aspect Foundation Exchange Programs
53, rue du Fbg. Poissonnière
75009 PARIS
Tel: 48 00 06 00
Fax: 48 00 05 94
Director: M. Peter SPIER

Association "Les Fauvettes"
10, rue Léon Jouhaux
75010 PARIS
Tel: 42 06 25 29
Fax: 42 06 51 35
Organizes stays in US families (with or without English lessons) for students aged 15 to 20

Association Internationale du Français par le Séjour
10, rue du Docteur Blanche
75016 PARIS
Tel: 46 47 92 74
Fax: 40 50 36 38
Director: M. DWYER
Language-oriented stays in France

Club USA
1, rue des Meuniers
94300 VINCENNES
Tel: 41 74 95 52
Organises American courses for French students

Council on International Educational Exchange (CIEE)
1, Place de l'Odéon
75006 PARIS
Tel: 44 41 74 74
Fax: 43 26 97 45

DIDAC
B.P. 1
92430 MARNE-LA-COQUETTE
Tel: 47 01 12 10
Fax: 47 41 00 66
Organizes studies in American universities for French students

Education USA
18, avenue des Champs-Elysées
75008 PARIS
Tel: 47 64 57 76
Fax: 47 63 35 89
GMAT, GRE, SAT, Business School applications

Experiment in International Living
89, rue de Turbigo
75003 PARIS
Tel: 42 78 50 03
Fax: 42 78 01 40
Director: M. Gilbert GUILLEMOTO
Linguistic and cultural visits for au pairs in the USA

Fondation Franco-Américaine
102, avenue du Maine
75014 PARIS
Tel: 43 35 04 81
Fax: 43 35 02 85
Awards, scholarships and grants

Franco-American Commission for Educational Exchange
9, rue Chardin
75016 PARIS
Tel: 45 20 46 54
Fax: 42 88 04 79
Director: M. Pierre COLLOMBERT
Administration of Fulbright Scholarship Program France-USA

Idfar
19, rue Clément Ader
51100 REIMS
Tel: (16) 26 82 92 74
Fax: (16) 26 82 92 75
Director: M. Pierre BARAST
Cross-cultural training for a successful business in France

Internships in Francophone Europe
Reid Hall
4, rue de Chevreuse
75006 PARIS
Tel: 43 21 78 07
Fax: 42 79 94 13
Director: M. RIVIERE-PLATT

Kaplan Educational Center
15, rue de Pondichéry
75015 PARIS
Tel: 45 66 55 33
Fax: 45 66 99 80
Director: M. Matt SYMONDS
Preparation of American exams: TOEFL, GMAT, SAT, GRE, LSAT

Learning Tree International
Espace Clichy
68, rue Villeneuve
92587 CLICHY Cedex
Tel: 49 68 53 00
Fax: 49 68 53 33
Marketing Director:
M. Pascal PATINEL
Technical and computer programming courses

MBA Services
39, Bd. Magenta
75010 PARIS
Tel: 42 45 11 11
Fax: 42 45 04 05
Preparation courses for American standardized tests (GMAT/TOEFL)

Women's Institute for Continuing Education (WICE)
20, Bd. Montparnasse
75015 PARIS
Tel: 45 66 75 50
Fax: 40 65 96 53
Director: Mme Lisa REDBURN
WICE is a cross-cultural non-profit institute offering English-language courses in Career Development, Arts & Humanities, Living in France, Women's Support Group

Wilson Learning Performance
2, rue Jacques Daguerre
92565 RUEIL-MALMAISON Cedex
Tel: 47 51 70 70
Fax: 47 51 58 02
Director: M. Jean-Pierre DUHAMEL

Air France Inter-Airport Bus Service
Tel: 49 38 57 57

Air France Vaccination Center
Tel: 43 20 13 50

Allô Curry
Tel: 46 26 79 29
Indian specialties delivered to your home

Allô Pékin
Tel: 41 19 90 09
Home delivery of Thai, Chinese and Vietnamese dishes

Alpha Taxis
Tel: 45 85 85 85

Ambulances de l'Assistance Publique
Tel: 43 78 26 26
Handles transportation from one hospital to another

Anti-Poison Center
Tel: 40 37 04 04
24-hour service

Arizona Pizza
Tel: 39 18 50 00
Home delivery of homemade US pizzas, brownies

Association des Urgences Médicales de Paris
Tel: 48 28 40 04
Medical emergencies

Atlas Couscous
Tel: 45 41 22 22
Home delivery of couscous

Burns (severe)
Tel: 42 34 17 58

Business Link Taxi
Radiophone: 46 89 06 77
English: 07 43 71 63

Central Post Office
52, rue du Louvre
75001 PARIS
Tel: 40 28 20 00
Open 24 hours

Cinema Booking Service
Tel: 40 30 20 10
Film programs and booking services by phone

Collect Calls to the US
Tel: 19 00 11

Directory Assistance for the US
Tel: 19 33 12 11

Elysées 1212
Tel: 43 59 12 12
Free booking service for hotels, restaurants, cabarets and cruises

Enfance et Partage
Tel: 05 05 12 34
Hotline for kids in trouble 09h00-21h00 (free)

Epicerie Russe
Tel: 40 54 04 05
Russian specialties brought to your doorstep

European Tourist Office
Tel: 36 68 07 47
Information about your stay in Paris in English

Fax Service
Tel: 40 28 20 00

Info Sida
Tel: 45 67 01 01
AIDS information service

Insurance needs
Tel: 47 97 64 80

Local Telecom Business Office
Tel: 14

Locksmith
Tel: 47 07 99 99
24 hours

Lost American Express Card
Tel: 47 77 72 00

Lost Carte Bleue or Visa Card
Tel: 42 77 11 90

Lost Diner's Club Card
Tel: 47 62 75 75

Lost Eurocard/Mastercard
Tel: 45 67 47 67

Lost Luggage (Orly)
Tel: 49 75 04 53

Lost Luggage (Roissy)
Tel: 48 62 10 46

Ludéric Service
Tel: 47 59 04 04
After-party cleaning-up service

Matin Croissants
Tel: 40 30 22 23
Breakfast pastries delivered to your home

Medical Emergencies
Tel: 15

Minitel Directory
Tel: 11

Objets Trouvés
36, rue des Morillons
75015 PARIS
Tel: 45 31 14 80
Lost and Found

Orly Airport
Tel: 49 75 15 15
Info: 49 75 52 52

Paris-Anglophone
Tel: 48 59 66 58
To order this book

Pharma Presto
Tel: 42 42 42 50
Medicine delivered to your house

Police Secours
Tel: 17

Pompiers
Tel: 18
Fire Brigade

Prefix for International Calls
Tel: 19

Prefix for Provinces
Tel: 16

Psychiatric Emergencies
Tel: 47 07 24 24

Rape Crisis Hotline
Tel: 05 05 95 95
Free

RATP Info
Tel: 40 46 42 12
Information on the Paris bus, metro and RER services

Roissy Airport
Tel: 48 62 12 12

SAMU Ambulances
Tel: 45 67 50 50
Tel: 15
24-hour emergency service

Sida Info Service
Tel: 05 36 66 36
AIDS help line

SOS Attack
Tel: 47 04 20 00
Assistance to assaulted victims

SOS Boulimia
Tel: 45 45 65 94

SOS Cardiologues
Tel: 47 07 50 50
Emergency service for heart patients

SOS Decès
Tel: 42 02 99 99
24h funeral assistance

SOS Dentistes
Tel: 43 37 51 00
24 hour emergency dental help

SOS Depannage
Tel: 43 31 14 14
Household emergencies

SOS Depression
Tel: 44 08 78 78

SOS Divorce
Tel: 45 63 11 13

SOS Help! Crisis Line
Tel: 47 23 80 80
Contact: Plum LE-TAN
A friendly listener daily 15h00-23h00

SOS Haemorrhoids
Tel: 42 85 17 00

SOS Locataires
Tel: 48 06 82 75
Help for tenants

SOS Médecins
Tel: 43 37 77 77
24h medical assistance

SOS Médecins
Tel: 47 07 77 77
24-hour emergency medical house calls

SOS Oeil
Tel: 40 92 93 94
Eye care

SOS Pédiatres
Tel: 43 94 35 01
Pediatric assistance

SOS Pregnancy
Tel: 45 82 13 14

SOS Vet
Tel: 47 55 47 00
Round-the-clock veterinary home visits

Taxis Bleus
Tel: 49 36 10 10

Taxis G7
Tel: 47 39 47 39

Taxis Radio Etoile
Tel: 47 39 47 39

Telemarket
Tel: 45 89 90 91
Home delivery service for groceries

Telephone Information
Tel: 12

Telephone Repairs
Tel: 13

Time
Tel: 36 99

Tourist Office of Paris
Tel: 49 52 53 56
Recording in English

Train Info SNCF
Info: 45 82 50 50
Res: 3615 SNCF

Urgences Dentaires Parisiennes
Tel: 45 35 41 41
Emergency dental service

VoiceAds
Tel: 36 68 92 68
Interactive small ads in English (for Sale, Baby Sitting, Housing, Practical Tips)

VoiceMail
Tel: 36 68 09 66
Interactive telephone service in English providing 24h contact and information

Wake-up Calls
Tel 55 plus the time in four digits (ex: 0800 = 8 a.m.), then # electronically programmed

Weather Info.
Paris: 36 65 00 00
Provinces: 36 70 00 00
International: 36 70 00 00

Youth Hostel Office
Tel: 43 57 55 60

International Operators
Communications Internationales

AT&T Dial Direct
Tel: (19) 00 11

British Telecom
Tel: (19) 00 44

MCI Direct
Tel: (19) 00 19

SPRINT
Tel: (19) 00 87

Selected International Country & City Codes

After dialing 19 and reaching the international dial tone, dial the appropriate country code and city code followed by the telephone number.

Australia	**61**
Melbourne	3
Sydney	2
Perth	9
Austria	**43**
Vienna	1
Belgium	**32**
Brussels	2
Canada	**1**
Montreal	514
Toronto	416
Vancouver	614
Czech Rep.	**42**
Prague	2
Denmark	**45**
Copenhagen	–
Finland	**358**
Helsinki	0
Germany	**49**
Berlin	30
Frankfurt	69
Hamburg	40
Munich	89
Greece	**30**
Athens	1
Hong Kong	**852**
Hungary	**36**
Budapest	1
India	**91**
Bombay	22
Ireland	**353**
Dublin	1
Iceland	**354**
Reykjavik	1
Israel	**972**
Jerusalem	2
Tel Aviv	3
Italy	**39**
Milan	2
Rome	6
Japan	**81**
Kyoto	75
Tokyo	3 or 33
Luxembourg	**352**
Malta	**356**
Mexico	**52**
Mexico City	5
Monaco	**93***
Netherlands	**31**
Amsterdam	20
New Zealand	**64**
Auckland	9
Norway	**47**
Oslo	2
Pakistan	**92**
Karachi	21
Poland	**48**
Warsaw	2 or 22
Portugal	**351**
Lisbon	1
Romania	**40**
Bucharest	1
Russia	**7**
Moscow	095
St. Petersberg	812
Singapour	**65**
Slovenia	**386**
South Africa	**27**
Cape Town	21
Johannesburg	11
Spain	**34**
Barcelona	3
Madrid	1
Sweden	**46**
Stockholm	8
Switzerland	**41**
Geneva	22
Zurich	1
UK	**44**
Birmingham	121
Edinburgh	131
Glasgow	141
London	171 or 181
Manchester	161
USA	**1**
Boston	617
Chicago	312
Los Angeles	213
Miami	305
New York	212
San Francisco	415
Wash., D.C.	202

*(use 16 instead of 19)

Gourmet Restaurants
Restaurants Gastronomiques

La Tour d'Argent
15-17, quai de la Tournelle
75005 PARIS
Tel: 43 54 23 31
Sanctuary of French cuisine.
Unique view of Paris

Lasserre
17, avenue Franklin Roosevelt
75008 PARIS
Tel: 43 59 53 43
Fax: 45 63 72 23

Taillevent
15, rue Lamennais
75008 PARIS
Tel: 44 95 15 01
Fax: 42 25 95 18

French Cuisine
Cuisine Française

Au Bon St-Pourçain
10, rue Servandoni
75006 PARIS
Tel: 43 54 93 63

Au Pied de Cochon
6, rue Coquillière
75001 PARIS
Tel: 42 36 11 75
Fax: 45 08 48 90

Aux Lyonnais
32, rue St. Marc
75002 PARIS
Tel: 42 96 65 04
Fax: 42 97 42 95
President: M. Pierre VALLEE

Café La Jatte
60, Bd. Vital-Bouhot
92200 NEUILLY-SUR-SEINE
Tel: 47 45 04 20
Features a 22-metre long dinosaur hanging from its ceiling

Canteen Bus
81, rue d'Alésia
75014 PARIS
Tel: 43 21 99 68

Chartier
7, rue du Fbg. Montmartre
75009 PARIS
Tel: 47 70 86 29
Fax: 48 24 14 68
Manager: M. ERIC
Authentic French bistro cooking

Daniel Métery
4, rue de l'Arcade
75008 PARIS
Tel: 42 65 53 13
Fish restaurant

Drouant
18, Place Gaillon
75002 PARIS
Tel: 42 65 15 16
Art Déco establishment popular among the literati

L'Apostrophe
36, rue St-Louis-en-l'Ile
75004 PARIS
Tel: 43 25 14 77

L'Auberge Nicolas Flamel
51, rue de Montmorency
75003 PARIS
Tel: 42 71 77 78

L'Espadon
Hôtel Ritz
15, Place Vendôme
75001 PARIS
Tel: 43 16 30 30

La Ferme St-Hubert
21, rue Vignon
75008 PARIS
Tel: 47 42 79 20
Wide range of cheese dishes

La Gauloise
59, avenue La Motte-Picquet
75015 PARIS
Tel: 47 34 11 64

La Langousterie
145, Bd. Montparnasse
75006 PARIS
Tel: 43 26 63 39
For lobster, crayfish and shellfish lovers

La Petite Tour
11, rue de la Tour
75116 PARIS
Tel: 45 20 09 97
Contacts: Christiane & Freddy ISRAEL

La Plaine aux Loups
43, rue de la Plaine
75020 PARIS
Tel: 43 70 36 60

La Poule au Pot
9, rue Vauvilliers
75001 PARIS
Tel: 42 36 32 96
Manager M. Paul RACAT
Restaurant open until 06h00 am

La Pêcherie
24, rue Pierre Lescot
75001 PARIS
Tel: 42 36 92 41
Fax: 42 36 02 65
Fish and seafood restaurant

Le Clos du Vert Bois
13, rue du Vertbois
75003 PARIS
Tel: 42 77 14 85
Traditional French cuisine at appetizing prices

Le Connétable
55, rue des Archives
75003 PARIS
Tel: 42 77 41 40
Fax: 42 71 69 21
Quaint first-floor dining room

Le Coupe-Chou
11, rue de Lanneau
75005 PARIS
Tel: 46 33 68 69

Le Durer
19, rue Yvonne Le Tac
75018 PARIS
Tel: 46 06 00 08

Le Dômarais
53bis, rue des Francs Bourgeois
75004 PARIS
Tel: 42 74 54 17
Fax: 42 77 78 17
Superb dining hall with domed ceiling

Le Marais du Bois
10, rue des Haudriettes
75003 PARIS
Tel: 42 72 10 43
Cosy French ambience

Le Pot au Feu
59, Bd. Pasteur
75015 PARIS
Tel: 43 20 79 80
Tasty cuisine in a cosy, unpretentious setting

Le Procope
13, rue de l'Ancienne Comédie
75006 PARIS
Tel: 43 26 99 20
Probably the oldest restaurant in Paris

Les Grandes Marches
6, Place de la Bastille
75012 PARIS
Tel: 43 42 90 32

Les Ministères
30, rue du Bac
75007 PARIS
Tel: 42 61 22 37
French specialties in a superb 1900 setting

Les Saisons
Hôtel Concorde Lafayette
3, Place du Général Koenig
75017 PARIS
Tel: 40 68 51 19

Maxim's Restaurant
3, rue Royale
75008 PARIS
Tel: 42 65 27 94
Fax: 40 17 02 91

Restaurant des Beaux-Arts
11, rue Bonaparte
75006 PARIS
Tel: 43 26 92 64

Restaurant L'Alisier
26, rue de Montmorency
75003 PARIS
Tel: 42 72 31 04
Fax: 42 72 74 83
Owner: M. DODEMAN
French gastronomic restaurant

Thoumieux
79, rue St. Dominique
75007 PARIS
Tel: 47 05 49 75

Vagenende
142, Bd. St. Germain
75006 PARIS
Tel: 43 26 68 18
Impeccable style and service

Other Restaurants
Autres Restaurants

Aquarius
40, rue de Gergovie
75014 PARIS
Tel: 45 41 36 88
Gastronomic vegetarian restaurant

Aux Iles Philippines
9, rue Pontoise
75005 PARIS
Tel: 43 29 39 00
Tel: 44 07 17 44
Contact: Nora V. DAZA
One of the best Asian restaurants in Paris

Bertie's
Hôtel Baltimore
1, rue Léo Delibes
75016 PARIS
Tel: 44 34 54 34
British cuisine

Chez Lucie
15, rue Augereau
75007 PARIS
Tel: 45 55 08 74
Martinique and Caribbean specialties

Chez Marianne & André
2, rue des Hospitalières St. Gervais
75004 PARIS
Tel: 42 72 18 86
Great deli and hospitality
(see advertisement)

Dominique
19, rue Bréa
75006 PARIS
Tel: 43 27 08 80
Russian restaurant

Flora Danica
142, avenue des Champs-Elysées
75008 PARIS
Tel: 44 13 86 26
Scandinavian cuisine in a pleasant setting

Higuma
32bis, rue Ste Anne
75001 PARIS
Tel: 47 03 38 59
Japanese restaurant

Il Fiorentino
26, rue de la Montagne Ste Geneviève
75005 PARIS
Tel: 46 34 71 61
Italian cuisine with a touch of Tuscany

Jo Goldenberg
7, rue des Rosiers
75004 PARIS
Tel: 48 87 20 16
Jewish delicatessen with small restaurant

Joyti
148, rue de Vaugirard
75015 PARIS
Tel: 47 83 45 45
Indian cuisine

La Bocca
59, rue Montmartre
75002 PARIS
Tel: 42 36 71 88
Contact: Perone
Italian restaurant

La Petite Légume
36, rue des Boulangers
75005 PARIS
Tel: 40 46 06 85
Healthy food, tasty vegetarian dishes

La Pirogue des Alizés
69, rue des Dames
75017 PARIS
Tel: 45 22 39 48
Spicy, exotic specialties from Africa and the West Indies

La Truffe
31, rue Vieille du Temple
75004 PARIS
Tel: 42 71 08 39
Natural cuisine made from fresh organic produce

La Varangue
27, rue Augereau
75007 PARIS
Tel: 47 05 51 22
Gratin specialties, vegetarian dishes, home cooking

Layali Phoenicia
170, rue St. Martin
75003 PARIS
Tel: 42 77 07 77
Lebanese restaurant

Mansouria
11, rue Faidherbe
75011 PARIS
Tel: 43 71 00 16
North African cuisine

Salades Folles
9, rue des Précheurs
75001 PARIS
Tel: 42 33 25 00
Salad restaurant

Sydney Restaurant
8, rue de la Grange Batelière
75009 PARIS
Tel: 47 70 05 02

Tokaj
57, rue du Chemin Vert
75011 PARIS
Tel: 47 00 64 56
Hungarian specialties

Vassanti
3, rue Larochelle
31, rue de Gaïté
75014 PARIS
Tel: 43 21 97 43
Contact: Mandjea
The art of Indian gastronomy in Paris

Villa Médicis
11bis, rue St. Placide
75006 PARIS
Tel: 42 22 51 96
Manager: M. Michel NAPOLI
The Italian family restaurant

American Cafés/Tex-Mex
Cafés Américains/Tex-Mex

American Pie & Company
15, rue des Archives
75004 PARIS
Tel: 48 04 76 79
Fax: 42 71 20 84

Arriba Mexico
32, avenue de la République
75011 PARIS
Tel: 49 29 95 40

Ay! Caramba!
59, rue de Mouzaïa
75019 PARIS
Tel: 42 41 23 80
Fax: 42 41 50 34
Mexican food, music and atmosphere

Bagel Café
76, rue Mazarine
75006 PARIS
Tel: 43 26 77 35
Contact: Laure
Delicatessen/Traiteur

Baskin & Robbins Ice Cream
1, rue du Four
75006 PARIS
Tel: 43 25 10 63

Bastille Corner
47, rue de Charenton
75012 PARIS
Tel: 43 47 12 17

Blue Jack Saloon
21, Bd. Arago
75013 PARIS
Tel: 47 07 01 15
American food and beer

Cactus Charly
68, rue Ponthieu
75008 PARIS
Tel: 45 62 01 77
Fax: 45 62 82 08
Director: M. SCHEPELERN
US Bar/Restaurant

Café de Mars
11, rue Augereau
75007 PARIS
Tel: 47 05 05 91
Contact: Catherine ALLSWAN
Californian cuisine: lunch, dinner and brunch at weekends

Café des Arts
92, Bd. Sébastopol
75003 PARIS
Tel: 48 87 05 59
American brasserie

Charly's Pub
26, rue de la Parcheminerie
75005 PARIS
Tel: 43 26 61 23

Chesterfield Café
124, rue La Boétie
75008 PARIS
Tel: 42 25 18 06
Manager: M. Arnaud DALAIS
Great cocktails, American specialties, live music

Chi-Chi's
27, Bd. des Italiens
75002 PARIS
Tel: 42 66 09 57
Mexican restaurant

Chicago Meatpackers
8, rue Coquillière
75001 PARIS
Tel: 40 28 02 33

Chicago Pizza Pie Factory
5, rue de Berri
75008 PARIS
Tel: 45 62 50 23
Free delivery in the 8th, 15th, 16th and 17th arrondissements

Chilis
114, avenue des Champs-Elysées
75008 PARIS
Tel: 42 89 87 87

City Rock Café
25, rue Quentin
75008 PARIS
Tel: 47 23 07 72
Fax: 47 23 07 46

Coffee Parisien
5 & 8, rue Perronet
75007 PARIS
Tel: 40 49 08 08
Tel: 45 44 92 93
Brunch all day

Coguns
151-153, rue du Chevaleret
75013 PARIS
Tel: 44 24 59 69
Live music: Jazz, Reggae, Folk, Blues...

Columbus Expresso Bar
13-15, passage des Princes
75002 PARIS
Tel: 40 15 98 99
Fax: 40 15 99 47

Conway's
73, rue St. Denis
75001 PARIS
Tel: 45 08 07 70

Crazy V.s
4, rue de l'Ecole Polytechnique
75005 PARIS
Tel: 43 54 98 09
American-style eatery

Daytona Café
10, rue de la Grande Chaumière
75006 PARIS
Tel: 43 29 00 60

Del Amingo
15, rue du Cygne
75001 PARIS
Tel: 42 21 10 57
Tex-Mex restaurant with terrace

Del Rio Café
2-4, rue de Sabot
75006 PARIS
Tel: 42 84 02 83
Plus other locations

Dicey Riley's
5, rue Montorgueil
75001 PARIS
Tel: 42 21 04 35

Domino's Pizza
50, rue Desbordes Valmore
75016 PARIS
Tel: 45 03 23 23
Director: M. ARRAG

Duke
19, rue de Ponthieu
75008 PARIS
Tel: 42 56 19 10
West Coast dining

El Rancho Grill
35, rue du Pont-Neuf
75001 PARIS
Tel: 45 08 45 21
Tex-Mex restaurant

Elliott
166, Bd. Haussmann
75008 PARIS
Tel: 42 89 30 50
American bistro, serves brunch

Frisco Bay
23, rue du Temple
75004 PARIS
Tel: 42 71 49 29
Fax: 42 71 10 87
Director: Dany SUTY
Californian cocktail bar and restaurant

Front Page
58, rue St. Denis
75001 PARIS
Tel: 40 39 92 77
Fax: 42 21 06 84

Hard Rock Café
14, Bd. Montmartre
75009 PARIS
Tel: 42 46 10 00
Fax: 42 46 49 70
Restaurant, bar, music memorabilia

Harry's Bar
5, rue Daunou
75002 PARIS
Tel: 42 61 71 14
Meeting place for Americans in Paris

Hayne's
3, rue Clauzel
75009 PARIS
Tel: 48 78 40 63

Henry J. Bean's
33, rue Quincampoix
75004 PARIS
Tel: 42 71 52 66

Henry's
189, rue de la Pompe
75016 PARIS
Tel: 47 27 25 75

Heritage Café
2, rue Linois
75015 PARIS
Tel: 40 59 97 97
Fax: 45 79 87 87
Contact: M. Sébastien TORRE
Restaurant and cocktail bar, live music

Hollywood Canteen
22, rue de la Roquette
75011 PARIS
Tel: 47 00 18 28
Fax: 47 00 18 38

Hollywood Savoy
44, rue Notre-Dame-des-Victoires
75002 PARIS
Tel: 42 36 16 73
Musical show every night, singing waitresses

Indiana Café
130, Bd. St. Germain
75006 PARIS
Tel: 46 34 66 31

Indiana Café
18, rue Quentin Bauchart
75008 PARIS
Tel: 40 70 96 89

Isa'Bar
12, rue Jean-Jacques Rousseau
75001 PARIS
Tel: 40 39 05 22

Joe Allen
30, rue Pierre Lescot
75001 PARIS
Tel: 42 36 70 13

King Opera
21, rue Daunou
75002 PARIS
Tel: 42 60 99 89

L'Hippocampus
81, Bd. Raspail
75006 PARIS
Tel: 45 48 10 03
Bar, restaurant, jazz club

La Ballena "Taco Loco"
116, rue Amelot
75011 PARIS
Tel: 43 57 90 24
Director: M. CAMPOS

La Cantina
10, rue Papillon
75009 PARIS
Tel: 42 47 05 21
Mexican restaurant

La Cucaracha
31, rue Tiquetonne
75002 PARIS
Tel: 40 26 68 36
Mexican restaurant

La Louisiane
176, rue Montmartre
75002 PARIS
Tel: 42 36 58 98
Fax: 42 36 05 30
American and Creole dishes

La Perla
26, rue François Miron
75004 PARIS
Tel: 42 77 59 40
Fax: 48 87 15 14

Las Ramblas
5, rue Puget
75018 PARIS
Tel: 42 58 67 31

Le Bar
27, rue Condé
75006 PARIS
Tel: 43 29 06 61
For backgammon buffs

Le Bar 23
23, rue de Rivoli
75004 PARIS
Tel: 48 04 96 90

Le Bus 35
35, rue Notre-Dame-de-Lorette
75009 PARIS
Tel: 44 53 94 16
Tex-Mex restaurant

Le Café Pacifico
50, Bd. du Montparnasse
75015 PARIS
Tel: 45 48 63 87
Mexican restaurant cantina

Le New Furstenberg
22, rue Guillaume Apollinaire
75006 PARIS
Tel: 42 86 00 88
Traditional American food

Le Restaurant au Tabac Bleu
117, rue du Fbg. St. Martin
75010 PARIS
Tel: 42 05 46 02
Late night bar with Country Music atmosphere. English and German spoken

Le Saloon
41, rue Victor Massé
75009 PARIS
Tel: 45 26 34 81

Le Western
Hôtel Hilton
18, avenue de Suffren
75015 PARIS
Tel: 44 38 56 00
Fax: 44 38 56 10

Main Street
68, avenue des Champs-Elysées
75008 PARIS
Tel: 45 62 30 86
Cellar pub with live music

Manhattan Delicatessen
65, avenue Félix Faure
75015 PARIS
Tel: 44 26 03 03
Director: M. Robert GRODMAN
New York-style sandwiches and salads

Marshal's Bar and Grill
63, avenue Franklin Roosevelt
75008 PARIS
Tel: 45 63 21 22

Mexico Café
1, Place de Mexico
75016 PARIS
Tel: 47 27 96 98

Montecristo's
68, avenue des Champs-Elysées
75008 PARIS
Tel: 45 62 30 86
Irish American pub

Movie's
15, rue Michel-le-Comte
75003 PARIS
Tel: 42 74 14 22

Mustang Café
84, Bd. Montparnasse
75014 PARIS
Tel: 43 35 36 12

Nantucket Café
37, rue du Roi de Sicile
75004 PARIS
Tel: 48 87 61 30
American café

New Haven Café
250, rue du Fbg. St. Antoine
75012 PARIS
Tel: 43 72 56 79

O'Cantina
161, avenue Daumesnil
75012 PARIS
Tel: 44 74 07 06
Tex-Mex cuisine

Pacific Palisades
51, rue Quincampoix
75003 PARIS
Tel: 42 74 01 17

Paul & Marcy Coffee Shop
52, rue du Fbg. Montmartre
75009 PARIS
Tel: 48 78 07 72

Pizza Hut
29, Bd. des Italiens
75002 PARIS
Tel: 42 65 16 00
For all locations: 05 30 30 30

Restaurant Mexicain Cielito Lindo
33, rue de Charonne
75011 PARIS
Tel: 47 00 16 44
Contacts: Maurice & Ana CALMARD
Typical Mexican cuisine

Rio Grande
24, rue Aubry-le-Boucher
75004 PARIS
Tel: 42 72 68 49

Sam Kearny
100, rue St. Lazare
75009 PARIS
Tel: 42 80 31 41
Tex-Mex restaurant with live music

Sam Pepper
32, rue Brey
75017 PARIS
Tel: 43 80 20 52
The American grill house

Sixty Six Café
8, rue de Lappe
75011 PARIS
Tel: 43 38 30 20
Original Tex-Mex food and drinks

Slice Pizza
11, rue de la Roquette
75011 PARIS
Tel: 43 57 66 67
Director: Stéphanie SARAF
New York Style pizza

Rosebud
11bis, rue Delambre
75014 PARIS
Tel: 43 35 38 54

Susan's Place
51, rue des Ecoles
75005 PARIS
Tel: 43 54 23 22
Contact: Mlle Susan
Tex-Mex restaurant -1st prize in Europe for chili con carne

T.G.I. Friday's
8, Bd. Montmartre
75009 PARIS
Tel: 47 70 27 20
Fax: 48 00 98 13

Tapas Nocturne
17, rue de Lappe
75011 PARIS
Tel: 43 57 91 12

Terrace West
12, rue de la Cossonnerie
75001 PARIS
Tel: 42 36 26 44

Tex-Mexon Square
42, rue Laborde
75008 PARIS
Tel: 45 22 08 36

Texas Blues
54, rue René Boulanger
75010 PARIS
Tel: 42 08 60 20

Texas Star
4, Place Edmond Michelet
75004 PARIS
Tel: 42 72 48 18
American bar and restaurant

The 16
16, rue Pastourelle
75003 PARIS
Tel: 44 59 85 25
Tex-Mex cuisine

The Studio
Société du 41
41, rue du Temple
75004 PARIS
Tel: 42 74 10 38
Fax: 42 77 19 90
Contacts: Monique & Alex
Paris' top American restaurant in a stunning 17th-century courtyard. Huge summer terrace

Tropical Café American Restaurant
5, Place Parmentier
92000 NEUILLY
Tel: 47 45 15 55
Fax: 47 82 24 37
Bar, grill, cocktails, American cuisine

Tucker
129, rue Lauriston
75116 PARIS
Tel: 44 05 15 15
Manager M. EVRARD
American restaurant, weekend brunch

West Side Café
34, rue St Ferdinand
75017 PARIS

Willi's Wine Bar
13, rue des Petits-Champs
75001 PARIS
Tel: 42 61 05 09
Fax: 47 03 36 93

Pubs
Pubs

Bedford Arms
17, rue Princesse
75006 PARIS
Tel: 46 33 43 54

Bière Academy
7, rue des Ecoles
75005 PARIS
Tel: 43 26 51 34

Bow Bells
33bis, rue des Bourdonnais
75001 PARIS
Tel: 45 08 55 99
Owner: M. Philip BELLAMY
London pub

Cambridge Tavern
17, avenue de Wagram
75017 PARIS
Tel: 43 80 34 12
Traditional British breakfast, daily specials

Carr's Restaurant & Bar
1, rue du Mont Thabor
75001 PARIS
Tel: 42 60 60 26
Fax: 42 60 33 32
Manager: M. Conall CARR
Irish Bar/Restaurant, private parties

Cockney Tavern
39, Bd. de Clichy
75009 PARIS
Tel: 48 74 80 80
Fax: 48 74 36 71
Manager: M. Roger TAILLANDIER

Connolly's Corner
12, rue Mirbel
75005 PARIS
Tel: 43 31 94 22

Cruiskeen Lawn
18, rue des Halles
75001 PARIS
Tel: 45 08 99 15

Edward & Son's
10, Bd. de Clichy
75018 PARIS
Tel: 44 92 90 91
Fax: 44 92 90 93
Contact: M. EDOUARD
Live Irish music Saturday and Sunday, open 16h00-05h00

Finnegan's Wake
9, rue des Boulangers
75005 PARIS
Tel: 46 34 23 65

Hall's Beer Tavern
68, rue St. Denis
75001 PARIS
Tel: 42 36 92 72

Hamilton's Fish & Chips
51, rue de Lappe
75011 PARIS
Tel: 48 06 77 92
Contact: Mme F. WATSON
A taste of Great Britain

Horse's Mouth
120, rue Montmartre
75002 PARIS
Tel: 40 39 93 66
Large screen satellite TV

Johnny's
55, rue Montmartre
75002 PARIS
Tel: 42 33 91 33
Irish pub

Kitty O'Shea's Pub
10, rue des Capucines
75002 PARIS
Tel: 40 15 00 30
Manager: M. Dermot TOQLAN

L'Aubergade
122, rue La Boétie
75008 PARIS
Tel: 42 25 10 60

La Taverne de Cluny
51, rue de la Harpe
75005 PARIS
Tel: 43 54 28 88
Typically British food and atmosphere

Le Formidiable
19, rue des Canettes
75006 PARIS
Tel: 43 26 44 27
13 international beers on draught

Le Mayflower
49, rue Descartes
75005 PARIS
Tel: 43 54 56 47
English beer pub and whiskey bar

London Tavern
3, rue du Sabot
75006 PARIS
Tel: 42 84 03 10
The English pub of St-Germain-des-Près

Molly Malone Lounge Bar
21, rue Godot de Mauroy
75009 PARIS
Tel: 47 42 07 77

Mulligan's
16, rue de la Verrerie
75004 PARIS
Tel: 40 29 03 89
Manager: M. Alain DETALLE
Irish Pub - Happy Hours 16h00-20h00

O'Neil
20, rue des Canettes
75006 PARIS
Tel: 46 33 36 66
Serves homemade pure malt non-pasteurized beer

Oscar
155, rue Montmartre
75002 PARIS
Tel: 42 21 09 61

Oscar Wilde
21, rue des Halles
75001 PARIS
Tel: 42 21 03 63

Piccadilly Pub
92, Bd. St. Germain
75005 PARIS
Tel: 46 33 51 16
Director: M. LEMEE

Pouchla
10, rue Mandar
75002 PARIS
Tel: 40 26 40 75
Good selection of beers

Pub 64 WE
64, rue de Charenton
75012 PARIS
Tel: 44 75 39 55

Pub Saint Germain
17, rue de l'Ancienne Comédie
75006 PARIS
Tel: 43 29 38 70
Open round the clock 7 days a week

Pub Winston Churchill
5, rue de Presbourg
75016 PARIS
Tel: 40 67 17 37
Fax: 45 00 88 12
Manager M. TYSSIER
The first English pub in Paris

Ryan's - Le Bistrot Irlandais
15, rue de la Santé
75013 PARIS
Tel: 47 07 07 45
Owner: M. SHIONER
Irish Pub/Restaurant

Saint Michel Pub
19, quai St. Michel
75005 PARIS
Tel: 46 33 30 41

Sous-Bock Tavern
49, rue St. Honoré
75001 PARIS
Tel: 40 26 46 61
Fax: 40 26 59 36
Well-stocked in beers and rare whiskeys

Stolly's Stone Bar
16, rue Cloche-Perce
75004 PARIS
Tel: 42 76 06 76

Sweeney Irish Pub
18, rue Laplace
75005 PARIS
Tel: 46 33 36 37

The Cricketer
41, rue des Mathurins
75008 PARIS
Tel: 40 07 01 45
Contact: Giles GOULDING
British pub with imported real ale and lunch specials

The Flann O' Brien Irish Pub
6, rue Bailleul
75001 PARIS
Tel: 42 60 13 58

The Frog & Rosbif
116, rue St. Denis
75002 PARIS
Tel: 42 36 34 73
The Paris Real Ale Brewery, open 7 days a week (see advertisement)

The Hideout
11, rue du Pot de Fer
75005 PARIS
Tel: 45 35 13 17
Irish watering hole

The James Ulysses Pub
5, rue du Jour
75001 PARIS
Tel: 45 08 17 04

The Mad Hatter's Pub
13, rue de l'Ecole Polytechnique
75005 PARIS
Tel: 43 54 18 48

The Quiet Man
5, rue des Haudriettes
75003 PARIS
Tel: 48 04 02 77

The Silver Goblet
11, rue du Cygne
75001 PARIS
Tel: 42 33 29 82

The Teeson Street
5, rue St. Sulpice
75006 PARIS
Tel: 43 54 11 48
Young Irish pub

Tony's
11, rue du Cygne
75001 PARIS
Tel: 42 33 29 82
Irish pub

Brasseries, Cafés, Tearooms
Brasseries, Cafés, Salons de Thé

Angelina
226, rue de Rivoli
75001 PARIS
Tel: 42 60 82 00
Tearoom renowned for its delicious hot chocolate and pastries

Antoine's
31, rue de Ponthieu
75008 PARIS
Tel: 42 89 44 20
Sandwiches, homemade pastries, fresh fruit cocktails

Au Bureau
4, rue du Fbg. Montmartre
75009 PARIS
Tel: 42 46 22 20
100 different beers

Au Diable des Lombards
64, rue des Lombards
75001 PARIS
Tel: 42 33 81 84
Fax: 42 33 73 99

Au Gamin de Paris
51, rue Vieille du Temple
75004 PARIS
Tel: 42 78 97 24

Au Père Tranquille
16, rue Pierre Lescot
75001 PARIS
Tel: 45 08 00 34

Bar L'Américain
57, rue Charlot
75003 PARIS
Tel: 48 04 78 72
Piano bar

Be Bop Café
35, rue Jouffroy d'Abbans
75017 PARIS
Tel: 40 53 07 13
Manager: M. Jean-Luc PEROTTI-VALLE
Salad and sandwich bar

Bistro Bizet
6, rue de Chaillot
75116 PARIS
Tel: 47 20 26 92

France Telecom welcomes you to France.
We hope the following information is helpful.

■ THE BASICS

Phone numbers in France currently have 8 digits. In Paris, numbers start with 4, and in the surrounding suburbs with 3, 5 or 6. To call from the provinces dial 16, wait for a tone; then dial the number. To call Paris from the provinces dial 16, wait for a tone, then dial 1 and the number. To call between the provinces, simply dial the 8 digit number. To telephone outside of France, dial 19, wait for a tone, dial the country and city code and then the number. National and international numbers starting with 05 are called “Numéros Verts” or free phone numbers.

In 1996, a ten digit dialling system will be put into place by France Telecom.

■ GETTING STARTED

To order a phone line, go to your nearest France Telecom Sales Office called “Agence France Telecom”. You will be greeted by a representative who will take your order and set up an appointment time for phone installation. The appointments are by time periods such as 8:30 am to 12 noon. It is therefore important to be available during the designated period. Phone bills are issued bimonthly and may be paid by check, automatic direct bank payment, at the Post Office (La Poste) or in person at any France Telecom Sales Office. You may request itemized billing (facturation détaillée) or star services (services conforts) such as call waiting (signal d’appel), three way conference calling (conversation à trois) or call forwarding (transfert d’appel), all for a nominal charge.

MINITEL

Minitel, a videotext service accessed through the telephone network, offers a multitude of services including directory assistance, chat lines, train/air reservations, financial and banking information and much more. Minitels can be rented or purchased from France Telecom. For access to Minitel's directory assistance, the first three minutes are offered free of charge, just dial "11". Charges for other Minitel services vary according to the service consulted. Sending a fax through the Minitel is easy with 3617 Fax or 3615 Super Fax.

TELECARTES

Télécartes (phone cards) allow you to call from any card pay phone without the hassle of dealing with change. These colorful cards are sold in units of 50 and 120 and can be purchased at Post Offices, Tobacco shops, France Telecom Sales Offices, airports, train & métro stations and kiosks displaying Télécarte stickers. Some Télécartes can be personalized and certain ones are even becoming collectors items!

For more information,
visit any of our "Agences France Telecom."
For an English speaking representative contact the:
International Business Center,
Forum des Halles, Porte du Louvre, 75001 Paris.
Métro : Les Halles or Châtelet.
Telephone : **N° Vert 05 05 05 75** APPEL GRATUIT
or (1) 44.76.27.28.

Orlyval. World's most advanced connecting system. For those who cannot afford to miss their flights.

With a single ticket, the RATP's Orlyval system gives you direct access from Orly airport to the Paris public transport network.
Departures are frequent - every 5 minutes during rush hours.
Whether leaving for holidays or business trips.
Orlyval assures you reliable connections : 30 min. from Châtelet to Orly ; 38 min. from the Arc of Triumph to Orly ; 60 min. from Roissy-Charles-de-Gaulle airport to Orly airport.

PARIS - CHARLES-DE-GAULLE AIRPORT DIRECT BY BUS.

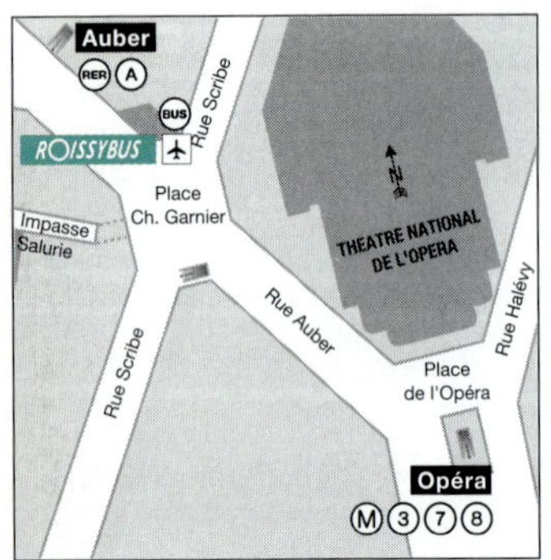

Opéra

Roissybus, the direct link between Paris and Charles-de-Gaulle Airport in 45 min. on average.
Departure from Opera and the airport every 15 min.
35 FRF. from March 1st, 1995.

Boutique à Sandwiches
12, rue du Colisée
75008 PARIS
Tel: 43 59 56 69
Director: M. SCHICK
Raclette, sandwiches

Brasserie Lipp
151, Bd. St. Germain
75006 PARIS
Tel: 45 48 53 91

Bread and Best
10, rue St. Marc
75002 PARIS
Tel: 40 26 56 66
Fax: 40 26 58 06
E-mail: 73631,1672@ compuserve
Contact: M. David BEST
High-quality English sandwich and salad restaurant (also provides home/office delivery)

Café de Flore
172, Bd. St. Germain
75006 PARIS
Tel: 45 48 55 26
The traditional meeting place for writers

Café de la Paix
12, Bd. des Capucines
75009 PARIS
Tel: 40 07 30 20

Café du Commerce
51, rue du Commerce
75015 PARIS
Tel: 45 75 03 27

Café Iguana
15, rue de la Roquette
75011 PARIS
Tel: 40 21 39 99
Trendy café near the Bastille with a pleasant decor

Café Oz
184, rue St. Jacques
75005 PARIS
Tel: 43 54 30 48

Café Pasta
30, rue Montorgueil
75001 PARIS
Tel: 40 28 49 78

Carpe Diem
4, rue Jaucourt
75012 PARIS
Tel: 43 43 27 44
Contacts: Jennifer & Pierre LEVEJAQ

Casta Diva
27, rue Cambacérès
75008 PARIS
Tel: 42 66 46 53
Tearoom serving light lunches, homemade pastries and a full range of teas and coffees in an elegant, cosy setting

Cave des Lombards
6, rue des Lombards
75004 PARIS
Tel: 42 71 04 04

Chez René
14, Bd. St. Germain
75005 PARIS
Tel: 43 54 30 23

Closerie des Lilas
171, Bd. Montparnasse
75006 PARIS
Tel: 43 26 70 50

Cosi
53, avenue des Ternes
75017 PARIS
Tel: 43 80 86 70
Fax: 43 80 86 65
Contact: M. LAVEAU
Italian sandwiches made with Cosi bread - choose your own filling!
2nd location at 54, rue de Seine, 75006

Cynthia Bread & Chocolate Bakery
31 rue Pétion
75011 PARIS
Tel: 43 48 06 84

Dammann's
20, rue du Cardinal Lemoine
75005 PARIS
Tel: 46 33 61 30
Director: M. Thomas DAMMANN
Tea room, ice cream parlour, salads, brunch

Fouquet's
99, avenue des Champs-Elysées
75008 PARIS
Tel: 47 23 70 60
Director: M. Joel MINOT

Häagen-Daz
144, Bd. St. Germain
75006 PARIS
Tel: 43 26 96 97
Many other locations in Paris

La Coupole
102, Bd Montparnasse
75014 PARIS
Tel: 43 20 14 20

La Rotonde
105, Bd Montparnasse
75006 PARIS
Tel: 43 26 48 26

Le Balzar
49, rue des Ecoles
75005 PARIS
Tel: 43 54 13 67
Traditional Parisian brasserie

Le Baragouin
17, rue Tiquetonne
75002 PARIS
Tel: 42 36 18 93

Le Comptoir
14, rue Vauvilliers
75001 PARIS
Tel: 40 26 26 66
Trendy meeting place

Le Select
99, Bd. Montparnasse
75006 PARIS
Tel: 45 48 38 24

Le Wepler
14, Place Clichy
75018 PARIS
Tel: 45 22 53 24
For its oysters and shellfish

Les Bouchons
19, rue des Halles
75001 PARIS
Tel: 42 33 28 73

Les Deux Magots
170, Bd. St. Germain
75006 PARIS
Tel: 45 48 55 25
Manager: M. DUPIN
The literary brasserie of St. Germain des Près

Les Mousquetaires
77, avenue du Maine
75014 PARIS
Tel: 43 22 50 46
Fax: 40 47 67 37

Lina's Sandwiches
50, rue Etienne Marcel
75002 PARIS
Tel: 42 21 16 14
Fax: 43 40 65 11

Lindsay's Tea Shop
4, rue Yvonne Le Tac
75018 PARIS
Fax: 42 52 74 09

L'Univers
116, Bd. Raspail
75006 PARIS
Tel: 45 48 24 74

Miremont Piccadilly Tea Room
10, rue Cambon
75001 PARIS
Tel: 42 60 74 12

Ned Kelly
8, rue des Ecouffes
75004 PARIS
Tel: 48 87 39 26
Australian bar

Orchid Café
18, rue Rosenwald
75015 PARIS
Tel: 42 50 06 05

Paris Bourse
10, rue St. Marc
75002 PARIS
Tel: 45 08 08 26

Pause-Café
41, rue de Charonne
75011 PARIS
Tel: 48 06 80 33
Salad Bar/Restaurant with sunny terrace in summer

Plein Sud
17, avenue du Cygne
75001 PARIS
Tel: 42 33 49 95

Shiro
49, rue du Fbg. St. Antoine
75011 PARIS
Tel: 44 75 78 78

Sydney Coffee Shop
27, rue Lacépède
75005 PARIS
Tel: 43 36 70 46

Tea Follies
6, Place Gustave Toudouze
75009 PARIS
Tel: 42 80 08 44
Fax: 45 26 38 22

The Lizard Lounge
18, rue du Bourg Tibourg
75004 PARIS
Tel: 42 72 81 34

Fast Food
Restauration Rapide

Burger King
84, avenue des Champs-Elysées
75008 PARIS
Tel: 42 56 34 20
Many locations around Paris

Kentucky Fried Chicken
31, Bd. Sébastopol
75001 PARIS
Tel: 40 26 61 14

La Croissanterie
48, Bd. St. Michel
75006 PARIS
Tel: 43 29 42 80

McDonalds France
34, Bd. des Italiens
75009 PARIS
Tel: 42 46 67 80
Many locations around Paris

Pomme de Pain
76, rue de Rivoli
75004 PARIS
Tel: 42 78 57 29

Quick Hamburger
8, rue du Fbg. Montmartre
75009 PARIS
Tel: 47 70 83 62
Many locations around Paris

http://www.paris-anglo.com

Welcome to the Paris-Anglophone Web Site!

This is **Business**. This is Culture. This is the **Art of** about **How** to **create**. This is about how to **Work**.

We are a publishing house, a **directory**, a **teepee**; we two editors, an **international** design team in a **Marais** **Resources** and know-how – more than **cash**. We're **revolutionaries**. We're a book with chapters that **Active** and Interactive. We're a **spontaneous** magazine, and **pictures**. We're both the **travel agency** and the trip. the word and we're a **daily**! We're a **data base**, a **radio** a commercial for ourselves and a lot of other businesses, **Singapour** and **Boston** and **Montreuil-sous-Bois** & **San** company, a health club, a **tv** station, a **library**, a **book** **Gallery** in the comfort of your office, a **museum** tour **democratic** idea run by a band of independent CEOs writers, **journalists**, stringers, students, **chefs**, developers **entrepreneurs**. We speak English, French, **html**, *argot* and **spreadsheets**. We're a bit older than you and some Steves without the **jobs**. We're **Ralph Petty**, the **Financial** **Mifflin**. We're Americans in Paris, Parisians elsewhere, **stock brokers**, information junkies and citizens of **new** We're **guerillas** and pandas and **leprechauns**. We grain **bread**, and cutting-edge **Projects of Quality**, knife. *(Download this message immediately; later* reinvent, and **reinvent** what we've invented. We are **cyber-Seine**, scaling our beloved **Notre Dame** of . and come and go like the tides. **Welcome** to the **New** from the **City of Halogen** and its international **suburbs** experiences, and **bank account** numbers. This is a new government **ministries**, the consumers, and **laptop** commercial globe-trotting and **table-hopping**. We have fill. What better place for art **&** commerce to **French** **functionality** to lock arms than on the gilded **Pont**

For more details on how to **get involved**-Call, Write,

Commerce. This is the Science of **Poetry**. This is

are a **bistro** & a **portable office**. A **troupe** of one or
flat, a page of **links** and a maze of trap doors.
ardently traditional. We are cool-headed
come apart, a collection of stories, **essays**, articles.
a group of unrehearsed yet **orchestrated** words
We're a monthly, a **quarterly**, a weekly. Give
station, a **documentary**, a drama, a **news flash**,
services, and projects. A Paris **café** in
Francisco & ***chez vous***. An **ad** agency, a moving
store, a therapist's office. We're a **Paris Art**
and **oyster bar** in the privacy of your **bedroom**. A
– and not a worker in sight! Editors, **publishers**,
song-writers, **corporate vice-presidents**, and
and bits of **Icelandic** and Farsi. We read **Beckett**
what younger. We're Bills without the **gates**,
Times, **Volvo**, Jacques **Chirac**, and **Houghton-**
decision-makers in **cyberspace**, culture brokers,
ideas. Welcome to the **PA Web Site**.
want to make **money**, friends, **babies**, whole
knowing that today's **cutting edge** is tomorrow's butter
it'll be another animal.) We are here to invent,
post-modern trapeze artists, swinging over the
Creative Aspirations. We share by edict, gobble by night,
& Old Paris, where like-and un-**like-minded** folks
seek definitions and **exchange** ideas, images,
time for the **encyclopedia** makers, the
voyagers. This is a new time for cultural &
the francophone world in site and a long menu to
kiss than on our **Ile Saint Louis**, for aesthetics &
Alexandre III?

Fax, **Email**, Dispatch a Carrier Pigeon, or **Drop** by.

David Applefield
Words

Cory McCloud
Bytes

http://www.paris-anglo.com

THE COMPLETE DIRECTORY OF THE ENGLISH SPEAKING WORLD IN PARIS

PARIS-ANGLOPHONE

L'ANNUAIRE DU MONDE DES AFFAIRES ANGLOPHONES A PARIS

The YES Form

____ **Yes,** I'd like to be listed in the 5th Edition of **PARIS-ANGLOPHONE**.

•

____ **Yes,** I'd like to order_____copy(ies) of **PARIS-ANGLOPHONE** (4th Ed.) @ 140 FF/$21.95 /£14.99.

•

____ **Yes,** I'd like to receive information on Sponsorship & Advertising opportunities in **PARIS-ANGLOPHONE**, book & on-line **Web Site**.

•

Name: ____________________

Company/Org: ____________________

Address: ____________________

____

City: __________ Code: __________

Country: ____________________

Tel: __________ Fax: __________

Email: ____________________

Brief description of activity: ____________________

____

When ordering copies please add 21FF/£2/$4US for postage

Amount enclosed: ____________________

Please make checks payable to:

Association Frank
32, rue Edouard Vaillant
93100 MONTREUIL/France
Fax: (33) (1) 48 59 66 68
Email: 100265.1435@compuserve.com